Boating from Bow to Stern

BOATING

from Bow to Stern

BY JAMES P. KENEALY

With drawings by James MacDonald and photographs

HAWTHORN BOOKS, INC.
Publishers
New York

BOATING FROM BOW TO STERN

All inquiries should be addressed to Hawthorn Books, Inc., 260 Madison Avenue, New York, New York 10016. This book was manufactured in the United States of America and published simultaneously in Canada by Prentice-Hall of Canada, Limited, 1870 Birchmount Road, Scarborough, Ontario. Library of Congress Catalog Card Number: 66-13607

Published by arrangement with Dodd, Mead & Company.

2 3 4 5 6 7 8 9 10

To Iris Vinton, who first put a pen in this sailor's hand, and Angie, my first mate

Acknowledgments

In the course of writing this book many people have given generously of their time, products and information. To them I am sincerely grateful. The following have been especially helpful: Iris Vinton who encouraged me to write this book; Ted Diamond and Conrad McGovern who were my sounding board while writing the rough draft; Dr. Burton W. Wilcke for his assistance in the first aid section; Allen Klots, Jr. for his patience and guidance; Charles H. Tracey, N. for editing Chapter 5, Compass, Charts, Piloting; James MacDonald for his invaluable assistance and guidance with the photography and art work; Richard Mack, President of Antico Marine Inc.; Bill Baker of Conley, Baker & Steward and Dick Trainer of the M. F. G. Boat Company for the use of special equipment; Joseph J. Graziano, George Benedetto, Philip Chiumiento, James De Salvo and Joseph DeVito who have been my shipmates for many years; the members of the Albany Yacht Club and Medford Boat Club for the use of their facilities; and a very special thanks to Angie, Nancy, Mike and Deane who patiently stayed ashore during many a fair wind while this book was being written.

I also wish to thank the following organizations and companies for their contribution of technical charts, photographs and drawings: The U. S. Coast Guard, U. S. Weather Bureau, New York State Division of Motor Boats, Danforth White Company, Buehler Corporation, The Garrett Corporation, Holsclaw Brothers Inc., Morse Instrument Company and the Molded Fiber Glass Boat Company.

Preface

In the past two decades pleasure boating in the United States and Canada has become a major recreational sport, catering to over fifty million participants. With this rapid growth many problems have arisen, mainly how to teach new boatmen proper boat handling techniques and safe seamanship procedures. Presently only a few of the many books on boating cover all of this material. The majority either specialize in one phase of the sport or are written in a highly technical style intended for the professional and expert sailor. This book will, however, give water oriented families, new and amateur boatmen, a complete training manual geared to meet their present and future needs. It covers all major phases of seamanship plus the operation and maintenance of powerboats, sailboats, and rowboats. And for the weekend skipper who plans to take advanced boating courses he will find this book an excellent reference text.

Contents

Boating from Bow to Stern

1

Your First Command

BUYING A BOAT

Buying a boat is an exciting time for a new sailor. Collecting boat advertisements, window shopping, and visiting marine dealer showrooms are all part of the fun. In a sense it is almost like buying a new automobile when you consider that construction, make, and design all play an important role. But unlike an automobile buyer a new skipper must also know what method of boating he or his family will enjoy best. This can be a problem, especially if you depend on friends or other boat owners for advice. Sailboat enthusiasts will spend hours extolling the thrills and excitement of sailing. Powerboat skippers, on the other hand, will quickly assure you that for fun, adventure, and versatility nothing compares to power. And for sheer enjoyment plus economy, listen to canoe or rowboat owners praise the virtues of their boats for quiet relaxation or exploring out-of-the-way waters. Surprisingly, they will all be 100 per cent right. Every type of boating offers fun, excitement, and adventure; the method depends on a person's likes and dislikes. To be sure you and your family make the right choice, spend some time afloat aboard different kinds of boats. Go out with friends who own boats or rent them at local boat marinas. Then when you are sure what method of boating you enjoy most, you are ready to decide on size, design, price, and construction.

SIZE

How big a boat do I need? Answer this question correctly the first time and you are well on your way to becoming an "old salt." Surveys show the average boating family trade in their boat after two seasons. The main reason given is "We outgrew it." Actually what they really mean is "The waters we are now sailing outgrew our boat." To avoid making this mistake sit down and figure out the maximum number of passengers and weight, outboard motor included, you expect to have aboard at one time. (Most manufacturers will show their boat's limitations regarding this, plus maximum horsepower rating, on an Outboard Boating Club of America [O.B.C.] capacity recommendation plate attached to the transom [Fig. 1].) Then list all the boating areas you

Fig. 1

CAPACITY
THIS BOAT IS BUILT TO ACCOMMODATE UNDER NORMAL CONDITIONS AN OUTBOARD MOTOR OF NOT MORE THAN
75 OBC CERTIFIED HORSEPOWER AND
6 PERSONS AT 150 LBS. PER PERSON
OR A PROPERLY LOCATED MAX. WEIGHT OF
1400 LBS. FOR PERSONS, MOTOR AND GEAR.
OUTBOARD BOATING OBC CLUB OF AMERICA

plan to sail on once you have acquired your sea legs. This information will give a clearer picture of the size (length, beam, draft, and freeboard) and design best suited to your needs. Excluding length, which is not a serious safety factor, your first major consideration should be *beam*. A boat with ample beam (width across its widest part) in relation to length assures comfort aboard and stability in rough seas. So, when all other factors are equal and seaworthiness is necessary, choose the boat with the widest beam (Fig. 2).

Freeboard, which is the height of a boat's sides that remain out of water when afloat, is the next necessary consideration. Look for freeboard high enough to keep a boat dry in moderate seas, yet low enough to prevent existing winds from pushing her out of control or making steering uncomfortably hard. Measure freeboard from the top of the gunwale down to the waterline. Do not include any superstructure above the gunwale. Although there are no set rules governing the height of freeboard, all well-designed hulls incorporate adequate freeboard to insure a fairly dry boat in rough seas while minimizing wind surface that could blow a boat off course. When outboard engine power will be used, measure the transom freeboard at the engine mount cutout. For

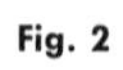

Fig. 2

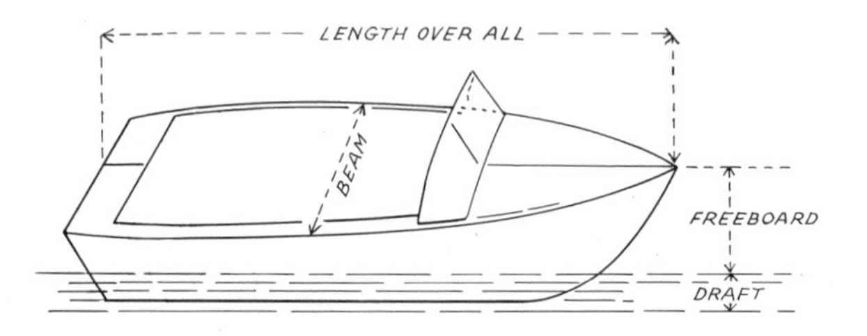

offshore boating, the height should be equal to, or within a few inches of, the freeboard where the hull and transom meet unless an inner transom is used. This extra height insures against a following sea coming in over the stern. Engine manufacturers provide extra-long drive shafts at little or no increase in price for these types of transoms.

Proper *draft* (how deep a boat sits under the surface of the water) is also important because it automatically regulates the depth of water you need to sail on. A five-foot keeled sailboat is useless on a shallow lake or bay, whereas the same boat with a three-foot centerboard might be perfect.

Other size factors to consider are trailability, storage, and mooring. Many states regulate the size and weight of boats that can be trailered by automobiles to insure safety on the highways. So check the laws of the states you plan to trailer in. Experience has shown that boats exceeding twenty-four feet in length, eight feet in beam, or weigh over two tons are too cumbersome and unwieldy to be pulled by the average passenger car.

If your boat is too large to be trailered, the problem of winter storage and summer docking or mooring must be considered. Check local boatyards and marinas to be sure they can handle your craft and what the cost of these services will be. If you trailer your boat, the chances are she will be stored in your garage or yard and transported to and from boating areas. This will eliminate the above costs.

INBOARD OR OUTBOARD

When a powerboat is your choice of craft, one other decision must be made: whether to use an inboard or outboard engine. Here again the deciding factor will depend greatly on the size boat needed, the areas to be sailed, and whether or not trailering is contemplated. In cases where six or less passengers will be the rule, and sailing confined to small lakes, rivers, and bays, outboard motorboats up to eighteen feet are the most practical. They are less expensive than comparable inboard models, give more room aboard because the engine hangs outside the boat, and can be trailered and stored much more easily. In fact, except for special cases, the use of inboard engines on small boats is a waste of space and money.

It is when you get into larger craft, twenty-five feet and over, such as sea skiffs and offshore cruisers, that inboard engines come into their own. To power these boats on long trips or to distant fishing grounds, large efficient inboard engines in the 145-horsepower-and-up class are needed. These power plants also serve as a power supply to run auxiliary motors, lights, pumps, etc., all of which are needed to operate offshore cruising craft.

The difficult decisions have, up until a few years ago, always centered on boats in the eighteen- to twenty-five-foot range. When either outboard or inboard power was used, one or more vantage points had to be eliminated. To overcome this problem, engine manufacturers developed a prototype engine. By using an inboard engine to power an outboard drive shaft housing and propeller, it became possible to gain the versatility of an outboard while retaining the operating efficiency and fuel economy of an inboard. These power plants, called in-outboard engines, start at about 90 horsepower and range up to over 200 horsepower. Designed primarily for boats in the eighteen- to twenty-five-foot range, they give the best performance and are competitive in price with comparable outboard or inboard models.

HULL DESIGN

Once size is determined, hull design becomes a factor, especially the shape of a boat's bottom. In recent years this area of boat building has evolved into a highly skilled science incorporating hydrodynamics and aerodynamics.

Unless a prospective boat buyer is trained in these professions, he can quickly become confused and end up purchasing a boat unsuited to his needs. To avoid this pitfall, keep in mind that all hull designs, regardless of bottom shape, fall into three categories: stepped hydroplaning hulls, displacement hulls, and planing hulls. Any other frills incorporated into a bottom are meant to complement one of the above shapes, and usually do when built by a reliable builder. Following is an explanation of each of these shapes telling you its purpose and what to look for.

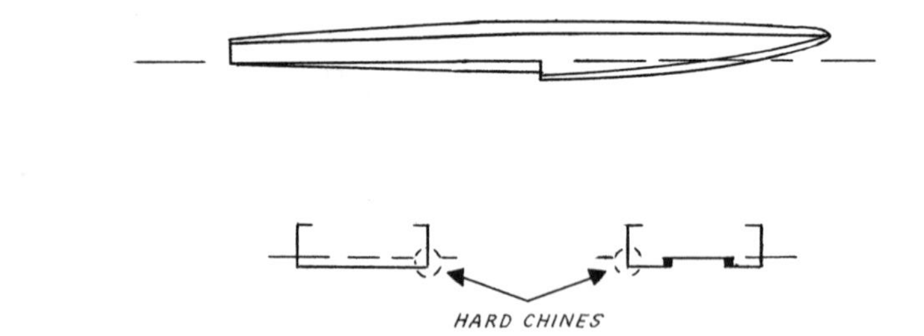

Fig. 3

Stepped Hydroplaning Hulls

In power-driven boats, when speed is the major requisite for racing, a hard-chine step-planing hull is recommended. This design has a flat single-stepped or multistepped bottom that lifts three-fourths to four-fifths of the hull above water at full throttle, reducing water friction and thereby allowing greater speed (Fig. 3). Although this type of hull is popular in racing circles, it is not considered seaworthy or safe enough for general use by families or on waters that build up during high winds or storms.

Displacement Hull

If all your cruising will be done on blue water (large open waters) a deep V- or round-shaped soft-chine displacement hull is recommended because it remains below the surface while under way (Fig. 4). During heavy seas this makes for a more seaworthy boat by lowering the center of gravity and lessening the tendency to porpoise (pitch and dip forward) or yaw (roll sideways.)

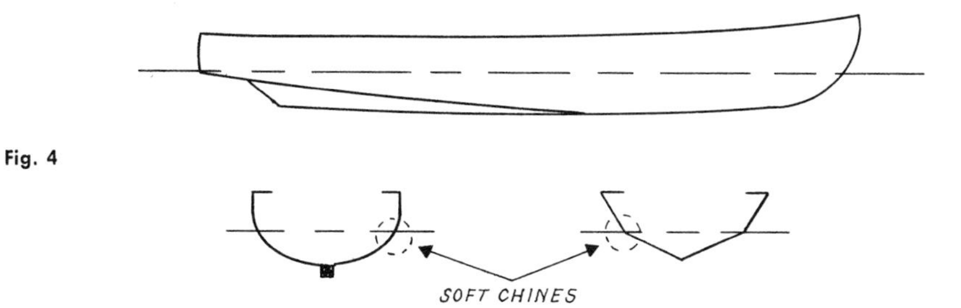

Fig. 4

Planing Hull

With the perfection of larger outboard engines, the demand for a hull that would give sufficient speed to pull water skiers and yet be seaworthy enough for families to cruise open waters brought about the design of the planing hull with a semisoft chine (Fig. 5). By incorporating some of the best features of both displacement and stepped-planing hulls, this design has become by far the most popular powercraft hull in use today. When not asked to perform beyond its limits, the planing design is without doubt the best buy for general use in the powerboating field regardless of the type engine (inboard, outboard, or in-outboard).

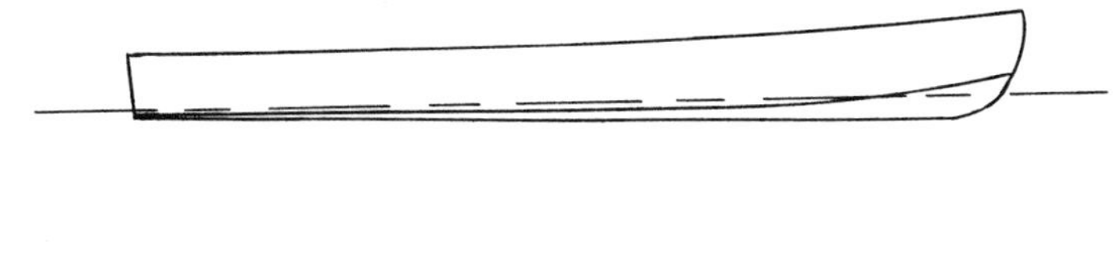

Fig. 5

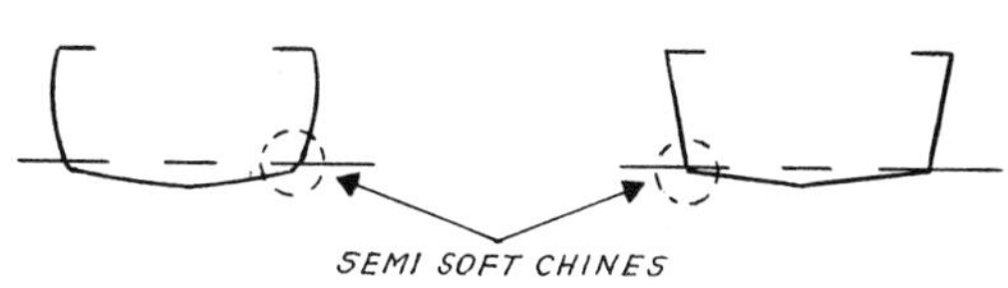

Hulls in General

The term "chine" refers to the angle and shape where the bottom and sides of a hull meet. "Hard," "soft," or "semisoft" chines refer to the angle of the chine found at the stern (back) or transom of a boat. On hard-chined boats this angle is around ninety degrees, making the aftersection of the hull bottom flat. Although this allows greater speed and lifting power, it tends to cause excessive pounding in moderate to heavy seas and skidding during fast turns, which can flip a boat over if the outside chine digs in.

Soft-chine hulls have rounded or V-shaped bottoms with an angle much greater than ninety degrees at the stern. This causes drag and lessens speed because the water does not break cleanly from the hull. Seaworthiness is increased, however, because the hulls bank rather than skid during turns, and allow heavy seas to roll under the hull rather than up and over.

The semisoft chine incorporates an angle greater than ninety degrees but less than that of a displacement hull. This gives a boat planing characteristics along with seaworthiness during heavy weather and high-speed turns.

Sailboat hulls have weighted keels or centerboards below the hull, thereby placing all but a few class-racing hulls in the displacement design category.

Rowboat hulls differ greatly in shape. Flat-bottom hulls with hard chines are designed for the quiet waters of small protected ponds and lakes; whereas V-shaped or round-bottomed hulls with soft or semisoft chines are designed for larger waters where seaworthiness is more important.

Catamaran hulls, although used by South Seas natives for centuries, are a recent innovation in modern powerboats and sailboats. The objective of attaching two hulls to a bridging deck is to give stability in heavy seas, plus the lifting power of a planing hull when moving at a high rate of speed (Fig. 6).

Boating advertisements to the contrary, *hull siding* is incidental. Lap strake, molded, planked, or a dozen other methods of construction have all proven seaworthy when made from quality materials and well built.

Cabins, windshields, and other *superstructure* built above a hull are designed for comfort and beauty rather than safety. Do not let these eye-appeals distract you from buying a safe, well-designed, and well-constructed hull.

CONSTRUCTION AND MATERIALS

Regardless of the type, size, or design of the craft you buy, quality workmanship and materials must be a major guiding factor in your selection. Too often new skippers are sold a fancy paint job with lots of chrome trim, only to find out later they bought a chronic repair bill. Keep in mind that often paint and trim are only beauty spots, not safety spots, and could be hiding inferior workmanship or materials. Inspections should be made under good light conditions with the proverbial "fine-tooth comb." Only then can you be sure of buying a safe boat that will give years of trouble-free performance.

Wooden boats should have oak or its equivalent for all framing members, unless the boat has a molded plywood hull. All plywood should be top marine grade. Hull siding and superstructure materials not built of marine plywood

Fig. 6

should be a good grade mahogany, teak, oak, or their equivalent. Fastenings, fittings, and hardware should be made of bronze, copper, anodized aluminum, monel, or stainless steel. Galvanized steel is acceptable but needs more care, as it tends to break down in salt water unless heavily painted. Check all joints and seams. Be sure they are well fastened, tight, and fit snugly, especially at the keel, bow stem, transom, and hull planking. Excessive seam or caulking compound are dead giveaways to sloppy workmanship. On boats carrying outboard motors, transoms should be extra strong and thick to absorb engine vibrations and stresses. This is important regardless of a boat's construction material.

Fiber glass, boating's new wonder material, also has its weak spots when not molded properly. Check for hairline cracks along the keel, transom, and bow that extend below the top smooth jell coat. They could be breaks in the glass cloth caused by improper removal of the boat from the mold. Feel for bubbles and thin spots in the hull by sliding your hands over the inner and outer sides. These represent spots that are not properly bonded or where an inferior grade glass cloth of uneven thickness was used. The formation of many hairline cracks, or crazing, on the outer hull means that the jell coat, which gives a fiber glass boat its smooth finish and color, dried too fast and will eventually chip. Although this will not weaken the boat, it does mean extra maintenance and upkeep.

On *aluminum boats* check metal thickness, rivets, and welds. A well-built aluminum boat should have a heavier-gauge metal on the bottom than on the sides to insure against dents, rips, and punctures below the waterline. Bow stems and transom joints should be welded. Rivets at these spots will loosen from vibration or excessive pounding. Hull rivets should be backed by washers or a permanent sealing compound; and most important, all aluminum boats using a soft antifouling bottom paint must have a protective prime coat between the aluminum and the antifouling paint to prevent electrolytic corrosion (*see* Chapter 13, "Fitting Out and Storage," page 229).

All boats regardless of material should be painted with an antifouling bottom paint if salt water sailing is anticipated.

Flotation Blocks

There's an old saying in boating that goes "boats don't sink, people sink them." Fortunately, this saying should not apply today when speaking of boats equipped with built-in flotation tanks or blocks. The tanks or blocks are permanently placed in a boat in such a manner that should the boat capsize or swamp, it will still float full of water, with passengers and equipment aboard. Every small craft should have this flotation to protect its passengers. When there is a choice between styrofoam blocks or airtight tanks, choose the styrofoam, because punctures or dents have no effect on their buoyancy. This

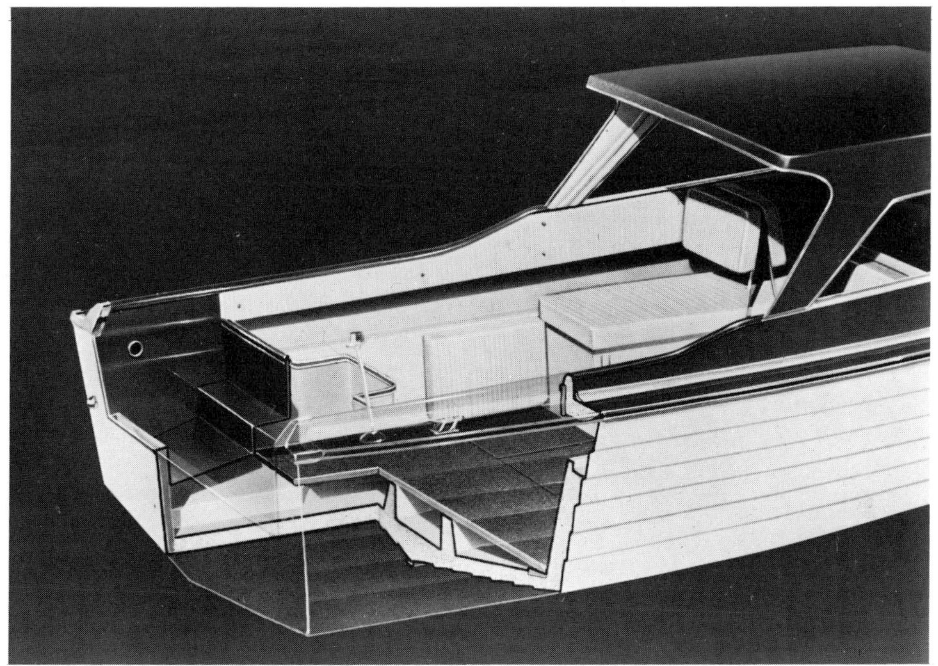

Fig. 7

buoyancy information is usually supplied in the manufacturer's technical sheet attached to the boat. If it is not available, ask the salesman to send for it. Do not buy any boat until you see these figures. Every quality boat builder will gladly supply them. Remember, as skipper you are responsible for the safety of your passengers and yourself, so be sure your boat can pass this test (Fig. 7).

SHAKEDOWN CRUISE

Probably the least understood part of boat buying is the final test, the shakedown cruise. No matter how well you like your choice of craft up to this point, the final decision should hinge on its performance under way.

You will notice the term "shakedown" is used instead of "test run." Shakedown, defined by the Navy, means a thorough check under way of all parts of a vessel under all conditions. Test runs, on the other hand, often mean a short spin on a sunny day. To insure a satisfactory shakedown, plan to hold it under the following conditions:

1. Bring along a friend who is an experienced boatman.
2. Read the chapter in this book on the type of craft you intend to buy. (This will give you a clearer understanding of what to look for.)

3. Have aboard the maximum number of passengers and equipment you plan to carry.
4. If powered by an outboard engine, have the engine you plan to buy as the power plant.
5. Bring along a pad and pencil to take notes on performance, working order of equipment, and any other items you may want to discuss or have fixed.
6. When possible make the shakedown run in two stages: the first on a good to ideal day for boating and the second under adverse conditions. Adverse conditions naturally do not mean going out in a gale or weather that might endanger those aboard. Depending on the size and use of your craft, pick a day that will give an indication of how it will handle in choppy or building seas and wind. During this second check *be sure* an experienced boatman is along.

While testing, keep the following factors in mind: safety, durability, speed, adaptability, and comfort. With the exception of safety, the other factors will have to be evaluated in the order of their importance to you.

Aboard a powerboat, watch for excessive slipping on turns, sloppy rudder control, excessive vibrations, sluggish throttle response at high and low speeds, porpoising, and a tendency to steer off course to the right or left. If porpoising and steering off course are found and cannot be corrected by trimming the motor or load, look for a hull deformity.

Rowboats and canoes are tested by paddling or rowing plus outboard power if it will be used. If they handle well when under way and meet your requirements as to design and construction, feel safe to buy.

Sailboats are tested by touch and feel. While under way, sail in all wind directions. Rudder and sail sheet handling should give positive control at all times except when "in irons," that is, when the bow is pointed directly into the wind. Excessive heeling (leaning) in light winds could mean the keel or centerboard does not have enough weight to compensate for sail area or the sails were cut too full.

During all test runs, check out auxiliary equipment, such as steering linkage, lights, rigging, wiring, anchors. If after the shakedown test the boat performs to your satisfaction and meets all other requirements, you can feel pretty sure that the boat is safe and sound.

PRICE TAGS

Fortunately for new and old skippers, boating has become such a large and competitive industry, price tags have been kept reasonable, making it possible to buy almost any type of boat to fit your budget. Following is a list of boats and their approximate price range. These prices do not include outboard engines, equipment required by law, or a trailer if you plan cross-country trips.

Dinghies and Prams, Price Range $90 to $450

Small size, seven to twelve feet, and light weight make these small boats excellent cartoppers or tenders for large craft. They are ideally suited as training craft for youngsters and will take up to a 3½ horsepower outboard engine. Many come rigged for sailing.

Canoes, Price Range $100 to $350

These lightweight craft, ranging in size from twelve to twenty feet, make good cartop or trailer boats. Long famous for guide and camp use the canoe is an ideal boat to explore out-of-the-way waters, for fishing or relaxation on small bodies of water. Because of their narrow beam, canoes tip easily, so users should be good swimmers. Engine brackets for small 1½ to 3 horsepower outboards and sailing rigs can be attached as auxiliary equipment.

Rowboats, Price Range $80 to $400

The workhorse of small craft sizes range from twelve to eighteen feet. Rowboats are one of the most popular boat in use today. Lightweight models, can be cartopped and will take outboard engines, up to 18 horsepower. In great demand by fishermen, it is a very safe boat when operated within its capacities.

Runabouts, Price Range $500 and Up

Looked upon as the sports cars of the waterways. A sleek design and high-speed output make these boats the favorite of daytime boatmen, racing fans, and waterskiers. Hulls come in both step planing and planing design, with the latter the most popular. Sizes range from thirteen to twenty-four feet. Depending on size, outboard engines of all horsepower can be used. Some larger models have inboard or in-outboard engines in the 100 horsepower and over class. Canvas and hardtop cockpit covers for sun and rain protection are usually available as accessories. Runabouts have outstanding trailering qualities.

Utilities, Price Range $250 and Up

Similar in design to rowboats, utilities have wider beam and more freeboard, adding to seaworthiness. Some have short forward decks and windshields. Depending on size, these boats will handle the complete range of outboard engines. Considered a general purpose boat, utilities are used for all boating sports except sailing and are easily trailered. Sizes range from twelve to twenty feet.

Sea Skiffs, $1,000 Up for Outboard Models, $3,000 Up for Inboard Models

Big brother of the utility design, the sea skiff is a very seaworthy boat for offshore fishing or day cruising. She can be bought equipped with bunks and a marine toilet placed under the forward deck. Sizes range from eighteen to over forty feet. Smaller models designed for use with large outboard engines can be trailered. Larger models have inboard or in-outboard engines. The famous offshore "bass" boats used on Cape Cod and the New Jersey coast are sea skiff designs especially built and equipped for sport fishing.

Outboard Cruisers, Price Range $1,200 Up

The reigning queens of powerboating. With the perfection of large outboard engines these boats have become second homes for hundreds of thousands of boating families. Depending on size, these miniature yachts will accommodate up to six persons in luxurious comfort. Everything from galley (kitchen) to sleeping quarters is available for long-range coastal cruising. When operated within their capacity, these boats display outstanding seaworthiness, yet most are light enough to trailer. Sizes range from sixteen to twenty-six feet. Single or twin outboard engines can be used with combined power ratings up to 200 horsepower.

Inboard Cruisers, Price Range $3,000 and Up (Including Engine)

Where outboard cruisers are the queens of powerboating, the inboard cruisers are kings. Because these boats are larger than the outboards, ranging in size from eighteen to sixty-five feet, they offer even greater comforts and luxuries. Smaller models are excellent long-range coastal cruisers. Larger models are capable of ocean crossings. Weight and size make trailering impractical. Power plants are available in both inboard and in-outboard engines.

Sailboats

Sailboats come in three basic types: class racing boats, day sailers, and sailing cruisers. The *class racers* come in literally dozens of class designs starting with the small nine-foot dinghies and lengthening out to the large meter classes. These craft are primarily for sailors who want the excitement of racing other boats of same weight, design, and specification as their own. Prices start at $200 and reach up into the thousands, with the majority falling within the $1,000 to $2,000 range. Before buying, check with local yacht clubs and racing clubs to find out what class designs are raced in your area. Otherwise you might find yourself with a discontented lady who has no one to run against. Most small centerboard models can be trailered.

Day Sailors

Day sailers are primarily family pleasure boats designed for seaworthiness, ease of handling, and comfort during daytime use. Size and design limit the waters where these boats can safely be sailed.

Sizes range from sixteen feet to over twenty feet and are priced from

$1,000. Small outboard engines can be used as auxiliary power on most models. Trailering can be done with the centerboard designs.

Sailing Cruisers

Ranging in size from twenty-two feet to over sixty feet, the sailing cruiser is the ultimate in sailing boats. Depending on size, these craft can weather any blow and travel all oceans. Accommodations compare favorably with power cruisers. Auxiliary power usually consists of small inboard engines with a few outboards for the smaller models. Weight and size make trailering for all but a few models impractical. Price range starts from $2,000 without auxiliary power and $3,500 with auxiliary power.

Special Note

Sailboat buyers should spend a season or two aboard the smaller class racers and day sailers before purchasing a sailing cruiser if they are not experienced sailors.

USED BOATS

When buying a secondhand boat, use the same check system as you would if you were purchasing a new boat. Just because the boat is used does not mean she need be any less seaworthy than a new one. An additional check on used wooden boats is for dry rot. Using a sharp instrument, press against any place where the wood is discolored or paint has blistered. Dry rot will feel soft and often crumble. These are weak spots, and unless you are able to repair them yourself, it's best to steer clear of such craft. On all metal, fiber glass, and wooden boats, check to be sure paint is not hiding cracks and open or loose seams. Beware of any large patch job done on a hull. Unless the repair was made by an expert, there is a good chance the hull is out of alignment.

On larger craft have a professional boat surveyor make the inspection. When a surveyor is not available, use as a guide the fitting out checklist, Appendix D, page 300.

BUILD-IT-YOURSELF BOATS

Boatmen skilled in the use of tools who wish to build their own boats have a large variety of precut kits and plans available. The kits vary from completely disassembled boats, which are the least expensive, to finished but unpainted hulls. Savings over the cost of a ready-built boat are said to be as high as 60 per cent. Unquestionably the better precut boats when built by a skilled workman compare favorably with similar ready-built boats. The trick is not to overestimate your ability by trying too complicated a kit. A good yardstick to go by is the following: only competent craftsmen should attempt the completely disassembled kits that call for complex angles and rounded chine lines. Handymen should purchase kits with the hull completely assembled or nearly so.

REGISTRATION

Most states require that all boats over a certain size, or those that use motors, must be registered and display a license number on the bow. Registration proves who owns the boat if she is lost or stolen. The numbers and letters should contrast in color to the hull. Check with your local boat dealer, U. S. Power Squadron or Coast Guard Station to find out where you register for a number in your state.

INSURANCE

Boating insurance is as necessary to a boat owner as automobile insurance is to a car owner. This statement often comes as a surprise to new boat owners, especially those who purchase small nonpowered craft. Accident statistics, however, bear it out. Approximately 30 per cent of all liability suits brought against boat owners involved a nonpowered boat less than sixteen feet in length. Boat owners in this same category were also involved in 10 per cent of all property damage suits. With these statistics in mind, all boatmen should carry ample insurance regardless of the type or size of their craft.

Patterned after automobile insurance, the policies available to pleasure boatmen are liability, collision, and extended coverage. The liability policy covers against personal and property injuries. Collision insurance protects against damage to your own boat. And extended coverage protects against a multitude of happenings such as fire, theft, and vandalism. Fortunately, these insurance policies are inexpensive, cost usually being based on size and type boat, and can be purchased as a package or individually from any general insurance agent.

2

Safety Equipment

Of all major recreational sports, boating holds one of the most enviable safety records. Surveys made by safety councils and insurance companies show three factors are responsible: well-built and well-designed boats, competent skippers and crews, and excellent safety equipment. The last, safety equipment, has become so important federal and state laws now require boats of different classes (lengths) to have certain safety and operating aids aboard at all times. Additional aids that can add to your fun and comfort afloat are also recommended.

The required equipment for Class A and I boats (under twenty-six feet in length) is a life preserver for each passenger aboard, running lights for boats operated between sunset and sunrise, a whistle or horn, a B-1 type fire extinguisher for boats with inboard engines, a flame arrester on all inboard engines, and bilge ventilators on boats with engines placed in the bilge or a covered area (Fig. 8).

On Class II boats (twenty-six feet but less than forty feet) an extra B-1 fire extinguisher, plus a bell is also required. On Class III boats (forty feet to sixty-five feet) a bell, plus three or more B-1 or B-2 fire extinguishers are required and only life jackets or life rings are allowed. Life vests or buoyant seat cushions are illegal.

Although the federal law does not, as yet, require an anchor, experience has proven it essential; therefore, one should be carried by all boats. Experienced skippers realize this and carry a spare anchor and line in case of an emergency.

Listed at the end of this chapter (page 20) are additional equipment rec-

Fig. 8

ommended by boating experts and some items required by state laws. Skippers should review this list and use the items that will make their time afloat safer and more enjoyable.

LIFE PRESERVERS

Every boat must carry a Coast Guard approved life preserver for each person on board. They can be of the jacket, vest, cushions or life ring, jackets preferred. On Class III boats, jackets or rings must be used. Each must carry a permanent official Coast Guard tag, and jackets must be Indian orange in color. Life preservers are considered the most important piece of safety equipment in boating, and therefore should be treated as such. To insure their proper use in an emergency, the following rules and habits should be observed.

1. Have every person try on his life preserver before going aboard. Be sure it fits properly and will support the weight of its wearer. Weight limitations should be clearly marked on the preserver or Coast Guard tag attached to it.
2. Nonswimmers and weak swimmers should wear their life preservers at all times when aboard or around docking areas. When in doubt of a person's swimming ability, consider him a nonswimmer. Don't let false pride on a passenger's part hinder you from enforcing this rule. Remember, under the

Lights Required on Motorboats Underway Between Sunset and Sunrise

MOTORBOATS: INBOARDS, OUTBOARDS, AND AUXILIARIES

Under Power alone	Auxiliaries under Sail and Power	Auxiliaries under Sail alone

INLAND RULES.—These lights may be shown only on Inland Waters, Western Rivers, and Great Lakes.[1]

Under 26 Feet

26 feet or over, but not more than 65 feet

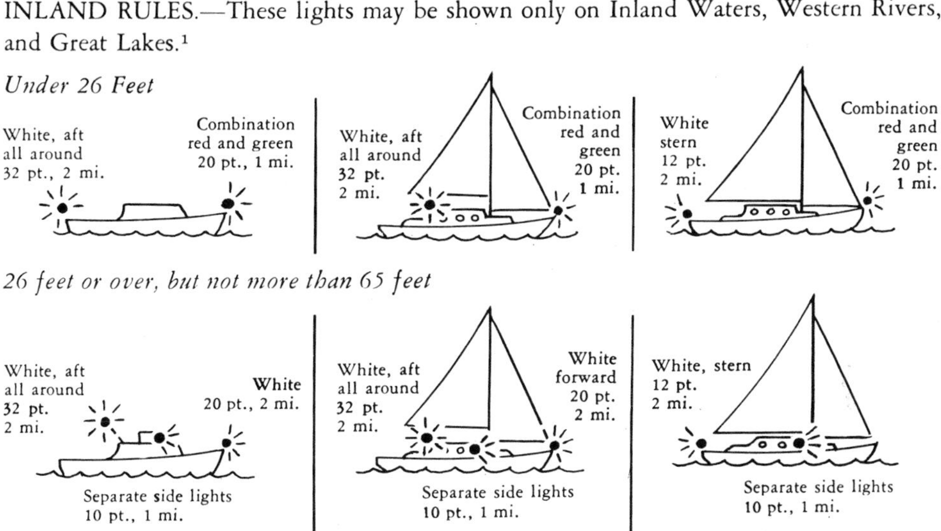

INTERNATIONAL RULES.—Lights under International Rules may be shown on Inland Waters, Western Rivers, and Great Lakes, and are required on the high seas.

Power vessel under 40 gross tons and sail vessels under 20 gross tons [2]

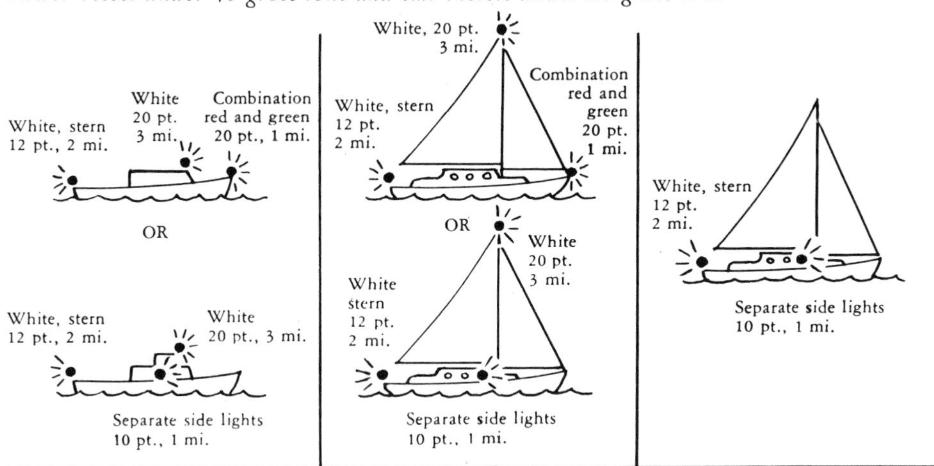

[1] A motorboat under sail alone on the Great Lakes is not required to display a stern light. All motorboats under sail alone must on approach of another vessel display a white light in the direction of the approaching vessel.

[2] Under International Rules powerboats of 40 gross tons or over must carry separate sidelights, visible 2 miles, and a 20-point white light visible 5 miles. Sailing boats of 20 gross tons or over must carry separate sidelights, visible 2 miles. Those less than 20 gross tons may use a combination lantern, if under sail alone.

Fig. 9

law, you, as owner or skipper, are responsible for the safety of your passengers and crew.

3. After each use in the water, life preservers should be dried out before they are stored or used again. This insures buoyancy and prevents rot.
4. Never sit on a wet life preserver, because weight will pack the stuffing and cause it to lose buoyancy.
5. Test each life preserver periodically. When one starts to lose its buoyancy, destroy it so a nonswimmer cannot find it.
6. Life preservers are not intended to be used as a swimming aid or for sport, and therefore should not be used for pleasure.
7. Make sure all life preservers stored aboard are easily and quickly accessible in an emergency.

LIGHTS

All boats are required to display lights from sunset to sunrise. These lights warn others of the presence of your boat and in many cases indicate to other boatmen the direction in which you are moving or the maneuver you are making. The two sets of laws regulating what lights must be used are called the Inland Rules and International Rules. Inland Rules cover all boats using Coast Guard controlled waters within the continental United States. International Rules cover all boats using the high seas and inland waters. Figure 9 shows the type, color, and placement of lights and how far they must be visible on different sizes and types of boats. The red lights mentioned always show on the port (left) side, and green lights always show on the starboard (right) side.

The term point (pt.) used in the illustration is based on the division of a complete circle into 32 points, the same as a compass. So when a light is said to have 10 points, it means it will reflect light that can be seen in only $^{10}/_{32}$ of a circle; a 12-point light appears in only $^{12}/_{32}$ of a circle; a 20-point light in only $^{20}/_{32}$ of a circle; and a 32-point light can be seen through the complete circle, or from every angle (Fig. 10).

Rowboats and canoes are not required to show any special running lights

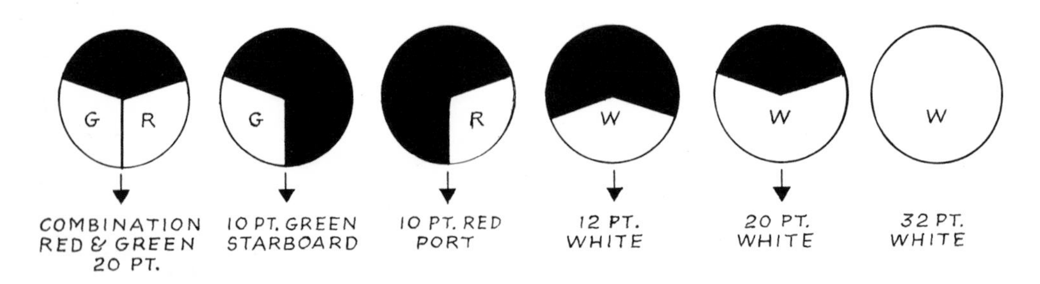

Fig. 10

but must carry a white lantern or flashlight. This light is shown when another vessel approaches.

Marine dealers can supply running lights showing the proper points and colors ready to mount.

WHISTLE OR HORN

The law states that only boats using engine power must carry a sound signal, but it recommends that all boats have a whistle or horn aboard to use for signaling during rules-of-the-road situations and emergencies (Fig. 11). To meet the requirements of the law, the whistle or horn must be able to sound a two-second blast that can be heard for at least one-half of a mile on Class A and I boats and one mile on Class II and Class III boats.

They can be either a hand, mouth, or power type for Class A boats, but must be hand or power type for Class I and II craft. While on Class III boats only powered horns or whistles are allowed. Class II and III boats must also carry a bell. The use of sound signals is an important part of safe boating and should be learned by everyone in the family.

Remember that "short blast" lasts one second, and "long blast" lasts two seconds or longer. Your horn or whistle must never be used except to signal. Use them only in the above situations; never play games with them or fail to pay attention to any signal. Properly used, they prevent accidents and save lives.

Sirens are forbidden on pleasure boats. Safety patrols and other emergency craft are the only boats allowed to use them, and then only in emergencies.

FIRE EXTINGUISHERS

Fires do happen aboard boats, especially motor boats. For this reason it is the law that all inboard motor boats must have a flame arrester on the motor's

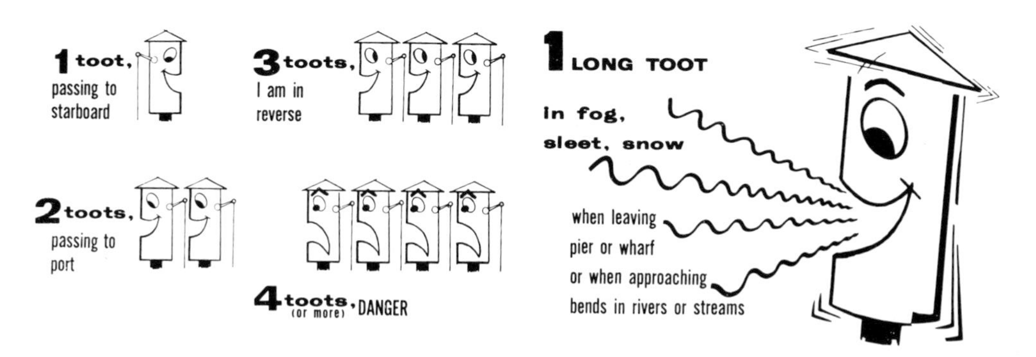

Fig. 11

carburetor. They must also carry one or more Coast Guard approved B-1 or B-2 fire extinguishers of the foam, carbon dioxide, or dry chemical type. Vaporized liquid extinguishers using carbon tetrachloride or chlorobromethane are forbidden because the fumes are toxic to humans. As yet the law does not apply to Class A and Class I outboard motorboats, but a smart skipper will have an approved fire extinguisher aboard regardless. The only exception to the above regulations is, when a boat has a built-in fixed fire extinguisher system. In such cases Class A and I boats are not required to carry a portable extinguisher aboard, while Class II craft need only one B-1 extinguisher and Class III boats only 2 B-1 or 1 B-2 extinguishers. Check your fire extinguishers periodically to be sure they are full and in working order.

VENTILATORS

Motorboats with enclosed areas, such as engine and fuel compartments, must have at least two cowled ventilators. The ventilators must be large enough to dissipate all inflammable or toxic fumes. Before starting your engine, check for fume odors around bilges, nonventilated areas and cabins.

ANCHOR

Although anchors are not as yet required equipment on small craft, smart skippers regard them as essential equipment. Along with being a parking brake, anchors often mean the difference between a wrecked boat and one that safely rode out the storm. Like most other equipment, anchors come in all shapes and sizes. When buying, be sure the type and size fit the design and weight of your boat and the waters she will be used in.

Just as important as your anchor is the anchor line. Make sure it is strong enough and long enough to anchor your boat safely. A good rule to follow is to have the line at least six to eight times as long as the depth of any water in which you will anchor.

A chart showing the types, sizes, weight, and holding power of anchors is shown in Chapter 12, "Anchoring, Mooring, Tying Up," page 199.

OTHER EQUIPMENT

Along with the minimum essential equipment required by law, the following *desirable equipment* should be carried aboard your boat: an extra flashlight and batteries, a first aid kit, extra paddle or oars, a tool kit and spare parts for making motor and other repairs, a bailer or bilge pump to bail or pump water from the boat in case of a leak, an extra anchor and coil of line when going on long trips, two or more boat fenders to protect the sides of your boat from chafing against docks or wharves when tied up, reserve fuel for long trips, a compass and charts when sailing strange waters, mooring lines, fresh water (this is especially important when boating on salt water), and emergency smoke flares for day and light flares for night.

If you plan to sail on large bodies of water, keep a roll of aluminum foil aboard at all times. Then if you should get lost offshore, spread the foil across the bow or any superstructure and it will act as a radar reflector for search boats. It is also a good idea aboard offshore cruisers that don't carry a "tender" (small boat) to store a navy type inflatable life raft.

STORING EQUIPMENT AND SAFETY DRILLS

Keeping equipment in working order and storing it properly are important. Flashlights with dead batteries or fire extinguishers inaccessible during a fire are useless in an emergency. Have permanent spots aboard for each item of equipment. Place them so they are out of the way yet readily available when needed.

Although no one wants trouble aboard, a wise skipper will hold periodic safety drills for fire, foul weather anchoring, abandoning ship, etc.

To a new boatman much of this equipment may sound extravagant. Unfortunately, most of it has come into use because of accidents and deaths, not to mention loss of vessels. Therefore, don't take any chances; start your boating career aboard a safe well-found craft.

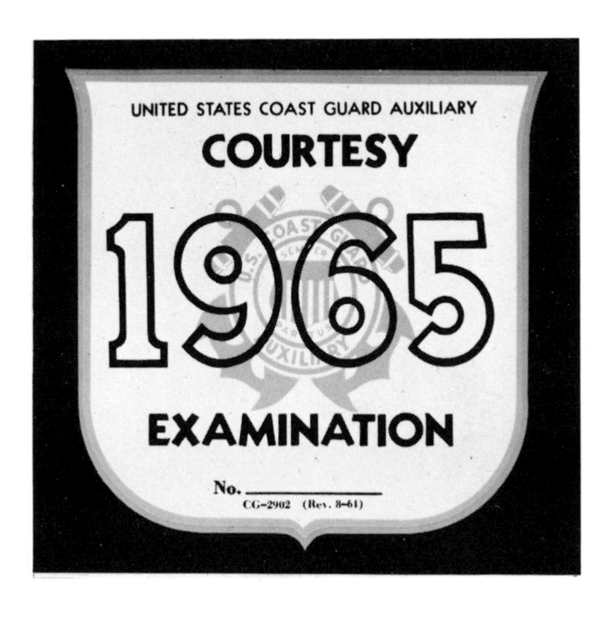

Fig. 12

U. S. COAST GUARD AUXILIARY INSPECTION

To promote safer boating in the United States, the U. S. Coast Guard Auxiliary offers a free safety inspection to all boat owners. New skippers will find this inspection especially helpful with regard to proper use and storage of emergency equipment. Boats that pass inspection receive a decal to place aboard showing they meet the high standards of safety required in all pleasure craft (Fig. 12). You can obtain a courtesy examination by getting in contact with the nearest U. S. Coast Guard Auxiliary Flotilla in your area.

3

Preparing to Go Afloat

Preparing to take command is as important to a new boatman as the studying a new driver must do to operate an automobile. Actually many of today's automotive traffic rules and regulations were formulated from maritime laws. This may come as a surprise, but just remember boating has been a part of civilization for thousands of years whereas automobiles have existed for only a few generations.

The time and study you and your family put into these seamanship rules will show up when you are afloat. Once mastered they will bring you automatic recognition from professional sailors and experienced boatmen. Probably the finest compliment you can receive in boating is to have an "old salt" tell you, "She's well found and you sail her well." A thorough knowledge of a few rules and procedures will earn you many such compliments.

SAFETY RULES AND HABITS

The most important rule of command is Safety for your passengers and boat. Obeying this rule means learning and practicing the following rules and habits. Be sure everyone you bring aboard knows and understands them.

1. Give your boat a safety check for seaworthiness and equipment before each cruise. (Chapter 13, "Fitting Out and Storage," page 229.)
2. Be sure everyone aboard has a Coast Guard approved life jacket. Poor

swimmers and nonswimmers should wear them all the time when aboard. In rough seas everyone should wear one. In case of an accident, a life jacket will keep you afloat when hurt or unconscious. (Chapter 2, "Safety Equipment," page 15.)

3. Always tell someone where you are going and what time you will be back. (Chapter 15, "Cruising America's Waterways," Fig. 254.)
4. Check the weather; stormy days are stay-ashore days! (Chapter 6, "Developing a Weather Eye," page 81.)
5. *No Standing room allowed in small boats.* Check the passenger capacity recommended by the builder of your boat. (Chapter 1, "Your First Command," page 1.)
6. When boating in strange waters, use your charts or bring someone familiar with the area. (Chapter 5, "Compass, Charts, Piloting," page 54.)
7. Always wear a hat for protection against sunstroke. If you sunburn easily, wear loose-fitting pants and shirt. (Chapter 11, "Rescue and First Aid," page 181.)
8. Respect the rights of others. Keep your speed and wake down near swimmers, fishermen, water skiers, and smaller boats. ("Courtesy and Common Sense," end of this chapter.)
9. When refueling afloat, always stop the boat. When possible drop anchor. Kneel, do not stand, while pouring gas. *No smoking.* (Chapter 9, "Powerboating," page 133.)
10. If your boat should tip or swamp, stay with the boat until help arrives. A boat should be able to hold her passengers when full of water. (Chapter 10, "Seamanship in Rough Weather," page 173.)

DAILY BOAT CHECK

Before each day's cruise give your boat a five-minute safety check. Bail out any water in the bilge (bottom). Check for leaks. Examine the hull for cracks, dents, and paint breaks. Test the motor and check the equipment list. Aboard outboard motor boats tighten the motor transom clamps and lock the safety chain. Copy the daily checklist in Figure 13 and place it in a conspicuous place aboard your boat as a reminder. (In Chapter 13, "Fitting Out and Storage," page 229), you will learn how to fit out your boat each spring plus how to make a weekly and monthly safety check.

NOTE: Use the check list below as a guide to develop a daily boat check for your craft.

DAILY BOAT CHECK

	OK	*REPAIRS
Hull		
1. Bilge Water		
2. Leaks		
3. Cracks—Breaks		
4. Paint Scratches		
5. Cleats—Chocks—etc.		
6. Other		
Sailboat Rigging		
1. Mast—Spars		
2. Stays—Sheets		
3. Sail Track—Halyards		
4. Sails		
Engine		
1. Gasoline Fumes		
2. Leaks (oil—water)		
a. Gasket		
b. Cracks		
3. Rust		
4. Missing Nuts—Bolts		
5. Gasoline		
6. Oil		
7. Transom Clamps		
(outboard)		
8. Safety Chain		
(outboard)		
9. Other		
***Repair Notes:**		
1.		
2.		
3.		

	OK	*REPAIRS
Controls		
1. Steering		
2. Throttle		
3. Shift		
4. Others		
Start Engine and Check		
1. Leaks (oil & water)		
2. Oil Pressure		
3. Cooling System		
4. Ammeter		
Instruments		
1. Compass		
2. Radio		
3. Other		
Equipment		
1. Life Preservers		
2. Fire Extinguishers		
3. Ventilators		
4. Lights		
5. Horn or Whistle		
6. Anchor—Line		
7. Other		

Fig. 13

SAILOR'S KNOTS

Among seamen, knots are considered a sailor's best friends. As you gain experience in boating this will become more and more apparent. The right knot, hitch, or splice in a line often becomes the difference between safety or tragedy. The following knots and splices are those used most in boating. Learn these now, and later you can learn many more from friends and other boatmen.

Fig. 14

1. REEF KNOT

1. Square or reef knot—used to tie two light lines of the same thickness together.

2. SHEET BEND

3. BOWLINE

2. Sheet bend—used to tie two lines of different thickness together.
3. Bowline—used to make a secure noose for tying up to a dock or pier. It can also be used to tie a line to an anchor.

4. CLOVE HITCH

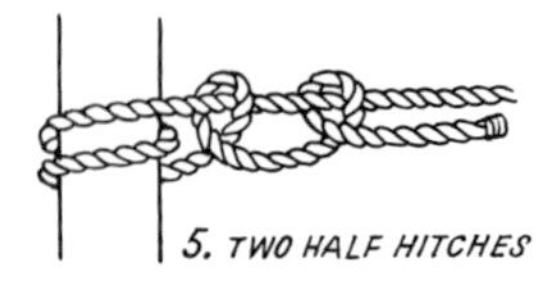

5. TWO HALF HITCHES

4. Clove hitch—used to make a line fast to a post or bollard temporarily.
5. Two half hitches—used to make a line secure to a post, bollard, or timber.
6. Cleat hitch—used to make fast to a cleat.

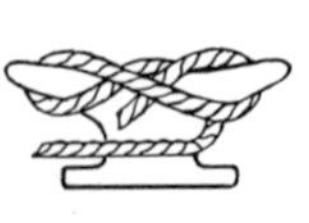

6. CLEAT HITCH

7. ANCHOR BEND

7. Anchor bend—used to secure a line to an anchor ring or other rings.

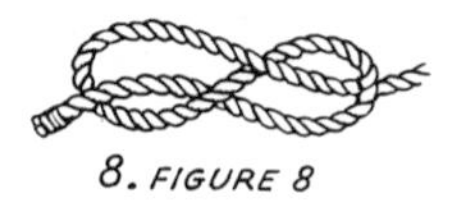

8. FIGURE 8

8. Figure eight—used as a stop at the end of a line running through a fairlead or eye.
9. Splices

9A. SHORT SPLICE

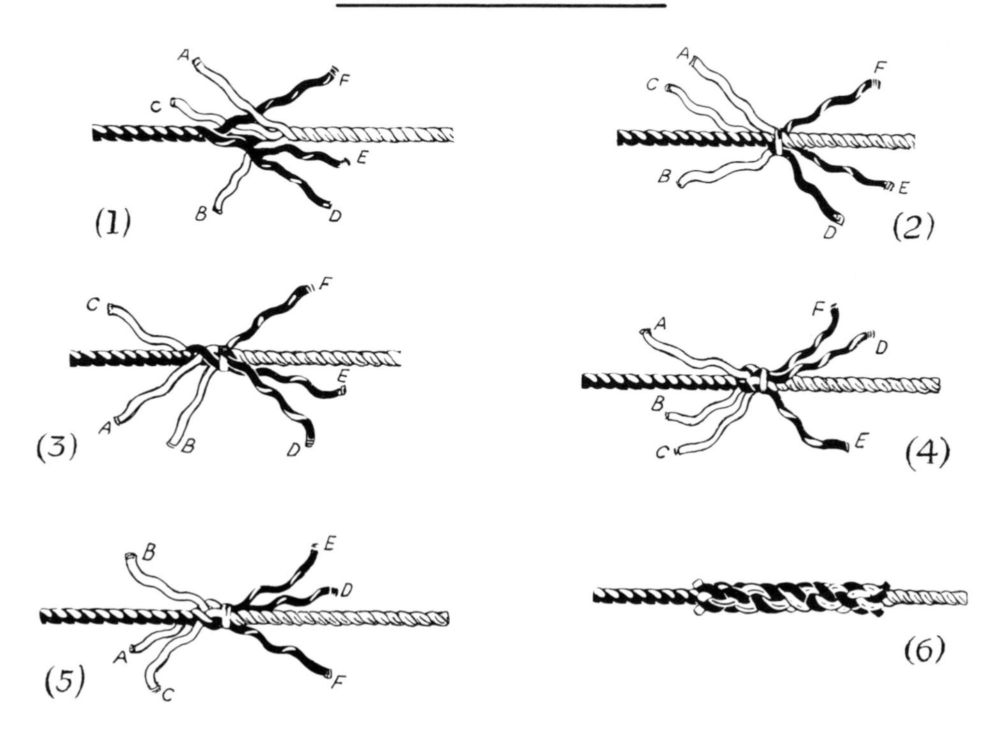

(1) Unwind each strand of line for 6 or 8 turns and whip end of each strand. Next bring both lines together so each strand of one line alternates with a strand of the other line.
(2) Bring lines tightly together and make a temporary seizing where they join.
(3) Take strand A and pass it over strand D and under strand E.
(4) Rotate the splice one-third of a turn away from you and make the second tuck. Pass strand B over strand E and under strand F.
(5) Rotate the splice once more one-third of a turn away from you and pass strand C over strand F and under strand D, this completes the first "round" of tucks.
(6) Repeat tucks 3, 4, 5 two or more times. Always over one and under one and be sure each strand lies snug with no kinks. Splice can be rolled smooth with foot or hand.

9B. LONG SPLICE

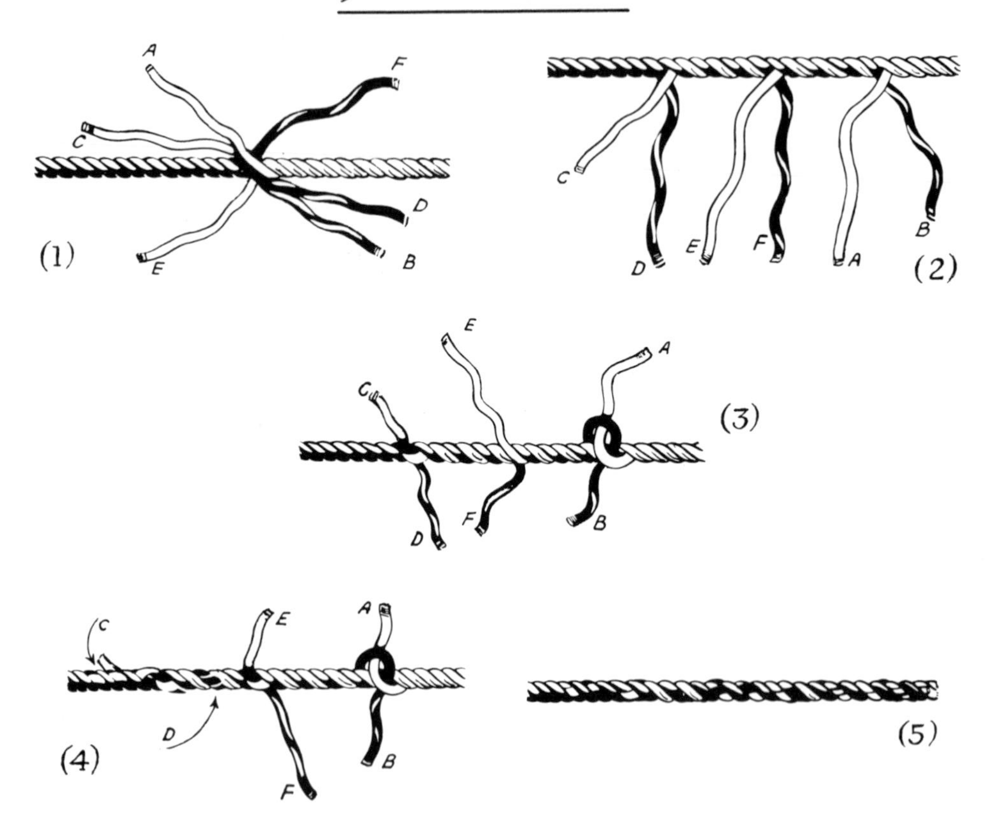

Fig. 14 (continued)

(1) Unwind each strand of line for 10 or 15 turns, whip end of each strand, then lock strands together.

(2) Take strands A and B, underlay strand A then strand B until less than a foot of strand A and B remains. Keep strand B tight during this stage—pulling it down firmly into strand A's former place. Repeat same operation with strands C and D, E and F.

(3) Tie each pair of strands loosely A and B. Then pull each pair down into the rope C and D.

(4) Tuck each strand twice over and under as if making a short splice. Strands C and D show how tuck should look. Where a smaller diameter splice is needed make two more tucks of each strand thinning out the strands as you tuck.

(5) Trim all strands close to line, then roll line on floor or table using a foot or hand to smooth it out.

Fig. 15

GOING ABOARD AND COMING ASHORE

Knowing how to enter and leave a small boat is important. The few minutes spent learning these operations will save a lot of lumps and bruises. The two most important rules to remember are: *Never jump into or out of a boat; and always have your hands free to hold the gunwale or transom.* When these rules are broken, a boat rolls or skids out from under you, throwing you backward into the water or dock.

Onshore

Most boats that are beached (pulled up onshore) have the bow resting on land. When boarding from this position, take hold of the gunwale (railing) close to the bow, and slide the boat out into the water until the bow is almost afloat, Fig. 15. Then gently step into the boat. Once aboard, crouch low over the keel line (center of boat) and move to your seat. When coming ashore use the same procedure in the opposite order. Sometimes, especially with lifeguard boats, the stern (back) of the boat will be beached. In such cases enter over the transom rather than the bow.

At Dockside

When a boat is tied to a dock, always enter and leave it amidships (middle of the boat). If the sides of the boat are above the dock, use the same procedure you would on shore, keeping in mind to enter and leave amidships. Fig. 16.

When a boat is tied to a high dock and you must step down into the boat, use the following procedure: Kneel on the dock at amidships; place one hand

Fig. 16

on the dock and the other on the gunwale of the boat. (To avoid a crushed thumb, *don't* put your thumb between the gunwale and dock.) Gently step aboard, as close to the keel line as you can, crouch low, and move to your seat, Fig. 17. Use the same procedure in the opposite order when coming ashore.

An added safety rule is to be sure the securing lines are tied bow and stern. They will keep the boat from sliding away from the dock.

At a Mooring

Frequently boats are tied to a mooring buoy offshore in deep water. To reach them you must row or motor out in a small boat called a tender. If the boat is moored bow and stern, so she does not head into the wind, always come

Fig. 17

Fig. 18

alongside on the leeward side (side furthest from the wind). This is the sheltered side, and the water is always calmer. Once alongside, tie up to the mooring buoy; put one hand on the gunwale of the tender and the other on the gunwale of the moored boat (remember your thumbs). Hold both sides together and gently step across into the moored boat (Fig. 18). Use the same procedure when leaving, only in the opposite order.

Loading Equipment

As skipper you are always the first to go aboard and the last to leave. Before helping your passengers aboard, stow all equipment. If you are using an outboard motor, take it aboard first and attach it to the transom. Then take aboard the remaining equipment stowing it out of the way, but accessible when needed.

RULES OF THE ROAD

Boats, like automobiles, have traffic regulations called rules of the road. On land, automobiles are guided by roads, traffic signs, and speed limits. Except in marked channels, boats, unfortunately, have no such signs and must travel on wide expanses of unmarked waters. Therefore, it is imperative that you and your family learn and obey these maritime traffic rules. Infractions call for fines up to $2,000 or a jail sentence. Be sure you know and understand each and every one before going afloat.

To simplify the enforcement and observance of these traffic rules, they have been divided into two sets of regulations, one for powerboats and the other for sailboats. The division is necessary because sailboats, depending on the wind, cannot sail in every direction and are less maneuverable than powerboats.

The first step in learning these rules of the road is to understand what composes a situation, a burdened boat, and a privileged boat.

A *situation* exists whenever another boat or boats approach you on a line that makes a collision possible.

A *burdened boat* is always the boat that must maneuver out of the way of another boat.

A *privileged boat* always has the right of way and must hold her course and speed, except when in danger of a collision.

When the burdened boat is a powercraft, she must sound a signal, letting the privileged boat know her intention (see pages 33-34). The privileged boat, if under motor power, must return the same signal, holding her course and allowing the burdened boat to pass. (Sailboats, canoes, and rowboats are not required to use sound signals during a situation.) The only time a privileged boat can return a signal different from the one given by a burdened boat is when it would be dangerous for the burdened boat to continue. This signal would be four or more short blasts, signifying danger. When this happens the burdened boat must slow down or stop until the privileged boat signals it is all right to continue by giving the original signal. When in doubt, repeat your signal and wait for an answer.

RULES OF THE ROAD FOR POWERBOATS

The most used rules of the road are those practiced by powerboats and recommended for canoes and rowboats. They are called the Inland Pilot Rules. Although these rules differ slightly on certain waters, the basic maneuvers are the same. Boatmen using the Great Lakes and western rivers will find these rules are applicable in all but a few sound signal cases. Coast Guard pamphlet CG-172 explains the Great Lakes Rules, and Coast Guard pamphlet CG-184 explains the Western Rivers Rules. Both pamphlets can be obtained by writing your nearest Coast Guard station.

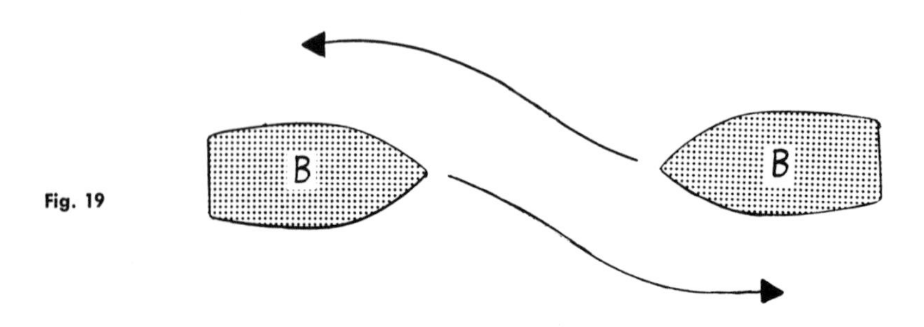

Fig. 19

Meeting Situation, Bow on Bow or Nearly So

In a meeting situation bow to bow both boats are burdened. Each must signal with one short blast, turn to the starboard (right), and pass portside (left) to portside, Fig. 19.

When the courses of the boats are so far to the port of each other that a bow-to-bow situation does not exist, each signals one short blast and continues on her present course.

However, when the courses of the boats are so far to the starboard (right) of each other that they are not in a bow-to-bow situation, a signal of two short blasts is given by one boat. When answered by the other boat, she is allowed to pass starboard to starboard, Fig. 20. This is the only time in a meeting situation you should pass starboard to starboard.

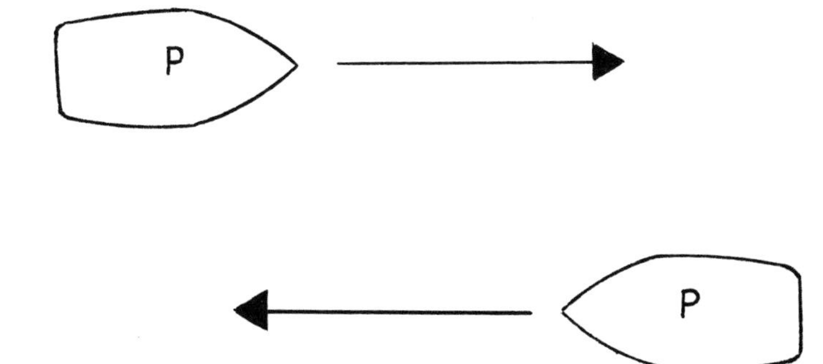

Fig. 20

Overtaking Situation

In an overtaking situation the lead boat is the privileged craft and must hold her course and speed. The burdened boat preparing to pass must signal with one short blast if she intends to pass on the starboard side of the privileged boat. When the privileged boat returns the same signal, the burdened boat turns to the starboard and passes, Fig. 21.

Occasionally a burdened boat may want to pass on the portside of the privileged boat. In such cases the signal would be two short blasts. Passing to the port, however, is not recommended as a general procedure.

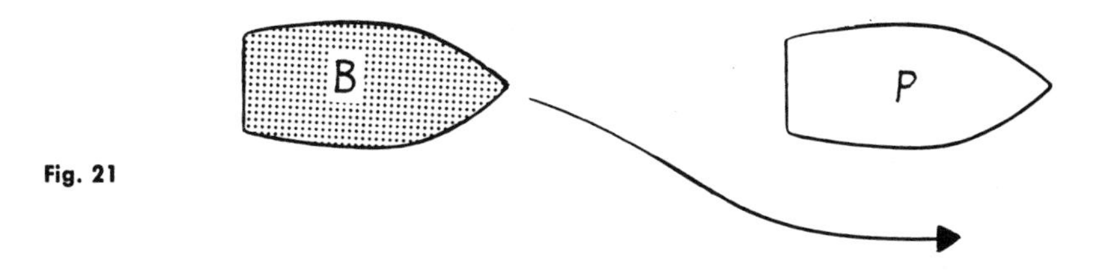

Fig. 21

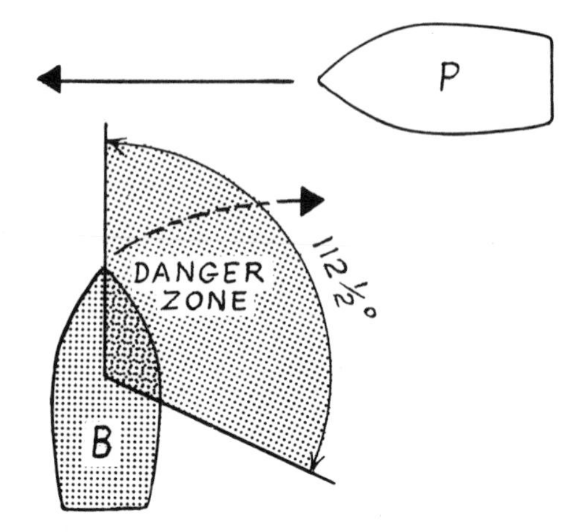

Fig. 22

Crossing Situation

A crossing situation takes place any time two or more boats approach each other at right angles or nearly so. In a crossing situation every boat has a danger zone from dead ahead to 112½ degrees aft on the starboard side (Fig. 22). When another boat enters this zone for your boat you automatically become the burdened craft. To avoid colliding, stop or turn your burdened boat to the starboard and pass to the rear of the privileged boat, who must hold her course and speed.

Although it is not mandatory, each boat usually gives a sound signal of one blast. This lets the privileged boat know the burdened craft will stop or pass to the rear.

SPECIAL SITUATIONS

To further insure the safety of all boats afloat, other rules for special situations have been established. They are:

1. Sailboats have the right of way over motorboats. Motorboats must pass astern or far enough to one side so as not to interfere with the sailboats course. The one exception to this rule is when a sailboat is overtaking a powerboat. In this situation the sailboat becomes burdened and must pass in the usual manner.
2. Keep to the right on channels, rivers, and streams.
3. Signal with one long blast (two seconds or longer) when rounding sharp bends, moving from slips, docks, berths, and prior to entering traffic channels.
4. Large oceangoing vessels, because of their great length and draft, require

more time to stop or turn. Therefore, small craft should always give them the right of way. Caution should be taken when passing to the stern of large ships. The heavy wake and suction caused by the churning propellers can swamp a small boat if she gets too close.

5. In a fog, mist, snow, or rain, signal with long blasts at one-minute intervals and slow down to a moderate speed. (Moderate speed has been defined as a speed no greater than will enable a boat to stop in half the distance of visibility.)

Common sense and safe speeds are integral parts of the rules of the road.

RULES OF THE ROAD FOR SAILBOATS

The direction of the wind largely determines a sailboat's maneuverability. Therefore, a separate set of rules of the road are necessary for sailing craft. Unless you have had previous sailing experience, chances are that these rules will seem strange and complicated when you first read them. Don't let this worry you. After you read the chapter on sailing, restudy these five rules and they will be clear and understandable.

1. A sailboat that is running free must keep out of the way of a sailboat that is close-hauled (Fig. 23).
2. A sailboat that is close-hauled on a port tack must keep out of the way of a sailboat that is close-hauled on a starboard tack (Fig. 24).

Fig. 23

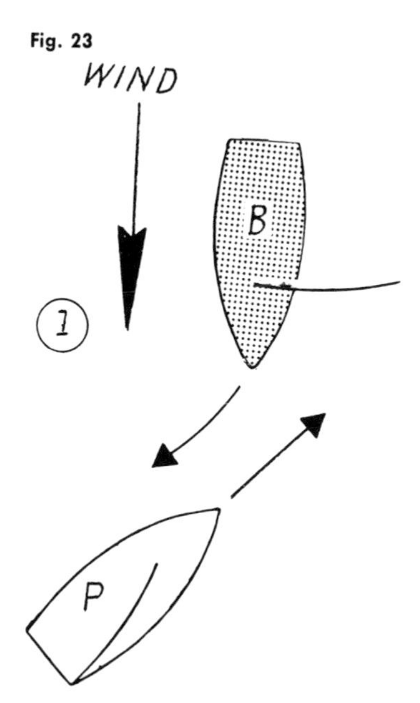

Fig. 24

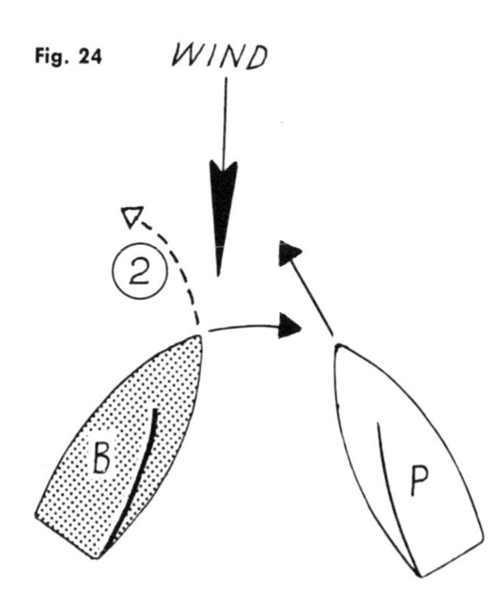

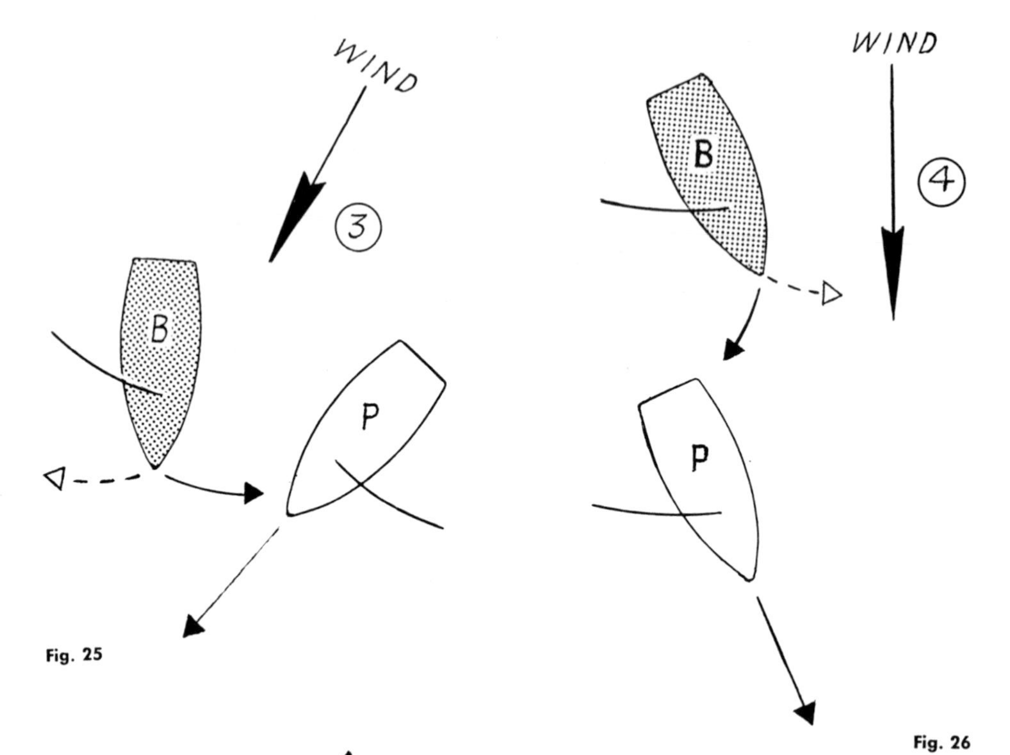

Fig. 25

Fig. 26

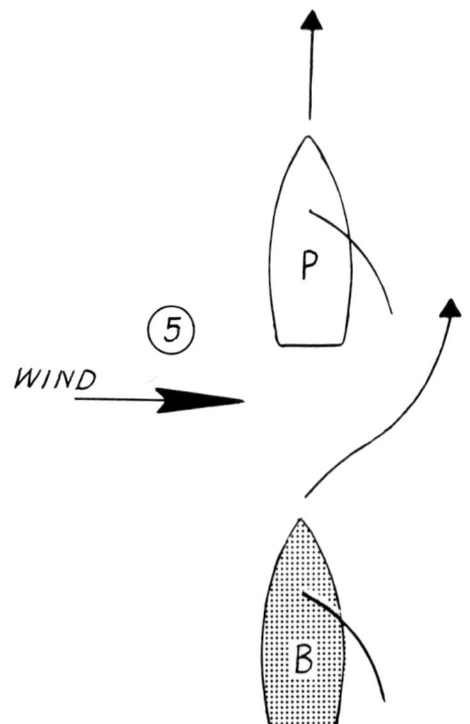

Fig. 27

3. When both sailboats are running free, with the wind on different sides, the boat that has the wind on the portside is burdened and must keep out of the way of the other (Fig. 25).
4. When both sailboats are running free, with the wind on the same side, the boat that is to the windward must keep out of the way of the boat that is to the leeward (Fig. 26).
5. A sailboat overtaking another on the same tack passes on the leeward side so as not to steal the wind. In racing, of course, you disregard this rule and try to steal an opponent's wind (Fig. 27).

In all sailing situations the boat that must keep clear is burdened, and the boat required to hold course is the privileged.

RIVER CRUISING

River cruising has a special magic for millions of boatmen who believe, as Mark Twain did, that an adventure lies around every bend. If you plan to become one of these "Mark Twains," the following are a few river "signs" you must understand to insure safety afloat.

1. On straight stretches of a river the deepest and best boating water is usually the darkest color and will be found in the middle.
2. At a bend on a river the deepest water is usually found at the outside of the bend.
3. Sand bars, mud flats, and shoals are apt to be found at junctions with streams or other rivers.
4. As water becomes shallow it lightens in color and tends to be more ripply in a breeze.
5. Avoid any dead calm river water. Usually it marks a shallow bar or flat.
6. Watch out for choppy water, swirls, or eddies in a current. The chances are they indicate a rock or other hazard just below the surface.

COURTESY AND COMMON SENSE

The fun and enjoyment associated with pleasure boating depend in large part on courtesy and common sense. Nothing ruins a day afloat more than an inconsiderate boatman who thinks a waterway is his private playground. Remember, you are only one of over one hundred and forty million people who use the waters in our country for their enjoyment. This means you must do your part to assure everyone his share of the fun. Observance of the following rules will make this possible.

1. Stay clear of swimmers and swimming areas.

2. Keep your speed and wake down when passing smaller boats, water skiers, and docks.
3. Don't hot-rod in heavily trafficked areas.
4. Stay clear of skin and scuba diving areas. A small red and white flag will be floating over these areas.
5. Don't show off at the expense of your passengers or other boats.
6. When docking or heading out, respect the rights of others.
7. Stay clear of fisherman and fishing boats that are trolling.

These are only a few of the many courtesy rules that make boating a pleasure. Common sense will dictate many more. Remember, your actions afloat are the key to safe, fun-filled boating.

LOCKS AND LOCKING THROUGH

To lengthen navigable rivers, Federal and State Governments have built locks around waterfalls, etc. in rivers and where necessary at canals to lift or lower boats between water levels. The locks are in a sense water elevators. A boat enters an open gate at one level, the gate is closed, and water is pumped in or drained off, raising or lowering the boat. When the boat reaches the desired level, a gate at the opposite end of the lock opens and the boat goes on its way.

Moving through locks, called "locking through," is regulated by certain safety rules that must be obeyed. These rules and regulations vary at different locks so it is important that you take the time to check out any locks you will be using. In some cases it is necessary to obtain lock passes beforehand. Four stages that are pretty much standard at all locks are: approaching, entering, position in the lock, and leaving. Procedures in each stage are as follows:

Approaching. Slow down or stop and wait instructions. These may be given by lights, horn, verbal, or written signs. If the lock is next to a dam keep well clear of the edge and stay alert. Put out your fenders and fender board (strong board that straddles fenders) on both sides.

Entering. Move up into the lock at slow speed following the traffic pattern as directed. Stay alert and be extra careful when large ocean vessels are also entering.

Position in the Lock. Once in the lock move to a position along one sidewall toward the front, unless directed otherwise. When in position turn off your engine and observe the "No Smoking" signs. Hold the boat, bow and stern, with a line that can be paid out or taken in as the water rises or lowers. Under no circumstances tie up tight. Rising water will snub you under, while lower-

Fig. 28

ing water can hang you up high and dry. Figure 28 shows a simple one man harness used by many small boats.

Leaving. When the water reaches the desired level the gate will open. Start your engine but wait until the lockmaster signals you to leave before getting underway. The usual procedure is to leave the same way you entered.

While locking through, the lockmaster has complete authority over the boats in his lock. Failure to obey his directions is an offense punishable by fine or prison.

DISTRESS SIGNALS

In the event your boat becomes disabled there are a number of recognized distress signals that will alert other boatmen to the fact that you are in trouble. What to use will depend on existing visibility, surface conditions, and equipment you have on board. Under no circumstances signal for help unless it is definitely needed. Such action can divert help from a boat that is in serious trouble. The following are the more commonly used distress signals. Learn to use and recognize them.

1. The official Coast Guard distress signal for small craft within sight of other boats is a crewman or passenger standing up and raising and lowering arms outstretched to each side.
2. Reverse your flag or ensign so that it flies upside down. Or fly a white cloth or pair of pants from the highest point on your boat.
3. Sound your horn or whistle repeatedly.
4. Blink a flashlight, white range light, or spotlight to signal SOS (three dots, three dashes, three dots, . . . — — — . . .)
5. Fire a gun at one-minute intervals.

6. Send up emergency rocket flares. Rocket kits are available at most marine dealers.
7. Light a fire in a metal pail placed on the bow or atop a cabin. Make it a smoky fire for daytime use and a bright flame for nighttime use. Do not use gasoline as a fuel.
8. When electronic communications are aboard (radiotelephone) follow the instructions on the set for sending a "Mayday" emergency call.

4

Navigational Buoys and Markers

As in automotive travel, boating has road signs and route numbers that tell the best and safest way to reach a destination. On the water these floating signposts are called navigational buoys and markers. Their primary functions are to mark channels (the highways and streets of boating), to warn of underwater hazards, such as shoals, reefs, and wrecks, and, in conjunction with charts, to locate a present position or plot courses. Under the direction of the United States Coast Guard all buoys used on navigable waters have been categorized into an easy-to-understand Lateral Buoyage System. This system employs a simple arrangement of colors, numbers, shapes, and light characteristics to show the side on which a buoy should be passed when proceeding in a given direction, "entering from seaward." Figure 29 shows the official U. S. Coast Guard Lateral Buoyage System.

ENTERING FROM SEAWARD

To simplify learning and consistently apply the Lateral Buoyage System, all official Coast Guard manuals and illustrations arbitrarily assume all buoys are approached or passed from seaward proceeding toward the head of navigation. This is stated as "entering from seaward." This term often confuses new boatmen, especially when channels run parallel to our coastlines, rather than inbound toward port or upriver. To avoid any confusion the following rules have been established for channels that run parallel to our coastline. On the Atlantic

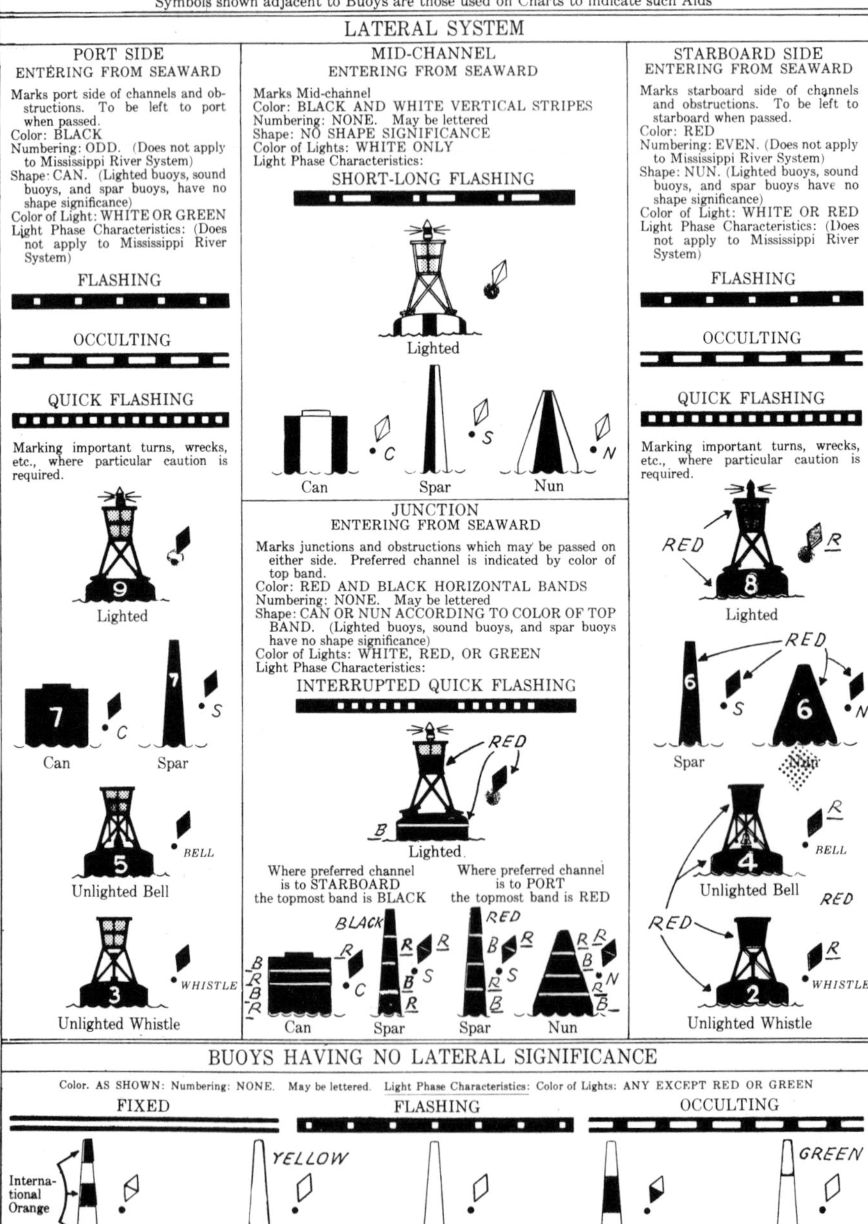

R DESIGNATES RED
B DESIGNATES BLACK

Fig. 29

Coast, "entering from seaward" means proceeding in a southerly direction; on the Gulf Coast in a northerly or westerly direction; and on the West Coast in a northerly direction. Looking at Figure 30 you will see this movement is in a clockwise direction starting at Maine and ending in Washington.

On the Great Lakes, "entering from seaward" means proceeding in a westerly or northerly direction on all lakes except Lake Michigan, where travel is assumed to be in a southerly direction. This is determined from the mouths to the head of navigation in each lake.

COLOR SIGNIFICANCE

All buoys are painted distinctive colors to indicate their purpose or, in the Lateral System, the side on which they should be passed.

Red buoys mark the starboard (right) sides of channels when entering from seaward and must be passed by keeping the buoy off the starboard side of your boat.

Black buoys mark the port (left) sides of channels when entering from seaward and must be passed by keeping the buoy off the port side of your boat.

Red and black horizontally banded buoys mark junctions in a channel, or obstruction. If the topmost band is black, the preferred channel will be followed by keeping the buoy off the port side of your boat entering from seaward. If the topmost band is red, the preferred channel will be followed by

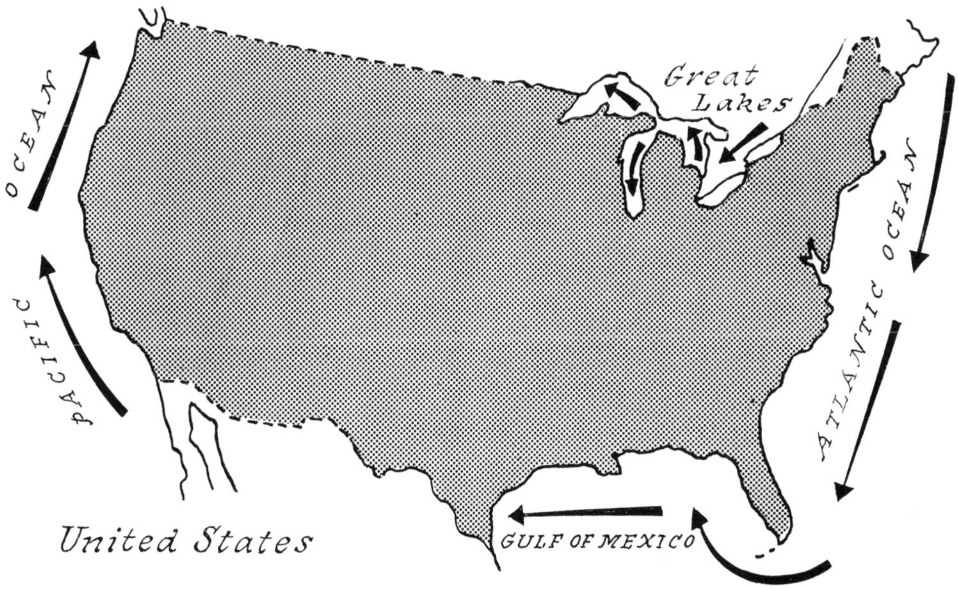

Fig. 30

keeping the buoy off the starboard side of your boat when entering from seaward. Occasionally it may not be possible, because of an obstruction, to pass close to either side of these banded buoys; therefore a local chart should always be consulted.

Black and white vertically striped buoys mark the fairway (midchannel) and should be passed close to, on either side.

The habit of painting a white band on the top of all buoys is becoming fairly common. This has no color meaning except to aid boatmen spot the buoy more easily at night with a searchlight.

NUMBERS AND LETTERS ON BUOYS

To further help boatmen identify buoys or plot their position, a numbering and lettering code is used on all buoys marking the sides of channels. Solid-colored red buoys marking the starboard side when entering from seaward will always be even-numbered. Solid-colored black buoys marking the left side will always be odd-numbered. Numbers increase from seaward and are kept in approximate sequence on both sides of the channel. A letter follows a numeral—such as 4A, 7a, or 1DR—to show that the buoy has been added as an additional reference point or to mark an important buoy, particularly isolated offshore dangers. An example of the latter is the Duxbury Reef Buoys (1DR) off the Massachusetts coast. The number 1 shows it must be kept on the left hand when passing from seaward, and the letters identify it as the Duxbury Reef on charts.

Occasionally letters without numbers will be found on buoys other than solid red or black side markers. Check local charts for their meanings.

The only instance where the above code system does not apply on navigable United States waters is in the Mississippi River Navigation System. In this system only lighted buoys are numbered to indicate the mileage from one point to another.

SHAPES OF BUOYS

Surprisingly, except for the conically shaped nun buoys and oil-drum shaped can buoys, the shape characteristic of buoys has no official meaning. This is because lighted and sound buoys, although used as day markers, are primarily designed for use in darkness and fog where the buoy itself is rarely seen. In nun and can buoys, which are considered only day markers, shape plays an important role with regard to placement.

Nun buoys when used as side markers are placed only on the starboard (right) side of a channel when entering from seaward and will be solid red with even numbers.

Can buoys when used as side markers are placed only on the port (left) side of a channel entering from seaward and will always be solid black with odd numbers.

When these buoys are painted with black and red horizontal bands as junction or obstruction markers, the top band on nun buoys will always be red and the top band on can buoys will always be black.

Midchannel markers painted with black and white vertical stripes can be either nun or can buoys. Shape has no significance in this instance.

Spar buoys, which are also used as day markers on either side of channels or as midchannel markers, have no shape significance. Although spar buoys were once widely used, they are slowly being replaced by nun and can buoys.

LIGHTED BUOYS AND LIGHT CHARACTERISTICS

To help boatmen navigate at night through channels and around obstructions, lighted buoys with coded flashing signals are used.

Red lights signify the right side of the channel entering from seaward.

Green lights signify the left side of the channel entering from seaward.

White lights mark midchannel and occasionally replace red or green lights at points where added brilliance is needed.

Fixed lights (lights that do not flash), flashing lights (-----), not more than thirty flashes a minute, and quick-flashing lights (.....), sixty or more per minute, all mark the sides of a channel. Quick flashes signify that special caution is required, as in bends or narrow areas.

Intermittent quick-flashing lights with dark intervals of about four seconds between groups (..... .....) signify channel junctions or obstructions. This flashing code will always be on red and black horizontally banded buoys.

Lighted fairway buoys marking midchannel use a short-long flashing code (-.-.-.-.-.), eight per minute.

In channels that have a lot of night traffic, nonlighted buoys will often have optical reflectors or reflective tape placed on them. This is merely to aid boatmen in finding them at night with a searchlight.

SOUND BUOYS

The use of sound on buoys by either bell, gong, or whistle dates back to the late 1800's. Their purpose is to assist boatmen in locating them in fog or poor visibility. Often a sound buoy will be combined with a light buoy to make location easier after dark.

RADAR REFLECTORS

In 1952, because of the increasing importance of radar as an aid to navigation, all buoy designs were changed to incorporate a corner radar reflector in the superstructure. Thus all buoys manufactured since that time have improved radar response.

SIZES OF BUOYS

The size of a buoy has no significance and should not be considered as important. Large buoys are usually anchored in large channels or offshore so they can be seen from a greater distance.

CHANNEL TRAFFIC

The flow of traffic in a channel always moves along the right-hand side. This means when entering from seaward you pass to the left of the even-numbered red buoys so as to keep them off your boat's starboard side, Fig. 31. An easy way to remember this is the three R's—Red buoys mark the Right-hand side when Returning from seaward, or Red-Right-Returning.

When leaving port heading out to sea or entering a parallel channel counterclockwise, the odd-numbered black buoys automatically become the right side of the channel. You also pass to the left of these buoys, keeping them off your boat's starboard side.

Red and black banded buoys marking an obstruction are usually placed in front of the hazard when entering from seaward. So caution should be taken to give these buoys plenty of berth when passing in either direction.

INTRACOASTAL WATERWAY

The intracoastal waterway is a group of natural and man-made channels that run along the Atlantic and Gulf coasts from New Jersey to the Mexican border. Called the "inland waterway," this route allows small cruising craft to travel in comparative safety while moving along either coastline. The buoyage system used is the Lateral System with one addition. All intracoastal markers will have some portion of them painted yellow. Buoys have a yellow band at the top and day markers will have a yellow border around the edges (Fig. 32). Channel junction buoys, marking the right side of the channel when traveling clockwise, show a yellow triangle, while buoys marking the left side will show yellow squares. When the intracoastal waterway joins another waterway buoyed in the opposite direction, the yellow symbols designate the side and type of buoy (Fig. 33). In such instances the black can buoys will have a

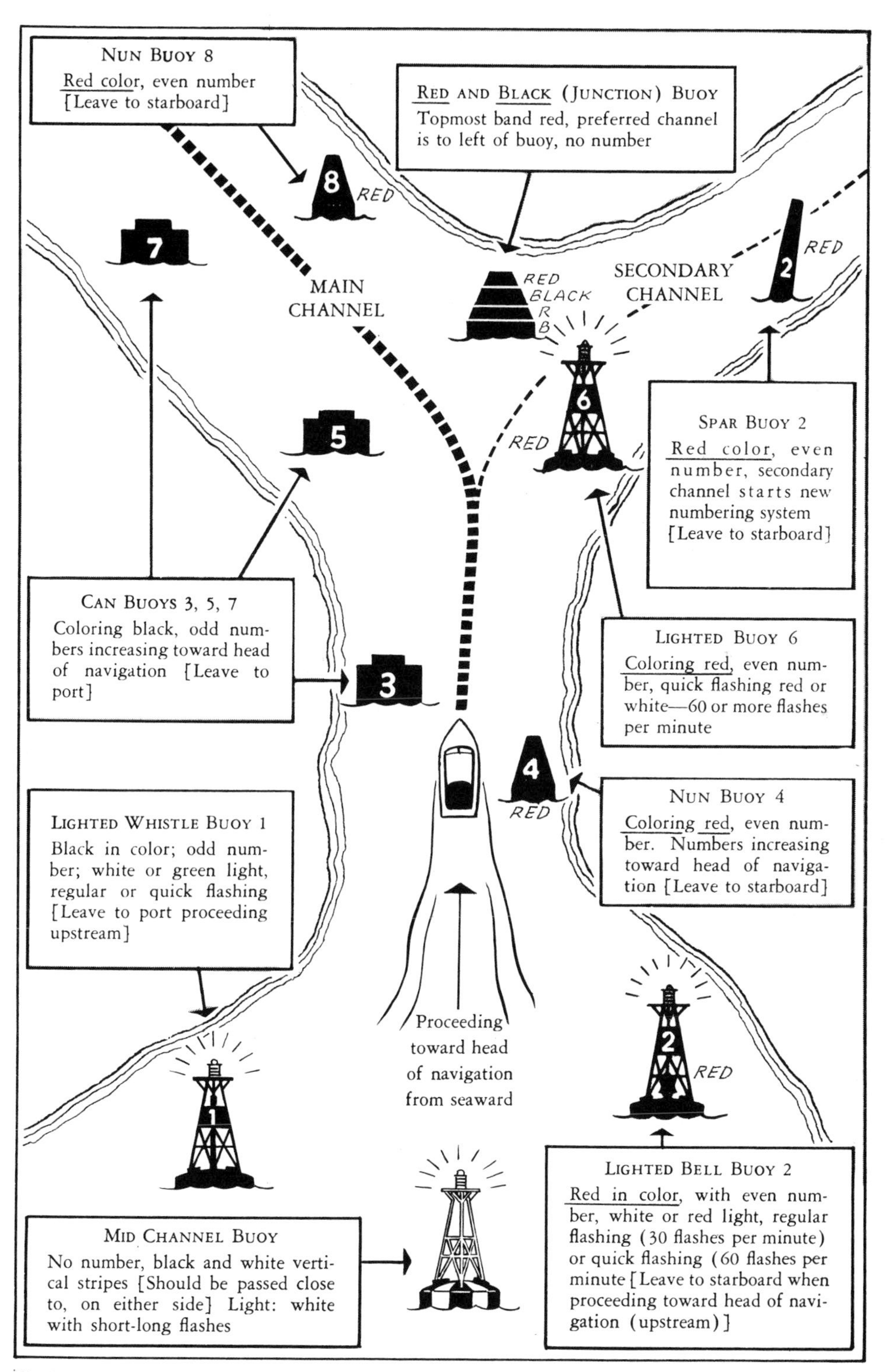

NUN BUOY 8
Red color, even number
[Leave to starboard]
RED AND BLACK (JUNCTION) BUOY
Topmost band red, preferred channel
is to left of buoy, no number
8
RED
7
RED
BLACK
R
B
MAIN
CHANNEL
SECONDARY
CHANNEL
2
RED
6
RED
5
SPAR BUOY 2
Red color, even
number, secondary
channel starts new
numbering system
[Leave to starboard]
CAN BUOYS 3, 5, 7
Coloring black, odd numbers increasing toward head
of navigation [Leave to
port]
3
LIGHTED BUOY 6
Coloring red, even number, quick flashing red or
white—60 or more flashes
per minute
4
RED
NUN BUOY 4
Coloring red, even number. Numbers increasing
toward head of navigation [Leave to starboard]
LIGHTED WHISTLE BUOY 1
Black in color; odd number; white or green light,
regular or quick flashing
[Leave to port proceeding
upstream]
2
RED
Proceeding
toward head
of navigation
from seaward
1
LIGHTED BELL BUOY 2
Red in color, with even number, white or red light, regular
flashing (30 flashes per minute)
or quick flashing (60 flashes per
minute [Leave to starboard when
proceeding toward head of navigation (upstream)]
MID CHANNEL BUOY
No number, black and white vertical stripes [Should be passed close
to, on either side] Light: white
with short-long flashes

Fig. 31

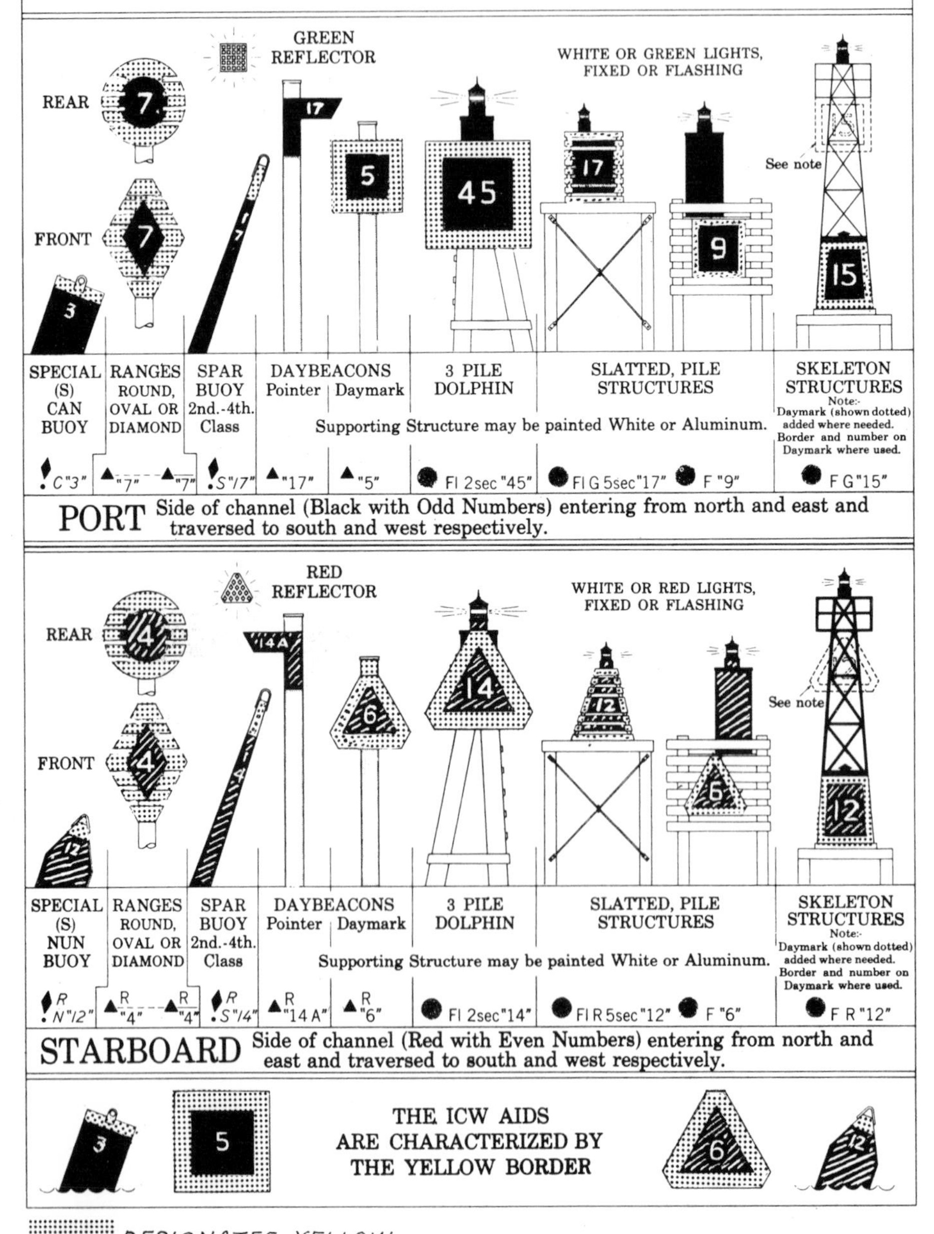
TYPES OF AIDS TO NAVIGATION
INTRACOASTAL WATERWAY
GREEN REFLECTOR
WHITE OR GREEN LIGHTS, FIXED OR FLASHING
REAR
FRONT
See note
SPECIAL (S) CAN BUOY
RANGES ROUND, OVAL OR DIAMOND
SPAR BUOY 2nd.-4th. Class
DAYBEACONS Pointer Daymark
3 PILE DOLPHIN
SLATTED, PILE STRUCTURES
SKELETON STRUCTURES
Note:- Daymark (shown dotted) added where needed. Border and number on Daymark where used.
Supporting Structure may be painted White or Aluminum.
C"3"
"7" "7"
S"17"
"17"
"5"
Fl 2sec "45"
Fl G 5sec"17"
F "9"
F G"15"
PORT Side of channel (Black with Odd Numbers) entering from north and east and traversed to south and west respectively.
RED REFLECTOR
WHITE OR RED LIGHTS, FIXED OR FLASHING
REAR
FRONT
See note
SPECIAL (S) NUN BUOY
RANGES ROUND, OVAL OR DIAMOND
SPAR BUOY 2nd.-4th. Class
DAYBEACONS Pointer Daymark
3 PILE DOLPHIN
SLATTED, PILE STRUCTURES
SKELETON STRUCTURES
Note:- Daymark (shown dotted) added where needed. Border and number on Daymark where used.
Supporting Structure may be painted White or Aluminum.
R N"12"
R "4" R "4"
R S"14"
R "14 A"
R "6"
Fl 2sec"14"
Fl R 5sec"12"
F "6"
F R"12"
STARBOARD Side of channel (Red with Even Numbers) entering from north and east and traversed to south and west respectively.
THE ICW AIDS ARE CHARACTERIZED BY THE YELLOW BORDER

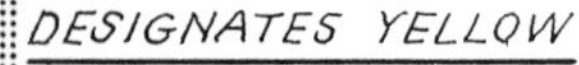
DESIGNATES YELLOW

DESIGNATES RED

Fig. 32

ILLUSTRATING THE SYSTEM OF DUAL PURPOSE MARKING WHERE THE ICW AND OTHER WATERWAYS COINCIDE

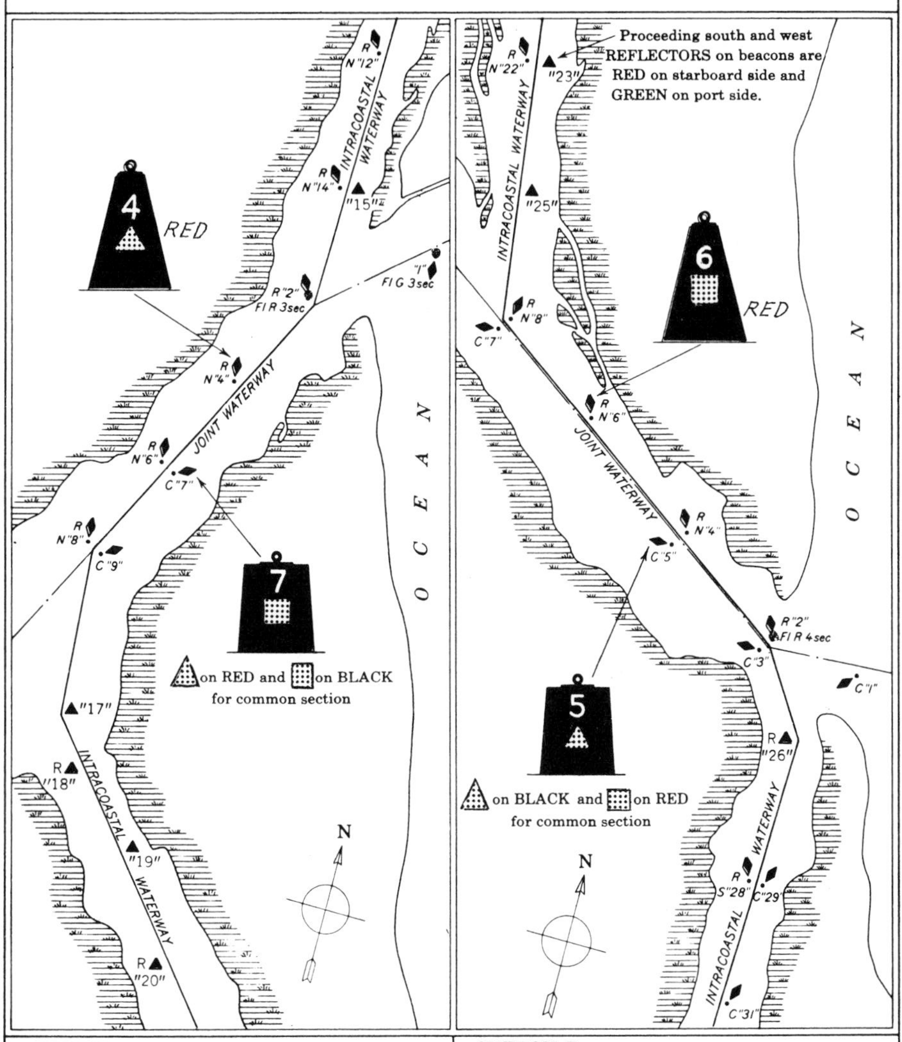

SKETCH A:

ICW joins another waterway, which is numbered from seaward, at buoy No. 2 and is common with it to buoy No. 9. ICW numbers and yellow borders are omitted in this section but the △ or ▦ is used on the regular aids to designate the ICW.

SKETCH B:

ICW joins another waterway at buoy No. 8 and is common with it to buoy No. 3. This section is numbered in the opposite direction to that of the ICW. The ICW numbers and yellow borders are omitted from the regular aids but a △ or ▦ is shown to designate the ICW.

DESIGNATES YELLOW

Fig. 33

yellow triangle painted on them representing a nun buoy in the intracoastal waterway, and the red nun buoys will have a yellow square representing can buoys.

NONNAVIGABLE WATERWAY BUOYS

The term "nonnavigable" means any waterway that ocean vessels cannot safely travel. Although such waterways are usually perfect sailing areas for pleasure craft, the Coast Guard does not maintain a buoyage system. For years this meant a hodgepodge of local marking systems put out by boat clubs or local residents. In recent years state governments have devised the following uniform small waterways buoyage system (Fig. 34).

The shape of the marker has no meaning; only color and symbols explain the purpose. All buoys are colored white with an orange band at top and bottom. Each buoy will have one of the following symbols placed on them: a diamond ◇ , a crossed diamond ◈ , or a circle ○ . The diamond warns of a danger area; the crossed diamond means keep out, waters closed to boating; and the circle indicates a restriction of some kind. Above or below the circle the restriction will be printed, such as Fishing Area or 5 Miles Per Hour. Although these buoys will eventually mark all small boating areas, check each waterway for other markers in case this system is not presently in use.

OTHER NAVIGATIONAL AIDS

In conjunction with the Lateral Buoyage System the Coast Guard also uses lighthouses, lightships, minor lights, range lights, and day beacons as navigational aides. These additional aids are used both within a buoyage system and as individual markers. Each is designed to do a specific job and has proved itself invaluable to boatmen.

Lighthouses

Lighthouses are placed on prominent headlands, entrances to some harbors, isolated danger areas such as nubs or rock formations, and at other points where a major light is needed to guide or warn boatmen. These structures are painted in such a way as to make them stand out against their background. Each light is given a distinctive characteristic (light, color, type, flashes, etc.) to distinguish it from other lighthouses. In addition to visual aids they usually are equipped with radio beacon and fog signals.

Lightships

Lightships serve the same purpose and are equipped with the same signaling devices as lighthouses. All lightships in United States waters except the Lake

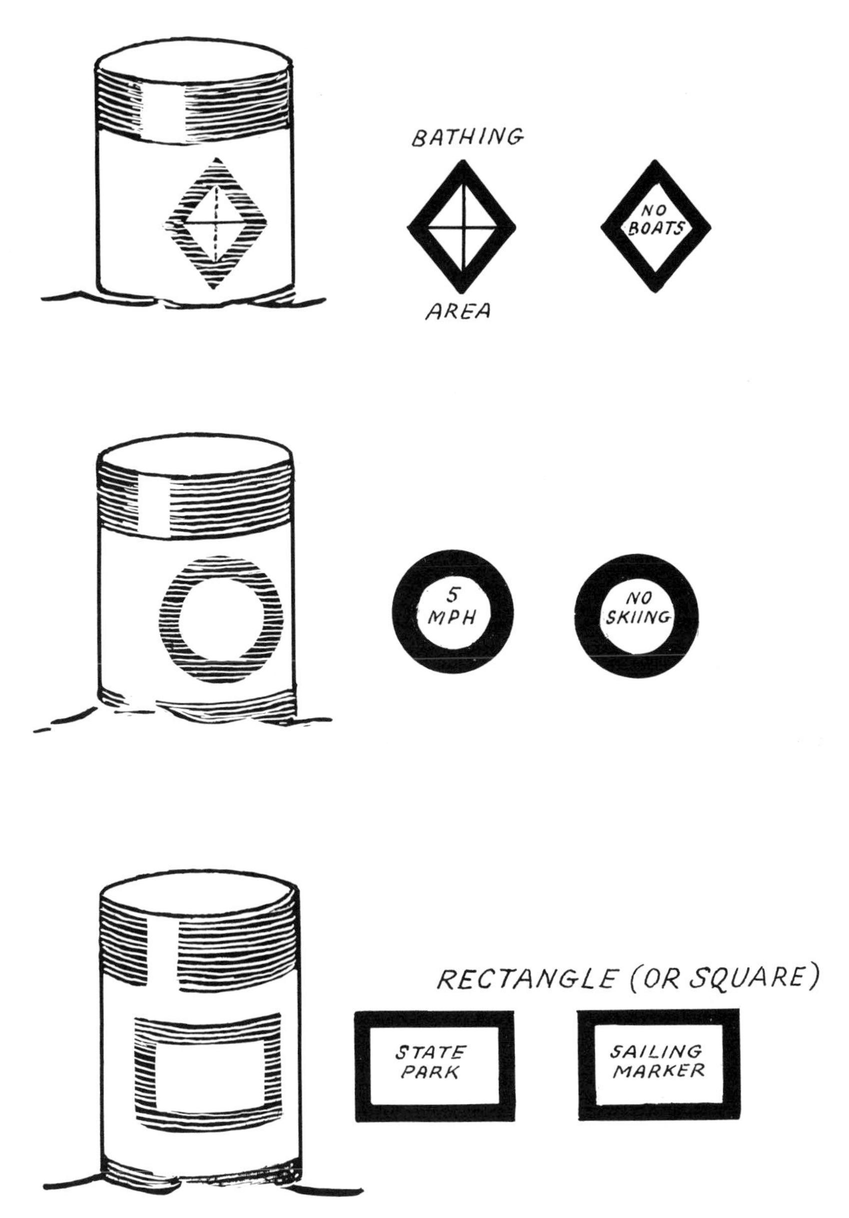

Fig. 34

Huron Lightship are painted red with the name of the station on both sides in large white letters. The Lake Huron Lightship is painted black. As with lighthouses, each lightship will have its own definite signaling characteristics. When under way, to or from repairs or an overhaul, lightships will fly the international code flag "PC" to show they are not at anchor and will only display the lights prescribed by the Rules of the Road.

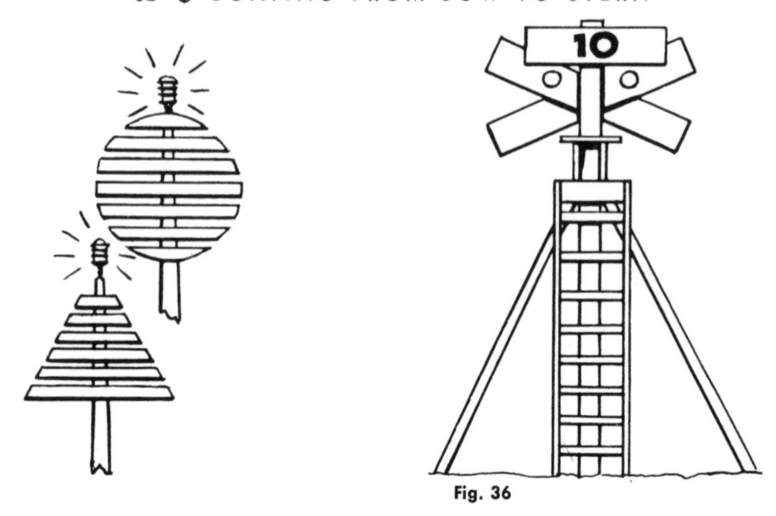

Fig. 35

Fig. 36

Minor Lights

Minor lights are in a sense small lighthouses and serve the same purpose as the larger markers. Occasionally because of their size minor lights will be placed on the sides of a channel. In these instances they will have the same color characteristics of side marker buoys in the Lateral System.

Range Lights

These are usually small lights on skeletonlike structures which, when in line (i.e., one over the other), indicate to a boatman that he is on a safe course. Generally they are visible in one direction only (Fig. 35).

By steering a course which keeps these lights in line (range-up) the boatman will remain within the confines of the channel. Just remember that a number of range lights are onshore and that is where you will be if you don't consult your chart as to where to change course.

The range lights may be white, red, or green and may also be fixed or flashing.

Day Beacons

These are aids to navigation in the form of unlighted structures. Design and construction vary (Fig. 36). A day beacon may simply consist of a single pile with a daymarker on the top.

These beacons are colored to distinguish them from their surroundings and to provide a means of identification. When they mark the sides of channels, coloring is the same as the Lateral Buoyage System.

Many day beacons are fitted with reflectors to help locate them at night by means of a searchlight.

CHART MARKINGS

Navigation charts are the road maps of boating and should be used in conjunction with buoys and markers, especially when afloat on strange waters. Buoys on charts are shown with a small diamond over a dot. The color, number, type, and light or sound characteristics are printed next to the diamond in abbreviated form or with the full word. These symbols are shown in the Lateral Buoyage System illustration (Fig. 29) and also in Chapter V on navigation (Fig. 46).

Boatmen who are interested in learning more about the history of United States buoyage, radio beacons, loran, and other electrical navigational aids will find a list of available books and pamphlets in Appendix B.

5

Compass, Charts, Piloting

Sooner or later every skipper, regardless of his boat's size, finds himself in the position of having to plot a simple course or, if socked in by fog or darkness, to feel his way home by compass. Therefore, compass and chart reading plus basic navigation must be included in the seamanship training of all new skippers. Probably the hardest part of learning these skills is getting started. For some unknown reason landlubbers have the notion that navigating by compass and chart is an exact science that takes years of study to master. This, of course, is not true. It is an exact science, but anyone with a sound background in high school math can learn basic navigation in a very short time—in fact, an evening or two spent studying this chapter. Once the basics are understood, one can go on to more advanced courses, such as those given by all U. S. Power Squadrons and Coast Guard Auxiliary units.

COMPASS

The first step is finding out the why's and wherefores of a marine compass.

The Marine Magnetic Compass

Today's marine magnetic compass is basically the same instrument, with a few construction refinements, that seamen have been using for centuries: one or more magnets that point toward the magnetic poles (north and south), balanced on a pivot point within a compass bowl. Attached to and above the magnet(s) is a compass card (Fig. 38) showing the degrees in a circle plus various compass points. This makes determining directions other than north and south much quicker and more accurate. Two major improvements in compass construction made during the past century and recommended for small craft use are the liquid-filled compass bowl, which makes the compass a liquid compass, and a semispherical glass top. The liquid, a special non-freezing fluid, performs two functions. It helps to float the compass card, reducing friction on the pivot point, and acts as a vibration damper. The latter is especially necessary aboard powercraft as engine vibrations, when under way, will start a "dry" compass dancing. The semispherical glass top acts as a powerful magnifier which in turn makes viewing and reading the card much easier. It also saves valuable space in a bridge or cockpit, as a magnified card means a smaller compass can be used. Other more recent improvements also recommended are the built-in deviation corrector used to correct deviation errors and a night light for after-dark boating. Figure 37 shows some of the more popular modern small craft compasses used today. Remember that when purchasing a compass it may very well save your life. So don't settle for an inferior make. Ask for, and get, a good instrument made by a reliable manufacturer.

Fig. 37

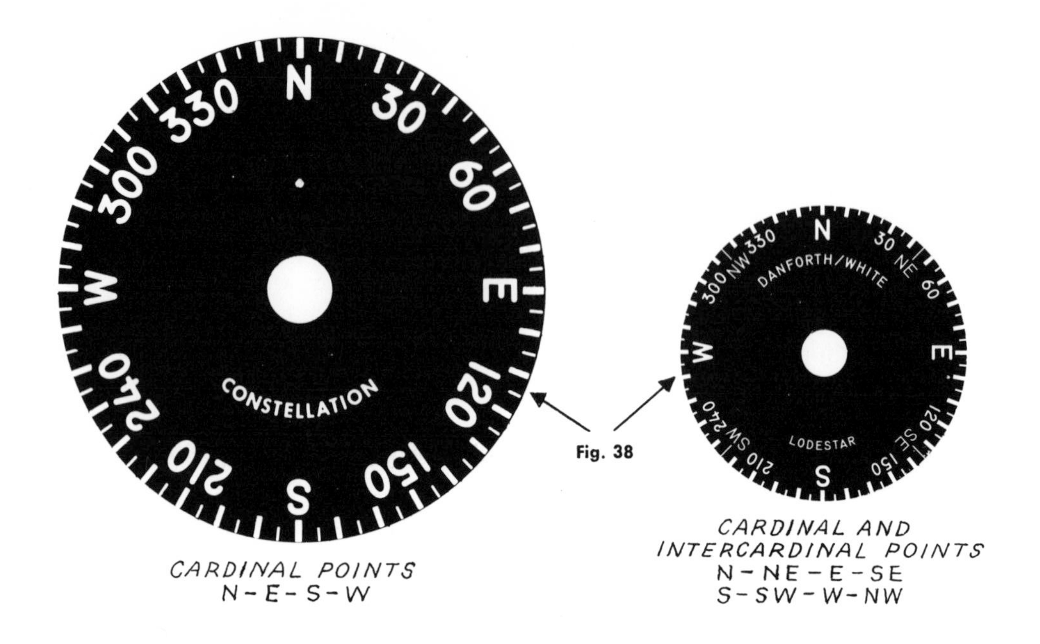

Fig. 38

CARDINAL POINTS
N-E-S-W

CARDINAL AND
INTERCARDINAL POINTS
N-NE-E-SE
S-SW-W-NW

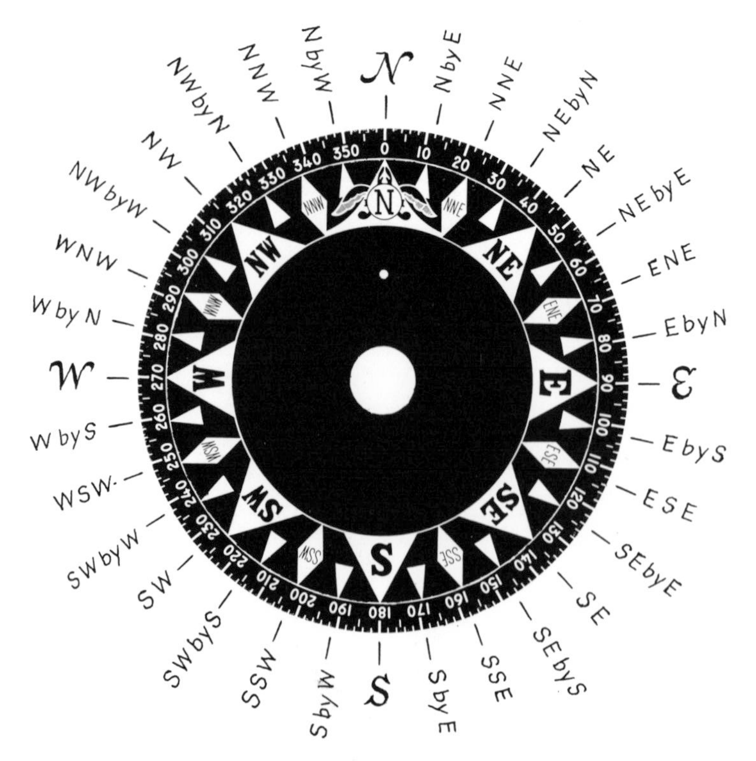

32 POINTS

Fig. 39

The Compass Card

The face or reading surface of a compass is called the compass card (Fig. 38). From it you read the direction in which the bow is pointed. The outer circumference is divided into 360 degrees representing a complete circle. The markings start at north 0° and move clockwise around the card to 360°. Most small cards will have every thirtieth degree numbered, and large cards every fifth or tenth degree. Just inside the degree markings the card is further graduated into compass points: north, east, south, and west, etc. Modern small craft cards, because they use degree markings to steer by, usually show only the four cardinal points—north, east, south, and west—plus the four intercardinal points—northeast, southeast, southwest and northwest (Fig. 38). Nowadays, compass points are used mainly for general direction, such as east 94°, and for wind directions. Large compasses, however, may show thirty-two or more points (Fig. 39).

Boxing the Compass

Old sailing masters depended on compass points rather than degrees to steer by, which meant every seaman learning navigation had to memorize and know the position of every compass point. This was and still is called boxing a compass. Although such knowledge is not necessary with a modern compass, any skipper worth his salt can, if called upon, box a compass "clipper style." For those interested in learning to box a compass, start by memorizing the names and positions of the cardinal and intercardinal points (Fig. 38). Next move on to the remaining 24 points which make up all 32 compass points (Fig. 39). And for the real diehard salt, Figure 40 shows the complete 128 points, the 32 whole points and the 96 quarter points.

Fig. 40

Installing the Compass

Proper compass installation and placement are the key to accurate piloting. Error in this respect can make the best and most expensive instrument useless, and in an emergency a contributing cause to disaster. Keep this in mind if you install your own compass, or should a yard do the job, be sure the installer is capable. Before starting the job, look down into the bowl and locate the "lubber line," a white or black line inscribed in the forward part of the compass bowl (Fig. 41). This is the mark used to indicate compass card directions and is the key to accurate compass steering. When possible try to place the compass directly over the boat's center line or keel, just forward of the wheel. If, however, the helmsman finds it hard to read the card in that position, move it to one side or the other. In either case it is imperative that the lubber line be parallel to the center line or keel. This is the only position which makes it possible for the lubber line and bow to point in the same direction, assuring positive course alignment. Figure 42 shows the right and wrong way to line up the lubber line. For easiest reading, try to have the compass card about two feet in front of the helmsman's eyes at a 20- to 25-degree angle. This permits easy viewing by the helmsman who can still be aware of what is ahead.

Most of the newer small craft compasses have some type of built-in gimbal (automatic leveling rings) and adjustable mounting brackets. A gimbal makes it possible to mount the compass on unlevel surfaces. The gimbals adjust to any angle, keeping the compass level, while the brackets can be mounted on almost any surface. The gimbal also holds the compass "steady" when a craft heels or pitches. When installing the compass, place it as far away as possible from any iron, steel, electric current, etc., because any material or object capable of becoming magnetized or setting up a magnetic flow of current will act as a secondary magnetic pole and pull the compass magnet away from magnetic north. Such deflection is called deviation and is present in varying

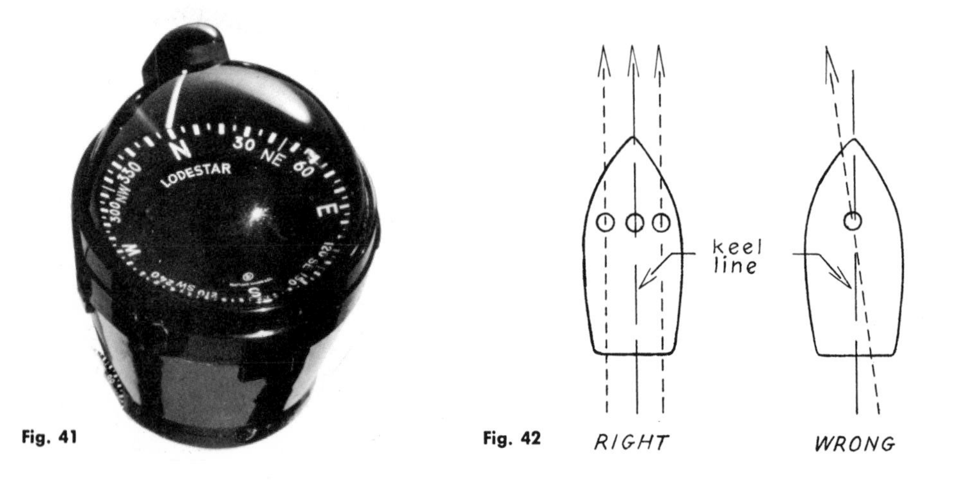

Fig. 41

Fig. 42

degrees aboard all small craft. How to correct for deviation is explained under compass errors. The object when installing is to try to keep deviation at a minimum.

Once a compass location has been chosen, fasten the compass temporarily with tape and secure the boat bow and stern so its heading remains constant. With trailered boats, the job can be done onshore. In either case, be sure there is no electric welding or heavy D.C. current being used in the vicinity that might alter the compass's magnetism. Next, check to see that all gear and equipment are stored or put in their proper places. When this is done, move each piece of magnetic metal equipment or gear not permanently fastened down, and see if it deflects the compass. This includes tool kits, cooking utensils, cutlery and tableware, portable tanks, cameras, etc. Offenders should be moved to a new location out of the compass's magnetic field. Next, operate any clutches or levers and turn the steering wheel from side to side. Turn on all electrical equipment and appliances one at a time, then in any series that might be used. If you note any deflection, move the offending piece out of range. When this is not possible, as with permanently secured equipment or an integral part of the boat, such as a steel-shafted steering column, try to find a new location for the compass. Wherever single wires rather than two-wire cables are used to connect a power unit, it is necessary to neutralize the single wires by twisting pairs together. While testing for deflection, keep in mind that magnetic lines of force can travel through solid material. So any magnetic metal objects in a drawer or cabinet must be treated as though they were exposed. The chances are that after you finally place your compass there will still be some minor deflection. Don't worry much about this, since it can be compensated for when you correct for deviation. The main objective is getting major offenders out of the compass's magnetic field.

Compass Calibration Check

Before starting to correct for deviation, calibrate your compass for errors that occasionally occur during transit to or from winter storage or at the factory. Take the compass ashore to a neutral area, free of local magnetic influences, and place it on a wooden table or other nonmagnetic level surface. Slowly rotate the compass housing until it reads north 0°. Make a small mark on the table just forward of the lubber line and another at south 180°. Now turn the compass until the lubber line is over the south 180° mark. The compass should read south 180°. If it does not, take a nonmagnetic screwdriver and turn the north-south (N.-S.) adjustment screw, found in the base or housing, until half the error is corrected. For example, a reading of 176° would be corrected to 178°. Next, return the compass to the north 0° mark. If any error is noted, make the correction again with the (N.-S.) adjustment screw. This time make a full correction. On a 2° error it would be brought back to 0°.

Repeat these corrections until you get a reading of north 0° and south 180°. Use the same system for correcting east 90° and west 270° by using the east-west (E.-W.) adjustment screw. Make full corrections at east 90° and half corrections at west 270°.

Deviation adjusters are built into all better-made modern small craft compasses. Check before buying to be sure your compass has this necessary improvement. A compass without it is either an older model or an inferior make.

Deviation Errors

Once your steering compass checks out, place it back on board and begin to correct for deviation error. The easiest way is by using a second compass that has also been checked for calibration accuracy. Place it on board in a

Fig. 43

Sample
DEVIATION ERROR COMPARISON CHART

Test Compass	Steering Compass	Deviation Error
000°	001°	001° W
015°	016°	001° W
030°	032°	002° W
045°	047°	002° W
060°	063°	003° W
075°	078°	003° W
090°	093°	003° W
105°	108°	003° W
120°	122°	002° W
135°	137°	002° W
150°	152°	002° W
165°	166°	001° W
180°	181°	001° W
195°	195°	000°
210°	209°	001° E
225°	224°	001° E
240°	238°	002° W
255°	253°	002° W
270°	267°	003° E
285°	282°	003° E
300°	297°	003° E
315°	313°	002° E
330°	329°	001° E
345°	345°	000°
360°	001°	001° W

nonmagnetic area with its lubber line parallel to the keel and steering compass. You can check for magnetic influence by taking a bearing on a distant stationary object and slowly turning the boat in a circle. If the bearing remains constant throughout the turn, the spot is free of local magnetic influence. If, however, deflection shows up, move the compass to a new spot. Once you find a neutral area, make another slow circle, checking the steering compass every 15° against the test compass. Write down each pair of readings under two columns, "Test Compass" and "Steering Compass" (Fig. 43). If no pair shows a deviation of more than 3°, you can make up a deviation card to compensate for error. If, however, deviations of 4° or more show up, it would be wise to correct the steering compass in the same manner that you checked for calibration. The only difference is that the compass remains on board in its permanent spot while you make the corrections. Should adjustment be necessary, make up a new set of readings after the steering compass is corrected.

Assuming, however, that there was no deviation greater than 3°, a simple deviation table, as shown in Figure 44 to be used when under way, can be made from your comparison reading list. The first column, "Magnetic Course," shows the twenty-four compass angles in degrees you used for readings. The middle column, "Deviation," will show the amount of deviation in degrees east or west of magnetic north. To determine whether the error is east or west, use the following formula. When the north pole of the steering compass moves to the right, or easterly, because of the boat's magnetic influence the error is easterly. When it moves to the left, or westerly, the error is westerly. The last column, "Steer Compass Course," will show what compass course to steer by. This is arrived at by adding westerly to, or subtracting easterly deviation degrees from, the magnetic course degrees. Just remember, "East is least; west is best." The deviation table in Figure 44 shows how this is done by using the comparison list in Figure 43.

Other methods for correcting deviation when a neutral spot cannot be found on board for a test compass are those using a pelorus, charts, and landmarks. These methods give excellent results but are more complicated. Should such methods be necessary, ask an experienced friend to help you or get a professional compass adjuster to make the corrections.

Variation Error

One other compass error that must also be compensated for is variation, the difference in degrees between magnetic north and true (geographical) north. This often confuses new skippers until they realize that true north pole is at the end of the earth's axis, while the magnetic north pole lies in an area north and west of Hudson Bay (Fig. 45). This variation causes magnetic compasses on the East Coast to point somewhat west of true north, and compasses on

Fig. 44

STEERING COMPASS
Deviation Table

Boat "Dreeki"
Compass Make: ______________________ Model __________
Port: ______________________________________
Variation: ______________________

Magnetic Course	Deviation	Steer by Compass Course
N 000°	001° E	359°
015°	001° E	14°
030°	002° E	28°
NE 045°	002° E	43°
060°	003° E	57°
075°	003° E	72°
E 090°	003° E	87°
105°	003° E	102°
120°	002° E	118°
SE 135°	002° E	133°
150°	002° E	148°
165°	002° E	163°
S 180°	002° E	178°
195°	000°	195°
210°	001° W	211°
SW 225°	001° W	226°
240°	002° W	242°
255°	002° W	257°
W 270°	003° W	273°
285°	003° W	288°
300°	003° W	303°
NW 315°	002° W	317°
330°	001° W	331°
345°	000°	345°
N 360°	001° E	359°

the West Coast to point somewhat east of true north. The amount of variation depends on how far south and east or west you are. Aboard a boat sailing on Blue Hill Bay, Maine, the variation would be 19° W. On the West Coast at Demarcation Point, Alaska, it would be 36° E. Actually the only location where variation is not a factor (less than 1° east or west) is the area running up through Knoxville, Grand Rapids, and Port Arthur. The reason for this is

Fig. 45

that these areas are in line with magnetic north and true north. Under these conditions, to steer a true north course, which is the normal procedure, a helmsman must know the amount of variation at the spot he is, or will be, sailing. Fortunately the degrees of variation are given on all coastal and lake charts at the center of each compass rose (Fig. 49). This makes compensating for variation while plotting a course a matter of simple addition or subtraction. How to compensate for variation is explained in the section on piloting (see page 72).

Steering by Compass

A compass, like any boating aid, is useless unless you know how to use it under all conditions. The quickest and best way to learn is by practicing until you can leave your wake astern straight as an arrow. On your first few practice runs, keep in mind that the compass card remains stationary with the north point always aligned with the magnetic north pole. The boat, compass bowl, and lubber line move around the card. This means that in order to change course you must drive or steer the lubber line around the stationary card to the desired degree. Should you forget and try to steer the card around to the lubber line, the boat will turn in the opposite direction. This is a common mistake among new helmsmen, as the card gives the optical allusion of moving when the boat turns.

When practicing, lay a course between two buoys or landmarks within sight of each other but at least one-half mile apart. Stand off one marker with your bow pointing at the other, and take a compass reading. Slowly get under way, steering by compass only. A crew member can act as lookout in case you drift too far off course. After a few runs you should be coming close enough to the second mark to hit it with a life ring. To be extra sure of your newly acquired ability, practice under various sea conditions: calm and rough, head and following, beam and quarter, currents, winds, etc. Once you master these conditions, you should be able to hold steady on any course. In fact, within a short time you will be holding steady with only an occasional glance at the card. Distant markers along the course will act as guide points, allowing you to scan the sea ahead. Actually the only time you really need a compass "watch" is while maneuvering through fog or darkness in a congested or hazardous area.

Compass Care

Marine compasses are precision instruments and need special care to insure giving accurate directions. Avoid any rough handling or treatment that might damage the pivot point, scratch the glass dome, or cause the bowl to leak. Clean the dome and housing with a soft cloth and mild soap in warm water. Never use harsh, abrasive cleaners. When around salt water a light coat of polishing wax is excellent protection against dried salt crystals. If the compass is mounted on external gimbals, keep the knife edges clean and dry. Never oil or paint these parts, as both tend to collect dirt, which retards free movement. When not in use, cover your compass with a cloth or canvas hood; this prevents the card and liquid from discoloring in the sunlight. When used in cold weather, a small bubble may appear in the compass bowl. This usually disappears once the weather warms up. If it doesn't or gets larger, the bowl is leaking and should be repaired by a qualified compass repair man. Don't try to fix it yourself, as special tools and liquid are needed.

Usually a well-made compass will go three or four seasons of average use before needing repairs. An excellent way of prolonging the life of a compass is by storing it upside down in a magnetic free area during the off-season. This prevents wear on the pivot point and jewel in case of movement from vibration or magnetic influence. If at anytime there is a doubt as to the accuracy of your compass, check it out and if necessary have it repaired.

CHARTS

Official nautical charts, like the compass, are essential aids to navigation. They show direction, distances, water depths, buoys and markers, channels, coastlines, hazards, and a host of other information necessary to safe boating.

In a sense they can be compared to the road maps used by motorists. Experience has shown that anyone capable of reading a road map will have no serious problems learning to read charts. The only major difference is that nautical charts give much more information in detail and have a greater need for accuracy. When using a chart for navigational purposes, be sure it is an official publication of the United States or the Canadian government, whose charts are considered the finest in the world. Other charts, such as those put out by oil companies and boating associations, are meant only as general guides and should never be used to navigate by.

Types of Charts

Three government organizations produce the bulk of all United States nautical charts: the Coast and Geodetic Survey, which issues charts of all U. S. coastal waters and tidal rivers; the U. S. Army Corps of Engineers, responsible for major inland rivers and waterways; and the U. S. Naval Oceanographic Office, responsible for offshore waters and the reprinting of foreign charts. Small craft skippers, for the most part, are concerned only with the Coast and Geodetic Survey charts, which are produced in six series. They vary from the small-scale blue water navigation (out of sight of land) charts to the large-scale small craft charts used by weekend skippers. Generally, all but the small craft charts are printed on strong water-resistant paper up to three by four feet in size. Small craft charts are bound in a portfolio for easy handling and storage. Following is an explanation of the Coast and Geodetic Survey charts:

1. *Sailing charts* are intended for navigation offshore or between distant points on a coast. They show offshore soundings (depths), outer buoys, major lights and landmarks that are visible from a great distance. Scales range from 1:000,000 and smaller (8.2 nautical miles per inch [N.M.I.] and up).
2. *General charts* are intended for coastal navigation by vessels usually within sight of land. Positions are fixed from landmarks, soundings, buoys, and lights that can be seen from a great distance. Scales range from 1:100,000 to 1:600,000 (1.4 N.M.I. to 8.2 N.M.I.).
3. *Coast charts* are intended for within-sight-of-land coastal navigation, entering large bays and harbors and certain large inland waterways. Scales range from 1:50,000 to 1:100,000 (0.7 N.M.I. to 1.4 N.M.I.).
4. *Harbor charts* are intended to meet the needs of piloting and anchoring within harbors. Scales range from 1:50,000 and larger (0.7 N.M.I. or less).
5. *Intracoastal waterway charts* are intended for navigational use on the intracoastal waterway, both Atlantic and Gulf coasts. Scale is 1:40,000 (0.55 N.M.I.).
6. *Small craft charts* were developed and intended for small craft use in and

SYMBOLS AND ABBREVIATIONS

(For complete list of Symbols and Abbreviations, see C. & G. S. Chart No. 1)

Navigation aids:

- Unlighted buoy (C. can, N. nun, S. spar, Bell, Gong, Whistle)
- Danger or junction buoy
- Fish trap buoy
- Mid channel buoy
- Mooring buoy
- Daybeacon (Bn)
- Lighted buoy
- Light (On fixed structure)
- R. Bn. radiobeacon
- Special-purpose buoy
- D.F.S. distance finding station

Light characteristics: (Lights are white unless otherwise indicated.)

F. fixed	Mo.(A) morse code	OBSC. obscured	Rot. rotating	R. red
Fl. flashing	Occ. occulting	WHIS. whistle	SEC. sector	G. green
Qk. quick	Alt. alternating	DIA. diaphone	m. minutes	
Gp. group	I. Qk. interrupted quick	M. nautical miles	E. Int. equal interval	

Bottom characteristics:

S. sand	rky. rocky	fne. fine	bk. black
M. mud	Co. coral	sft. soft	bu. blue
Cl. clay	Sh. shells	hrd. hard	gn. green
G. gravel	Oys. oysters	stk. sticky	br. brown
Rk. rock	Grs. grass	wh. white	gy. gray

Dangers:

Sunken wreck   Visible wreck   + ✳ * Rocks

21 Wreck, rock, obstruction, or shoal swept clear to the depth indicated

(2) Rocks that cover and uncover, with heights in feet above datum of soundings

AUTH. authorized; Obstr. obstruction; P.A. position approximate; E.D. existence doubtful

Currents:

E 0.6 kn ← ebb current with average maximum velocity of 0.6 knot.

F 0.5 kn → flood current with average maximum velocity of 0.5 knot.

FOG SIGNALS

WHILE UNDERWAY

Motorboats: Prolonged blast every minute.

Sailboats: When on starboard tack one blast, port tack 2 blasts and wind abaft of beam 3 blasts.

Boats towing or towed: One prolonged and 2 short blasts every minute.

AT ANCHOR

All boats: 5 seconds of bell every minute.

Fig. 46

around congested waterways. These charts give much more detail and local information than found on regular charts. For example, all depths are in feet; scales are given in nautical miles, statute miles, and yards; color is used to emphasize objects and areas; shore facilities are listed, as well as information on rules of the road, currents, tides, and weather. As a further aid, small craft charts are bound in a semistiff cover ring binder portfolio for easy storage and use in small cockpits. To date, small craft charts are available only in certain areas. They will include eventually, however, all major small craft boating areas.

Small craft skippers will find the last four types of charts the best suited for their purposes.

Reading Charts

Although chart reading does not require any special knowledge or skills, a certain amount of study is necessary. Like road maps, nautical charts depend on coded symbols, abbreviations, colors, etc., to give maximum information in a minimum amount of space. Start by purchasing a chart, preferably of

Fig. 47

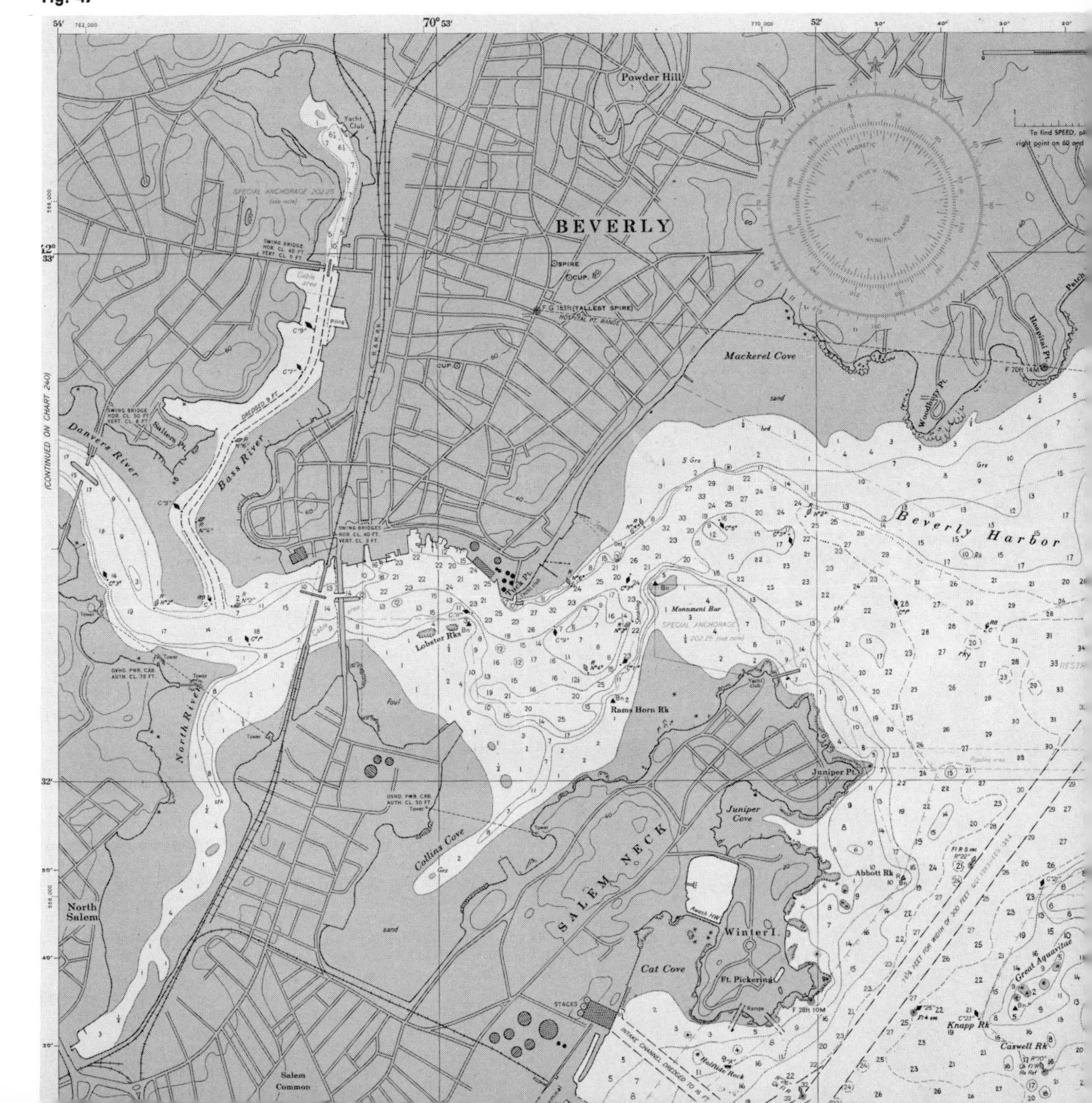

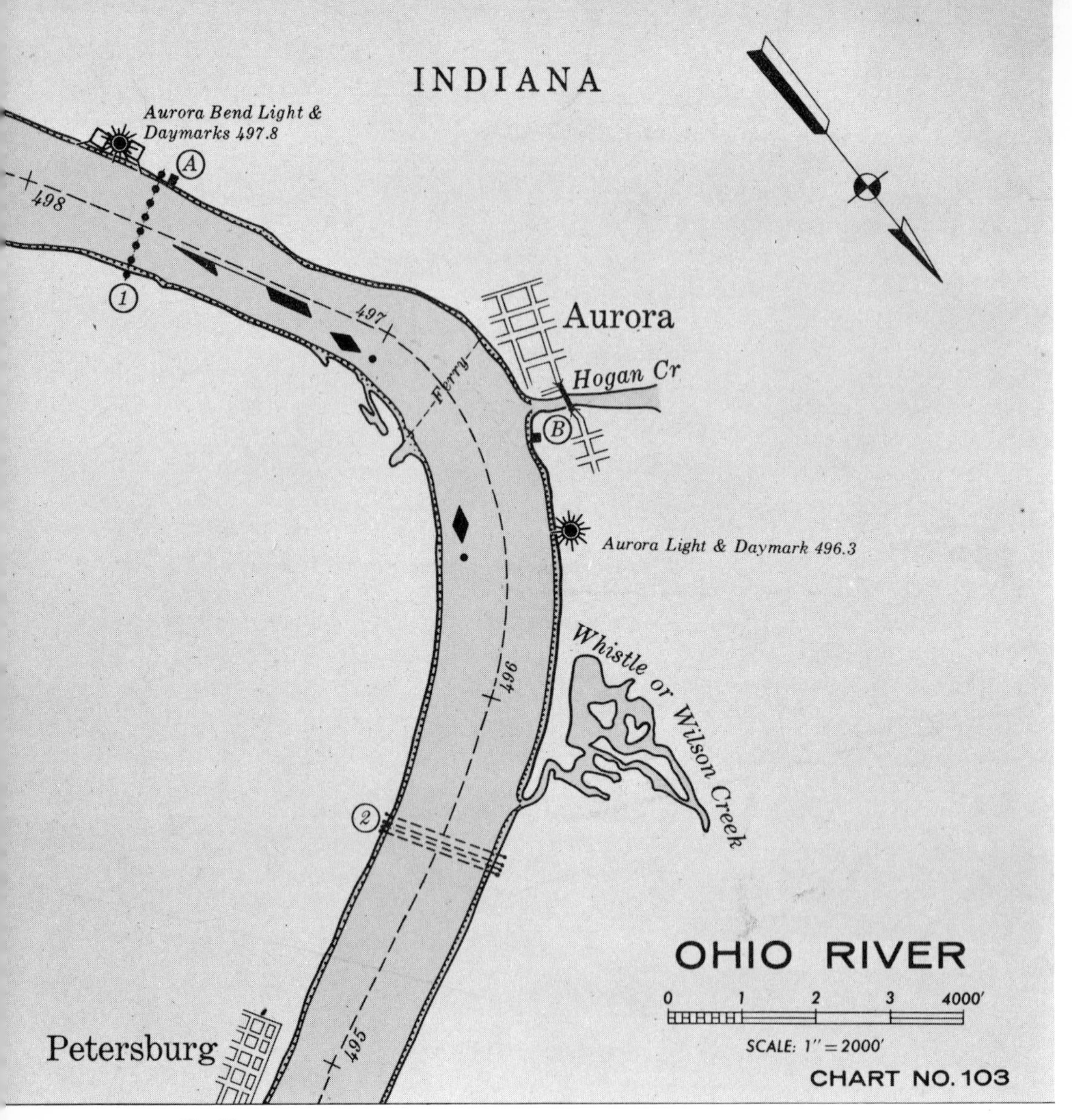

Fig. 48

local waters, and familiarize yourself with its content and layout. Then learn the meaning of the various symbols and abbreviations which represent the different aids and hazards to navigation. Figure 46 shows these in legend form as they appear on small craft charts. Similar legends, but not as complete, are also printed on most other types of U.S. Government charts. An excellent reference booklet called *Chart #1*, recommended for all cruising libraries, gives a complete interpretation of every chart marking used on U. S. Coast and Geodetic charts. It may be obtained from any U. S. chart-issuing agency.

The charts shown (Figs. 47 and 48) are examples of how U. S. nautical charts are marked. Sample A, taken from a harbor chart, is typical of all U. S. Coast and Geodetic charts. Sample B, taken from a river chart, is representative of charts issued by the U. S. Army Engineers. As you can see, one differs greatly from the other. Coast and Geodetic charts give accurate compass directions necessary to coastal and lake navigation. North is normally at the top of the chart. Meridians and parallels complete with distance scales, measured in degrees, minutes, and seconds, are shown at the outer edges. Longitude lines running north and south are measured at right and left sides. In addition, a series of compass roses are placed at suitable spots. The outer circle shows true north 0°; the inner circle with an arrow, magnetic north; while the center gives the amount of variation, year, and amount of annual change (Fig. 49). River charts omit most of this information. The flow and direction of streams are shown by arrows, which replace the compass roses, since compass direction has little value on rivers. North can be at any angle on the chart, and distance scales are missing from the longitude and latitude lines. Other noticeable differences involve water depths, markers, hazards, and mileage scales. Coast and Geodetic charts give the varying water depths at mean low tide in either feet or fathoms, as marked on the chart. Buoys are labeled to signify their purpose, hazardous areas are plainly marked, and distance scales are usually in nautical miles. River charts, on the other hand, give

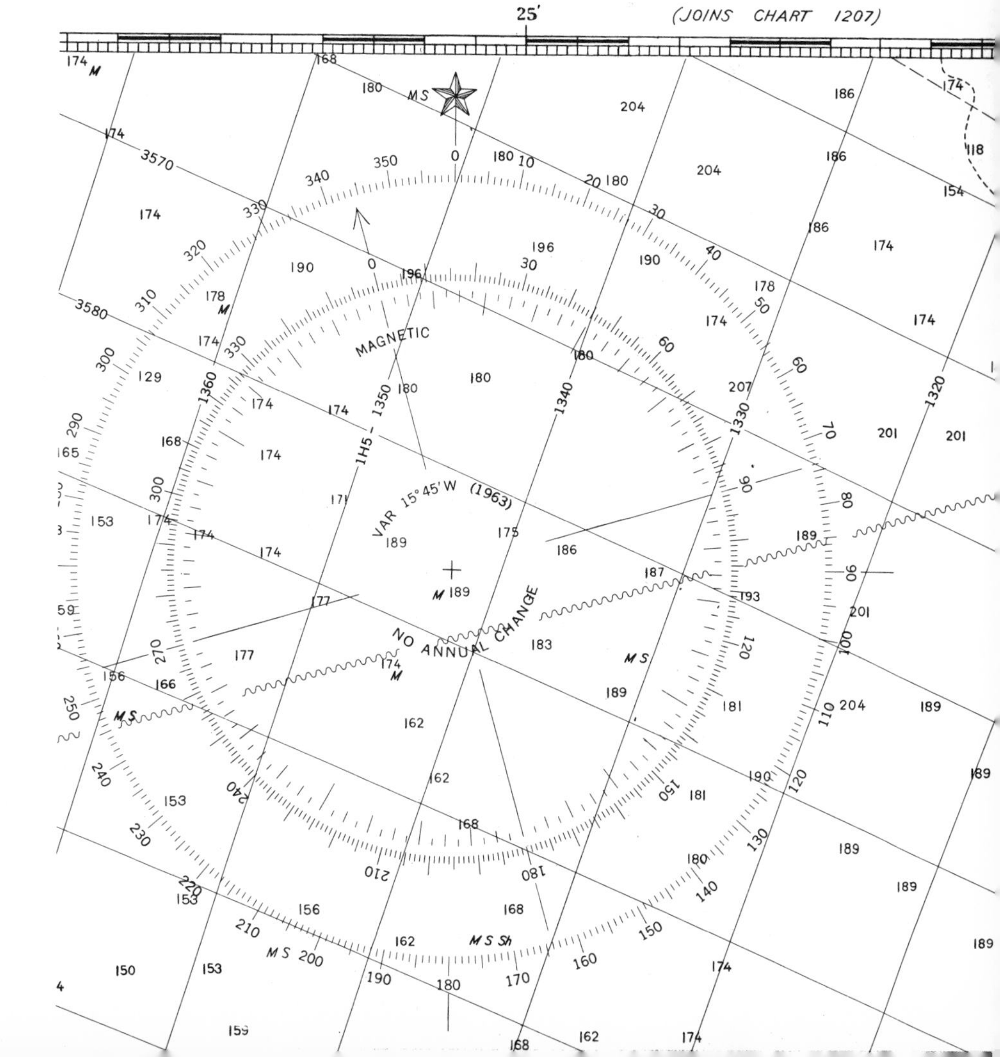

Fig. 49

distance in statute miles, show only buoys marking the navigable course of the river and water depth.

Using Charts

Once you understand and can read charts, using them to determine a position or to reach a destination is simple. For basic piloting you need only a few tools: pencil, ruler or straightedge, course protractor, dividers, parallel rules, and a watch with a sweep second hand (Fig. 50). These are used in finding direction, distance, position, etc. Other instruments are available, but at first only the tools mentioned above are essential. Additional equipment can be purchased later, if necessary, when you can better judge the difference between a bona fide navigational instrument and a gimmick.

To determine direction of a course line or between two points, place one edge of the parallel rules along the line or between the points. When in position, slowly walk the rules across the chart to the center of the nearest compass rose. The center will be marked with a +. In this position follow the edge resting on the center mark up through the magnetic and true circles. These are the magnetic and true directions of the line or points. The parallel rules in Figure 50 show a direction in degrees magnetic north and degrees true north.

Direction can also be determined with a course protractor. Place the center of the protractor directly over your position, and slowly pivot the straightedge, without moving the protractor, until the center edge lies over the center of the nearest compass rose. Note the degree the straightedge cuts across the chart rose's true scale. Then holding the straightedge steady, slowly revolve the course protractor until it and the chart rose are aligned. The course protractor is now an auxiliary chart rose. To find the direction of your proposed course,

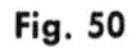

Fig. 50

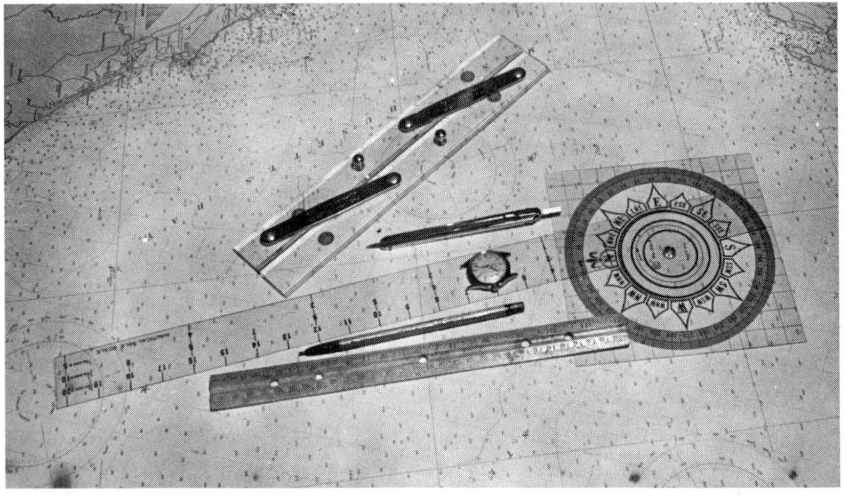

simply pivot the straightedge until it lies along the course line. Then read the degrees as a true scale at the point it cuts through the protractor compass.

To determine the distance between two points or along a course line, use the chart scale and dividers. Spread the dividers until the tips touch each point. Then without changing the spread, place the dividers on the chart scale and read the distance. On long spans, start by measuring off five or ten miles on the scale with the dividers. Then walk the dividers from the starting point along the course line to the destination. As an example, on a twenty-three-mile course line the dividers set for five miles, would be walked four times (twenty miles) then spread down to the course destination and remeasured on the scale, which would show the new spread to be three miles. When using projection charts (Coast and Geodetic Survey and Lake Survey) north-south distances can be measured from the latitude scales at each side.

To describe or note a position, give the degree of latitude and longitude. The easiest way to do this is with dividers. Spread the dividers from the position to the nearest longitude line. Then without changing the spread, place the dividers on the same line at the edge of the chart, and add or subtract the minutes or fractions of minutes. Repeat the same process for latitude.

Another method of finding longitude and latitude is with a straightedge: Run the straightedge from the position to the longitude and latitude scale at the edge of the chart, and add or subtract as you would with dividers. Be sure when using this method that the straightedge is perfectly aligned with the nearest parallel or meridian. Failure to do so will give an incorrect reading. This latter method is most often used on a large chart table where a T-square and right angle can be used. When describing a position relative to another point note the mileage and direction, followed by a reference point (1.3 miles, 48° true from nun buoy #4 at Bowditch Ledge). Be sure the reference point is clearly defined and cannot be mistaken for a similar point, which would be possible, for example, in an area of two or more buoyed channels.

When doing chart work, use the latest edition or revision in the series that gives maximum scale of the area you are plotting. This insures having up-to-date information and the sharpest detail. The edition date of publication will be printed at the lower left-hand corner: thus "4th ed., June 4/63, Revised 11/12/64." Important changes on revised charts, except intracoastal waterway charts, are usually hand corrected and will always be noted in the publication, *Notice to Mariners*. This makes it possible to keep your older charts up to date. *Notice to Mariners* is published weekly, and can be had free of charge by writing to the commander of your local Coast Guard district.

Where to Obtain Charts

All U. S. government nautical charts are available from the issuing agencies and their local outlets. A call to any nearby yacht club or marine store will get you the name and address of the outlet in your area. Cruising skippers will find it advantageous to have catalogues of the different types of charts. These are available from the issuing agency and tell what area each chart covers, whether it is sold singly or in a set, how much it costs, and where it can be purchased. Following are the names, addresses, and types of chart produced by each chart-issuing agency:

U. S. Coastal Charts (including tidal rivers and the intracoastal waterway) issued by U. S. Coast and Geodetic Survey, Washington 25, D. C.

Offshore, Ocean, and Foreign Charts, issued by U. S. Naval Oceanographic Office, Washington 25, D. C.

Great Lakes and Connecting Waters (including New York State Barge Canal System, Lake Champlain, St. Lawrence River to Cornwall, Canada, and the Minnesota-Ontario Border Lakes) issued by U. S. Army Engineer District, Lake Survey, 630 Federal Building, Detroit 26, Michigan.

Lower Mississippi River Charts (including Gulf of Mexico to Ohio River: St. Francis, White, Big Sunflower, Atchafalaya, and other rivers) issued by U. S. Army Engineer District, Vicksburg, P. O. Box 60, Vicksburg, Mississippi.

Middle and Upper Mississippi River and Illinois Waterway to Lake Michigan, issued by U. S. Army Engineer District, Chicago, 536 S. Clark Street, Chicago 5, Illinois.

Missouri River, issued by U. S. Army Engineer District, Missouri River, P. O. Box 1216, Downtown Sta., Omaha 1, Nebraska.

Ohio River, issued by U. S. Army Engineer Division, Ohio River, 315 Main St., P. O. Box 1159, Cincinnati, Ohio.

T.V.A. Lakes, issued by Maps and Engineering Section, Tennessee Valley Authority, Knoxville, Tennessee.

Canadian Coastal and Great Lakes Waters, issued by Chart Distribution Office, Canadian Hydrographic Service, Surveys and Mapping Building, 615 Booth Street, Ottawa, Ontario, Canada.

PILOTING

Once you feel at ease with compass and charts, the art of piloting should be the next phase of your seamanship. This method of navigation is used along the coast and inland waterways. It is ready-made for small craft skippers, as it utilizes navigational aids and landmarks to plot courses and take fixes. It is also the foundation for advanced offshore navigation for those who wish to continue their studies. With this in mind, practice piloting whenever the opportunity arises. Make a habit of taking a fix when anchored in strange waters and while running a course. During long winter evenings plot a few chart courses to those faraway spots you hope to visit. Such practice cannot help but make you a better navigator and safer boatman.

Laying a Course

The accepted rule when laying out a chart course is to show it as a true (geographical north) heading, for example, T-160°. To find a compass steering course from such a heading you must compensate for any deviation and variation errors. This also holds true when the situation is reversed, plotting a true course from a compass heading. To assist navigators with these problems certain formulas and easy-to-remember sayings have been worked up. The formulas tell whether to add or subtract the errors, while the first letter in each word of the sayings gives a step-by-step key to the answer. The first formula, used to find a compass steering course from a true course, is *Add westerly errors, subtract easterly errors.* Along with the formula memorize the saying, "*T*imid *v*irgins *m*ake *d*ull *c*ompanions." Following is an example of how the formula and saying are used.

From a true course of 160°, a variation error, at the closest compass rose, of 19° W., and a deviation error, found on your deviation card, of 2° E., find the compass course.

*T*imid (true course), T-160°
*V*irgins (variation), V-19° *W* (add westerly errors)
*M*ake (magnetic course), M-179° (true course plus variation)
*D*ull (deviation) D-2° *E* (subtract easterly errors)
*C*ompanions (compass course) C-177° (magnetic course minus deviation)

Naturally, you would not write out each word. But it is a good idea to jot down each letter in its proper order: T.V.M.D.C. This helps avoid mistakes when in a hurry.

The second formula, used when you know the compass course and want to lay it out on a chart as a true course, states: *Add easterly errors, subtract westerly errors.* The phrase to memorize is: "*C*an *d*ead *m*en *v*ote *t*wice." Following is an example of how the second formula and phrase are used.

From a compass course of 177°, a deviation error, shown on your deviation card, of 2° E., and a variation error, at the closest compass rose, of 19° W., find the true course.

*C*an (compass course), C-177°
*D*ead (deviation error), D-2° *E* (add easterly errors)
*M*en (magnetic course), M-179° (compass course plus deviation)
*V*ote (variation error), V-19° *W* (subtract westerly errors)
*T*wice (true course), T-160° (magnetic course minus variation)

To be sure you understand how both formulas work, look at Figure 51. The first two legs of the course are plotted from a true and a compass heading. The last leg is not computed. Work this out yourself. The answer can be found

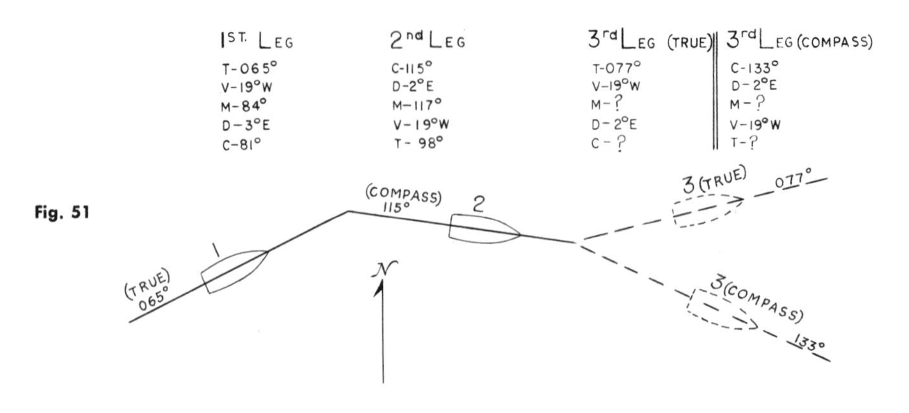

Fig. 51

at the end of this chapter. (When variation is shown in degrees and minutes, use the closest whole degree, for example, 15° 45′ = 16°.)

Time × Speed = Distance

The ability to determine the distance traveled and a boat's over-the-bottom speed is necessary in the art of piloting. From such information you can estimate time of arrivals, get position fixes, find distance off, etc. Distance traveled is found by multiplying over-the-bottom speed by time elapsed. Example: 15 m.p.h. (speed) × ½ hour (time elapsed) = 7½ miles (distance traveled). Over-the-bottom speed is calculated by making a series of timed runs over a measured mile course. Most major boating areas have such courses. When a tachometer, which gives r.p.m.'s (revolutions per minute of the propeller), is used to indicate a boat's speed, make three runs per reading and average the time in seconds. Then divide the average into 3,600 seconds (one hour), which will give you speed in miles per hour (m.p.h.). Example: If on three measured mile runs at 3,800 r.p.m.'s the times were 155, 149, and 146 seconds, the average run would be 150 seconds. Divided into 3,600 seconds, the speed at 3,800 r.p.m.'s is 24 m.p.h. On longer runs, minutes can be substituted for seconds.

By making a series of such runs at different tachometer readings, you can work up a speed conversion card (Fig. 52) to get various actual over-the-bottom speeds while under way. For easy reference place it near the wheel.

Aboard boats using marine speedometers a conversion table is still necessary, since most small craft speedometers tend to register a bit on the fast side. In areas without a measured course, a second boat that has an accurate conversion table can be used to lay out a temporary course. Don't use navigational buoys shown on charts except as a last resort, for they are rarely placed in the exact spots indicated on the chart. Be sure when using charts that show distance in nautical miles only that the measured course is a nautical mile

Speed Conversion Card

Boats Name________________ Hull Type________________ Gross Weight________________

Engine Horsepower____________ Type & Size Propeller____________

Tachometer Reading R.P.M.	Speed M.P.H. or Knots
500	3
1000	4.5
1500	6.
2000	11.
2500	16.5
3000	22
3500	25
4000	27
4500	29

Fig. 52

(6,076 ft.). In such cases your speed would be in knots (1.13 statute miles) rather than m.p.h.

When working up a tachometer conversion table, keep in mind that it is figured on the gross weight of the boat as is, while being tested. Any engine, propeller, structural design, or weight change will upset the table. So make your computations with the normal number of crew and equipment aboard.

Wind, Tide, Current

Unfortunately a boat's over-the-bottom speed and conversion table speed are rarely the same. Usually interference from wind, tide, or current, either singularly or together, act to slow or speed up a boat's forward progress. Under such conditions, in order to get actual over-the-bottom speed, the element velocity must be added or subtracted from conversion table speed.

Example: tidal current 3 m.p.h., boat's conversion table speed 20 m.p.h. When going against the current subtract: $20 - 3 = 17$ m.p.h. over-the-bottom speed. When moving with the current add: $20 + 3 = 23$ m.p.h. over-the-bottom speed.

Crosscurrents are computed with special formulas, but as a general rule on short runs they can be treated as a minus factor (moving against). Quartering currents also have special formulas, but generally they can be treated as a minus factor when on the bow quarters and a plus factor when on the stern quarters.

Learning to judge and estimate element velocity is at best a matter of cockpit observations gained from years of experience, so don't be upset when running a course if your estimated time of arrival is a few minutes off schedule. Give yourself time to develop a weather eye and get acquainted with your boat. In areas where tides and currents can be predicted, tide and current tables are extremely helpful. These books, available from the U. S. Coast and Geodetic Survey, give daily tide times, mean high and low water, current velocity, directions, etc. The Beaufort Scale (Chapter 6, Fig. 64) is an excellent guide for wind velocity.

Fig. 53

Position Fixes

The necessity of position fixes becomes apparent once you realize the adverse effect wind, tide, and currents have on a boat's progress. To plot a fix, take one or more bearings on stationary objects by sighting over your steering compass or a pelorus. The pelorus, a direction finder (Fig. 53), is used when the steering compass lacks sighting vanes or is situated in a spot that is awkward to reach. Following are a few fixes used by small craftsmen. They will for all practical purposes meet your present needs. As in all other phases of piloting, practice makes perfect, so make a habit of taking a fix whenever the occasion arises.

Dead Reckoning

The simplest method of taking a position fix is by dead reckoning, basically a speed-time-distance problem. To determine your position, simply calculate your speed against time under way and apply the distance to your course line. Example: If you are cruising at 15 m.p.h. and have been under way 30 minutes, your position should be 7½ miles along the course line (Fig. 54). The major drawback to dead reckoning is the effect of wind, tide, and currents. These elements, if present, must be allowed for, as there is no other line of position (L.O.P.) to fix on.

Fig. 54

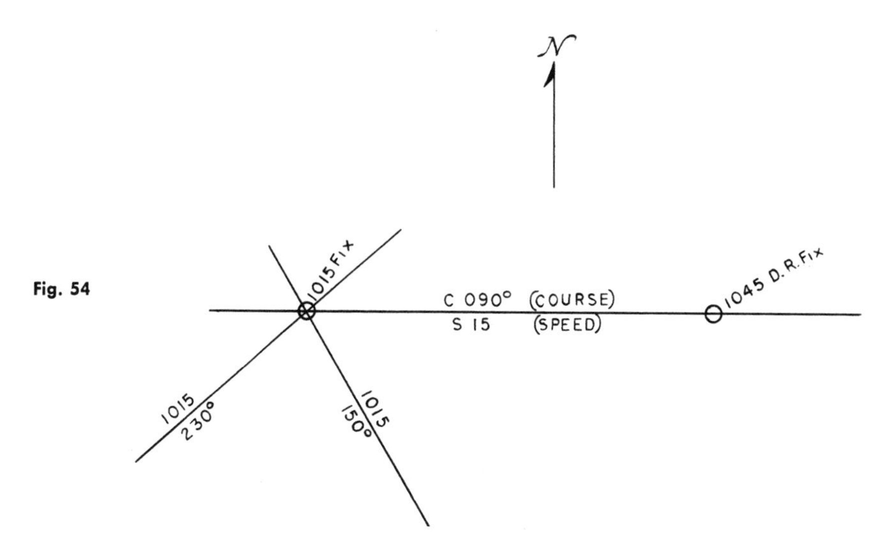

Two-Bearing Fix

A much more accurate fix can be made by using two stationary objects. Take the bearing by sighting over your compass or pelorus on each object. Once you have the bearings, transfer them to the chart by drawing a line of position (L.O.P.) through the two objects at the corrected angle of degrees. Corrected angle of degrees is found by computing deviation and, when a true bearing is wanted, variation. The spot both L.O.P.'s intersect is your position. Label each L.O.P. with the corrected degrees. Also note the time you made the fix, in 2400-hour nautical time rather than 1200-hour A.M. or P.M. land time. (Example: 3:00 P.M. = 1500 hours; 4:30 P.M. = 1630 hours.) (Fig. 55.) This avoids the confusion of two 12-hour days.

Fig. 55

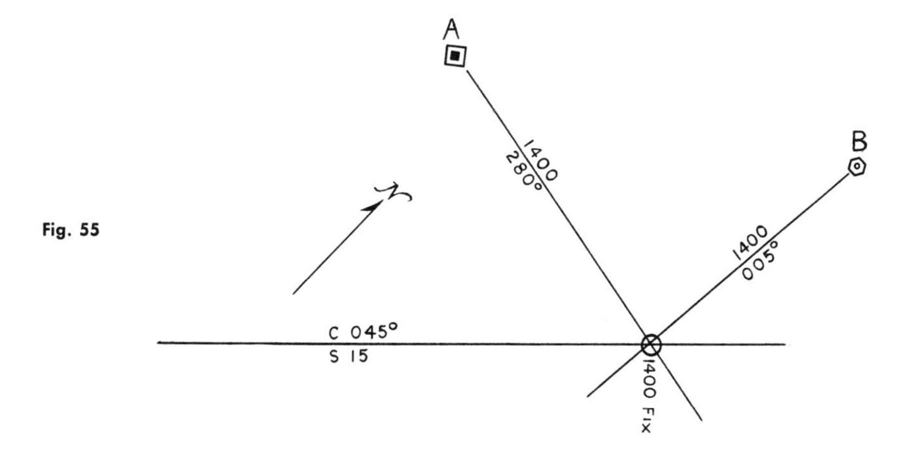

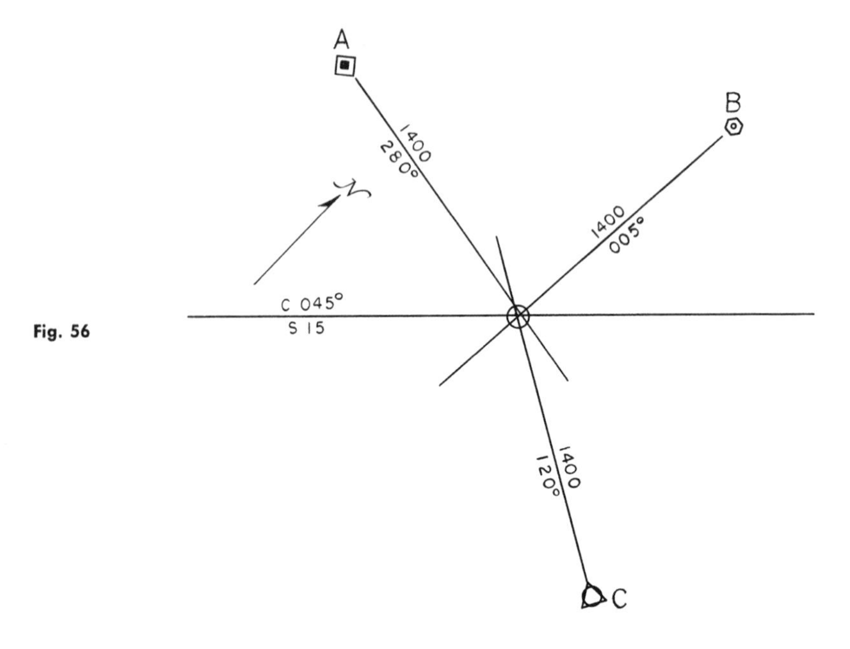

Fig. 56

Three-Bearing Fix

By adding a third L.O.P. bearing to a two-bearing fix, you pinpoint the position even more accurately. The method and formula are the same as taking a two-bearing fix, the only difference being that your position will be inside the L.O.P.'s triangle rather than where the lines intersect (Fig. 56). Both two- and three-bearing fixes make excellent anchor fixes. When taking bearing fixes try to have the L.O.P.'s intersect at right angles or nearly so. Lines close to parallel increase the distance of an error.

Running Fix

Occasionally you must take your fix from a single object or when a time lapse occurs between bearings. In such instances you make a running fix. Advance the first L.O.P. along the course line the same distance your craft has traveled at the time you establish a second L.O.P. This is done by using the speed × time = distance formula, keeping in mind the effect of wind, tide, and currents. In its advanced position, the first L.O.P. is used the same as in a regular two-bearing fix.

Example: At 1300 (1:00 P.M.) cruising at 12 m.p.h. on a 45° course you take bearing A-170°. Thirty minutes later at 1330 (1:30 P.M.) you take bearing B-80°. To advance bearing A from its 1300 position to a 1330 estimated position you find the distance traveled. In this case: 12 m.p.h. × ½ hour = 6 miles. Scale off 6 miles from the 1300 E.P. along the course line and plot a new 170° L.O.P. (Fig. 57). Your position is at the intersection of both L.O.P.'s.

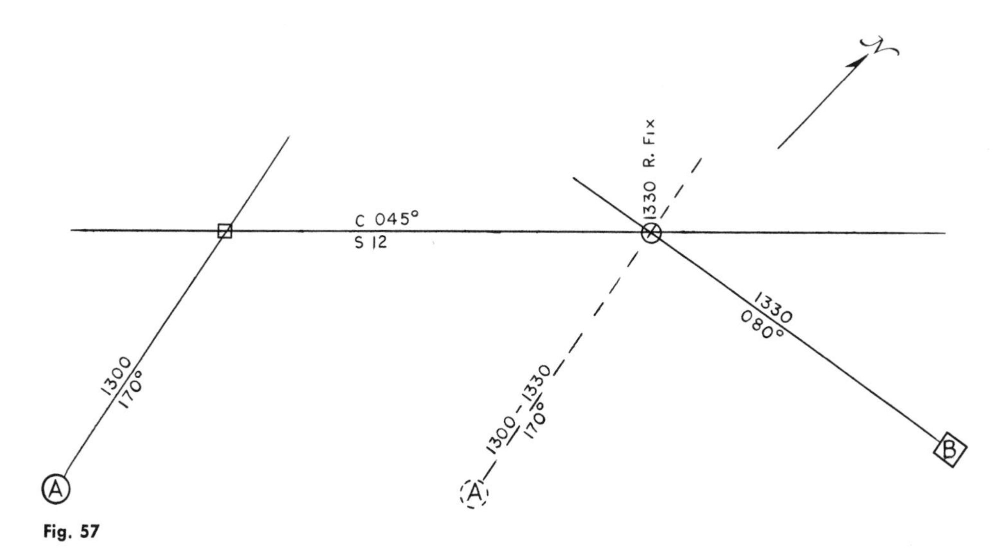

Fig. 57

The same method of advancing an L.O.P. is used when making a fix from a single stationary object.

Bow and Beam Bearing

Often while cruising you will want to check your distance from a certain stationary object. This is done by taking a bow and beam bearing on the object selected. As you move into range, note the time and your speed when the object bears 45° off the bow. Continue on course, holding the speed constant, and make another time check when the object is 90° abeam of you. The distance run (speed × time = distance) between the two bearings will equal the distance between your craft and the bearing object.

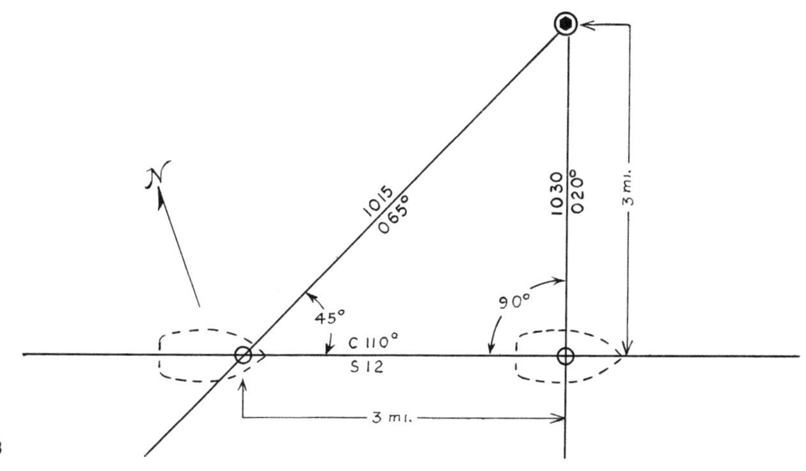

Fig. 58

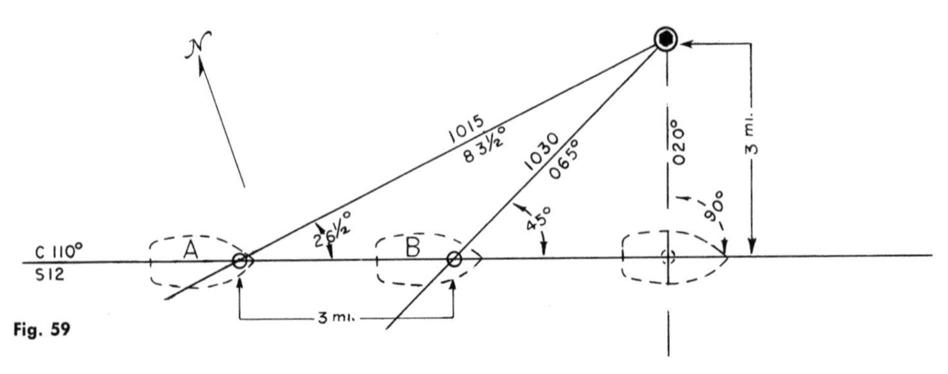

Fig. 59

Example: At 1015 (10:15 A.M.) Portland light bears 45° off your bow. Fifteen minutes later at 1030 (10:30 A.M.) Portland light bears 90° abeam of you. Assuming your speed was 12 m.p.h. during the run, you would have traveled 12 × ¼ hours, or 3 miles (Fig. 58). This puts your distance off Portland light at 3 miles.

26½° - 45° Bearing

Another procedure, similar to the bow and beam method is the 26½°-45° bearing. This formula in the same way tells how far off from an object you will be when you come abeam of it (Fig. 59). Such information is extremely valuable when cruising strange waterways or approaching hazardous areas.

* Answer to question on page 74:

True	Compass
M — 96°	M — 135°
C — 94°	T — 116°

6

Developing a Weather Eye

Seafaring men have long been famous as weather prophets. Dating back to early civilizations, ancient writings tell of sea captains' renown for their ability to predict the weather before important battles or ceremonial feast days. Of course, the reason why these men understood the weather is quite simple. Every sailor in his basic seamanship training learns to use the elements and instruments to predict the weather. Unlike land dwellers, who can take cover during a storm, sailors must be able to forecast storms in time to heave to and secure their ship or reach a safe harbor.

DAILY WEATHER MAPS

The fact that you have now entered the exciting world of wind, sails, and water means that you, too, must develop a weather eye. The first step in this direction is learning to use the daily weather map found in all newspapers. Once you master this lesson, general long-range forecasting up to a week in advance is often possible. This is especially helpful when planning a trip afloat next weekend. Looking at the weather map in Figure 60 you will notice many curved lines, with the heavier ones showing little black triangles ▲▲▲▲ or half circles ◓◓◓ placed on either side. The light lines are called isobars (lines of equal barometric readings), and the heavy lines with the symbols represent the boundary lines of moving and stationary cold or warm air masses called frontal systems. The direction of these frontal movements is

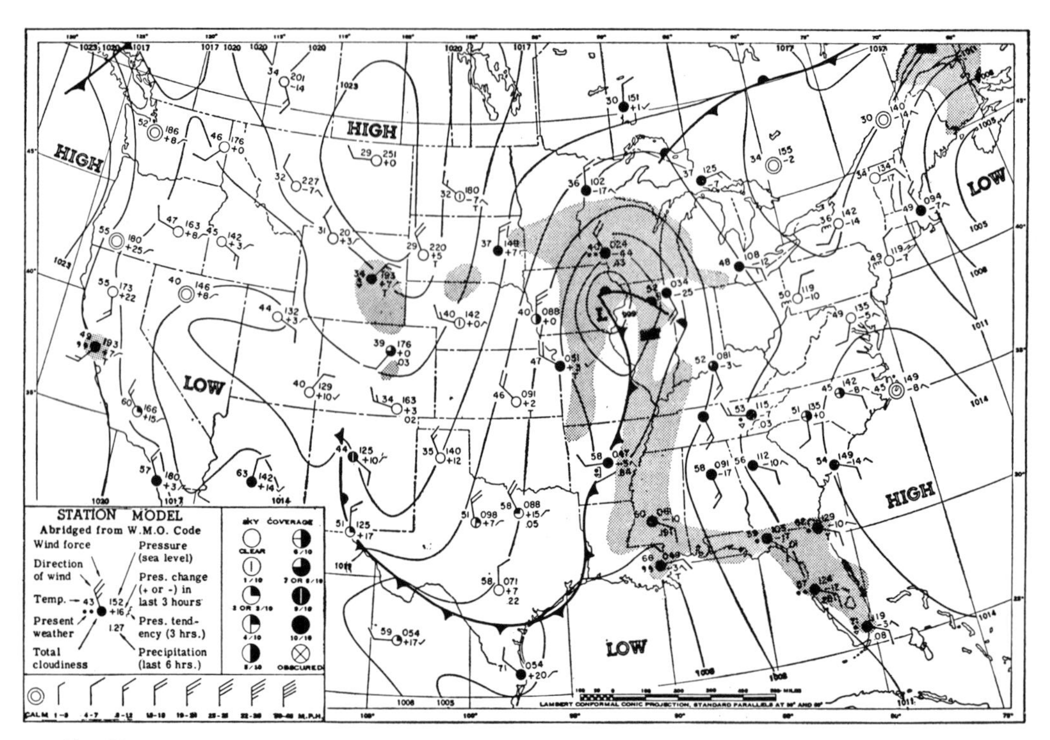

Fig. 60

indicated by the side of the line on which the symbols are placed. Usually they will be on the eastern side, because most of our weather makes up in the west and moves in an easterly direction. Thus the saying, "Look to the west for weather at its best." The symbols and meanings of these frontal systems are as follows:

Cold front—The boundary of relatively cold air of polar origin advancing into an area occupied by warm air.

Warm front—The boundary of relatively warm air advancing into an area occupied by cold air.

Stationary front—The boundary between a warm and cold front, which shows little tendency to advance one on the other.

Occluded front—A line along which a cold front has overtaken a warm front at the ground level.

Squall line—Represents a line of thunderstorms or squalls usually accompanied by heavy showers and shifting winds.

Behind these fronts are high and low barometric pressure areas shown by the letters H for high, and L for low. High-pressure areas usually bring good weather, while low-pressure areas, shown in gray, usually bring bad weather.

These symbols and meanings show the basic weather pattern as it moves across the country. By watching these movements for a day or two it is often possible to forecast the weather up to a week in advance. Should you want to learn more about daily weather maps, write to the nearest U. S. Weather Bureau and ask for a Sunday weather map with explanations on the reverse side.

RADIO AND TV

The easiest way to learn today's or tomorrow's probable weather is, of course, through the radio or TV. Every boatman should make a habit of tuning in the weather forecasts before going afloat. Fortunately today all boatmen can carry an inexpensive portable radio aboard and receive hourly reports of local conditions. A word of caution: Be sure the station you are tuned to is local (within fifteen miles); otherwise the forecast is useless except for general forecasting.

BAROMETER AND WIND

Ask a professional boatman what his most important weather instrument is, and the answer will always be a barometer. This instrument, called a "glass" by sailors, translates the atmospheric high- and low-pressure areas into barometric inches and millibars. By knowing what pressure system is on its way, a boatman can pretty much tell what the weather will be in his area within the

Fig. 61

next twelve to twenty-four hours. A falling barometer indicates an approaching low-pressure system (low), usually containing bad weather. A rising barometer indicates an approaching high-pressure system (high), usually bringing fair weather. And a steady barometer usually means you can expect the present weather to stay a day or longer.

Fig. 62

Sample
WEATHER LOG

Date	Time	Reading
10-4-65	0800	30.54
10-4-65	1400	30.61
10-4-65	2200	30.89
10-5-65	0700	31.11
10-5-65	1200	30.96
10-6-65	0900	30.75
10-6-65	1200	30.67

Learning to use a barometer is quite simple. You will notice in Figure 61 there is an inner and outer scale plus two hands. The outer scale gives atmospheric pressure readings in terms of inches of mercury. The inner scale gives readings of atmospheric pressure in millibars. The long arm attached to the inner workings gives the present pressure reading. The shorter arm, which can be turned by hand, is the setting indicator. By placing this indicator directly over the pressure arm you can make periodic checks to see how far, if at all, the atmospheric pressure has fallen or risen. The setting indicator remains stationary, allowing you to add or subtract any rise or fall in pressure. Although the pressure arm will fluctuate continuously with the passage of highs and lows, do not expect a wide variation in readings. It is unusual for readings to change as much as an inch in twenty-four hours, and such a change would mean a serious disturbance moving into your area at a rapid rate. In fact the record range of barometric readings for the past sixty-six years on file in Philadelphia is only 2.48 inches (84 millibars). The highest range was 31.02 inches (1050.5 millibars), and the lowest range 28.54 inches (966.5 millibars.) When making readings it is a good idea to record them in a weather log kept next to the barometer (Fig. 62).

Many barometers have the words Rain-Change-Fair printed on their dial and only show the mercury scale. Without the millibar scale these barometers are confusing when listening to or reading a weather forecast that uses the

Fig. 63

THE WIND AND WEATHER
Amateur Forecasting Hints

When the wind sets in from points between south and southeast and the barometer falls steadily, a storm is approaching from the west or northwest, and its center will pass near or north of the observer within 12 to 24 hours, with wind shifting to northwest by way of south and southwest. When the wind sets in from points between east and northeast and the barometer falls steadily, a storm is approaching from the south or southwest, and its center will pass near or to the south of the observer within 12 to 24 hours, with wind shifting to northwest by way of north. The rapidity of the storm's approach and its intensity will be indicated by the rate and the amount of the fall in the barometer.

Wind Direction	Barometer Reduced to Sea Level	Character of Weather Indicated
SW to NW	30.10 to 30.20 and steady	Fair, with slight temperature changes, for 1 to 2 days.
SW to NW	30.10 and 30.20 and rising rapidly	Fair, followed within 2 days by rain.
SW to NW	30.20 and above and stationary	Continued fair, with no decided temperature change.
SW to NW	30.20 and above and falling slowly	Slowly rising temperature and fair for 2 days.
S to SE	30.10 to 30.20 and falling slowly	Rain within 24 hours.
S to SE	30.10 to 30.20 and falling rapidly	Wind increasing in force, with rain within 12 to 24 hours.
SE to NE	30.10 to 30.20 and falling slowly	Rain in 12 to 18 hours.
SE to NE	30.10 to 30.20 and falling rapidly	Increasing wind, and rain within 12 hours.
E to NE	30.10 and above and falling slowly	In summer, with light wind, rain may not fall for several days. In winter, rain within 24 hours.
E to NE	30.10 and above and falling rapidly	In summer, rain probable within 12 to 24 hours. In winter, rain or snow, with increasing winds, will often set in when the barometer begins to fall and the wind sets in from the NE.
SE to NE	30.00 or below and falling slowly	Rain will continue 1 to 2 days.
SE to NE	30.00 or below and falling rapidly	Rain, with high wind, followed within 36 hours by clearing, and in winter by colder.
S to SW	30.00 or below and rising slowly	Clearing within a few hours, and fair for several days.
S to E	29.80 or below and falling rapidly	Rain, with high wind, followed within 36 hours by clearing, and in the winter by colder.
E to N	29.80 or below and falling rapidly	Severe northeast gale and heavy precipitation. In winter, heavy snow, followed by a cold wave.
Going to W	29.80 or below and rising rapidly	Clearing and colder.

It must be remembered that the above statements are based on average observations, that much of the time storms depart from their usual behavior, and in such cases the above statements will be wholly or partially misleading.

millibar system. Unless you can convert inches into millibars it is almost impossible to read the barometer. So when purchasing a barometer (prices start at about $5.00), ask for an aneroid barometer with a mercury and millibar scale. Don't worry if the words Rain-Change-Fair are missing. They are meaningless and only clutter up the dial.

WIND AND PRESSURE

Inasmuch as barometric pressures are the main key in forecasting weather, the winds these pressures ride in on are also important. Over the years meteorologists have found that certain wind directions, combined with pressure changes, are responsible for local weather situations applicable to all parts of the United States. To assist amateur weather forecasters the U. S. Weather Bureau has incorporated these findings into a statement and table called, *The Wind & Weather-Amateur Forecasting Hints* (Fig. 63). A weather-wise boatman will copy this information and place it beside his barometer as a forecasting key.

Wind direction also predicts wave storms that cause the sea to become a churning roller coaster even though the sun is shining in a cloudless sky. Such disturbances are caused by violent storms far out to sea or earthquakes hundreds of miles away from your boating area. If the wind in these storms is blowing in your direction, the waves will, unless changed by other winds or land masses, roll across the ocean, reaching you a few days or a week later. Coast Guard, Weather Bureau, and local boating reports will keep you informed about these storms.

BEAUFORT SCALE

Along with a wind's direction its speed in either miles per hour or knots is also important to boatmen. The higher the wind the more violent the storm. While afloat the movement of surrounding water is the key to wind speed. By using the Beaufort Scale (Fig. 64), which interprets the wind's effect on a body of water, boatmen can judge a wind's speed and safely reach shore before a blow. Experience has shown that the average small craft should start to take precautions at Beaufort #4. Naturally this is not a hard-and-fast rule. Canoes, rowboats, or small outboards will find the seas uncomfortable at #2 or #3, whereas larger offshore cruisers with experienced skippers will be able to operate safely up to #6 or #7.

CLOUD FORMATIONS

Long before weather instruments were invented man used nature and the clouds to aid him in predicting the weather. Although many of nature's signs

TA 610-0-3
(Formerly WB Form 4042A)
(5-55)

U. S. Department of Commerce, Weather Bureau

BEAUFORT SCALE OF WIND FORCE

May 9, 1955

Beaufort Number	Miles per Hour	Knots	Wind Effects Observed at Sea	Terms Used In U.S.W.B. Forecasts
0	Less than 1	Less than 1	Sea like a mirror	Light
1	1-3	1-3	Ripples with the appearance of scales formed, but without foam crests	
2	4-7	4-6	Small wavelets, short but pronounced; crests appear glassy, do not break	
3	8-12	7-10	Large wavelets with crests beginning to break; foam appears glassy. Perhaps scattered white horses (white foam crests)	Gentle
4	13-18	11-16	Small waves, becoming longer; fairly frequent white horses	Moderate
5	19-24	17-21	Moderate waves of a pronounced long form; many white horses, possibly some spray	Fresh
6	25-31	22-27	Large waves begin to form; white foam crests more extensive everywhere; probably some spray	Strong
7	32-38	28-33	Sea heaps up; some white foam from breaking waves blows in streaks along the direction of the wind	
8	39-46	34-40	Moderately high waves. Edges of crests begin to break into spindrift. Well-marked streaks of foam blow along direction of wind	Gale
9	47-54	41-47	High waves. Dense streaks of foam along direction of wind. Spray may affect visibility	
10	55-63	48-55	Very high waves with long overhanging crests; great patches of foam blow in dense white streaks along direction of wind. Sea surface takes on a white appearance. Visibility affected	Whole gale
11	64-72	56-63	Exceptionally high waves; sea completely covered with long white patches of foam lying along direction of wind; edges of wave crests everywhere blown into froth. Visibility affected	
12 or more	73 or more	64 or more	Air filled with foam and spray; sea completely white with driving spray. Visibility very seriously affected	Hurricane

Fig. 64

are still used, most have been proven untrustworthy. Cloud formations, on the other hand, are still considered excellent weather forecasters.

The three main types of clouds that tell of approaching weather changes are:

1. *Cirrus* (Fig. 65). These are thin wispy clouds that travel across the sky at heights of 20,000 feet and higher. They are carried by winds that reach speeds of 500 to 700 miles an hour, and are the advanced warning signals that other clouds are on the way. If they approach on west or north winds, good weather can be expected. But if they approach from the east or south, expect bad weather within twenty-four hours.

Fig. 65

2. *Cumulus* (Fig. 66). These clouds develop vertically and constantly change shape as they roll across the sky. When they are white fluffy cotton balls in a blue sky it means a fair day. However, if they should start to grow into mountains and develop heavy gray rolls, prepare for a thunderstorm or shower shortly.

Fig. 66

3. *Stratus* (Fig. 67). These clouds lay horizontally in layers covering wide geographical areas and are usually the cause of overcast skies.

When either cumulus or stratus clouds become saturated with moisture they

Fig. 67

develop into storm clouds and are called cumulonimbus or nimbostratus—the word nimbus meaning "rain."

Cumulonimbus (Fig. 68). Commonly known as thunderheads, these clouds bring thunderstorms, showers, and line squalls. They develop from fair weather cumulus clouds that build vertically in the sky developing into what look like dark mountains off in the distance. Often they will have an anvil (flat) top resembling a plateau on a mountain. Weather-wise skippers make for shore when they sight these clouds developing, because along with rain and hail they often pack winds up to sixty miles an hour. When caught too far off-shore to reach port safely, heave to, secure ship, and prepare to ride it out (*see* Chapter 10 "Seamanship in Rough Weather," page 173). Special care should be taken against cumulonimbus clouds on hot sultry days, especially late in the afternoon if the temperature starts to drop.

Fig. 68

Nimbostratus (Fig. 69). Heavy rain, light rain, drizzle, or mist all are caused by nimbostratus clouds. Called "weekend limbos" because they ruin so many boating holidays, these clouds hang overhead in overcast skies bringing rain that often lasts three or four days. Unlike cumulonimbus clouds, which

Fig. 69

Fig. 70

are localized, nimbostratus clouds cover large areas and are usually predicted well in advance of their arrival.

Fog. Although everybody dislikes bad weather, boatmen have a special pet peeve when it comes to fog. When this gray soup rolls across the water, offshore boatmen make final position checks and prepare to navigate "blind." While near shore, skippers run for port knowing that in a short while distinctive landmarks will dissolve into gray shapeless masses. The most common type of fog along our coastlines and the Great Lakes area is advection fog. This culprit develops as warm air passes over colder water or land forming a blanketing stratus cloud (Fig. 70). Another type of fog often found in a river valley and over shallow lakes and ponds is called steam fog or sea smoke. Cold air passing over warmer water or land causes this fog. Depending on how cold the air is, this steam fog may rise upward hundreds of feet. The morning mist so common in early spring and fall is an excellent example of steam fog.

SPECIAL WEATHER SIGNS

Back before the days of meteorologists, men associated certain signs in nature with weather changes. Although many of these signs have proven false or unreliable, others make excellent weather forecasters. Following is a list of these signs that boatmen can usually rely on:

1. Vivid red sky at sunset—fair weather tomorrow.
2. Vivid red sky at sunrise—poor weather today.
3. Clear sky at sunset—fair weather tomorrow.
4. Gray sky at sunset—poor weather tomorrow.
5. Bright moon—fair weather tomorrow.
6. Dull or haloed moon—poor weather tomorrow.

7. Smoke that rises straight up—high-pressure area, fair weather.
8. Smoke that hugs the ground—low-pressure area, poor weather.
9. Rainbow in the morning—rain later in the day.
10. Rainbow in the afternoon—fair tomorrow.
11. Heavy dew on the morning grass—fair weather today.

STORM SIGNALS

To alert boatmen of approaching storms the U. S. Weather Bureau with assistance from numerous boating organizations has developed a visual warning system composed of flags and lights (Fig. 71). These warnings are flown at most boating areas when advised by the Weather Bureau. Boatmen should respect these signals at all times.

The small craft warnings are for all boats sixty-five feet and under.

Boatmen who would like to learn more about the weather will find a list of books and pamphlets available from the United States Weather Bureau in Appendix B of this book.

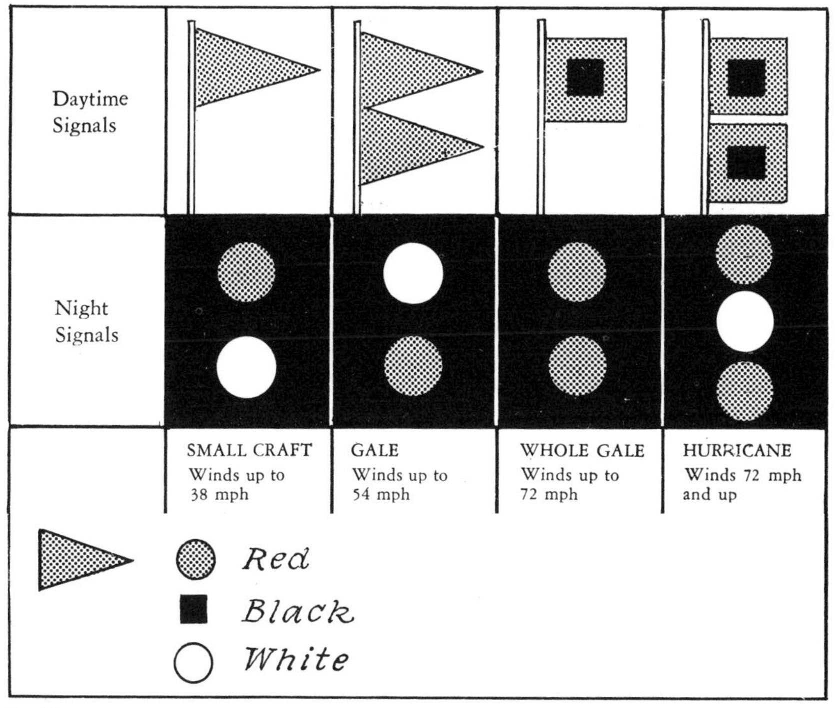

Fig. 71

7

Rowing

Rowing is one of the most popular methods of boating in America and the world. Not only lots of fun and an ideal physical conditioner, rowing is also the safest and easiest way to learn basic seamanship. Each year thousands of new boatmen train themselves in this manner as better skippers. Other thousands look to rowing as the best method of exploring remote waterways or quietly reaching a favorite fishing ground. All of these reasons add up to one thing: every boatman worth his "salt" must be able to handle a rowboat.

NOMENCLATURE

There are only a few parts in a rowboat to learn. As in all boats the front end is called the bow, and the back end the stern. The piece that goes across the stern is called the transom. Gunwales are built along the top edge of the boat's sides. Oarlock fittings are fastened to the gunwales, which hold the oarlocks. Usually there are three thwarts (seats), called bow, rowing, and stern. At the bow there will be a short line called a painter, used to tie up the boat. To make rowing easier many rowboats have an adjustable stretcher. This is a narrow board fastened crosswise on the floor between the stern and rowing seat, allowing the rower to brace his feet while rowing. Every rowboat should have flotation tanks or blocks, buoyant enough to keep the boat afloat with its allowed number of passengers while full of water (Fig. 72).

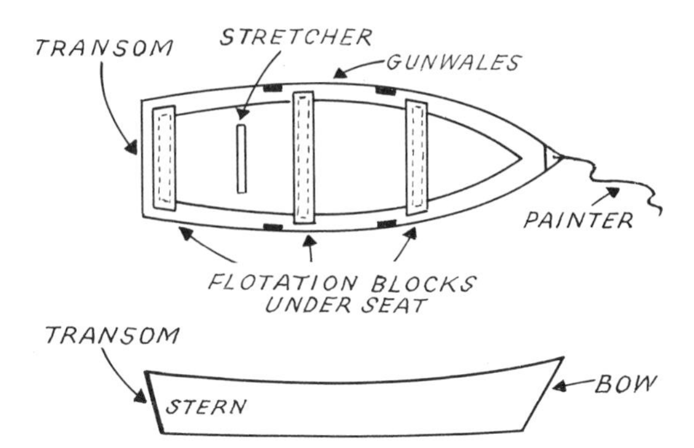

Fig. 72

OARS

Oars are usually made from selected ash or spruce woods. The three parts of an oar are the handle, loom, and blade. The handle is at the top, the loom is the round tapered shaft between the handle and blade, and the blade is that thin flat part which goes into the water. Occasionally oars will have a piece of leather wrapped around the loom where the oars fit in the oarlocks. They are called leathers and buttons and prevent the oars from slipping through the oarlocks (Fig. 73).

Often when people go rowing they grab any pair of oars handy and later complain that the boat handled poorly. Chances are they took a pair of oars too long or too short for the boat. A good yardstick to follow when choosing oars is: on boats eight to ten feet use oars five and a half to six and a half feet long; on longer boats, up to sixteen feet, use oars seven to seven and a half feet long.

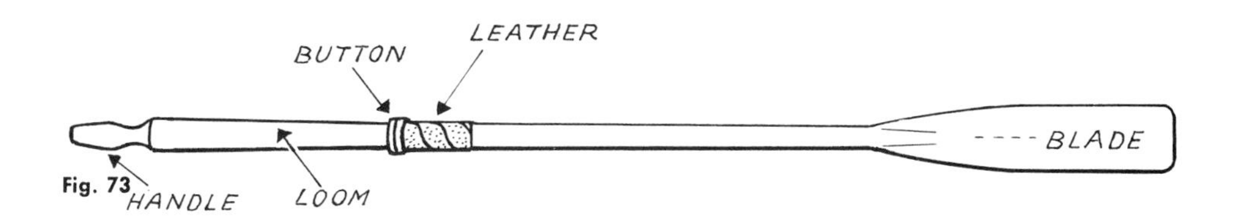

Fig. 73

OARLOCKS

The majority of oarlocks used today are made of either brass or galvanized iron. To row properly an oarlock should swivel when the oar moves on a stroke. Do not let anyone put permanent or pin oarlocks on your boat. It is impossible to learn to row properly with them.

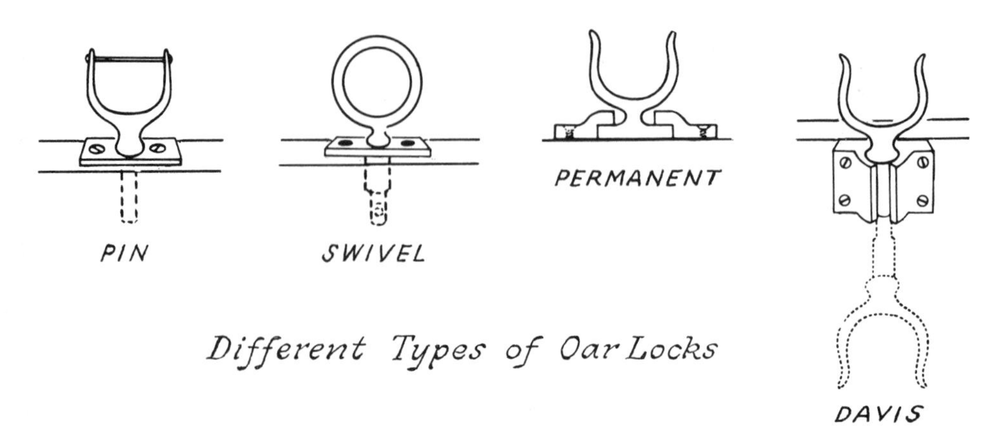

Fig. 74

Davis oarlock—swivels with each stroke and allows you to feather your oars. When not in use they hang out of the way below the gunwale. Good oarlock (Fig. 74).

Swivel oarlock—fits into a socket in the gunwale allowing oar to swivel with each stroke. One type of swivel has a crutch top like the Davis. The other type has a ring top used with oars having leathers and preventers. The oar is put into the ring; then the preventer is put on so the oar cannot slip out. Good oarlock (Fig. 74).

Permanent oarlock—does not allow oar to swing free, wears out oars. Poor oarlock (Fig. 74).

Pin oarlock—does not allow oar to be feathered. Weakens oar where pin goes through loom. Poor oarlock (Fig. 74).

LET'S GO ROWING

Now that you know the important parts of a rowboat and oar, let's go aboard and start your first lesson. Untie the painter, gently step aboard, and sit on the rowing seat facing the stern. Notice how the boat sits in the water at an awkward angle, one side higher than the other with the bow or stern too deep in the water. This shows the boat is untrimmed (Fig. 75). Trimming is the nautical term for balancing a boat. To operate efficiently and handle with a minimum of effort, all boats must be trimmed—even sailboats, though in a different manner. Rowboats are trim when both gunwales are the same height over the water, and the stern sits a little deeper in the water than the bow (Fig. 76). When alone, sit in the middle seat facing the stern (in rowing you are always looking backward) directly over the keel, which runs from bow to stern down the center of the boat. In this position your boat will be trimmed and ready to row. If passengers are aboard, distribute the extra weight so you

Fig. 75

Fig. 76

will have the same trim as when rowing alone. Heavier passengers sit on the stern seat because it holds more weight. Lighter passengers sit forward on the bow seat so the bow will not dip too much. Keep the weight over the keel or balanced evenly on each side; otherwise the boat will lean sideways (list), making it untrimmed (Fig. 77).

CHANGING POSITIONS

Usually in the course of a trip afloat those aboard take turns rowing. This means shifting of personnel from one seat to another. Aboard rowboats this can be dangerous unless done in a safe manner because the shallow draft and low freeboard invite tipping. Under no circumstances should anyone stand or walk upright while changing seats. The safest and easiest method is as follows. Before a change is made, the rower always ships his oars (places them inside

Fig. 77

the boat parallel to the sides). He then slides over to one side of the boat, remaining on the rower's seat. Once the rower has slid over, the new rower grasps the gunwale and leaves his seat in a hunkered-down position. This keeps his weight low in the boat, allowing the center of gravity to remain unchanged. He then "duck walks" to the rowing seat, sliding his hand along the gunwale for balance. On reaching the rower's seat he simply pivots and sits down, if he came from the stern, or gently steps over the rower's seat and then sits down, if he came from the bow seat. Once the new rower is seated, the former rower returns to the vacant seat using the same method. The main thing to remember is: *Never* stand or walk upright.

STROKES

Every time you move an oar through the water it is called a stroke. In rowing there are two basic strokes, a sweep stroke and reverse stroke. Once these are mastered the other fundamentals such as turning, approaching a dock, and leaving a dock become child's play.

REST POSITION

Every stroke in rowing, except sculling, starts and ends from the rest position. To get in this position, sit on the rowing seat facing the stern. Place the oars in the oarlocks, grasp the handles firmly, swing the oar blades out over the water, and pull the handles together until they almost touch. The oars should now be at right angles to the boat, about waist high with the thin edge of the oar blades vertical to the water's surface. Holding the oars in this position, your arms will be at your sides, bent at the elbows, with your wrists straight. Now sit up straight and brace your feet against the stretcher on floorboards. Most people find it easier to row if they keep their feet together. You are now in the rest position and ready to move to a stroke position (Fig. 78).

Fig. 78

Fig. 79 (A-E)

Fig. 80

SWEEP STROKE

The first stroke to learn is called a sweep. From the rest position lean slightly forward, extending your arms out in front of you. The oar blades are now behind you toward the bow of the boat. Now raise your hands about chest high until the oar blades dip three-quarters submerged in the water. You are now ready to pull. Slowly lean back, pulling the oars until your back is straight, elbows at your sides, and hands close to your chest. Now drop your hands to your waist, and the oars will leave the water. You are again in the rest position. Rest for a moment and let the boat glide forward. You have just completed a sweep stroke. Practice sweep strokes until you are sure of each movement. With the boat moving forward, occasionally look over your shoulder to see where you are going. Watch your hands and you will see they are making a counterclockwise oval. Cut the oval into pieces and you can see each part of a sweep stroke (Fig. 79 A to E).

When practicing, keep the oval in mind and repeat during each stroke, lean forward–dip oars–lean back–rest. Repeating this rhythm will help you develop a smooth even sweep. Study the illustrations and you will see the complete stroke using the oval.

CATCHING A CRAB

Most new rowers have a tendency to dip the oar blades too deep, making the water pressure so great on the blades that an oar jumps out of the oarlock throwing the rower backward (Fig. 80). This is called "catching a crab." To avoid this, make sure only three-quarters of each blade is submerged in the water when you dip oars and lean back.

You can regulate the oars dip by watching the blades for a few strokes to see how high or low your stroke oval should be. When the blade is at the right depth, your hands will be at the top of the oval in the lean-back position.

FEATHERING YOUR OARS

Once you have mastered the sweep you are ready to start feathering the oars. Feathering simply means turning the oar blades from a vertical to parallel position during the lean-forward movement. This allows the blade edge to cut through the air with the least amount of wind resistance when rowing against the wind or on a choppy day. Starting at the rest position, turn your knuckles up toward your chest. This will pivot the blades from vertical to parallel over the water. Continue through with your lean-forward motion. Just before you dip oars bring the blades back to vertical by dropping your knuck-

Fig. 81

Fig. 82

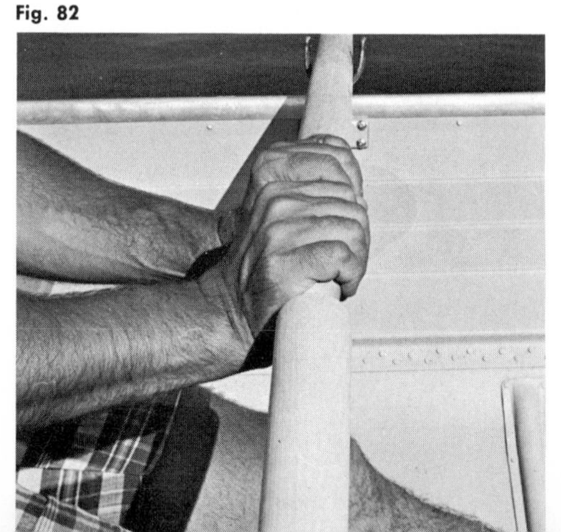

les to their original position. Then continue through with a regular sweep stroke. Feathering is one of the fine points of rowing that separate the amateurs from the pros. So take an extra few minutes to master this skill. Boatmen using pin oarlocks will find it impossible to feather because the oars cannot pivot. Should your boat be so equipped, replace the pin oarlocks with swivel oarlocks (Fig. 81) (Fig. 82).

Fig. 83

STOPPING

Now that you are sweeping and the boat is moving forward, you must learn to stop. Fortunately stopping is easy and will only take a minute to learn. To stop, go to the rest position and just raise your hands to your chest. This movement will make the oar blades dip into the water and act like a brake. The pressure of the water will try to push the blades toward bow or stern depending which way you are moving. To counteract this pressure, hold the oar handles steady. This will keep the blades in the same position and the boat will stop (Fig. 83).

ROWING IN A STRAIGHT LINE

By this time you have most likely found that trying to row in a straight line is almost impossible. The boat keeps going in a wide circle. Don't worry, all beginners have the same problem. What is happening is that your strong arm is pulling harder than your other arm. For right-handed people this is usually their right arm, and for left-handed people their left arm. To offset the uneven pull and to row in a straight line, use the following technique.

Line up the boat's bow directly at your destination. Then sight over the center of the transom and pick out a stationary object onshore or in the water, such as a tree, pole, or buoy. This puts the bow, your head, the center of the

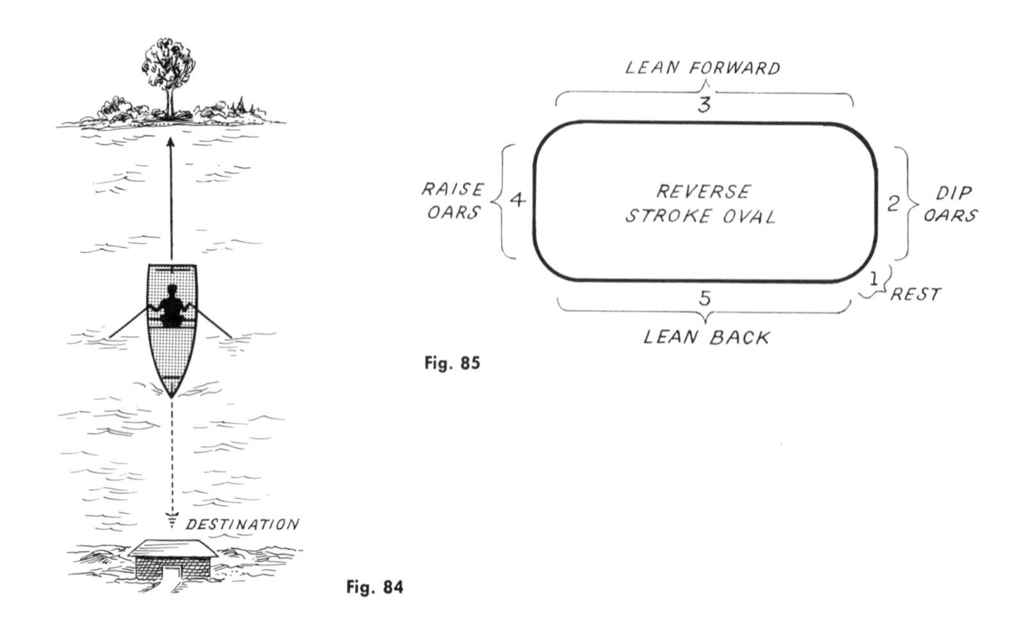

Fig. 84

Fig. 85

transom, and the object all in a straight line. As long as you keep the object centered over the middle of the transom your course will be straight toward your destination. If the object starts drifting to one side of the transom, just pull a little harder with the oar on the same side as the direction in which the object is drifting, and you will straighten right out. Many rowboat owners paint or scribe a mark on the transom to use as a guide (Fig. 84).

REVERSE STROKE

Often while rowing you will want to move the boat through the water stern first. This is called backwatering. Lifeguards and fishermen often backwater because it is easier to keep an eye on swimmers or nets. The movements used in this stroke are just the reverse of a sweep stroke. Hence the name reverse stroke. From a rest position make your oval in reverse (Fig. 85).

Raise your hands to your chest until the oars are three-quarters submerged in the water, then lean forward extending your arms; this will push the oar handles toward the stern and the blades through the water toward the bow. Now drop your hands to waist level, and the blades will leave the water. Feather the blade by turning your knuckles down instead of up, and lean back to rest position. You have just completed a reverse stroke. Practice until you are sure of each movement.

TURNS

When making a turn in a rowboat you must remember that your left hand is holding the right oar and your right hand is holding the left oar. This may be confusing so pay special attention to the next paragraph.

The way to find the starboard (right) or port (left) side in any boat is to face the bow when aboard. Your right hand will be on the boat's starboard side and your left hand on the boat's port side. So when you sit with your back to the bow, such as in rowing, the port and starboard sides remain the same on the boat; but because you are facing the stern, your left hand will be on the starboard side of the boat holding the right oar, and your right hand on the port side holding the left oar. To be sure you thoroughly understand this, take a minute and read this paragraph again. Most of the collisions in rowing are caused because people turn in the opposite direction when someone yells port or starboard in an emergency.

Wide Turns

The simplest turn in rowing is a wide turn. All you do is sweep with one oar and keep the other oar at rest position, and the boat will make a wide arc. To make a starboard (right) turn, just sweep the left oar with your right hand. To make a port (left) turn, sweep the right oar with your left hand. An easy way to remember is, on a right turn pull with your right hand—Right turn, right-hand pull. On a left turn pull with your left hand—Left turn, left-hand pull. Practice until you turn in either direction automatically. Having a friend call out directions is a good way to practice.

Pivot Turn

You can always tell a rower's ability by the way he turns. Beginners will make wide turns while experienced rowers will make pivot turns. In pivot turns the boat turns within its own length, or as the saying goes, spins on a

Fig. 86

dime. A pivot gives the quickest response, therefore is the best turn to use in most turning situations. From a rest position put one oar in a sweep pull position and the other in a reverse push position. Dip both oars, pull with the sweep oar and push with the reverse oar, and the boat will spin around as if it was balanced on a pivot or pole. For direction use the same system you learned for wide turns, just add a push. On a starboard (right) turn, sweep the left oar with your right hand and reverse the right oar with your left hand—right hand pull, left hand pushes. A left turn is just the opposite—left hand pulls, right hand pushes. Pivoting takes a while to learn so do not get discouraged if it takes longer than the strokes or wide turn. Stick with it, and you will shortly be classified as an expert rower (Fig. 86).

USING AN OARMATE

There are many reasons why you would row with an oarmate. Rowing against a current, tide, or wind, rowing over a long distance, or to row faster are just a few. The only difference between rowing alone and with a partner is you only handle one oar. Have your oarmate sit next to you on the rower's seat, each of you hold one oar with both hands, check to see the boat is trim, and row away. Every stroke is the same as rowing alone, the only thing to watch for is that you both pull together and during turns remember which side of the boat you are sitting on (Fig. 87).

SCULLING

Have you ever thought how you would get back to shore if an oarlock broke? You could sit at the bow facing the stern and paddle canoe style—hard work but you would eventually reach land. A much easier way would be to scull from the transom or good oarlock. This method of rowing with one

Fig. 87

Fig. 88

oar is used in many lands instead of the conventional two-oar method. Look on the top center of the transom and see if there is a U-shaped nitch cut out. If there is, it is called a sculling cup. Boats without a sculling cup can attach a swivel oarlock fitting and use the oarlock.

Sit in the stern seat facing the bow, or kneel just forward of the stern seat facing the transom. Do not stand. Sitting or kneeling is much safer and more comfortable. Put the oar in the sculling cup; place one hand on the handle and the other about one foot lower on the loom. Dip the blade, thin edge vertical, and move the handle in a figure 8 motion from side to side. This movement will make the boat move forward almost as fast as using two oars. Sculling from an oarlock is done in the same fashion. When docking against a current you can scull sideways into the dock with the outside oar after the inside oar has been shipped. Sculling is as much fun as rowing, so take a few minutes and learn (Fig. 88).

CURRENTS, TIDES, AND WINDS

A current, tide, or wind can help or hinder a boat, depending on its direction. When a boat and these elements are moving in the same direction they help push the boat along. Rowers can take advantage of this extra help by resting longer at rest position during each stroke. But if the boat is moving against these elements they act as a brake, and a rower must use short fast strokes with little or no rest at rest position. Rowing against the wind is one instance where feathering oars are important.

Moving across currents, tides, or winds, putting them at right angles or nearly so to the boat poses an altogether different problem. Drift and how to compensate for it must be solved.

The following is an example of drift when crossing a current. Tides or wind pose the same problem.

If you start to row at A, traveling at two miles per hour to B, straight across a river two miles wide that has a current of two miles per hour, you would end up two miles below your destination at C.

Looking at Figure 89 you can see how the boat was pushed two miles down-river by the current.

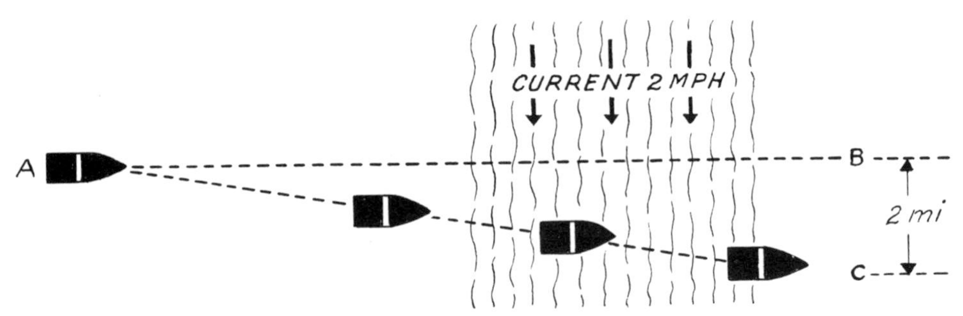

Fig. 89

As you become more experienced in boating you will learn how to plot a course compensating for currents, tides, and winds by using navigational instruments. Until then you can use a simple system called angling up. To do this you angle the bow of your boat up into the current at a point above your destination. This angle allows you to row into as well as across the current, offsetting its force on the boat. A simple way to determine the angle is to look across your shoulder at your destination while rowing. If the middle of the boat starts to drift below your destination, increase the angle, up into the current. After a little practice you will be able to angle up correctly into any current, tide, or wind.

PULLING AWAY FROM A DOCK

When a current, tide, or wind is offshore, moving toward open water, the problem of pulling away from a dock is simplified. After your equipment and passengers are aboard, just cast off and let the boat drift with the current, wind, or tide away from the dock (Fig. 90). If the current is weak, use an oar and shove against the dock. This will push you far enough out to maneuver both oars.

When a current, tide, or wind is onshore holding your boat against the dock, use the following method to pull away. After casting off take the oar farthest from the dock and start to reverse stroke. This will swing the bow out toward

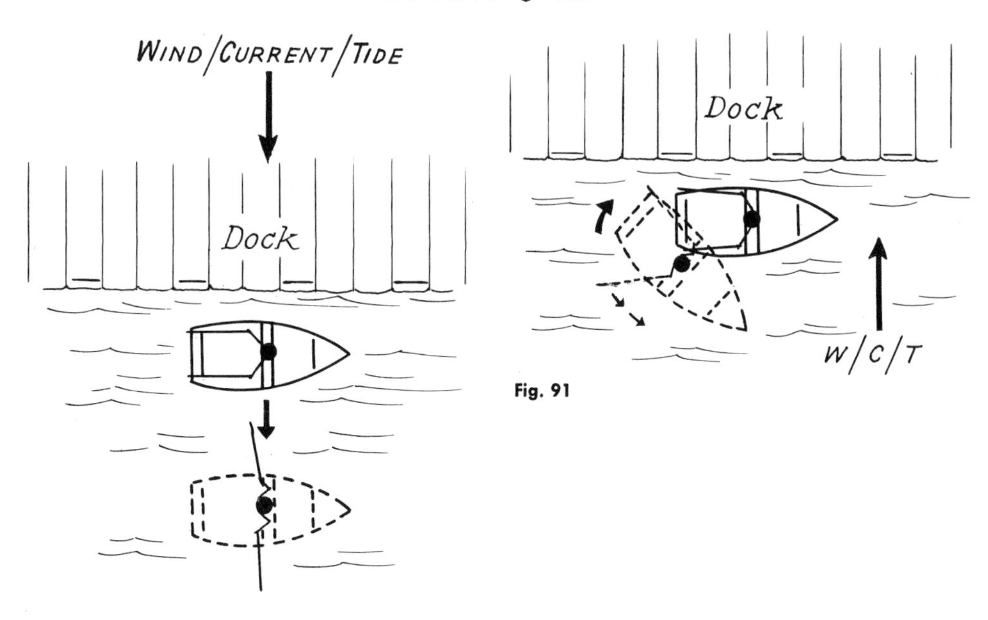

Fig. 90

Fig. 91

open water and the transom in toward the dock. To protect the transom from bumping the dock, hold the inside oar blade against the dock. Once the boat swings around far enough to use both oars, start to sweep toward open waters (Fig. 91).

DOCKING

Docking, like pulling away from a dock, can be easy or difficult depending on the direction of the current, tide, or wind. When the current, wind, or tide is onshore moving toward the dock, swing your boat around to docking position a few yards away from the dock and let the boat drift in. Use an oar to fend off the boat to keep it from banging into the dock. Many boatmen have a bad habit of fending off with their hand. This is an easy way to have your hand or fingers crushed between the dock and gunwale, so remember to use an oar (Fig. 92).

When docking with the current, wind, or tide offshore moving toward open water, there are two ways to dock. The easiest method after you learn to scull is the following. Row as close to the dock as you can, pivot turn putting the boat parallel to the dock, ship the inside oar, and scull with the outside oar moving the boat sideways into the dock (Fig. 93).

The other docking method is called angling and can also be used if the current, tide, or wind is moving at an angle to the dock. Row up into the current toward the dock at an angle great enough to use both oars. Gently touch

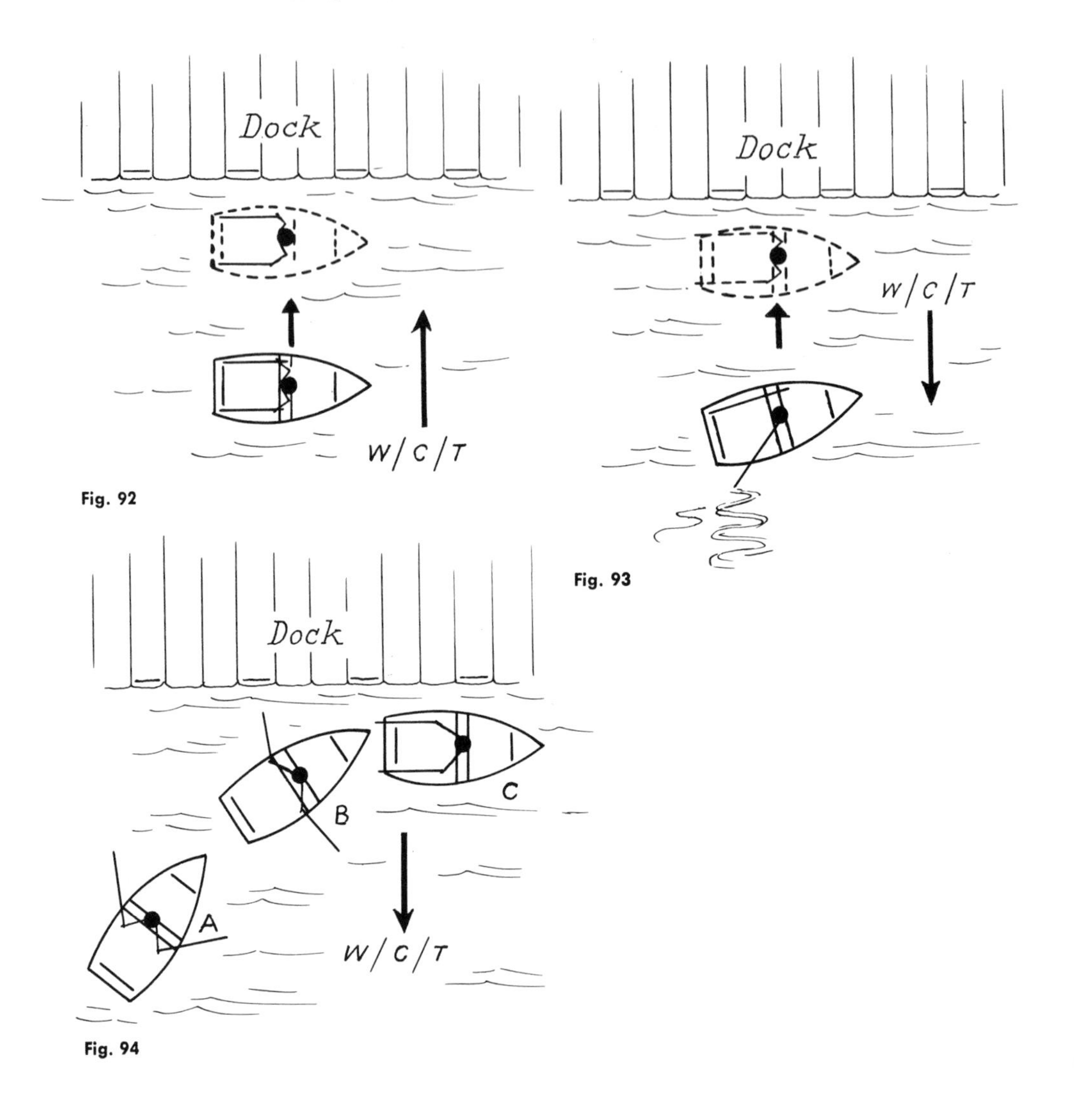

Fig. 92

Fig. 93

Fig. 94

the bow into the dock, ship the oars, and reach over and hold the dock. When passengers are aboard, have the man in the bow hold the dock (Fig. 94).

After you have docked, tie up bow and stern and put fenders out to protect the boat's side from banging against the dock.

LEAVING FROM SHORE

Often a rowboat is pulled up onshore instead of tied in a docking area. If the bow is resting onshore, lift the bow and slide the boat out into the water. When the stern is afloat, step aboard over the bow, sit in the rower's seat, and reverse stroke until you can turn the boat and start sweep stroking.

If the stern is resting onshore, slide the boat out into the water until the bow is afloat, step in over the transom, sit in the rower's seat, and sweep stroke away.

LANDING ON SHORE

When you land a boat onshore it is called beaching. Regardless of whether you come in bow or stern first, use the following method. Row slowly until you feel the bow or stern touch bottom, stop rowing, move to the bow or stern, and step ashore, then pull the boat one-third out of the water. Never row fast onto shore. It will scrape the paint on the boat's bottom or crack the hull. Always watch out for rocks or other obstructions that would harm the bottom.

REFLOATING WHEN CAPSIZED

When a rowboat capsizes in deep water, use the following methods to empty out the water and get back aboard. Swim to one side of the rowboat and roll it over until it is sitting upright in the water. A gentle pull will do this.

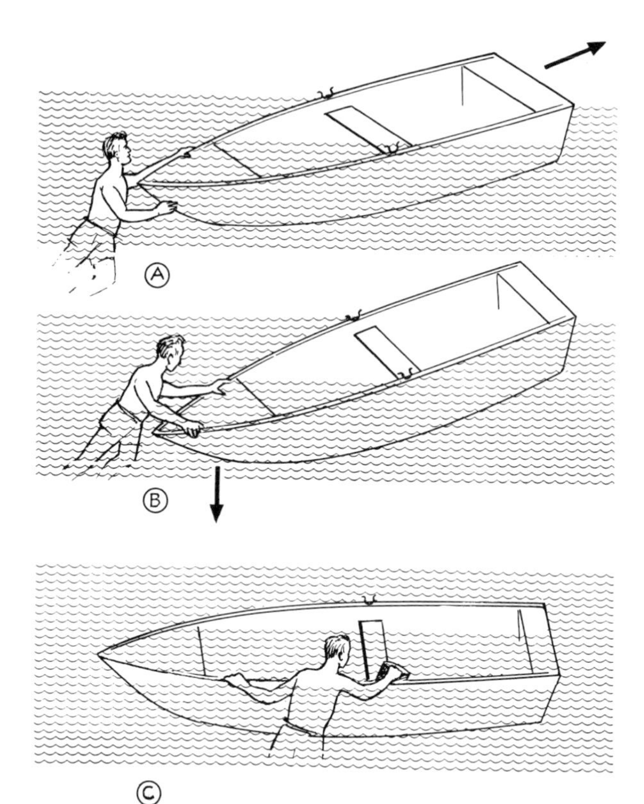

Fig. 95

Once upright, gather the oars and wedge them under the seats. Then move to the bow and start swimming, pushing the boat backward. Once the boat is moving, push the bow down underwater and give a hard shove. This will cause the stern to pop up out of water and the boat to lunge ahead emptying one-third to one-half of the water from the boat. Now swim to the side, holding on to a gunwale, and start bailing with your hand or the bailer, which should be tied to a seat. Be careful the gunwale does not go underwater. After the boat is two-thirds empty, gently climb in over the transom, bail out the rest of the water, and row ashore (Fig. 95).

When close to land, push from the stern while swimming until you reach shore.

If you are too tired to empty the water out and too far offshore to push the boat in, climb aboard over the transom and sit on the floor in the center of the boat to rest. After you have rested, start paddling with your hands toward shore or wave to attract attention.

When passengers are aboard, check to see all are all right immediately after you capsize. Everyone, including you, should be wearing life preservers. Anyone injured or unconscious should be cared for by a good swimmer. If you plan to empty the boat, use the same procedure explained above, plus the help of passengers on both sides to bail.

If for some reason you do not empty the boat, have the injured and weak swimmers gently climb aboard and sit or lie in the middle of the boat. Good swimmers can either hang on to the gunwales or also climb aboard. The main thing to remember is *stay with the boat.* Never try to swim to shore. This cannot be stressed too strongly. *Stay with the boat.*

Fig. 96

8

Sailing

Beauty, excitement, and challenge! All three make sailing the favorite pastime of thousands of pleasure boatmen and their families. The beauty of a sailboat with sails billowed high overhead is usually the first introduction to sailing for most new skippers. Once aboard, the excitement of handling the tiller and mainsheet as your boat races over the water, driving to a mark, quickly proves you made the right choice. And last, the challenges found in racing other boats or cruising offshore waters, once you have acquired your sea legs, turns you into a "diehard" canvas sailor.

To learn this great sport and get you aboard and sailing in the shortest possible time, a one-sail (cat-rigged) boat is recommended, such as the one shown in Figure 97. These small craft are ideal trainers because they handle easily, are extremely seaworthy within their limitations, and are inexpensive to buy. As all sailboats work on the same principles, you can, if you wish, step up into a sloop design (one mast with two sails) or other type after just one season in a "cat."

If you have access to a sloop (Fig. 118) and plan to use it as a trainer, only the mainsail should be used for the first few lessons. Later when you start practicing "coming about" and "tacking," the jibsail, which is called a jib, will have to be raised, as sloops react sluggishly without it when turning across the wind. How to work and handle a jib is explained at the end of this chapter.

Regardless of the type of boat you learn in, the important thing to remember is to concentrate on the basic steps. The finer points and techniques will come

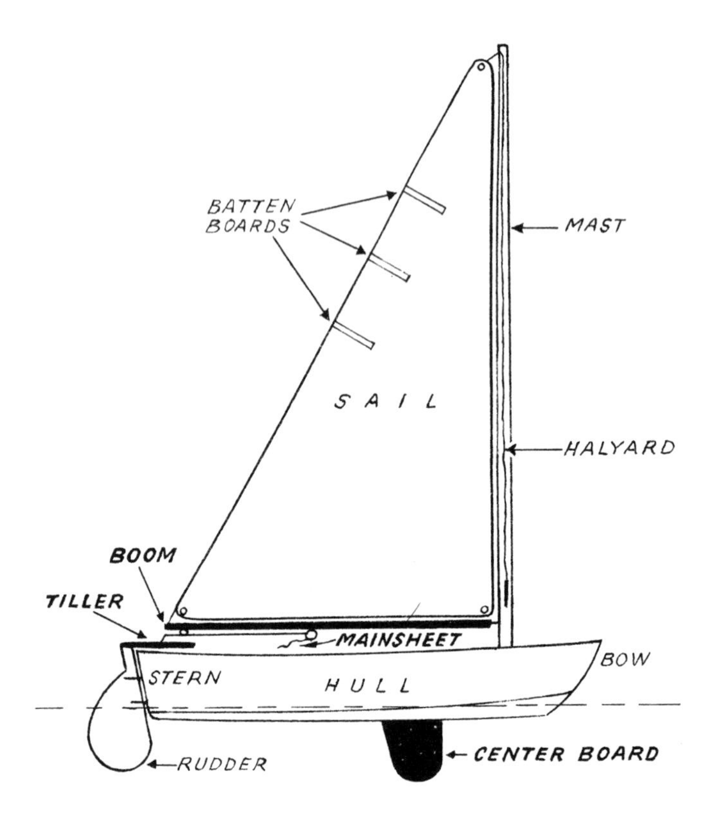

Fig. 97

automatically later, with practice and observation. In the meantime you will be enjoying the fun and excitement of skippering your own craft.

SAILBOAT NOMENCLATURE

In Figure 97 you will notice that only four parts of the sailboat are labeled in heavy print: the centerboard, tiller, mainsheet, and boom. They are the teaching parts of the boat. Once you understand their functions and master their operation you will be able to handle any sailboat, for all sailing craft work from these same four major parts.

The first is the *centerboard*, which hangs below the boat and acts as a slipping brake. Without this awkard-looking slab of iron, steel, or wood it would be impossible to sail into or off the wind. When in a down position the centerboard counteracts the wind pressure that would normally push a boat sideways causing it to slide downwind. The only exception to this is when sailing free with the wind coming in over the stern. On such a course the wind can only drive the boat forward.

Some boats, especially high-masted ocean sailing models, have a much heavier and larger permanent iron and lead keel instead of a centerboard, the object being to add more ballast (weight) and surface area.

The next and most important parts you must learn to use are the *tiller*, *mainsheet* and *boom*. They are the steering wheel, throttle, and engine mount of your boat. Two of them, the tiller and mainsheet, are held in your hands to steer and control the boat. And the third, the boom, holds the foot (bottom edge) of the mainsail and is controlled by the mainsheet. These three parts are the key to all sailing points and maneuvers.

The *tiller* is the sticklike handle attached to the rudder. When you move the tiller the rudder also moves, steering the boat. There are two movements with the tiller that are necessary to understand. So take your time and be sure you know what they are, and what they do.

1. When you move the tiller toward the sail the bow of the boat moves up into the direction of the wind. This is called heading up or pointing up (Fig. 98A).

2. When you move the tiller away from the sail the bow of the boat moves away from the direction of the wind. This is called bearing off (Fig. 98B).

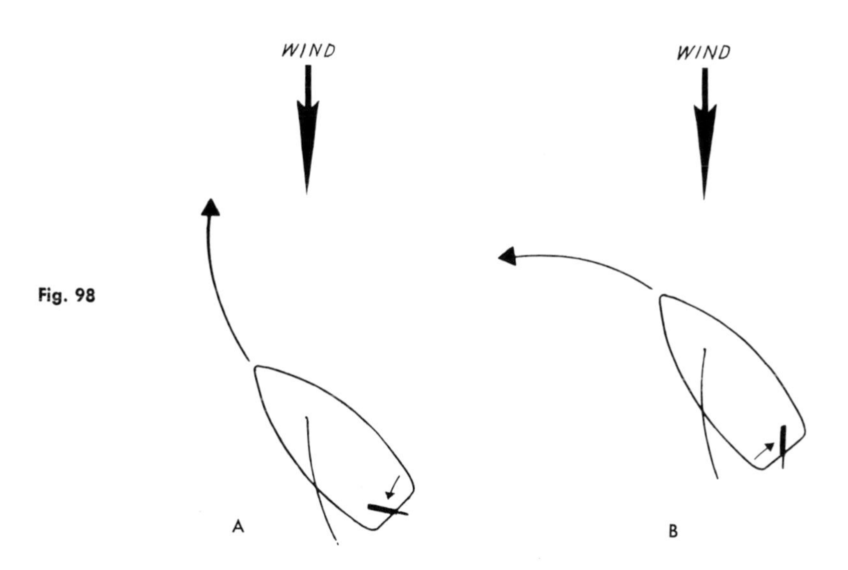

Fig. 98

Just remember: "Into the sail, into the wind." "Away from the sail, away from the wind."

Of course, when the tiller is parallel to the bow, the boat steers straight ahead.

The *mainsheet* is the line (rope) attached to the boom, with which you set and trim the sail by pulling in or letting out the boom. On sailboats all lines used to control sails are called sheets.

The *boom* is the horizontal pole on which the foot (bottom edge) of the mainsail is secured. One end is attached to the mast with a gooseneck. The other end is allowed to swing free controlled only by the mainsheet.

Fig. 99

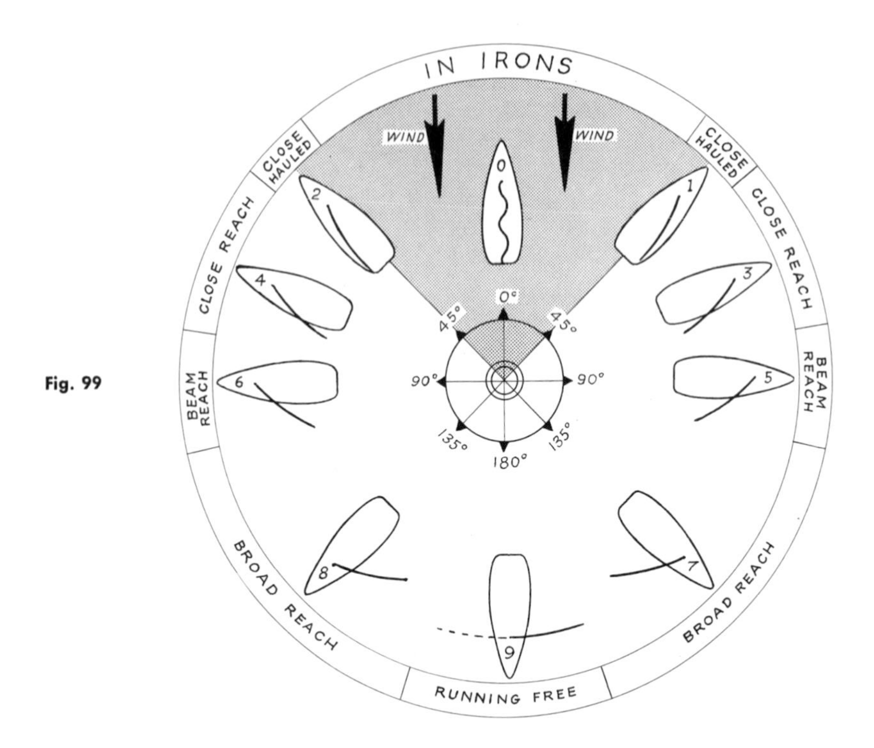

SAILING POINTS

Once you know and understand the important parts of a sailboat all that remains before hoisting sail is to learn the terms used when sailing at different angles to the wind. Among sailors these are known as sailing points and must be thoroughly understood in order to make your boat perform safely and efficiently.

Although each point will be explained in detail, once you have learned to set a sail it is to your advantage to know beforehand what they are and mean. So study Figure 99 and the explanations. Then when you go aboard, your lessons will progress much faster and more smoothly. Pay special attention to the wind and sail angle on each boat as you will shortly be trying to copy them.

1. *In irons*—when a boat is facing directly into the wind and will not move (Fig. 99, #0). When "in irons" the boom will be parallel with the keel, and the sail will be flapping. This is called luffing.
2. *Close-hauled*—sailing as near as you can directly into the wind, approximately 45 degrees, without going into irons (Fig. 99, #1 and 2).
3. *Reaching*—sailing in any direction except close-hauled or running free (Fig. 99, #3, 4, 5, 6, 7, and 8).
4. *Running free*—sailing before the wind, with the wind blowing in over the stern (Fig. 99, #9).

HOISTING SAIL

To save time when aboard let's learn how we put the sail on the mast and boom, or in sailor's jargon, "bend the sail." First secure the sail head to the line on the mast which is called a halyard; then slide the clips attached to the luff onto the mast track. Do not hoist the sail yet. Now attach the foot of the sail at the clew end to the outhaul sheet. Pull it along the boom and tie it down. Next check to be sure the batten boards are in the batten pockets and that the boom can swing free. If everything checks out, take the halyard and bend away. Remember, do not hoist sail until the foot is stretched on the boom and the batten boards are in. Forget, and the sail will be flapping in the breeze like a flag, making it impossible to secure the foot to the boom (Fig. 100).

CHECK THE WIND BEFORE CASTING OFF

The first thing a smart sailor does before leaving shore is to check the weather and wind. From the start you must realize the wind is your partner. How well you learn to work with it decides your ability to handle a sailboat. Before going out on the water, check to see in which direction it is moving and how strong it is blowing. There are many simple ways to do this. Look at trees, the water, flags, or smoke, and see which way they are blowing. A tell-tale made from a piece of bright-colored yarn or feather should be tied high on the mast or a stay of every sailboat. It shows the wind direction even in a light breeze (Fig. 101).

And speaking of breezes, make sure your learning and practicing is done in gentle winds. Stiff winds call for a stiff boat and expert handling. Winds up to twelve miles per hour (Beaufort #3) are the best and safest to develop a gentle

Fig. 100

Fig. 101

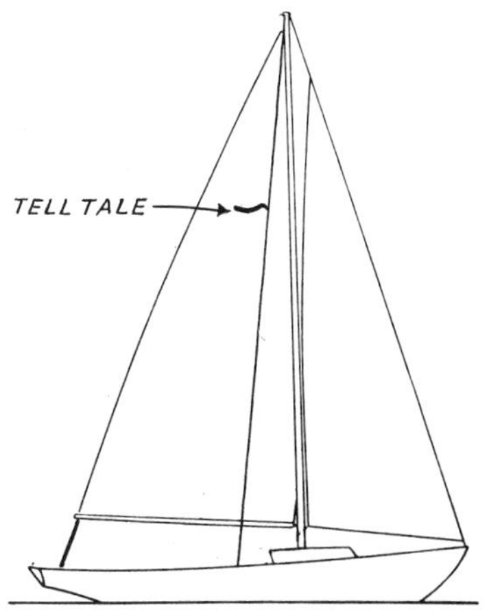

touch and trim sail. (Wind velocity is discussed in Chapter 7, "Developing a Weather Eye," page 92.)

LET'S GO SAILING

Well you are finally aboard and ready to get under way. So cast off and row or paddle far enough away from the dock and other boats to insure safe maneuvering. Once clear, turn the boat at a right angle to the wind (Fig. 99, #3 or 4), drop the centerboard, and hoist sail. Remember, make sure the mainsheet can run free so the sail can swing parallel to the wind.

If at any time the boat goes into "irons" (bow directly into the wind) (Fig. 99, #0) and won't move, just grin and bear it, and paddle or row the boat back at a right angle to the wind. After you learn to set a sail we will discuss "in irons."

Sit on the side of the boat that has the wind blowing on your back, just forward of the tiller. This is called the weather side because it is closest to the wind. In this position you will be sitting opposite the sail, which is always on the lee side (farthest from the wind), and can easily move the tiller either way. Once under way you will find that sitting opposite the sail helps balance the boat and makes it easier to watch the sail (Fig. 102). The only time you ever sit on the lee side is when the wind is just barely blowing and your weight is needed to heel (lean) the boat slightly to keep the sail on the lee side.

Now pick up the mainsheet with one hand and grasp the tiller with the other. Hold the tiller parallel to the bow and slowly start pulling the sail, which should be luffing (fluttering like a flag Fig. 103A), toward you with the mainsheet. As the wind starts to fill the sail the luffing will stop, and the pressure

Fig. 102

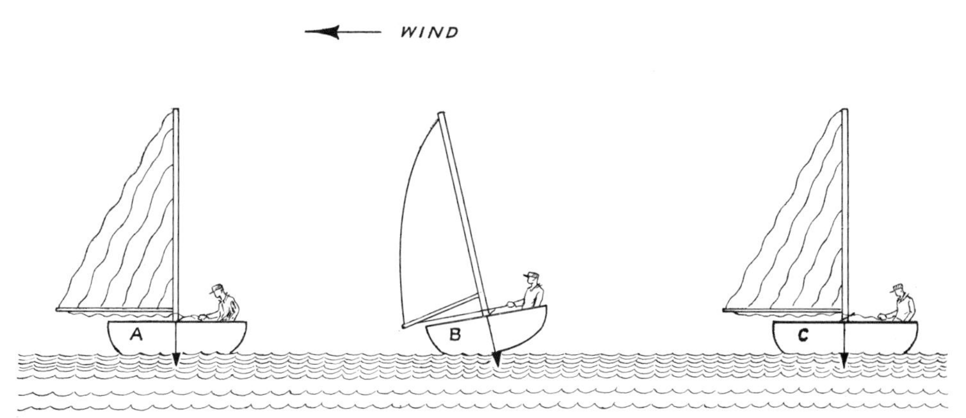

Fig. 103

will make the boat lean over (Fig. 103B). Don't be frightened; this is called heeling and happens on every sailboat. In fact a certain amount of heel is necessary on most sailboats to acquire top performance. Now let the mainsheet slowly slide through your hand, allowing the sail to move away from you. Notice how the boat has stopped leaning and is again flat in the water (Fig. 103-C). What happened is, as the sail moved away from you, the wind spilled out. With no wind in the sail there was no pressure to make the boat heel. Practice this a few times until you get the feel of the heeling action of the boat. If at anytime the boat leans too far over, or starts moving too fast, just drop everything, duck, and relax. The sail will automatically swing into a luffing position, and the boat will quickly flatten out. This is the fastest and safest way to stop a sailboat while learning. Make sure the loose end of the mainsheet is clear and not tangled on some equipment or your foot. Another safety point to remember is: Never tie or cleat down the mainsheet in a small sailboat. Breaking this rule is a sure way to end up with wet sails and a capsized boat.

SETTING THE SAIL

Once you get accustomed to the heeling motion, your next lesson is setting the sail. Start with the boat at a right angle to the wind (Fig. 99, #3 or 4) and the sail luffing. As long as the sail is luffing, the boat will not move forward. Now slowly pull in the sail with the mainsheet until the luffing just stops and the sail is gently curved and full of wind. Your sail is now set and in the best sailing position. It is just as easy as it sounds.

Holding the set when running a course is a matter of touch and feel that comes with practice. When sails are set properly the tiller will have a gentle touch with just a slight tendency to pull toward the lee side of the boat, while the feel of the mainsheet will be even and steady. Any excessive pulling or pressure by the tiller combined with excessive heeling shows the sail is trimmed too tight (pulled in too far) and is trying to force the boat to swing upwind. This is called pinching and can be corrected by letting out the sail a bit with the mainsheet. On the other hand, if the sail is not trimmed tight enough, the boat will start slipping sideways downwind. Correct this by pulling in the sail a few inches and watching your wake astern. When the wake stops drifting upwind and becomes a long straight line behind you, the slipping has stopped and the sail is properly trimmed.

A trick used by all expert sailors in setting sails and keeping them set is: look only at the lower third of the sail next to the mast. This is called the trouble or instrument panel because it quickly tells you when your sail starts to luff and saves you from getting a stiff neck, by looking high up on the sail (Fig. 104).

Fig. 104

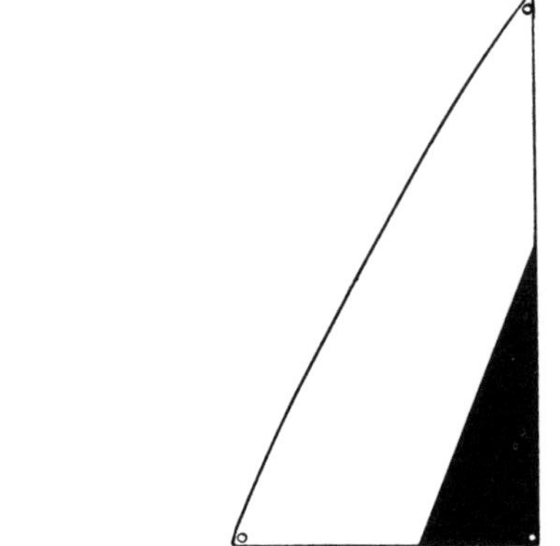

POINTING AND TURNING

At this point in your lessons you should feel at home in your boat and be ready to start the serious side of sailing. From here on you will be learning to use the sailing points discussed earlier, also the turns necessary to cross the wind. The time you devote to mastering these maneuvers will decide how good a skipper you become. If sailing only means an occasional day of fun afloat, practice each point and turn until you can hold a steady course and cross the wind bow up (coming about) and bow down (jibing). Then if an emergency arises, you can safely maneuver away from danger. On the other hand, if sailing means the challenge and excitement of racing or cruising, my best advice is practice, practice, and practice. This is the only way to develop the skills necessary to become a top-rated racing skipper or cruising captain.

When practicing each point and turn, keep an occasional eye on the telltale so you will know the wind angle on your boat and sail.

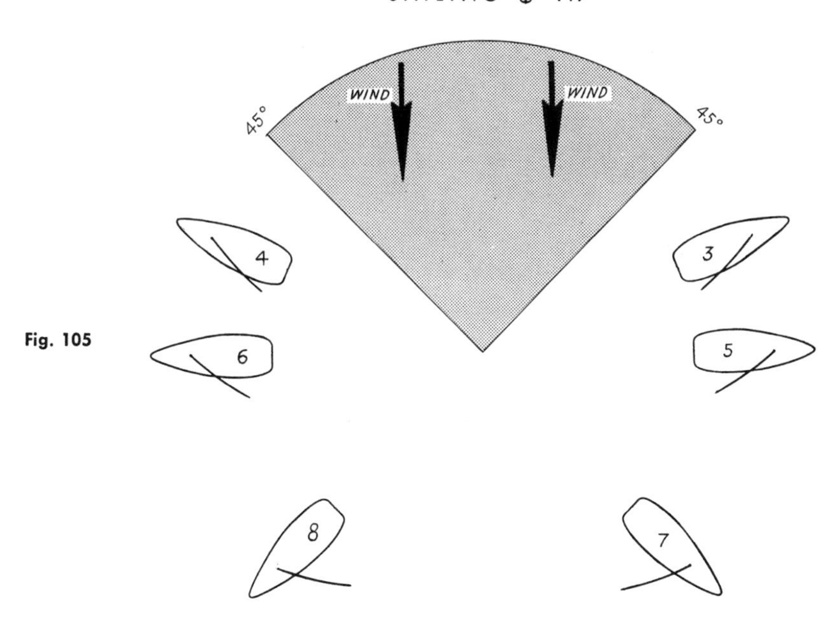

Fig. 105

REACHING

Reaching is the easiest to learn, the most used, and the fastest of all sailing points. In fact, you have already mastered one reach, a beam reach (90 degrees to the wind) (Fig. 105, #5 and 6), while learning to set a sail and hold steady on course. The remaining two, a close reach and broad reach, are simply variations of the beam reach. On a close reach you sail a course more than 45 degrees but less than 90 degrees off the wind (Fig. 105, #3 and 4). On a broad reach (Fig. 105, #7 and 8) you sail a course more than 90 degrees but less than 180 degrees off the wind.

Setting and trimming a sail on these variations is done exactly the same way as on a beam reach.

Example: If from a beam reach you want to point downwind on to a broad-reach course, simply move the tiller away from the sail and slowly let out the mainsheet. When on the desired course, reset the sail and hold the tiller parallel to the bow "steady as she goes." When pointing upwind into a close reach, simply move the tiller toward the sail and slowly pull in the mainsheet. Once on the desired course, trim the sail and hold the tiller parallel "steady as she goes."

Not only easy to learn, reaching is also the safest position to sail. The only hazard is an occasional strong gust of wind that could overturn your boat if the mainsheet is not slacked off in time (beginners: drop, duck, and relax). So take advantage of this built-in safety factor and learn to point up and bear off in the reach positions. Then when you start sailing "close-hauled" and "free," the tiller and mainsheet will be old friends.

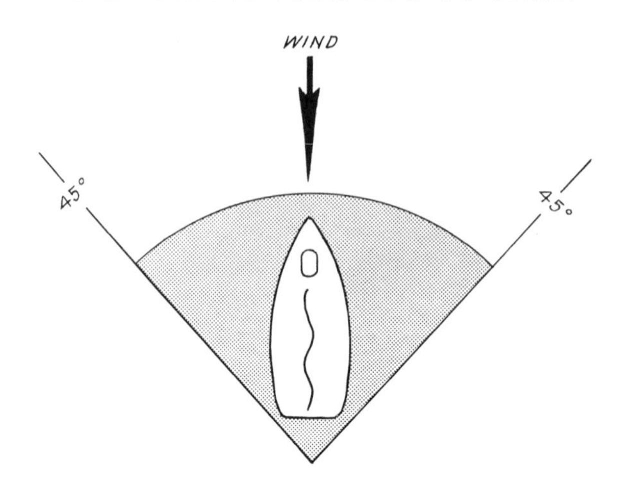

Fig. 106

IN IRONS

The chances are, much to your frustration and unwanted paddling, you have discovered that a sailboat cannot sail directly into the wind. The reason is that when the bow points dead into the wind, the wind blows along both sides of the sail with equal force, causing it to luff (Fig. 106). When this occurs the boat is said to be "in irons," a sailor's term for running out of gas.

When this happens, and it does to all new sailors, just ease off (let out) the mainsheet and start fishtailing the rudder. Fishtailing* is done by slowly moving the tiller away from you, then quickly pulling it back. Continue this action until the pressure exerted by the rudder against the water swings the stern upwind, and the bow downwind. As the bow bears off, trim in the sail until it starts to draw (fill with wind), and you will be out of "irons."

Another method used to get out of irons is by reversing the rudder angle. This is done by moving the tiller toward the sail so the rudder will cause the bow to swing off as the boat slips backward.

Sloops using a jib can get out of irons by holding the jib over the weather side of the bow (Fig. 107). This will swing the bow downwind, allowing the mainsail to draw.

Although going into irons can be embarrassing when it happens unexpectedly, it can, on occasion, be used to your advantage, especially if you must slow down or stop quickly to avoid a collision or when docking. While sailing, make a habit of occasionally pointing up into irons and recovering by bearing off before your boat stops. After a week or two you will be surprised at how easy this maneuver will become. It will also help you master the next sailing point, "close-hauled."

* Fishtailing is illegal when racing because it can be used to move a boat across the finish line. But because it is so easy to do, it is recommended procedure for all new sailors when caught in irons aboard cat rigged boats.

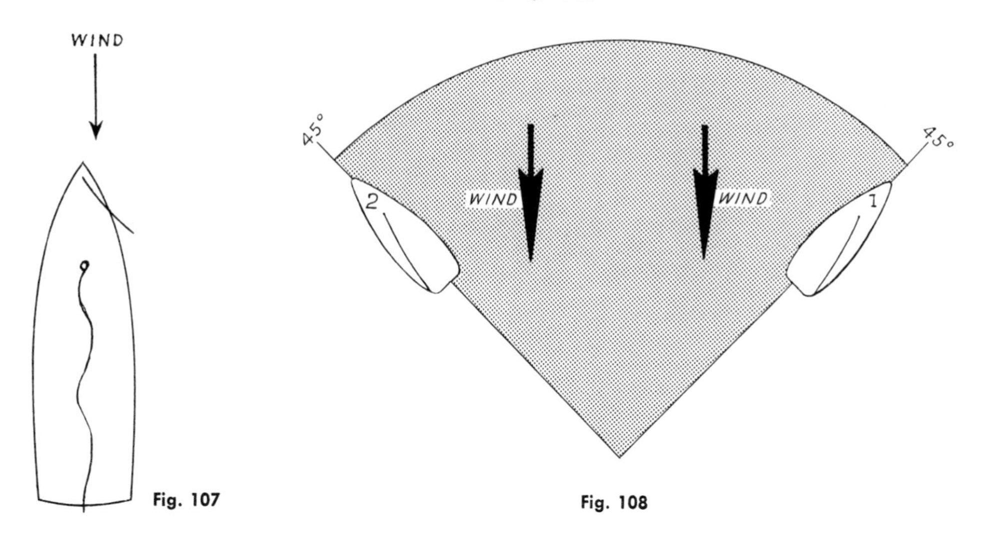

Fig. 107

Fig. 108

CLOSE-HAULED

The problem of reaching a mark directly into the wind starts to be solved with the next sailing point, "close-hauled." This point means to sail as high as possible into the wind without going into "irons." On such a course, also called "beating," your boat sails along the edge of the in-irons area, approximately 45 degrees off the wind. The sail is set when the boom is closely hauled in over the stern (back) corner of the boat on the lee side. Figure 108, #1 and 2, shows the correct wind-boat angle and sail set when sailing close-hauled.

Learning this point is a simple matter after you have mastered the close-reach positions (Fig. 108, #1 and 2). Except for pointing higher into the wind and setting the sail a bit tighter, sailing close-hauled is just an extension of a close reach. Tiller movement, setting the sail, and holding steady are all done exactly the same way. So when practicing to sail close-hauled, just point up as high as possible from a close reach, trim the sail until the boom is about over the lee corner of the stern, and hold steady.

If the sail starts to luff, the bow is pointed too high and is slipping into irons. Correct by moving the tiller away from the sail a few inches. Don't rush this operation. Give the rudder time to bite and swing the bow downwind (bear off). A common mistake made by most new sailors is to move the tiller further away if the boat does not respond immediately. This action sends the boat into a close-reach position causing excess heeling. When excess heeling does occur, the boat is too far off the wind for the set of the sail. To correct this situation point up a bit by slowly moving the tiller into the sail until the boat returns to a normal heel. This generally occurs when the tiller stops fighting and holds easy.

The importance of being able to point close-hauled will become more and more apparent as your knowledge of sailing increases. In racing, the skipper who can point the highest when tacking on a windward leg is the winner seven times out of ten. Pleasure sailors, on the other hand, quickly learn that a good close-haul point gives them a better command of their boat, making sailing much more fun. And most important the close-hauled points combined with coming about are the key to tacking, which makes reaching a mark directly into the wind possible. So don't be satisfied until you can point up into a close-hauled course quickly and easily. This is best accomplished by sailing's most famous teacher, Captain Practice.

COMING ABOUT

Once you can sail the reach points, close-hauled, and get out of irons, you are ready to start your first turn, "coming about." This maneuver makes it possible to turn a boat, bow up, across the wind without going into irons. As the wind comes in over the opposite side of your boat, lee and weather side are reversed. Figure 109 shows how this new wind-boat angle happens. After coming about, a boat is said to be on a new "tack" (direction). This is how the term "Taking a new tack" originated.

To come about bring your boat upwind in a close-reach or close-hauled position. When the sail is trimmed and the boat moving smartly, push the tiller, hard, toward the sail. This action combined with the boat's forward momentum will swing the bow up, across the wind, through the in-irons area, out the other side onto the opposite close-hauled or close-reach course. Speed is essential during this turn to carry the boat up and through the in-irons area. So make sure your boat has plenty of headway or else it will end up wallowing in irons. Figure 109 shows each phase of a boat coming about, with proper tiller movement.

Looking at Figure 109 you will see that the sail and boom have swung over to the new lee side of the boat. This new sail position is the result of the new wind angle on your boat. Fortunately, in coming about this swinging movement happens slowly giving you plenty of time to avoid the moving boom. The proper way to prepare for this action is as follows. When the boom starts to swing, duck your head, let it pass over you, then pivot your body over to the new weather side. Sitting on the new weather side, facing the sail, readjust the tiller, set the sail to your new course, and hold steady. When sailing a series of close-haul tacks, only tiller adjustment is needed because the same degree of sail angle is used on both sides.

During the time your boat is going through the in-irons area the sail will, of course, be luffing (Fig. 109, #0). Don't let this disturb you. If your speed is sufficient it will start drawing on its new wind angle in a second or two.

When a crew or passengers are aboard they must be warned each time you come about. Otherwise the swinging boom will crack them on the head or knock them overboard. Warnings consist of yelling, "Ready about!" when preparing to come about. This tells those aboard to get ready to duck and pivot. Then, as you push the tiller into the sail, yell, "Hard a lee!" This lets them know you have started to turn and the boom is swinging to the new lee side of the boat.

In your next lesson, "tacking," you will learn that coming about combined with sailing close-hauled lets you sail a boat to a mark directly into the wind. Therefore, it is necessary to practice this turn until you can come about quickly and in shipshape fashion.

If you are using a sloop-designed boat as a trainer, the jib (front sail) must be used to come about properly. The jib is necessary because on a sloop the mast holding the mainsail is stepped too far aft to swing the bow all the way through the in-irons area. How to handle a jib is explained at the end of this chapter.

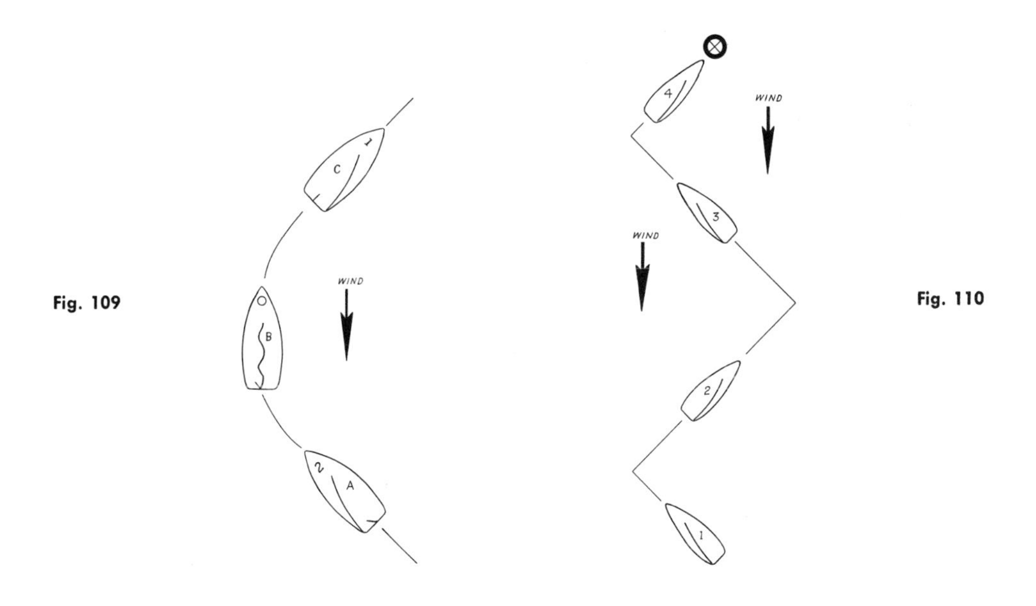

Fig. 109

Fig. 110

TACKING

"Tacking" is the sailing term used to describe the zigzag course a sailboat must take to reach a mark directly into the wind. The key to this zigzag course is a series of coming abouts and sailing close-hauled as shown in Figure 110. Start by picking out a buoy or some other mark off in the distance that lies dead into the wind. Point up your boat onto a close-hauled course and sail as high as possible toward the mark. After holding steady on this course for a few minutes you will find you are getting closer but are sailing off to the side of your target. To get back on course, come about and sail the opposite close-hauled point until you pass the mark and lay off its opposite side. Come about again and assume your original course. Keep tacking in this manner until your boat reaches a course directly in line with the mark. Notice in Figure 110 the boat has lined up and is ready to shoot its mark on the fourth tack.

When practicing tacking, start with long close-haul runs that take you some distance off your mark. Then, after you get the feel of zeroing in on target, shorten the runs and come about more often. This latter method of tacking is helpful when beating out through narrow coves or channels. It is also important in racing, where one leg is always to the windward. Tacking is also called "beating to the windward."

Direction of Tack

Wind direction and boat position determine the direction of a tack. When the starboard (right) side of a boat is on the weather side (closest to the wind), the boat is on a starboard tack. When the port (left) side is on the weather side, she is on a port tack. This is important to understand in passing situations with other sailboats. Notice that in Figure 110 tacks 1, and 3 are starboard tacks, while tacks 2 and 4 are port tacks.

RUNNING FREE

"Running free" or "before the wind" completes the circle of sailing points every canvasman must master before calling himself a helmsman. When running free a boat sails at or almost 180 degrees off the wind. On this course the wind blows in over the stern pushing the boat downwind as shown in Figure 111. Surprisingly this is the only time the wind actually pushes a sailboat. On all other points a sailboat is, in a sense, being pulled by the wind. ("What Makes a Sailboat Go?" on page 131, explains this phenomenon.)

Therefore on a running-free course it is possible to raise the centerboard, lessening the drag resistance, because the boat cannot be pushed sideways causing slippage. While learning, though, keep the centerboard down, as it makes steering easier.

To reach a running-free course, simply bear off as if you were going into a broad-reach course. Move the tiller away from the sail toward the weather side, and let out the sail. Continue on by the broad-reach position until the boat is almost 180 degrees offwind and the sail almost at a right angle to the boat. Set the sail as you would on any other point.

Notice that in Figure 111 boat B in dotted lines is exactly 180 degrees offwind and shows the sail out over both sides. This is possible because at 180 degrees there is no lee side to a boat. Therefore the sail can be set on either side. Although sailing on this point looks easy, it is deceptively dangerous. Any change in wind direction can slam the sail and boom across the boat at

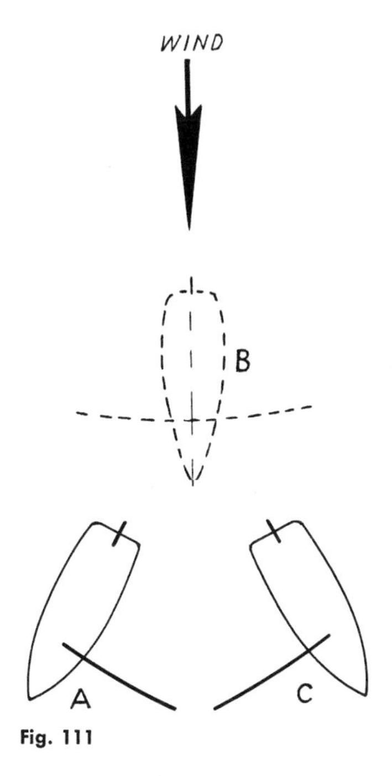

Fig. 111

Fig. 112

great speeds causing an accidental jibe (Jibing and accidental jibes are explained next). Because this danger is always present, it is best to practice running free with the wind blowing in over a stern corner (Fig. 111, boat A and C). This puts your boat about 170 degrees off the wind, still giving you a lee and weather side which will help prevent accidental jibes. Later, when you can jibe (turn across the wind, bow down) and feel an accidental jibe coming, will be time enough to sail at 180 degrees off the wind.

One of the great thrills of sailing to look forward to after developing your sea legs is flying a spinnaker sail while running free. Spinnakers are the large, parachutelike sails that literally pick up boats by their bows and fly them downwind (Fig. 112).

JIBING

"Jibing" is another way of turning across the wind, the most dangerous way. The danger lies in the fact that while jibing the bow is pointed away from the wind and the sail must swing across the boat in an arc of about 180 degrees (Fig. 113). Controlling the speed of the swinging boom is the key to success. A slow even swing is perfect. A fast swing that slams the boom across the cockpit can, and often does, break a mast, capsize the boat, or do physical harm to those aboard.

How a sail and boom can slam across a boat during a jibe is best explained

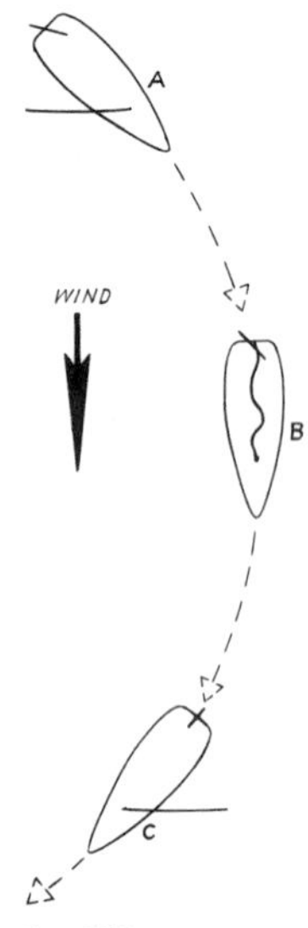

Fig. 113

Fig. 114

by the following example. Picture a flag with a steady boom flapping on a flagpole. As long as the wind moves across the end hitched to the pole, nothing exciting happens. The flag just flutters and flaps. This is what takes place when a boat coming about goes through the in-irons area. Now picture the same flag if the wind should suddenly shift and come in from behind. The unhitched free end of the flag is caught by the wind and violently thrown across the pole onto the opposite side. This is what can happen if you jibe haphazardly. With this in mind, pay special attention to the following instructions as unprofessional as they may seem. In twenty years of teaching I have found them the best way for a beginner to learn to jibe. Even after you learn, practice jibing only in very light winds.

Start by kneeling down facing forward with your head below the level of the boom. Let the tiller rest against your side which is toward the weather side away from the sail (Fig. 114). Now take the mainsheet in both hands and lean against the tiller. When you feel the mainsheet start to pull easy, haul in the sail as fast as you can until it is directly overhead. If the mainsheet pulls hard or the boat starts to heel excessively, lean a bit more on the tiller. Once the sail is overhead, wait for the first tug of the wind in the sail. As soon as you feel the tug, let the mainsheet run out through your hands and pivot your body over to the new weather side of the boat. Reset the tiller, trim the sail, and you have jibed.

When practicing a jibe if the boom starts to lift or swing across the boat faster than you can haul in the mainsheet, drop everything, duck, and relax. And, of course, if a crew or passengers are aboard they must be warned. Before jibing yell, "Stand by to jibe!" Then as you move the tiller toward the weather side yell, "Jibe-Ho!" These commands give those aboard plenty of time to duck below the level of the swinging boom.

A hazard common among new sailors while jibing is a snubbed mainsheet. Make sure your mainsheet is free to run all the way out and will not tangle on a foot or piece of equipment.

Unexpected Jibes

Occasionally when running free, especially at 180 degrees, the wind will shift and come in behind the sail, sending it slamming across the boat. This is called an unexpected jibe and must be constantly watched for. The first warning usually comes when the mainsheet suddenly goes slack and the free end of the boom starts to lift vertically.

Prevently an unexpected jibe is done by quickly moving your tiller into the sail as soon as the mainsheet slacks off. This action turns the boat upwind, sending the sail into a luff. While trying to recover, make sure you duck your head and warn anyone aboard by yelling, "Jibe-Ho!" Even if you do recover it is better to be safe than sorry.

MOORING AND DOCKING

When approaching a mooring buoy or dock always try to land into the wind. The wind acts as a brake and helps to slow down the boat. On a mooring point this is easy because the mooring will be offshore and you can go around it if necessary (Fig. 115). The only precaution necessary is the following. Make sure your boat has come to a complete stop before reaching for the mooring ring. If the boat is still moving when you grab the ring, the chances are you will be pulled off the boat or, even worse, break an arm.

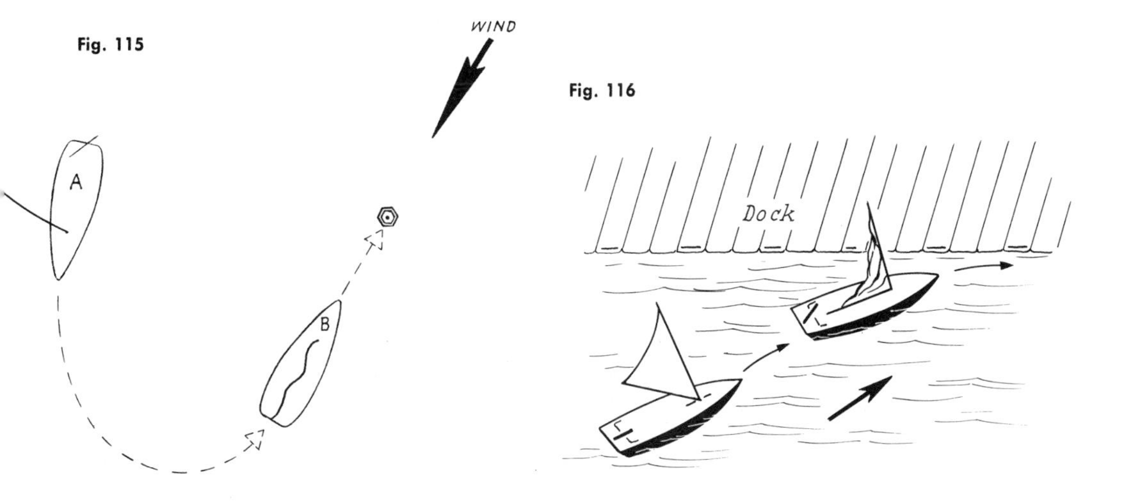

Fig. 115

Fig. 116

Landing at a dock can present an altogether different problem. When the wind cooperates, just point up into irons and slowly glide in as you would on a mooring buoy. Be sure you don't hit any other boats tied up. If, on the other hand, the wind is blowing in a reach or running-free position, your best bet is to lower the sails about two or three boat lengths away from the dock and let the wind push you in (Fig. 116).

The easiest way to learn docking is by practicing out on a mooring area free of other boats. Pick out a mooring buoy and approach it from all wind angles. When you can do this to perfection, then you will be able to "shoot" a dock like an old salt.

SECURING THE BOAT

Before going ashore after tying up you must secure your boat. Lash the sail to the boom if you are planning to use it again the same day. Otherwise, take it off and put it in your sail bag. Tie the boom to the tiller or boom crutch so it cannot swing free. If the rudder is removed and there is no boom crutch, secure it to the traveler or transom. Check to see that all the lines are fastened and bail or sponge out any water in the boat. If you are at a dock, put out bumpers on the side next to the dock to protect the boat's side. Figure 117 shows a sailboat properly secured and tied to a dock.

CAPSIZING AND REFLOATING

Inasmuch as sailboats travel in a heeled-over position most of the time, they are more prone to capsizing than other types of boats. Therefore, in such an emergency, it is necessary to understand the procedure used to insure the

Fig. 117

safety of your boat and crew. This information is fully covered in Chapter 10, "Seamanship in Rough Weather" (page 173) and should be read and understood before you go out in a sailboat. Chapter 11, "Rescue and First Aid" (page 181) should also be read as it tells the proper way to pick up a man overboard and explains emergency first aid treatment for the most common boating injuries.

Refloating a sailboat is done in the following manner. Once you have checked the safety of your crew (all should be wearing life preservers), swim to the mast and slide the sail down it. Lower the jib, if you are using one, down the front stay. Leave the foot of the mainsail attached to the boom and the jibsail clipped to the stay. This prevents the sails from sinking or floating away. After the sails are down, swim to the opposite side of the boat and stand on the centerboard or keel. From this position grab the gunwale or shroud and roll the boat upright. When she is upright, gently climb aboard and lash down the sails and any other equipment nearby. Don't swim after any equipment being carried away by a current or the wind. Swimming back may tire you out. Also, if a current or wind is moving the boat away from shore, drop the anchor if possible. This will stabilize your position and make it easier for rescuers to find you. On some small boats it is not necessary to lower sails when refloating. New self-bailing, self-rescue designs allow recovery within a few minutes after a blow down.

On boats too large to turn upright, have everyone lie across the hull. In boats small enough to turn upright but too large to empty out the water, have the poor swimmers climb aboard and sit on the bottom over the keel. Good swimmers can also go aboard or hold on to the gunwales. On boats small enough to empty, use the same procedure to empty the water out as explained in Chapter on rowboats. Regardless of the boat's size the main thing to remember is *stay with the boat.* A capsized boat can be spotted much more quickly than swimmers. If you have the boat turned upright and cannot remove the water from it, fly a shirt, pants, or bright-colored seat cushion from the mast top. Such objects are recognized distress signals and can be seen from great distances.

USING THE JIB

Flying a jib (front sail) is in a sense like adding another engine to a boat. Aboard sloops this extra working sail increases speed, makes pointing higher into the wind possible, and, when tacking, carries a sloop through the in-irons area quickly and efficiently. The techniques used to handle the jibs are similar to those used for the mainsail with two exceptions: jibs use two jibsheets (lines) rather than one, and often a boom is used only when running free.

To hoist the jib, rig it in the following way. Attach the clips on the luff

Fig. 118

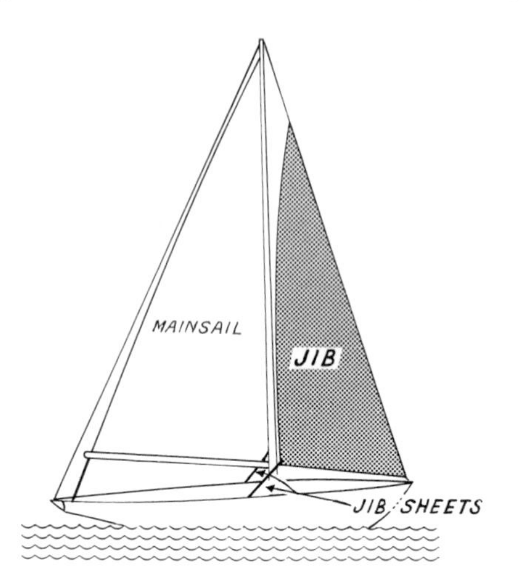

(front) edge to the headstay, the tack (front corner) to the tack ring on the bow, and the head (top) to the jibhalyard. Next take the two jibsheets attached to the clew (back corner) and run them through the fairleads (eyebolts) placed about opposite the mast on the port and starboard sides of the boat. Further aft on the gunwales or centerboard trunk you will find a cleat(s) to secure the "lee jibsheet" when under way. Figure 118 shows all the above-mentioned parts.

Always hoist the jib before raising the mainsail. This procedure insures against an accidental jibe if you are standing or sitting by the mast when hoisting the jib.

Fig. 119

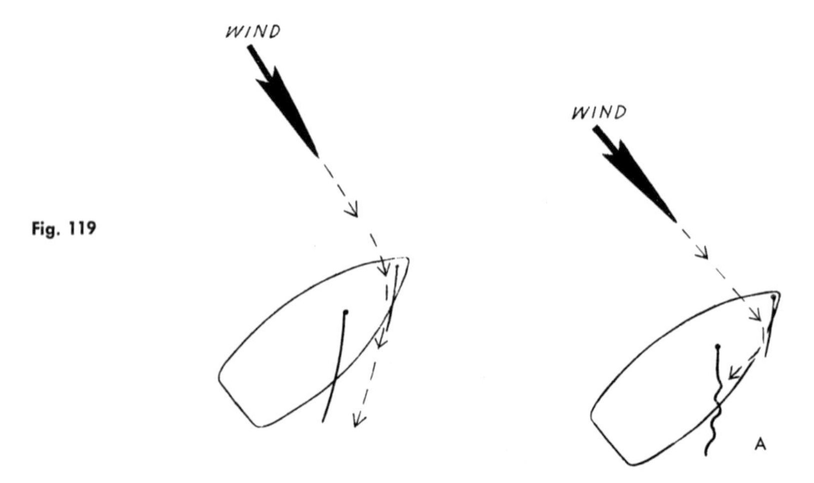

After casting off, set the mainsail in the usual manner, then prepare to set the jib. Take the jibsheet on the lee side of the boat and haul it in until the jibsail just stops luffing. The jib should now be set and will be about parallel to the mainsail (Fig. 119). If the mainsail starts to luff, the jib is trimmed too tight. This is called backwinding (spilled wind onto the mainsail, Fig. 119A) and is corrected by letting out the jib until the luffing stops. On the other hand, if the jib is too slack (let out too far), the tiller will fight you, or the boat will start slipping sideways. This condition is corrected by slowly trimming in the jib until the tiller holds easy and the wake flows out behind the boat in a long straight line. You would probably have met both these problems when learning to use the mainsail, so you know that with a little practice they can easily be overcome. Once both sails are set, properly secure the jibsheet on the jibsheet cleat. Under normal conditions you can forget about it until you change course by making any minor correction with the tiller. Naturally, at first you will find your self unhitching and resetting the jib often. But here again a little practice will quickly enable you to hold a steady course.

Coming About

When coming about unhitch the jibsheet just as the boat is ready to swing up into irons. Then as you move through the in-irons area let the jibsheet run free. Once on your new tack, reset the mainsail, then the jib, by using the second jibsheet, which is now on the new lee side. After trimming, cleat it down and "hold steady" (Fig. 120).

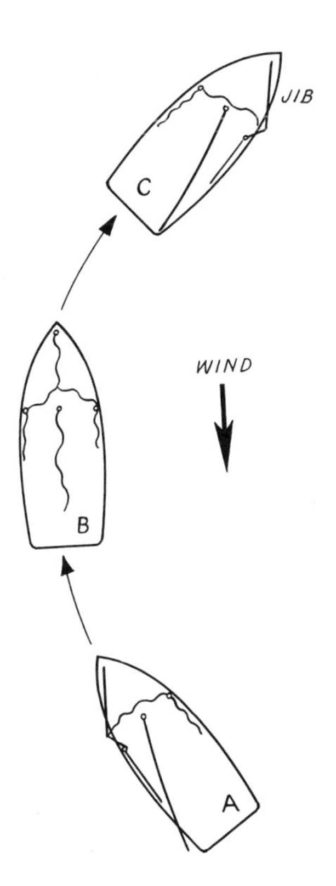

Fig. 120

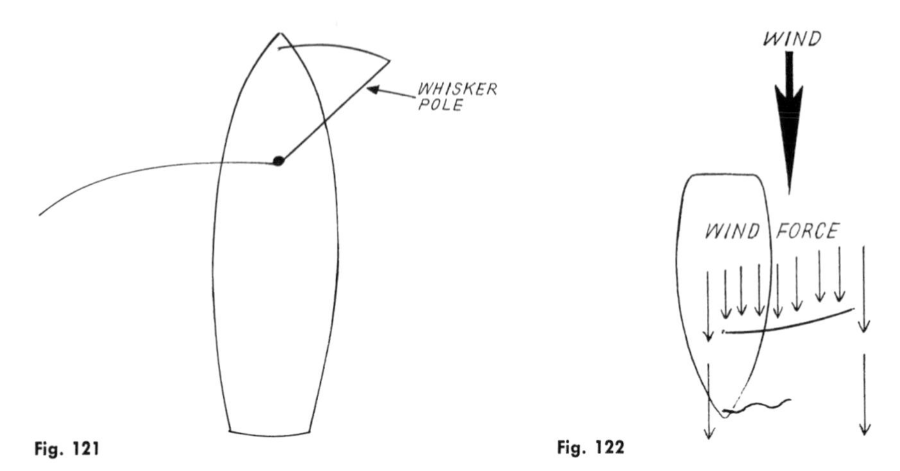

Fig. 121

Fig. 122

Running Free Wing on Wing

On a running-free course the jib is most effective when flown in a "wing-on-wing" position (off the weather side, opposite the mainsail) (Fig. 121). The reason for this odd position becomes clear when you realize the jib would be blanketed (not getting any wind) by the mainsail if flown in the regular way off the lee side (Fig. 122). To get the best results and easiest handling, a whisker pole (small boom) should be used as a temporary jib boom. The whisker pole attaches to the mast and runs out to the clew (back corner). This added stiffness makes setting and trimming the jib while running free much simpler.

Crew

Inasmuch as sloops are designed to carry more than one person, the jib is usually handled by a crewman (Fig. 123). This extra hand speeds up jib control when resetting the jib and tacking. In racing this is especially important,

Fig. 123

as seconds are often the difference between victory or defeat. So if you plan to do any racing, train your own jibman until you and he work as a well-oiled unit.

WHAT MAKES A SAILBOAT GO?

No treatise on sailing is complete without answering the question, "What makes a sailboat go?" The wind, of course, is the answer. But how it performs this act often baffles the neophyte skipper. Actually the wind both pushes and pulls a sailboat forward. The amount of push or pull depends on the wind-sail angle of the boat. Consider for a moment the wind-sail angle when beating on a close-hauled course (Fig. 108). In this position it is impossible for the wind to push the boat forward. At best only a sideways movement can be accomplished, and this is prevented by the centerboard or keel. So the boat has to be pulled forward. This is done in the following way. As the wind passes across the sail it forms a vacuum pocket on the front side causing a suction which literally pulls the sail into the void (Fig. 124). As the wind-sail angle increases, the vacuum pocket becomes smaller and the push factor greater, until, when running free, the vacuum disappears and the boat moves forward solely by the push of the wind.

Looking at Figure 125, you will see the push-pull ratio at each sailing point. Notice on a beam reach both factors are about equal. This is why a sailboat moves fastest on a beam reach. Figure 125 also shows why proper sail set and trim are so important. Unless the right sail curve is present, the vacuum pocket loses most of its effectiveness, causing the boat to become sluggish.

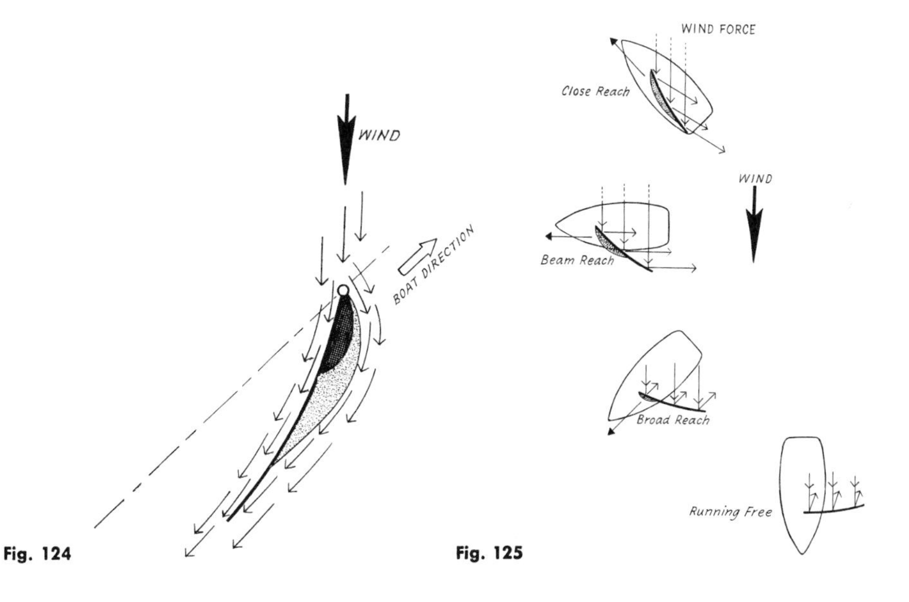

Fig. 124

Fig. 125

SAILING TIPS

Here are a few sailing tips to help you on the road to becoming a first-rate sailor. Watch and listen to learn many more from friends and acquaintances who are advanced sailors.

1. Only sail in water that is two or more feet deeper than your centerboard at low tide.
2. Keep the bilge (bottom of the boat) empty of water. Water rolling around the bilge makes a boat sluggish and hard to steer.
3. Dry out your sails after each day afloat. Damp cotton sails will mildew; nylon or Dacron sails get shabby looking. Never put sails over a clothesline or use clothespins to hang sails; unless hung properly sails will sag like a wet sweater. The easiest method is to spread them out on the ground or other flat surface.
5. Always be prepared for an emergency. The surest way to do this is to carry all necessary equipment and make sure each piece is in working order.
6. If the mast should break, reef your sail (lower the sail below the break and tie the excess sail to the boom).
7. If the boom breaks, use the boat hook or an oar and lash it to the boom as a splint.

SAIL HO

Now that you understand the basic fundamentals of sailing, a whole new world of fun and excitement awaits you. Whether you stay in a cat boat or move up to sloops, yawls, ketches, or schooners matters little. The fundamentals you are now learning are the same for all sailing craft. As you master each one through practice, the finer points that make expert sailors look like magicians of wind and sail will suddenly become easy. And one day soon, you will find yourself master of the wind and free as a soaring bird.

9

Power Boating

Powerboating is unquestionably the most popular method of boating in America today. The reasons can be attributed to engineering advances, wide versatility in hull design encouraged by modern engines, and ease of handling. Engineering was the key, starting with the development of an efficient compact gasoline engine. Later the introduction and perfection of the outboard "motor" put boating within reach of millions of wet-footed landlubbers. And once afloat, because of the similarity with the automobile, most Americans found they could quickly master the skills of powerboat handling. Add to these the excitement of racing over the water under full power, getting under way for a long planned family cruise, or tying into a "lunker" while trolling across a fishing hotspot, and it is easy to see why powerboating rates as Number 1.

To master the skills of powerboat handling you must also have a working knowledge of engine power and if necessary be able to make minor emergency engine repairs. To accomplish this end this chapter is divided into two sections, "Power Plants" and "Powerboat Handling." Study each section before going afloat to insure a safe boat and a competent skipper.

POWER PLANTS

Once you decide on a powerboat the next decision is, what type of power plant to use? This is best answered by the size, design, and weight boat it must power plus the kind of boating you plan to do. If the boat comes equipped with a factory-matched engine, there is rarely a problem, as all reliable boat and engine manufacturers go to great lengths to insure top performance and customer satisfaction. In such cases only specialized accessories may be needed. When a power plant must be purchased separately, however, experienced boatmen and controlled tests have come up with the following recommendations.

Inboards

In large craft, twenty-four feet and over, inboard engines give the best performance and operating economy (Fig. 126). These power plants are fastened to an engine bed inside the hull about amidship. The engine is mounted at a slight angle so the drive shaft can extend down through the bottom and turn the propeller (Fig. 127).

The size (horsepower) engine needed will depend on the size, weight, and design of the boat. Normally this information is supplied by the builder or designer. If it is not, do not buy until you see it in writing. The kind of boating you plan to do is also a factor. Weekend cruising, long day trips, or fishing excursions call for a low fuel burning engine that is economical to run. Fast speeds, necessary to racing or pulling water skiers, call for high-speed power plants, notorious as fuel burners. If, however, you are like most boat owners and want to do a bit of everything, look for a compromise engine. One that is fairly economical to operate on cruises yet fast enough to lift one or two skiers. Here again advice from an expert and a shakedown cruise (see Chapter 1, "Your First Command," page 1) are the surest way to match a power plant to your craft.

Outboards

Smaller boats, eighteen feet and under, perform best with outboard "motors." These compact engines, up to 100 horsepower, are self-contained power units that clamp to a boat's transom (back) (Fig. 128). This frees the area normally taken by an inboard, giving more cockpit space. Trailering is also simplified, as the lower units can be swung up out of the way, leaving an unobstructed "clean" bottom (Fig. 236, Chapter 14, "Trailers and Trailering," page 246).

Fig. 126

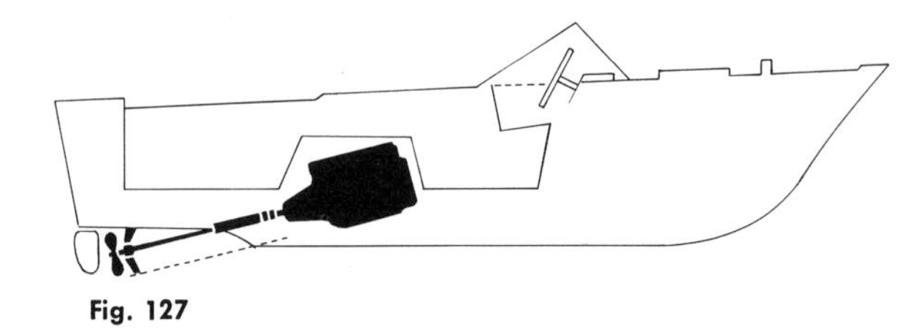

Fig. 127

Fig. 128

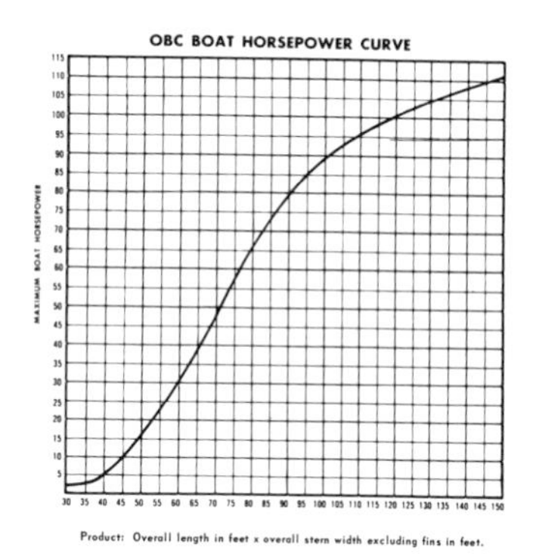

Fig. 129

The size motor (horsepower) needed, like that for inboards, is determined by the size, weight, and design of the boat it must power. Outboard boat owners will find a wealth of expert information on this subject, the best of which is the Outboard Club of America's "O.B.C." plates attached to the inside transom of all reputable manufacturers' boats (Fig. 1, Chapter 1, "Your First Command," page 2). These plates, which give recommended maximum horsepower and load capacities, have become the accepted guidelines used by most marine dealers in matching a boat to an engine. Another excellent guide, also developed by the O.B.C., is their maximum horsepower chart (Fig. 129). To relate the correct maximum horsepower to boat size, multiply boat length by stern width, then match the answer to the figure at the bottom of the graph. Next, follow the perpendicular line above the answer until it bisects the horsepower curve. The figure to the left in line with the curve and perpendicular line is the maximum horsepower your boat will safely accommodate. Example: A boat 14 feet long × 5 feet wide at the stern equals 70. The line above 70 bisects the horsepower curve at a reading of 50 to the left. Fifty horsepower is the maximum size engine recommended for this boat. Where the curve falls between two maximum horsepower numerals use the highest figure.

A more general reference, which follows, gives engine size and weight, with the recommended types and model craft.

Under 5 H.P., 17–36 lb. General use: Small light boats fourteen feet or less (prams, sailboats, canoes, etc.) Operation: Manual starting and controls, integral fuel tank.
5 H.P. to 9.5 H.P., 37–60 lb. General use: Light boats sixteen feet or less (rowboats, small utilities, large square-sterned canoes, sailboats). Operation: Manual starting and controls (accessories for remote control available); forward, neutral, reverse gearshift; separate fuel tank.
10 H.P. to 20 H.P., 65–77 lb. General use: Utilities and small runabouts (larger models will lift one water skier if boat's gross weight is held to a minimum). Operation: Manual starting and controls (electric starter optional on some larger models; accessories for remote controls available); forward, neutral, reverse gearshift; separate fuel tank.

25 H.P. to 45 H.P., 100–165 lb. General use: Medium-sized utilities and runabouts (larger models will lift two water skiers under ideal conditions). Operation: Manual and electric starting; manual and remote controls; generator-alternator standard or optional on most models; separate fuel tank.
50 H.P. to 100 H.P., 142–270 lb. General use: Large utilities and runabouts, ski boats, hydroplanes (racing), outboard cruisers, houseboats. Operation: Electric starting and remote controls standard equipment; generator-alternator standard or optional on all models; separate fuel tanks. Special convenience and racing accessories are available with many of these large engines.

Outboard "motors" are generally classified in two groups: portable and nonportable. The portables, up to 20 H.P. (77 lb.) can be transported and handled quite easily to and from boating areas. Larger models, because of weight and size, are usually left on the transom all season. This should be considered if you do not own your own boat or must remove the motor after each use.

In-Outboards

A third type of engine which has won wide favor in boats eighteen to twenty-four feet is the in-outboard engine. This power plant is a hybrid of both the inboard and outboard. An inboard engine is fastened at the stern with an outboard lower unit attached to it through the transom (Fig. 130). The inboard allows higher horsepower, surer performance, and usually more economical operation, while the outboard lower unit gives excellent maneuverability and unmatched versatility because of the tilting drive. Before this development, boats in the eighteen- to twenty-four-foot range were orphans, too big for outboards, yet too small for inboards. Today, however, it's not uncommon to find a twenty-two-foot craft with the cockpit space of a twenty-six-footer that trailers with the ease of a sixteen-footer.

When selecting the size engine (horsepower) needed, follow the same pro-

Fig. 130

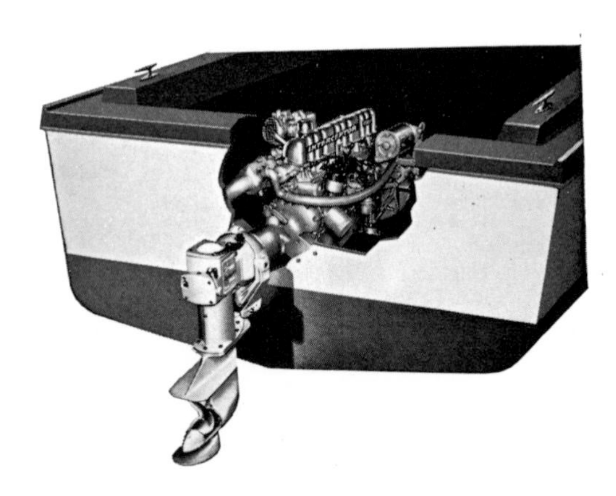

cedure recommended for matching an inboard engine.

All of the aforementioned power plants are gasoline fired two- or four-cycle internal combustion engines and should not be confused with diesels, electric, or gas turbine engines. These latter types, compose less than 10 per cent of the power plants used in today's small craft, therefore are rarely a factor when selecting an engine. If, by chance, one could become your boat's power plant, use the same guidelines as for gasoline engines and have a qualified person on hand for guidance.

Power Safe Zone

Regardless of the type of engine you use, it must fall within a safe power zone, strong enough to meet sea conditions, yet small enough not to endanger boat or crew by being overpowered. For example, A twenty-eight-foot cabin cruiser powered by a 115 H.P. engine might perform excellently with a four-man crew in a calm to moderate sea, yet be dangerously underpowered with six aboard in a light blow. The so-called underpriced, stripped-down bargain specials used as advertising bait often fall into this category. At the other end of the wharf watch out for the overzealous salesman who believes every sports runabout should be powered for Gold Cup competition. Never exceed the recommended horsepower for your boat. Too much engine can cause a craft to flip on turns, race out of control, swamp by porpoising or stern submersion, and will always cost more to operate.

Single or Twin Installation

With large boats you often have a horsepower option of using two small engines in place of one large engine. The pros and cons of such installations have always been a subject of debate. Two-engine advocates claim the additional engine gives an extra margin of breakdown safety, especially when offshore, more speed, and better maneuverability around docks and crowded waterways. Those opposed contend two engines only increase costs as two of everything are needed and must be maintained. They claim that today's marine engines rarely break down if properly maintained, and a single installation is only a fraction slower than a twin while being much cheaper to operate. My own feelings side with the single-engine advocates, except on large cruising craft where cost would not be a factor.

Engine Break-In

New marine power plants, like all engines, need a break-in period to allow the various parts to "seat" and wear off initial stiffness. Operating procedure, running time, and lubrication during this period are thoroughly explained in every manufacturer's engine manual. Be sure to read this important information. Otherwise you may end up with a "weak" engine or the need for an engine overhaul. Major things to guard against are overheating (running too fast), moving under power while the engine is still cold, and using a type of oil not recommended by the manufacturer. Other don'ts include prolonged idling, steady speeds (slow or fast) for long periods, and fast full-throttle acceleration.

After operating under break-in conditions for the recommended hours, have the engine gone over, similar to an automobile 3,000-mile check. This catches any loose or lost wires, nuts, bolts, screws, etc., and is an excellent time for an engine tune up.

Tune Up

To insure top performance and economical operation, your power plant should be kept at peak efficiency. This is done by tuning up whenever the need arises, usually during fitting-out time and following a period of steady use or disuse. The term "tune up" means a systematic inspection, with repairs, replacements, and adjustments as needed, of all an engine's operating elements. These would include electrical system, spark plugs, fuel system, carburetor, compression, and cooling system. Only a trained mechanic should tune an engine, as most of the adjustments and settings are critical. If you qualify as such, study the service manual available from the manufacturer to learn the recommended procedures. Most manufacturers suggest a tune up be made in the following order: Electrical system (battery, generator or magneto, wiring, coil, distributor parts, etc.); cylinder compression; spark plugs; fuel system (tank, lines, pump, etc.); cooling system; and any special accessories.

After a tune up, follow the recommended care and maintenance procedures as outlined in your owner's manual.

Preventive Maintenance

Just a few minutes of engine care before, during, and after each day afloat will give you many extra hours of top engine performance. Before getting under way observe the following practices: 1. Check for strong gasoline fumes (a sign of poor ventilation or leaks. Don't start the engine until the fumes are gone). 2. Check the oil and gasoline level. 3. Check for cracks, loose fittings, and leaks. 4. Warm up the engine, per starting instructions. 5. Recheck gasoline and oil lines for leaks. 6. Listen to general engine sounds. 7. Check out all auxiliary engine equipment.

While under way use the throttle sensibly. Constant running at top speeds wears out an engine much faster than operating at recommended cruising speeds. Slow down engine speed when shifting to reverse. And before turning off the engine, let it idle a while to cool down.

After a day afloat make it a habit to wipe the engine clean of any accumulated dirt, grease, or oil. While cleaning, look for loose fittings, cracks, or leaks that might have developed during the day.

If you find any trouble, fix it or have it fixed immediately. Minor troubles tend to become major breakdowns when ignored.

Troubleshooting

Engine trouble at dockside is at worst an inconvenience that could cancel a day or two of boating. Trouble offshore, however, can be a serious threat to the safety of your boat and crew. Learning to cope with such situations should be a part of every powerboat skipper's seamanship training. To accomplish this, an understanding of the theory and basic operating principles of your boat's engine, found in the service and owner's manual, is necessary.

Once you understand the how's and why's of your engine, it is a fairly simple matter to troubleshoot a breakdown. The easiest method is by the process of elimination. Start with the symptom (engine won't start, overheats, misfires, etc.), then systematically eliminate each probable cause until the trouble is corrected. This formula has proven so effective over the years that all manufacturers include a troubleshooting section in their manuals.

Following is a general troubleshooting guide for use with marine gasoline engines.

Inboard Engines

Symptom: Engine Won't Start (starter turns over)

Fuel: 1, out of gas; 2, fuel line valve shut off; 3, fuel line kinked, split, or broken; 4, fuel filter clogged; 5, water or other foreign matter in gas tank; 6, carburetor choke stuck closed; 7, carburetor defective; 8, fuel pump defective.

Ignition, ammeter reads zero while starter turning: 1, disconnected or broken ammeter wire; 2, wires to distributor disconnected or broken; 3, distributor points stuck open; 4, defective ignition switch.

Ignition, ammeter discharges while starter turning: 1, distributor points

Fig. 131

stuck closed; 2, bare wire in distributor shorting out.

Ignition, ammeter oscillates while starter turning: check the spark to each spark plug by holding the connecting distributor wire about one-fourth inch away from the spark plug terminal (Fig. 131). To avoid a shock be sure to hold the wire at a dry insulated section.

If sparks to each plug are strong, check for: 1, wet or oil-soaked wires; 2, loose or disconnected spark plug wires; 3, broken or cracked distributor cap; 4, broken or defective distributor rotor.

If sparks to each plug are weak or there is no spark, check for: 1, spark from coil wire to distributor cap; 2, defective coil; 3, defective condenser.

Symptom: Engine Won't Start (starter turns over slowly)

Check for: 1, battery charge low; 2, battery cables need tightening; 3, battery cables worn; 4, defective starter; 5, engine oil too heavy (cold weather).

Symptom: Engine Won't Start (starter doesn't turn over)

Check for: 1, battery dead or needs charging; 2, battery cables broken, disconnected, worn, or loose; 3, ignition or starter wires disconnected or defective; 4, ignition switch or starter button defective.

Symptom: Engine Sputters or Coughs then Stops

Check for: 1, out of gasoline; 2, no oil (overheating); 3, loose or broken wires; 4, clogged fuel line; 5, clogged oil line; 6, water or antifreeze low (overheating); 7, water or impurities in fuel; 8, defective fuel pump; 9, fouled propeller.

Symptom: Engine Stops Dead

Check for: 1, same causes as when engine sputters or coughs then stops; 2, broken or defective distributor or coil; 3, a locked gear (transmission).

Symptom: Low or No Oil Pressure

Check for: 1, low oil level in crank case; 2, broken or leaking oil line; 3, disconnected or loose wire to oil pressure gauge; 4, defective oil gauge; 5, defective oil pump. Once you notice lack of oil pressure, stop the engine at once. Failure to do so will cause overheating and eventual engine burn-up.

Symptom: Engine Overheating

Check for: 1, low oil level in crankcase (lack of lubrication); 2, low or no water or antifreeze in cooling system; 3, cooling system clogged; 4, engine room not properly ventilated; 5, defective water pump; 6, engine overworking from one of the following reasons: (a) oil too heavy in cold weather, (b) transmission lacking grease or oil, (c) grease or oil too heavy for cold weather use, (d) drive shaft binding, (e) propeller fouled.

Symptom: Engine Backfires

Check for: 1, low on fuel; 2, crossed spark plug wires; 3, water or impurities in gasoline; 4, blown head gasket; 5, late ignition timing; 6, a stuck valve or broken valve spring.

Symptom: Engine Misfires Regularly

Check for: 1, loose, broken, or crossed spark plug wires; 2, broken or cracked distributor cap; 3, fouled spark plugs; 4, blown cylinder head gasket; 5, broken valve spring; 6, a sticking or burned valve; 7, burned distributor points; 8, improperly gapped distributor points.

Symptom: Engine Misfires Irregularly

Check for: 1, flooding carburetor; 2, too rich a fuel mixture going into carburetor; 3, air leaks in fuel line; 4, water mixed with gasoline; 5, loose or cracked wires; 6, defective fuel pump; 7, broken contact brush in distributor cap; 8, burned distributor points; 9, improperly gapped distributor points.

Symptom: Engine Knocks

Check for: 1, engine overheated; 2, spark plugs gapped wrong; 3, wrong type spark plugs; 4, advanced ignition timing; 5, loose bearings; 6, loose flywheel; 7, loose propeller; 8, gasoline octane rating too low.

Symptoms: Engine Vibrates

Check for: 1, bent or nicked propeller; 2, bent drive shaft; 3, loose engine mount bolts; 4, loose propeller.

Outboard Motors

Symptom: Motor Won't Start

Check for:

Fuel: 1, out of gasoline; 2, fuel shut-off valve closed; 3, fuel line hose pinched, loose, or connected wrong; 4, loose or broken fuel line; 5, choke not closed (cold motor); 6, motor flooded (warm motor); 7, water or impurities in fuel tank; 8, fuel filter plugged; 9, too much oil in fuel mixture; 10, carburetor needle valves improperly adjusted; 11, carburetor linkage improperly adjusted.

Ignition: 1, spark plug wire disconnected, loose, or broken; 2, spark plug wire shorting out on motor housing; 3, fouled spark plug; 4, spark plug porcelain (insulators) cracked or broken; 5, no spark from magneto to plugs; 6, magneto breaker points dirty or need setting.

Symptom: Motor Won't Idle

Check for:

Fuel: 1, carburetor needle valves out of adjustment; 2, dirty fuel filter; 3, water or impurities in fuel tank; 4, stale fuel (old); 5, improper oil to gas fuel mixture.

Ignition: 1, fouled spark plugs; 2, spark plug porcelain (insulators) cracked or broken; 3, wrong type spark plug; 4, spark plug wires loose; 5, insulating covering on spark plug wires cracked or oil soaked; 6, weak spark; 7, magneto breaker points not set properly.

Other: 1, blown intake valve gasket; 2, motor set too deep in water.

Symptom: Motor Loses Power

Check for: 1, carburetor needs adjustment (either too rich or too lean); 2, improper oil to gas fuel mixture; 3, spark plugs fouled; 4, wrong type spark plugs; 5, water or impurities in fuel tank; 6, fuel line clogged; 7, dirty fuel filter; 8, cooling system clogged; 9, poor compression.

Symptom: Motor Runs but Boat Makes Little or No Progress

Check for: 1, weeds fouling propeller; 2, bent or broken propeller; 3, motor not deep enough in water (cavitation); 4, broken shear pin or drive pin.

Symptom: Propeller Doesn't Turn

Check for: 1, broken shear pin or drive pin; 2, worn slip clutch; 3, loose propeller nut; 4, broken propeller, propeller shaft, or drive shaft.

Symptom: Motor Overheats

Check for: 1, clogged cooling system; 2, defective water pump; 3, motor not deep enough in water to cover water intake opening; 4, lack of lubrication, not enough oil in fuel mixture; 5, lower unit running dry, needs oil; 6, blown exhaust gasket.

Symptom: Motor Freezes Up

Check for: 1, lower unit running dry, needs oil; 2, fouled propeller or propeller shaft or drive shaft; 3, not enough oil in fuel mixture; 4, rust on cylinder walls (not lubricated when stored).

Symptom: Motor Knocks

Check for: 1, propeller loose; 2, flywheel nuts loose; 3, spark advanced too far; 4, preignition due to overheating; 5, worn or loose bearings, piston pin, rings, or connecting rod.

Symptoms: Motor Vibrates Excessively

Check for: 1, transom clamps loose; 2, swivel bracket loose; 3, propeller fouled; 4, propeller bent or badly nicked; 5, carburetor needs adjustment.

Starting Submerged Outboard Motors

When an outboard motor falls over the side or is dunked on a capsized boat get it out of the water and cared for as soon as possible. Most motor manufacturers agree that three hours after recovery is the maximum waiting period before service must be started. After this length of time rust will almost certainly make a major overhaul necessary.

In instances where the motor is recovered quickly the following procedures will often get it running without the need of a major overhaul: 1. Remove motor cover. 2. Remove spark plugs. When disconnecting spark plug leads make sure to detach rubber spark plug lead covers and ground lead terminals by attaching them to motor block. This grounds the motor when you pull the starter handle. 3. Work out as much water as possible by pulling manual starter handle several times. Tilt up the motor so the water will drain out of the spark plug openings. When the water is out pour a small amount of oil through spark plug holes into each cylinder and pull manual starter handle several times to distribute the oil. If when pulling the manual starter you feel the motor bind, stop. It indicates a bent connecting rod and under no circumstances should any one try to start the motor. Get it to a repair station as soon as possible. 4. Remove cover from magneto. Do not disturb timing belt. 5. Blow air through the inspection hole to remove water from the magneto. Wipe magneto dry with a clean cloth, being sure no water remains between contact points. 6. Remove distributor cap and rotor, blow out all traces of water, and wipe dry with a clean cloth. 7. Drain carburetor bowl. 8. Reassemble all parts removed and follow starting instructions. 9. If motor will not start, remove spark plugs to check for water between electrodes. Remove any water from electrodes and reinstall plugs or replace with new ones.

When a motor is submerged in salt water follow the same procedure as above. The only difference is that you should still have it serviced as soon as possible since salt water will cause excessive corrosion on electrical and other parts.

In-outboard Engine

Troubleshooting an in-outboard engine is done basically the same way you troubleshoot an inboard engine and the lower unit of an outboard motor.

Tool Kit and Spare Parts

Most engine trouble can be repaired on the spot if the necessary parts and tools are on board.* The problem is knowing what parts and tools to carry.

* All tools and parts should be stored in a moisture-proof toolbox to protect against rust and corrosion. Before returning tools to the box, wipe them with an oily rag.

This is best solved by assembling a basic repair kit plus any special tools or equipment necessary for your particular power plant. A basic kit that might be carried by small cruising craft would consist of:

Inboard Engine: *Tools:* 1. A set of open-closed end wrenches; 2, spark plug socket wrench; 3, various-size screwdrivers plus a Phillips type if needed; 4, pliers (two regular, different sizes, and a longnose); 5, hammer; 6, jackknife; 7, six-inch file; 8, ignition kit; 9, drift pin; 10, tape (friction and electrical); 11, small roll of soft wire; 12, service manual. *Spare Parts:* 1, a set of spark plugs; 2, fuel pump or fuel pump kit; 3, distributor kit (points, motor, cap, condensor); 4, coil; 5, insulated wire; 6, water pump impeller; 7, V-belt (if necessary); 8, waterhose and clamps; 9, assorted nuts, bolts, and screws; 10, oil and lubricating grease (grease gun if necessary); 11, spare propeller; 12, small can of gum and grease dissolving cleaner.

Outboard Motor: Tools: 1, set of open-closed end wrenches; 2, spark plug socket wrench; 3, various-size screwdrivers including a Phillips if needed; 4, pliers, regular and longnose; 5, hammer; 6, jackknife; 7, small file; 8, drift pin; 9, tape (friction and electrical); 10, small roll of soft wire; 11, service manual. *Spare Parts:* 1, set of spark plugs; 2, fuel pump or fuel pump kit; 3, shear or drive pins; 4, spare propeller; 5, insulated wire; 6, magneto breaker points, condensor, and coil; 7, assorted nuts, bolts, and screws; 8, oil and lubricating grease; 9, a small can of gum and grease dissolving cleaner.

In-outboard: Use the same tools and spare parts recommended for inboard engines plus any special tools or parts for the outboard lower unit.

Factors to consider when assembling a repair kit are the size of your craft, and the type boating you will do. For example, a runabout on a small lake would not have the space nor need to carry an extensive repair kit, whereas a large offshore cruiser would be considered unsafe without one. Some engine manufacturers supply tool kits with their engines or as an extra. Spare parts are available from the engine dealer.

Propeller Selection

Chances are when you bought your boat or outboard engine (new) it came equipped with a factory-installed propeller. Under normal use these propellers do an excellent job and should not be replaced. If, however, you intend to use your boat for a special purpose (racing, long slow cruising, etc.), make a below-water hull change, or change the engine gear ratio (inboards), replacement may be necessary. In such cases you need expert advice to assure getting a prop that will "match" the need. If your local yard or marine dealer cannot advise you, write directly to the engine or propeller manufacturer. In your letter include the following information: 1, engine horsepower; 2, reduction ratio (if any); 3, recommended maximum engine r.p.m.'s; 4, size and type of your hull; 5, gross weight of your boat; 6, largest-size (diameter) propeller your boat will take; 7, new use, hull change, gear ratio, etc., you plan to make.

Under no circumstances install a different size or style of propeller until it has been recommended by a competent person or source. To do so can seriously harm the engine or decrease a boat's operating and safety efficiency.

Propeller Maintenance

Propellers, like engines, should be inspected and, if need be, repaired at regular intervals, usually after so many hours of operation and whenever they strike a floating or submerged object. With inboards this inspection must be conducted when the boat is out of water or, in an emergency, with scuba (self-contained underwater breathing apparatus) equipment. Outboards and in-boards, however, with their tilting lower unit, can be checked anytime. Inspection should include: 1, a close examination of the propeller for cracks, dents, bends, and corrosion; 2, the drive shaft (inboards) for looseness, bends, and corrosion; 3, the stuffing box (inboards), where the drive shaft extrudes through the hull, for leaks; 4, the rudder(s) for looseness, cracks, bends, corrosion, and missing nuts or bolts; 5, the lower unit of outboards and in-out-boards for cracks, breaks, corrosion, missing fittings, and lack of lubrication.

When making the inspection, write down any needed repairs and have them made as soon as possible. With serious disorders don't run the engine until the repairs are made. Failure to observe this rule could ruin the engine and transmission. Inspection periods are also an excellent time to clean, paint (anti-fouling), and lubricate parts as needed.

When outboards or in-outboards are kept in the water all season, make a habit of tilting the lower unit up out of the water when not in use. This prevents marine growths (grass, weeds, barnacles, etc.) from fouling the propeller and other underwater parts.

Cavitation

To drive a boat forward or backward the propeller must bore into a smooth even flow of water. Any interference with this flow will create a partial vacuum around the propeller causing it to lose the thrust developed by the blades. When this occurs it is called cavitation and can, if not corrected immediately, ruin the propeller and/or overheat the engine. Cavitation on inboard or outboard boats is quickly recognized by a churning wake at the transom with little or no thrust, a loud sucking noise at the propeller, or excessive vibration.

The causes of cavitation fall into two categories: temporary and chronic. The temporary occurs whenever a propeller is momentarily lifted or partially lifted from the water. This is usually caused by: 1, improper trim (bow heavy); 2, running too fast in rising seas; the stern is lifted out of the water by wave action plus speed; 3, making tight turns at high speeds; the boat heels (leans) too far over, raising the propeller to the surface. These temporary causes can be remedied by practicing safe seamanship and boathandling habits. Chronic cavitation, however, develops from poor design, crude below-water hull repairs, or a propeller flaw, each of which can be corrected only by a design change, repairs, or replacements. The most common chronic flaws are: 1, hull obstructions ahead of the propeller caused by repair work, too wide a keel, or poorly designed fins; 2, the wrong type, size, or pitched propeller; 3, a bent, nicked, or broken propeller or outboard lower unit. Outboard propellers also cavitate when the motor is not properly "set" on the transom (Fig. 140B, page 151) when not deep enough in the water (drive shaft too short), or occasionally from a slight weight shift (trim). In the latter case (trim), the installation of a cavitation plate just above the propeller will usually cure the problem. Where chronic cavitation exists, let a qualified person check it out and make the necessary modifications or repairs.

Fig. 132

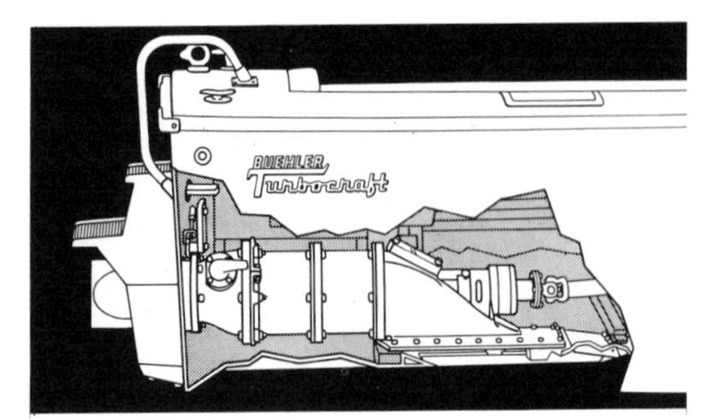

Fig. 133

Other Propulsion Systems

On shallow, weed-infested or rocky waterways a propeller is often incapable of doing the job intended. For such waters, specialized propulsion units have been developed. The two most popular are air drives and water jets. Air drives use a pusher-type airplane propeller mounted above the stern of a very shallow-draft boat (Fig. 132). This leaves the hull bottom "clean," allowing it literally to skim over water and weeds. Air drive boats are used extensively in the Florida Everglades. Water jets use water pressure from a high-velocity pump, usually a three-stage axial-flow pump, to propel the boat (Fig. 133). First used on rocky waterways and to run up rapid infested rivers, water jets are now used on all waterways. Their main advantages are safety around swimmers, nets, etc., because there is no spinning propeller, and their ability to operate in shallow, obstructed areas.

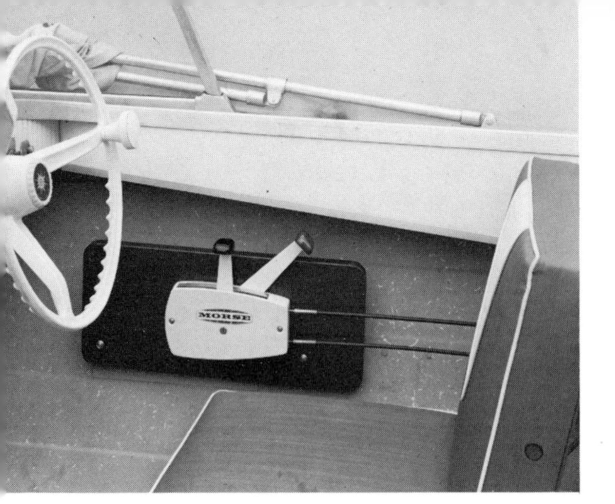

Fig. 134

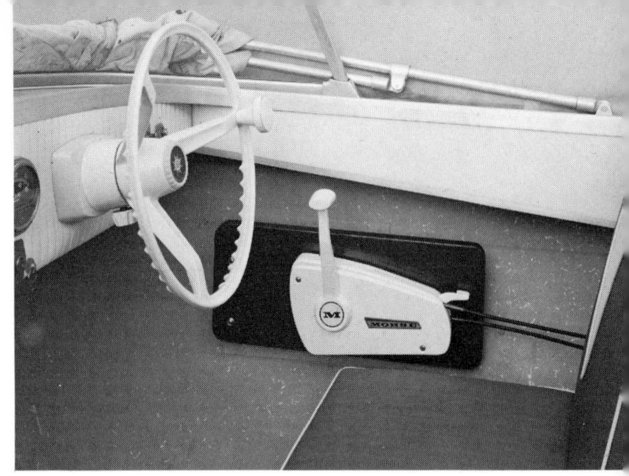

Fig. 135

Operating Controls

The control system that operates the throttle (speed) and gearshift (forward, neutral, reverse) should be considered a part of the overall engine complex. On today's small craft either a two-lever or single-lever control is used in all installations, except for small tiller-controlled outboards. The two-lever system (Fig. 134) uses one lever for throttle control and the other for shifting. The new single lever system (Fig. 135) incorporates both throttle and gearshift into one operation. The standard hook-up between the lever(s) and engine is a push-pull cable enclosed in a self-lubricating jacket.

When buying a boat, if you have a choice of controls the single lever is considered the easiest to operate. To shift into forward gear and forward drive you simply push the control lever forward. To shift into reverse gear and reverse drive simply pull the control lever backward (Fig. 135A). Neutral is in the center, between forward and reverse.

Two-lever controls are still favored by many skippers who predate the single-lever system and by many boat rental agencies. The latter feel that separately marked controls stand up better and are safer for the average novice who rents their boats. This might be a consideration if your boat will be operated by many others.

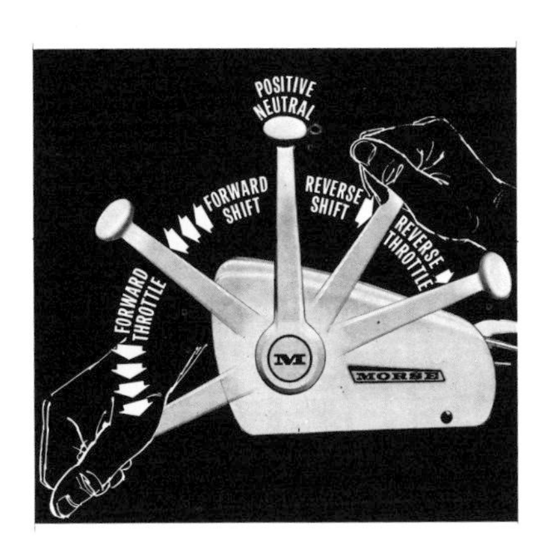

Fig. 135A

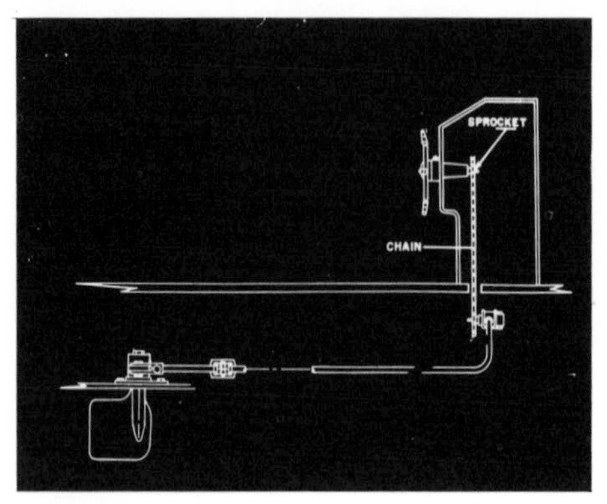

Fig. 136

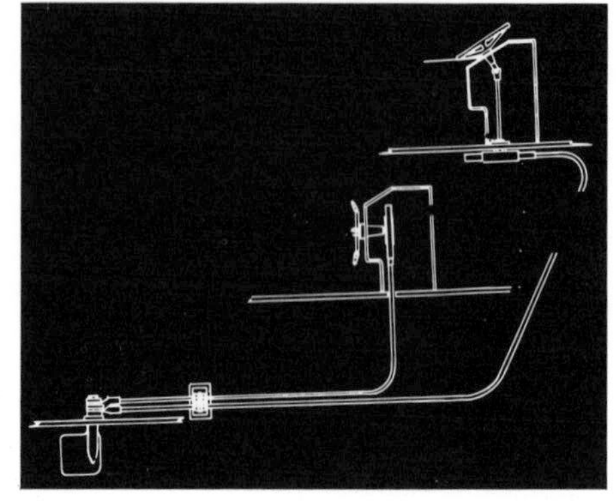

Fig. 137

Steering Controls

Although a boat's steering system is not considered a part of the power plant it is a good idea to familiarize yourself with the controls. This prepares you to analyze a breakdown and make emergency repairs. When possible (always on new craft) have a schematic drawing and troubleshooting chart of the system. This is usually included in the service or owner's manual for inboard craft. If it is not available, trace out the system and learn the various parts and their operation.

On modern inboards the sprocket and chain or rack, pinion, and cable sort of steering controls is the most popular. Figure 136 shows one type of sprocket-chain installation while Figure 137 shows a dual rack-pinion-cable installation for a "sport fisherman" with a flying bridge. Both these systems are classified as reversing controls. Any water pressure exerted on the rudder is transmitted back to the steering wheel. This means that to hold a steady course the helmsman must be at the wheel to apply a counteracting force. On

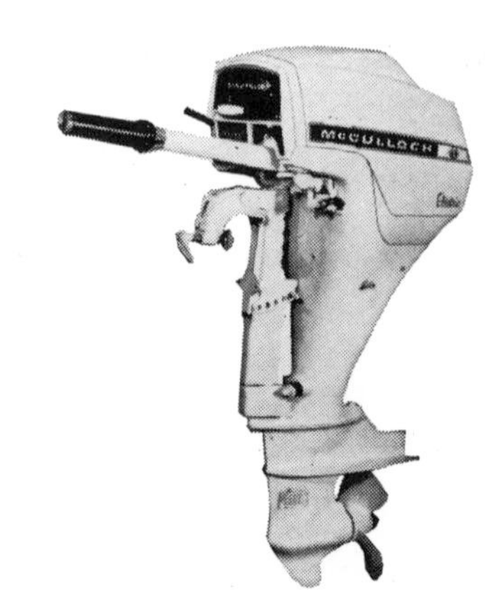

Fig. 138

Fig. 139

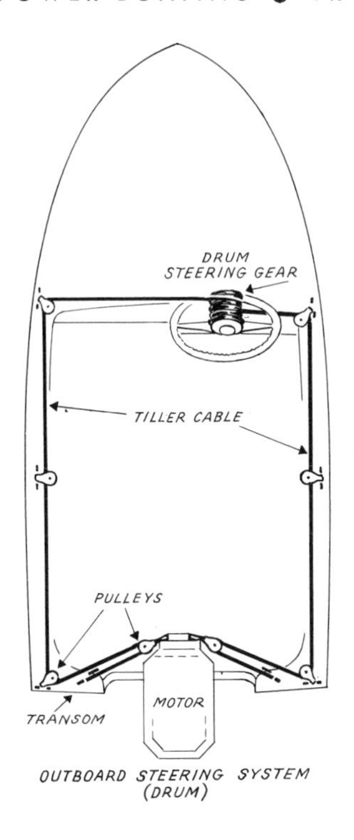

OUTBOARD STEERING SYSTEM
(DRUM)

large inboard craft, nonreversing type controls (worm gear-rod or hydraulic systems) are often used. In either system water pressure against the rudder has no effect on the wheel.

On outboard craft the steering controls are designed to turn the engine rather than to operate a rudder, and the engine steers the boat by directional propeller thrust. On most small boats, under fourteen feet, a direct tiller drive is the normal steering gear. The tiller (steering handle) connects directly to the motor (Fig. 138) and when moved to port or starboard by the helmsman steers the boat. Figure 161 shows how this is done. On large outboard craft the standard controls are the wheel drum and cable system or the rack-pinion-cable system. With some very large boats and dual motor installations having a rod and gear system. The wheel drum and cable controls utilize a steering wheel with spindle drum attached, rope or cable, and pulleys. The cable is secured at the drum, run along the port and starboard sides of the hull, and connected to the motor with a pulley rig (Fig. 139). When the wheel turns, the engine turns. The rack-pinion-cable type controls are similar to those used on inboards, the major difference being that the cable is attached to the engine, not the rudder. When a choice of drum or rack-pinion controls is available, choose the rack-pinion-cable system. Although it is more expensive there is no wheel backlash common to some styles of wheel drum controls. This makes for somewhat easier steering in close quarters.

POWERBOAT HANDLING

The operation of a powerboat is in many ways similar to that of an automobile: you steer with a wheel (except in small outboards and specially designed inboards where a tiller is used), control the rate of speed through a throttle, and change directions from forward to reverse by moving a shifting lever. Here, however, the similarity ends, and this is where most new skippers run into trouble. Powerboats, unlike automobiles, have no brakes, turn from the stern (back) rather than the bow (front), must compensate for tides, winds, and currents, and need a much surer hand when maneuvering in traffic (around docks and crowded waterways). Unfortunately, these unfamiliar aspects are rarely realized by a new skipper until he is confronted with them afloat, and often they dampen his enthusiasm. To avoid this problem take the time now to learn how your boat should be handled while under way. Then when you go afloat as helmsman, guesswork is replaced by know-how. To make learning easier and get you afloat in "jig" time, this section is divided into two parts, inboard boat handling and outboard-inboard handling. The division is necessary as there is a marked difference in the handling qualities of rudder-steered boats (inboards) against propeller-thrust steered boats (outboards and in-outboards).

Once you read and understand how your type of craft will handle, go aboard and head for a practice area. While practicing keep in mind that know-how plus practice is the key to becoming a top-rated skipper.

Trimming the Boat

To obtain the best and safest operating efficiency every powerboat is designed to ride at a balanced angle or plane while at rest or under way. The bow is somewhat higher than the stern, and both sides have equal freeboard (Fig. 140A). In such a position the boat is said to be trim or trimmed. Boats not trimmed properly steer hard, handle sluggishly, and are prone to swamping and tipping. Trimming a modern powerboat is mostly a case of distributing passenger and equipment weight in such a way that the manufacturer's static trim (built-in fixed weight) is unaffected. The designed seating arrangement will, in most cases, distribute passenger weight properly. Storage areas for equipment or gear can be found quickly by shifting items around during a practice run. Be sure not to exceed the manufacturer's recommended maximum weight-carrying capacity. Things to guard against are: 1. Too much weight forward: A bow-heavy boat responds to controls sluggishly, can cause cavitation (see page 145), and at high speeds or in head seas will take water in over the bow. 2. Too much weight aft: A stern-heavy boat steers hard in a wind, squats in the water, and when running in a following sea will take water

Fig. 140

in over the stern. 3. Too much weight on either side: A tilting or leaning powerboat steers hard, tends to roll from side to side, and is prone to flip during tight turns.

Size and weight of a boat when empty must also be considered. The smaller and lighter a boat, the finer the passenger and equipment trim must be. For example, on a small boat one passenger moving from the port to starboard side or sitting forward on the bow deck could upset the trim. Whereas on a large heavy cruiser with plenty of built-in ballast, passenger movement would have little or no effect on trim. Before buying a powerboat check out its static trim during the shakedown cruise (Chapter 1 "Your First Command," page 1). Occasionally, even the best manufacturers make design mistakes.

Trimming an Outboard Motor. Along with boat trim, outboard skippers must also check the mount and trim of their motor. Properly set, the motor should be mounted at the center of the transom so the drive shaft, when under power, is almost perpendicular with the transom (Fig. 140A). In this position the propeller develops maximum thrust parallel to the boat's line of travel. Engineers term this the angle of greatest efficiency. When this angle is upset, performance and safety are reduced. For example, if the motor's lower unit tilts too far forward, the bow digs in and plows. This makes steering hard, allows water in over the bow at high speeds, and can cause cavitation (Fig. 140B). If, on the other hand, the motor's lower unit tilts too far back (away from the transom), the bow will be forced up, causing the stern to "squat" (Fig. 140C). In this position the slightest breeze will affect steering, the bow will pound, and water from following or cross seas will come in over the stern.

To make motor trim adjustment easy on various types and sizes of outboard craft, motor manufacturers have built a tilting mechanism into the mounting bracket (Fig. 140A). On large motors this mechanism is often hydraulically controlled, whereas on small motors it is manually operated. Before getting under way be sure you can operate this control.

Changing Seats

Usually in the course of a trip afloat those aboard will stand a trick at the helm or move from one seat to another. Aboard medium and large size craft (eighteen feet and over) such movement comprises little or no danger. On small powerboats, however, changing positions can be dangerous unless done properly. Under no circumstances allow anyone to stand or walk upright while moving from one seat to another. Any sudden boat movement could throw him overboard or in a shallow draft narrow beam craft capsize the boat. The recommended and safest procedure to follow is: 1. Slow down or stop the boat before the change is made. 2. Have the person closest the bow move first. This moves the extra weight towards the stern which can support more. 3. To move, simply slip out of your seat in a "hunkered" down position and "duck walk" holding a gunwale to your new seat. By moving in this fashion your weight is kept low without changing the center of gravity. 4. When you arrive at your new seat have the person occupying it slide over so you can slip in. 5. Once seated have the person whose seat you took move to your old seat using the same "duck walk" procedure.

Often seat changing as explained above is considered childish, especially by new boatmen or landlubber passengers. As skipper don't let them jeopardize the safety of your boat. Remember that when an accident occurs you are held responsible regardless of fault.

Leeway

(Combined effects of wind—waves and current on a boat's course) While underway keep in mind that the effects of wind, tide, and currents can help or hinder your boat's progress. When the wind/current is from behind it will help push the boat forward. When from ahead it will slow the boat down. And when abeam or off a quarter it will push a boat off course. The first two directions, behind and ahead, effect only elapsed time along a course line from one point to another. The third direction, abeam or quarter, called leeway effects the course of a boat by pushing it down wind/current. This latter

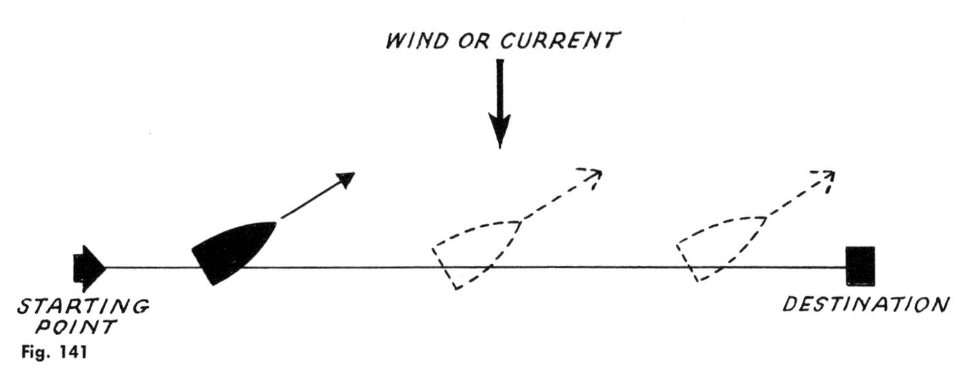

Fig. 141

factor is of primary importance to boatmen who do their boating in current and tidal waters or make long cruises where navigational markers are spread far apart. Unless allowed for, leeway in these instances can force a boat far off course. To compensate for this drift factor you must head up into the prevailing condition at an angle great enough to offset its force (Fig. 141). When wind or sea conditions prevail, allowance for leeway is pretty much a matter of personal observation and judgment acquired from experience afloat. A thorough understanding of how your boat performs under various sea conditions is also helpful. In cases where tides or currents of a known speed and direction prevail, leeway can be computed. Between short distances this is rarely necessary as there are usually navigational or other markers to steer by. On long cruises in strange waters, however, special piloting and navigation formulas are used.

Chapter 5, "Compass, Charts, Piloting," is an excellent introduction to plotting such courses and should be read by every power boatman.

Refloating a Capsized Boat

On occasions power boats do tip over or capsize. How to handle yourself and passengers in such a situation is explained in Chapter 9, "Seamanship in Rough Weather," under the section on capsizing. Often when this does happen, if the sea is fairly calm, the boat is small enough or when close to shore, the boat can be refloated. In cases where the boat is close to shore use the following procedure: 1. After you have cared for the safety of crew and passengers swim to one side of the boat and roll her upright in the water. Usually a gentle pull will do this, even with an outboard on the transom. 2. With another strong swimmer push the boat, by the stern, into shore. Tilt up the motor, pull the boat up until the gunwales are afloat, then bail out the water. 4. Try to start the motor. (*See* "Starting Submerged Motors," page 143, under the section "Outboard Motors").

If the boat is a small inboard light enough to push ashore, bail her out, stay on shore but set out an anchor if in tidal waters and put up a distress signal. Don't try to start engine.

In instances where the boat is in deep water too far to reach shore, attempt the following, depending on the type and size boat: With inboards or large outboards stay with the boat until help arrives. With small outboards using low horsepower motors try to remove the water from the boat by the following method: 1. Roll the boat upright as explained in #1 (on shore landing) above. When upright tilt the motor up. 2. Move to the bow and with another strong swimmer start pushing the boat down wind/current, stern first. 3. When you have the boat moving, push the bow down underwater and give a hard shove forward. If done properly this will cause the stern to pop up out of the water and the boat to lunge ahead, emptying one-third to one-half of the water from the boat. 4. Have the good swimmers move to each side of the boat. Gently take hold of a gunwale, which will now be above water and start bailing with a hand or bailor still secured in the boat. When holding the gunwale be careful it does not go under water. 5. After the boat is ⅔ empty of water have one person climb aboard, being extra careful not to submerge a gunwale, and bail out the remaining water. 6. When the boat is bailed bring passengers aboard one at a time, injured and non-swimmers first. Raise a distress signal. Try to start engine per submerged motor instructions. (*See* page 143). In calm water a rocking motion from side to side can be used to empty water in conjunction with #4 above. Just be careful not to submerge the gunwales or transom.

Inboards

In the course of learning to handle an inboard powerboat certain basic facts and maneuvers that are used repeatedly should be memorized. They are:

1. When aboard, looking forward toward the bow, starboard (right-hand side) is on your right, while port (left-hand side) is on your left. These designations never change and should not be confused when moving in reverse or facing aft (rear).

2. Whenever the wheel turns, the rudder also turns.

3. Steer, both forward and reverse, as you would an automobile. Turn the wheel in the same direction you want to go (Fig. 142).

Fig. 142

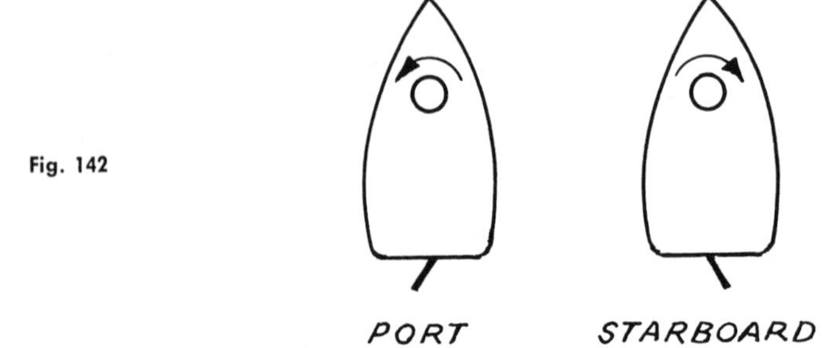

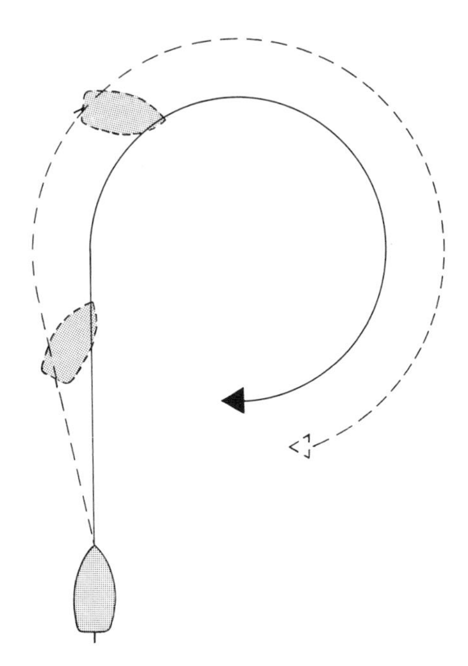

Fig. 143

4. When turning, the stern (back) will swing out much further than the bow (front) (Fig. 143). This is just the opposite of an automobile and must be kept in mind when maneuvering in close quarters.

5. As speed increases, rudder response quickens. At very slow speeds rudder response is very sluggish and must be compensated for when shoving off or docking.

6. Find out which way your boat's propeller rotates. Boats with propellers that rotate clockwise (right-hand propeller) turn best to the port (left). Boats with propellers that rotate anticlockwise (left-hand propellers) turn best to the starboard (right). Most boats use right-hand propellers. On twin-engine installations one propeller will be left-handed and the other right-handed.

7. To increase speed, push the throttle forward. To slow down, pull the throttle back. In a single-lever control, shifting gears is combined with the throttle, push for forward gear, pull back for reverse gear, neutral is upright in the center position (Fig. 135A). In two-lever controls, one lever is the throttle and the other a forward-neutral-reverse shift.

8. As boats have no brakes, they must glide to a stop by shifting to neutral of if necessary reverse. Learning to judge stopping distance is necessary for docking and maneuvering in crowded waterways.

Nomenclature. To make you familiar with the various parts of an inboard powerboat, Figure 144 shows a top and side view of a typical stock model thirty-foot cruiser. The items labeled in heavy print indicate the working parts

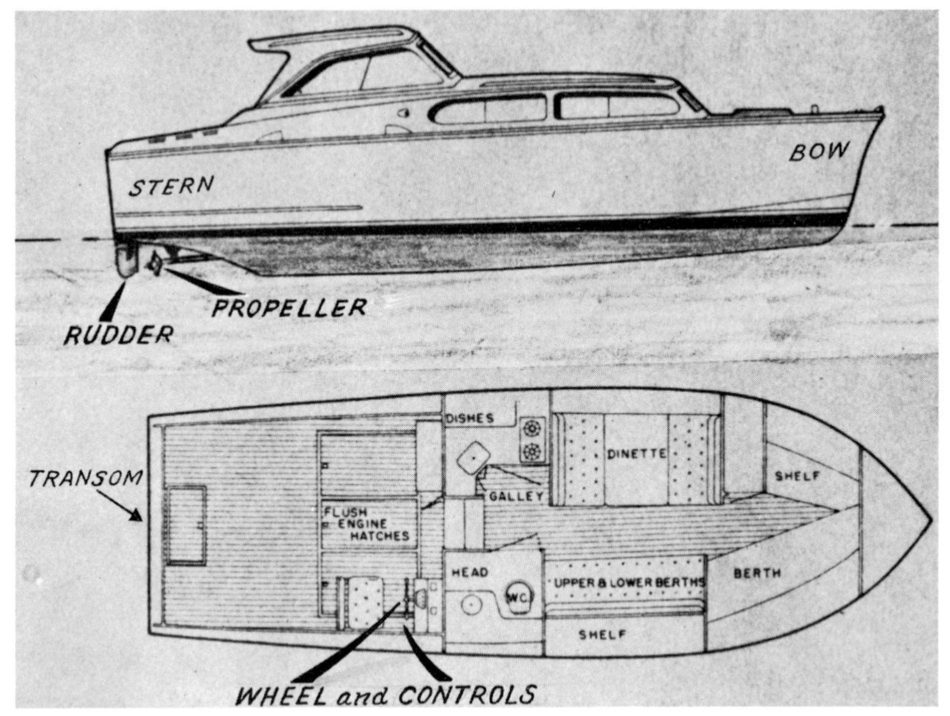

Fig. 144

(rudder, propeller, wheel, and control levers) used to control speed and direction. The remaining sections and parts, in light print, are standard for this type of craft. Additional equipment or superstructures (flying bridge, etc.) are normally listed as extras.

Getting Under Way. Before going aboard and getting under way, be sure to read Chapters 2, "Safety Equipment," and 3, "Preparing to Go Afloat." They explain what safety equipment should be aboard, rules of the road, safe boating habits, etc., all of which are necessary to safe boating. There should be an experienced skipper aboard on your first few practice runs. All reliable marine dealers include boat-handling lessons free when needed. If you are a novice don't let pride keep you from this instruction.

Once aboard make the required daily boat and engine check; then start the engine according to instructions. Don't bother waiting for it to warm up, as engines warm up better at half speed while under way. Prolonged idling in neutral tends to overheat an engine and wears the clutch. Cast off your lines and push or let the wind move the boat away from the dock. Be careful not to bump the dock or another boat. After you get the feel of the wheel and maneuvering in open water you can master the art of docking.

When clear of the dock and other boats, shift into forward and slowly start moving out to a practice area free of heavy traffic. At the practice area, while still moving slowly, feel out the steering wheel by turning it a bit to the right then the left. Don't be surprised if the boat does not respond immediately like an automobile. Remember that at slow speeds the rudder reacts sluggishly, and as speed increases, rudder reaction will quicken. This must be kept in mind, as speed is always a factor when turning. Next slowly increase speed up to the recommended cruising range, and once again turn the wheel a bit to port, then starboard. Notice how much more quickly the rudder responds.

The chances are that the boat will also heel (lean) a bit into the turn. This is normal and should be expected. Heeling increases with speed and the tightness of the turn. This is why at high speed, tight turns can be dangerous. Spend the next few minutes speeding up, checking headway (slowing down), and making slight direction changes at different speeds, all below cruising range.

If while under way the wheel and boat tend to pull to the left, don't become alarmed. This pull is only the effect of the rotation of a right-hand propeller. Left-hand propellers will pull a boat to the right. While practicing be sure to keep a watch for other boats.

Stopping. Once you have the feel of the wheel bring the boat to a stop. Throttle down to idling speed and shift into neutral. How quickly you stop will depend on how fast you throttle down, your speed, and surface conditions (wind, current, sea, etc.). Don't look for the sudden or skidding stops associated with an automobile. Instead you will feel a sudden sinking sensation as the boat loses her plane, settles in the water, and slides to a stop. The sinking sensation is more pronounced at higher speeds, somewhat like the initial drop in an elevator. Practice stopping at different speeds and surface conditions until you can judge the distance needed to stop under various conditions. An excellent way to practice is by dropping a small floating object overboard to use as a marker.

Quick or Emergency Stops. On occasion you must make a fast stop. To do so, quickly throttle down to idle, shift into reverse, then throttle up until you stop. The trick is throttle control. With practice you will soon develop the feel of how far to throttle down and up again at various speeds. Remember once you stop, throttle back to idle and shift into neutral. Otherwise the boat will start moving in reverse. Here again practice with a floating marker will help you judge stopping distance.

Reversing. Boats, unlike automobiles, won't back up in a straight line by centering the wheels or rudder. The reason is propeller rotation. Right-hand propellers pull the boat to the left, and left-hand props pull the boat to the right. To compensate for this pull, which is more pronounced in reverse than forward, you must turn the rudder a bit in the opposite direction (Fig. 145). Just how much rudder is needed will depend on hull design, speed, and sur-

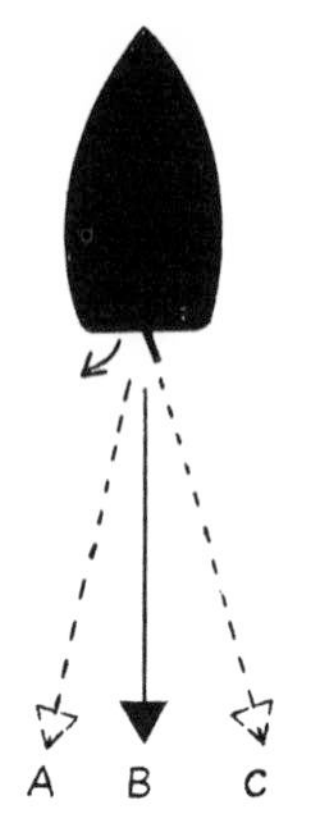

Fig. 145

A — Direction of propeller thrust
B — Desired course
C — Course to steer to make desired course

face conditions. As when moving forward, rudder response in reverse increases with speed. While turning in reverse the same factors hold true. Left turns are made most easily with right-hand propellers, and right turns are made most easily with left-hand propellers. To master these maneuvers correctly, spend a little extra time practicing. On your first few tries concentrate on judging rudder "set," then go on to holding a straight course and turning. Some reversing tips used by professional skippers are: Set the rudder before getting under way, and where possible plan turns so they favor propeller rotation.

Turns. When turning either to the port or starboard, move the steering wheel in the direction of the turn as when steering an automobile. Make your first few turns wide slow S's, circles and ovals. Then as you gain in confidence and skill, the turns can be tightened until the boat comes around in a fairly small radius (a few boat lengths).

While practicing, pay special attention to how far the stern swings out past the bow (Fig. 143). This knowledge will be important when docking or maneuvering from potential hazards. During the course of practicing, the chances are that the boat will seem to turn more easily in one direction than the other. This is caused by propeller rotation as mentioned earlier. When possible take advantage of this knowledge, especially when docking or maneuvering in tight quarters.

Kick Turns. Often you will be required to make a tight turn in narrow or crowded waters. This maneuver, called a kick turn, is made in the following way: 1. Bring your boat to a near or dead stop. 2. Turn the wheel hard over in the direction you wish to go. 3. Throttle up quickly in forward gear. This will "kick" the stern around with little or no forward boat progress. 4. Before the boat begins to move forward, throttle down, shift into reverse, then throttle up again to stop any forward progress. 5. Throttle down and shift into neutral. 6. Repeat steps 1 through 5 until turn is complete (Fig. 146). How adept you

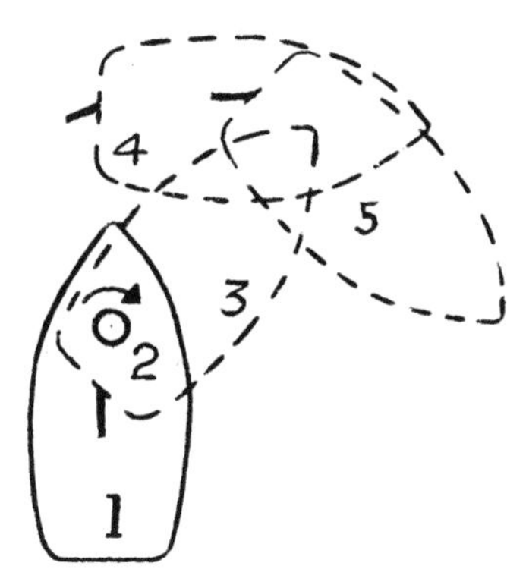

Fig. 146

become at making a kick turn will depend to a great degree on the amount of time spent practicing. Your ultimate goal should be the ability to turn almost within the boat's length.

Docking. As pleasure boating grows in popularity, anchorge areas become increasingly overcrowded. This makes the art of docking all the more important. New skippers should be especially concerned with learning this maneuver, as nothing is more embarrassing or frustrating than a scratch, scrape, and bump session with a pier or other boat while docking. The first step in mastering the art of docking, once you feel at ease at the wheel, is a review of certain powerboat characteristics and a knowledge of basic docking situations. Once these are thoroughly understood it is a case of practice makes perfect.

Always keep in mind the fact that a boat has no brakes, so approach any landing area with caution and allow plenty of "elbow" room to maneuver. Have fenders (bumpers) out with bow and stern lines fast, ready to be brought ashore. Also remember that powerboats, unlike automobiles, steer from the stern (back), which means the stern will swing out past the bow when turning into a dock or slip. Remember, too, that propeller rotation can be a help or hindrance when maneuvering. Plan ahead when possible to take advantage of propeller rotation. And lastly check existing surface conditions (wind, current, or tide). Whenever possible land into the wind or current (whichever is the stronger). This allows better control over your boat in that you can keep under power longer, stop more quickly, and maneuver more easily. In cases where there is a choice between propeller rotation or landing into the wind or current, choose the latter.

Following are illustrations with explanations showing the best way to handle basic docking situations under various wind/current directions. On calm days treat the situation as a head-on wind/current. For simplicity all boats are shown portside to the docks. If they were in the opposite position (right side to the docks), the rudder positions would be reversed but the directions and engine speeds would remain the same.

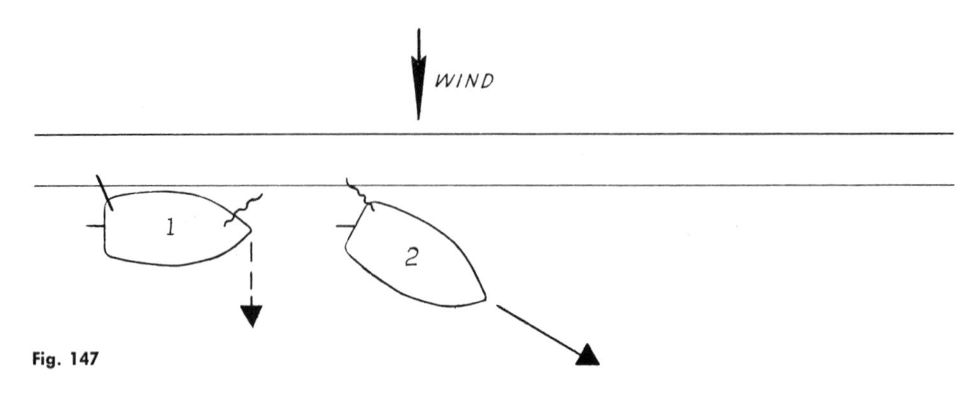

Fig. 147

Leaving a Dock

Wind/current off the dock (Fig. 147):

1. Cast off the bow line and let the wind/current swing the bow out. Ease off on the stern line as the bow swings out. This will clear the stern.
2. Once clear, cast off the stern line and get under way.

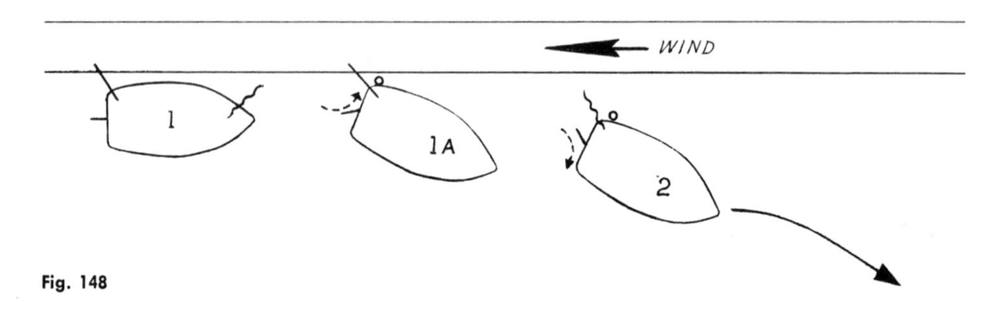

Fig. 148

Wind/current ahead (Fig. 148):

1. Cast off the bow line and let the wind/current swing out the bow. If the bow won't swing out on its own, use a boat hook or quick spurts of forward power, rudder hard right. Have a bumper out and a crewman with a fending pole (boat hook) at the port quarter.

Never fend off with your hands. A sudden surge from surface conditions or inboard power could break or crush your hand or arm. Always use a pole, oar, etc.

2. When the bow has swung out 20 to 25 degrees, cast off the stern line, turn the rudder hard left, and with a few spurts of forward power kick the stern clear.
3. Once clear, get underway. Be careful while moving out not to use too much right rudder or the stern will be pushed back into the dock.

Wind/current behind (Fig. 149):

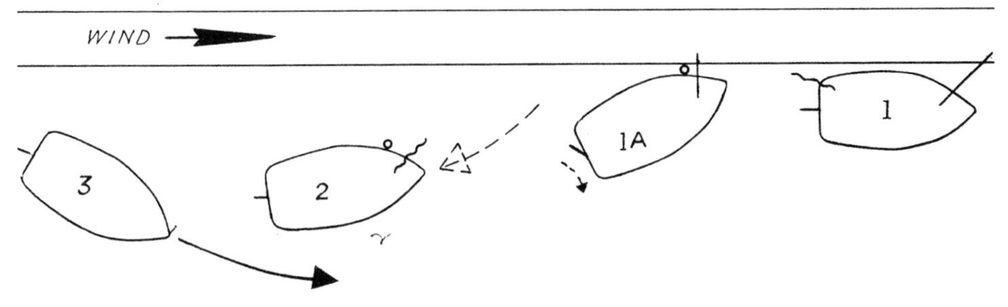

Fig. 149

1. Cast off stern line and let wind/current swing out stern. If the stern won't swing out on its own, use a boat hook or quick spurts of forward power, rudder hard left.
2. Once the stern has swung clear, cast off bow line and back out under reverse power.
3. When well clear, shift into forward, steer with an easy right rudder, and get under way.

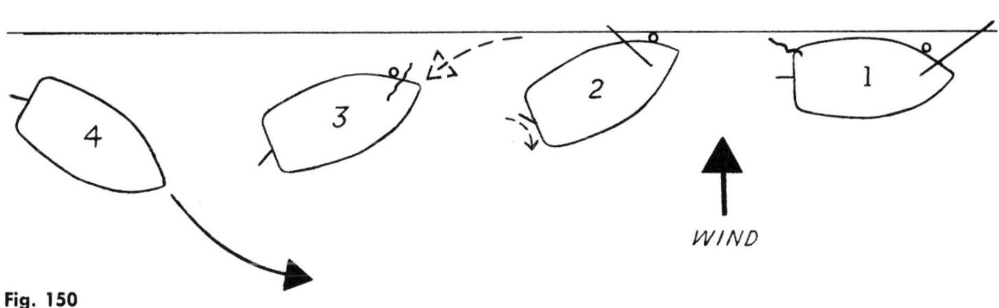

Fig. 150

Wind/current on the dock (Fig. 150):

1. Cast off stern line and place bumper and crewman with fending pole (boat hook) at bow.
2. Turn rudder hard left and power forward in quick spurts until the stern swings out.
3. Once the stern has swung clear, cast off the bow line and back out under reverse power.
4. When well clear, shift into forward, steer with an easy right rudder, and get under way.

During this operation the wind/current will be trying to push the boat back into the dock, so remain under power at all times.

Leaving a Slip (Fig. 151)

The following maneuvers can be used in all wind/current situations. The

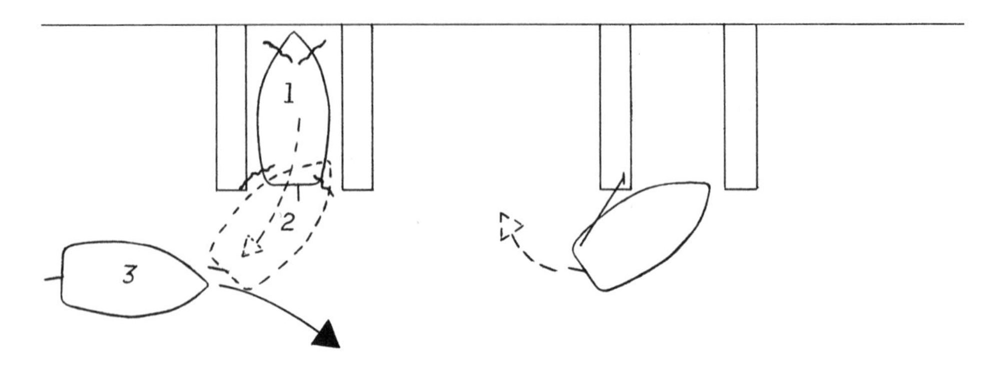

Fig. 151 Fig. 152

only variation would be the degree of power or rudder.

1. Cast off all lines. Back out under reverse power until clear of slip.
2. Once clear, hard left rudder under reverse power until the bow swings around. (Use right rudder if boat has left-hand propeller).
3. Shift into forward and get under way.

In tight quarters with boats astern use the port quarter line eased out a bit to pivot around (Fig. 152).

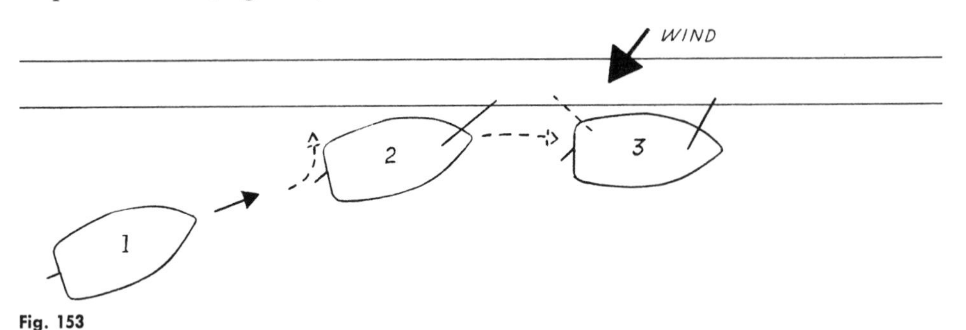

Fig. 153

Landing at a Dock

Wind/current ahead or off the dock (Fig. 153):

1. Approach the dock slowly at a thirty-five- to forty-five-degree angle.
2. Come to a stop with bow about twelve to eighteen inches from dock and put bow line ashore.
3. When bow line is secured, steer hard right rudder and power forward in short spurts until stern swings into dock.
4. Secure stern line and if necessary spring lines.

Wind/current on the dock (Fig. 154):

In a light breeze or current dock as follows:

1. Approach dock almost parallel (bow in) about two or three yards off from it.

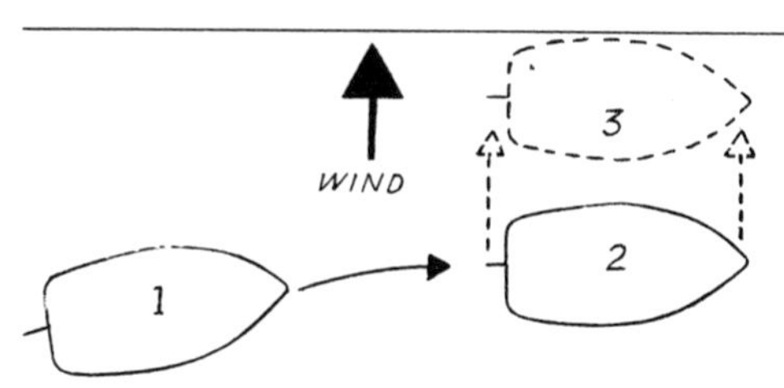

Fig. 154

2. Come to a stop and let wind push you in.
3. Secure bow line and stern line, in that order. Then spring lines if necessary.

If, however, there is a heavy wind/current use the following docking procedures (Fig. 155):

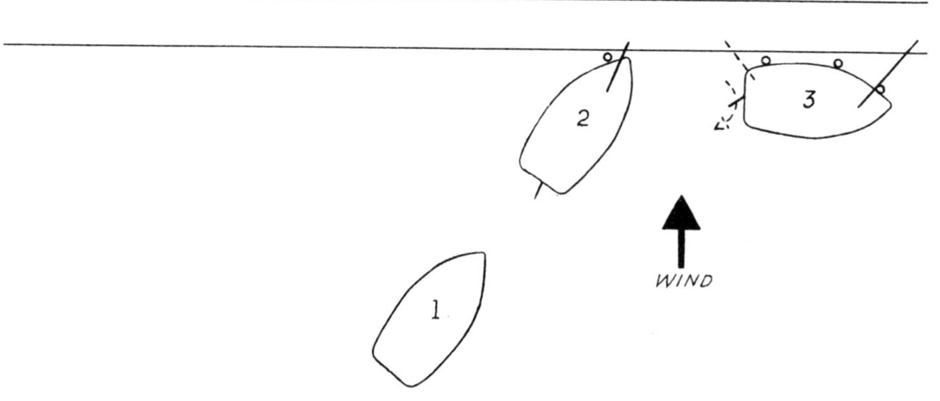

Fig. 155

1. Approach the dock at a steep angle, sixty to seventy-five degrees.
2. Come to a reverse power stop when the bow is about twelve to eighteen inches off the dock and put the bow line ashore. Have a crewman at bow with finding pole (boat hook).
3. Let wind/current push the stern toward the dock. To brake against the wind/current use a hard right rudder with short spurts of reverse power as needed. Have extra fenders out and a crewman at stern with fending pole.
4. Secure stern lines and if necessary spring lines.

Practice this landing in light winds. Then when needed in a heavy blow you will be prepared.

Wind/current behind (Fig. 156):

1. Approach the dock almost parallel (bow in).
2. When about two feet off the dock, steer right rudder with quick spurts of

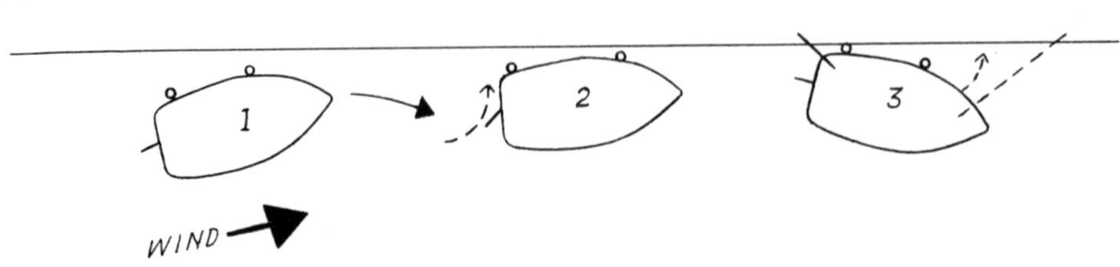

Fig. 156

forward power until stern starts to swing into dock. Have crewman to fend off.

3. Put stern line ashore, let wind/current swing bow in and put bow line ashore. If necessary put out spring lines.

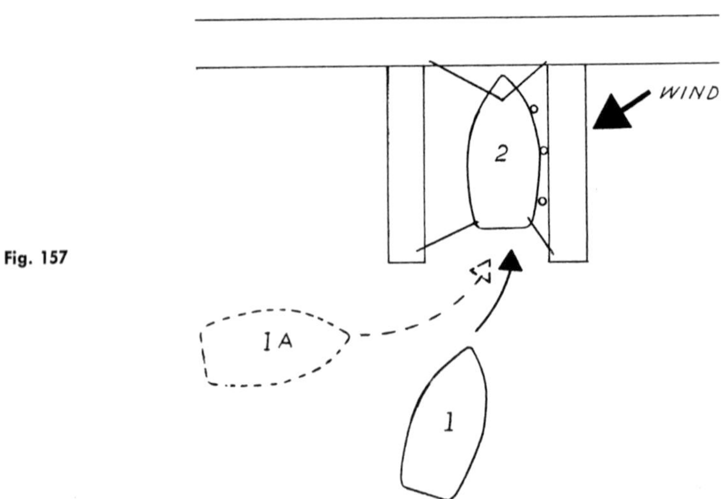

Fig. 157

Entering a slip (Fig. 157):

1. Approach the slip parallel or nearly so, favoring any cross wind by maneuvering more closely to the windward side.
2. Come to a stop twelve to eighteen inches off the windward dock.
3. Put ashore windward side bow and stern lines, then leeward side bow and stern lines.

Moorings. At most anchorage areas many boats use mooring buoys anchored in deep water for tying up (see Fig. 211, Chapter 12, "Anchoring, Mooring, Tying Up"). If your boat should ever be on a mooring buoy use the following procedures to cast off and land.

Fig. 158

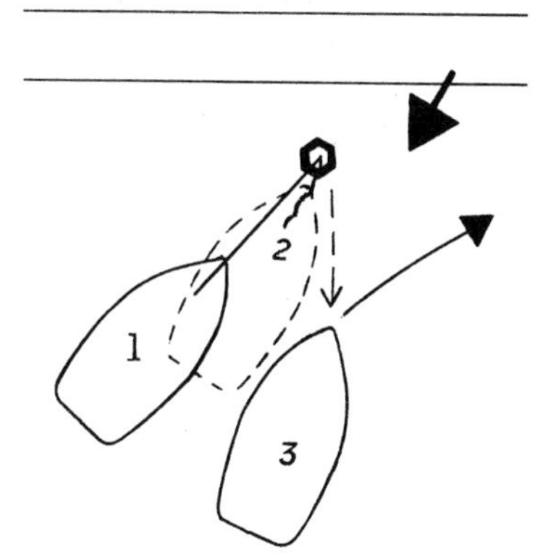

Casting Off from a Mooring (Fig. 158)

1. Edge up to the mooring buoy under power until the mooring line is slack and can be cast off. Normally a crewman in the bow does this job.
2. Cast off the mooring line, throttle down, shift to neutral, and let the boat drift clear of the buoy. On a calm day you will have to back away under power. Be careful of boats behind you.
3. Once clear of the mooring get under way, making sure not to run over the buoy or line.

Fig. 159

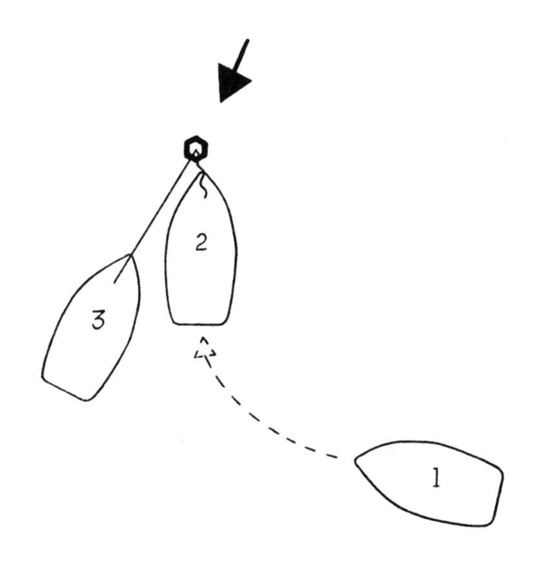

Landing at a Mooring (Fig. 159)

1. Approach the mooring buoy into wind/current. A look at your tender or

other boats moored nearby will show which direction the wind/current is moving.

2. Power up to within one or two feet of the buoy and hold steady. Have a crewman, stationed at the bow, pick up the pennant line with the boat hook, bring aboard the mooring line, run it through a bow chock, and then secure it to a bow cleat or bit.
3. Let the boat settle back against the mooring line, make sure the line is fast, secure the boat, and go ashore.

Under no circumstances allow a crewman to grab the pennant line while the boat is still under way. Such action can pull him overboard, break an arm, or worse.

When a tender (small boat used to reach the mooring and come ashore) is tied at the mooring, have the crewman in the bow fend it off with the boat hook as you power up to the buoy.

Beaching-Grounding. Inboard powerboats, having an affixed shaft-propeller-rudder assembly below the bottom of the hull, are not built for beaching (running up gently, bow first, on a soft beach). If, however, you should run aground in strange waters without causing major damage, proceed in the following order:

1. If the propeller and rudder are free (still afloat) try to back off under power. Move all passengers and crew aft to raise the bow. When the propeller or rudder is grounded, don't try to reverse under power. Such action only causes more damage.
2. Aboard small light craft, pole off or have some crewmen, wearing protective footwear and life jackets, go over the side and push the boat free.
3. On a rising tide, wait until the tide floats you free.
4. On a large craft with a tender, attach the bitter (loose) end of the anchor line to a stern cleat or bit and row the anchor, paying the line from the tender, out to deep water. Set the anchor a bit to the starboard of the stern for boats with right-hand propellers (the port for boats with left-hand propellers). Then use reverse power if the propeller and rudder are free. The propeller rotation when powered in short spurts works against the anchor line and often sets up a wiggling or rocking action that will work the boat free.
5. Request assistance from other craft nearby, preferably a larger, more powerful boat.
6. On a falling tide that keeps you fast aground, put an anchor off one side to help refloat her in case she lays over in sticky mud.

Outboards and In-outboard Boats

Outboard and in-outboard craft handle alike and therefore can be grouped under the same heading. In learning to handle these craft certain characteristics and maneuvers that are used repeatedly must be understood before going aboard. They are:

1. When on board, looking forward toward the bow, the right-hand side of the boat is called starboard, while the left side is called port. These designations never change and must not be confused when facing aft or moving in reverse.

2. Outboards obtain their steering power from propeller thrust, which eliminates the need of rudders. When you turn the steering wheel (or tiller) the engine or lower unit also turns. This form of power steering makes outboards extremely maneuverable and easy to handle.

3. On boats equipped with a steering wheel, steer both forward and reverse by turning the wheel in the same direction in which you want to go (Fig. 160). If, however, a tiller is used in place of a steering wheel, move it opposite the direction in which you want to go. For example, when turning to the port, move the tiller toward the starboard side. When turning to the starboard, move the tiller toward the portside (Fig. 161).

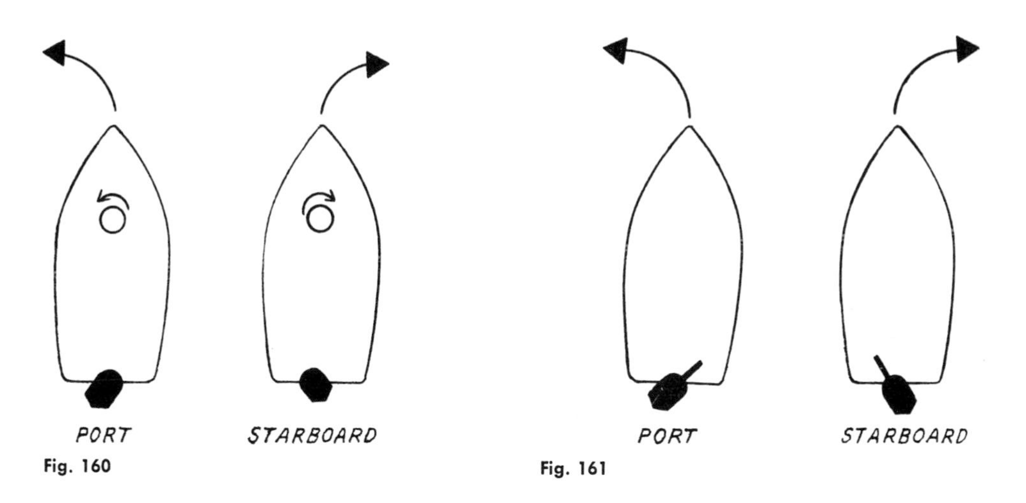

Fig. 160

Fig. 161

4. During a turn the stern will swing out past the bow. This reaction is just the opposite of an automobile and must be kept in mind when maneuvering in tight quarters.

5. As speed increases, steering response quickens. At high speeds most outboards become very "tender" and need an experienced hand at the controls.

6. All powerboats have no brakes; they must glide to a stop by throttling down and shifting into neutral or reverse. Learning to judge the distances needed to stop at various speeds and surface conditions of wind, current, and

sea is necessary for safe docking and maneuvering.

7. Find out which way your boat's propeller rotates. Boats with propellers that rotate clockwise (right-hand propellers) turn best to the port (left). Boats with propellers that turn counterclockwise (left-hand propellers) turn best to the starboard (right). Most outboard motors turn right-hand propellers. On twin-engine boats the port engine will usually swing a right-hand prop, while the starboard engine will swing a left-hand prop.

8. To increase speed push the throttle control forward. To slow down, pull the throttle control back. In a single-lever control, shifting gears is combined with the throttle; push for forward gear, pull back for reverse gear, neutral is upright in the center position (Fig. 135A). On some outboard installations, push buttons act as the shifting lever. When a two-lever control is used, one lever acts as the throttle and the other the shifting gear.

9. Outboard craft are usually much lighter (weight) than comparably sized inboards; therefore they are more susceptible to wind pressures while maneuvering.

Nomenclature. To illustrate the various parts of outboard and in-outboard craft, Figures 162 and 163 show a stock model outboard runabout and in-outboard sports utility. The items labeled in heavy print are the working parts (propeller, wheel, throttle, and shift) used to control speed and direction. The remaining parts, in light print, are standard for these types of craft. Additional equipment is normally listed as extras.

Getting Under Way. On your first few practice runs try to have an experienced skipper along. His presence will save a lot of time and effort in the "how to do it" department. Be sure also that you have read Chapters 2, "Safety Equipment," and 3, "Preparing to Go Afloat." They explain what

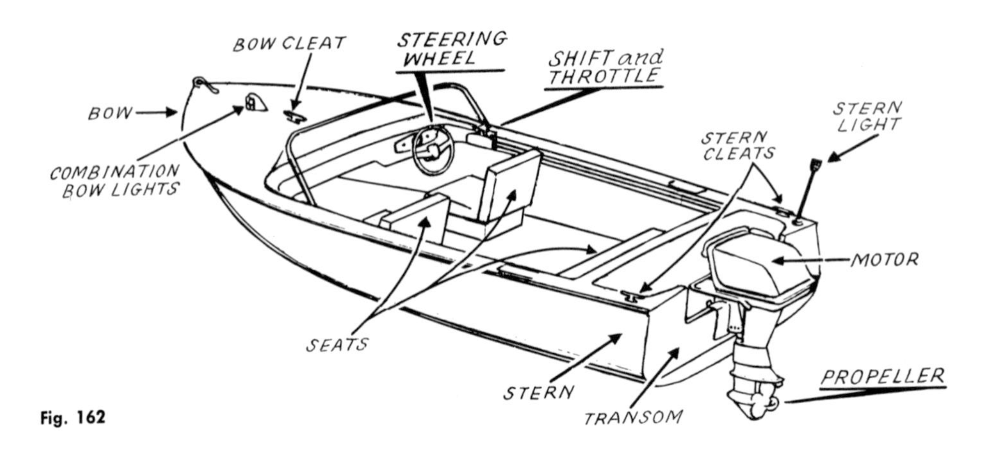

Fig. 162

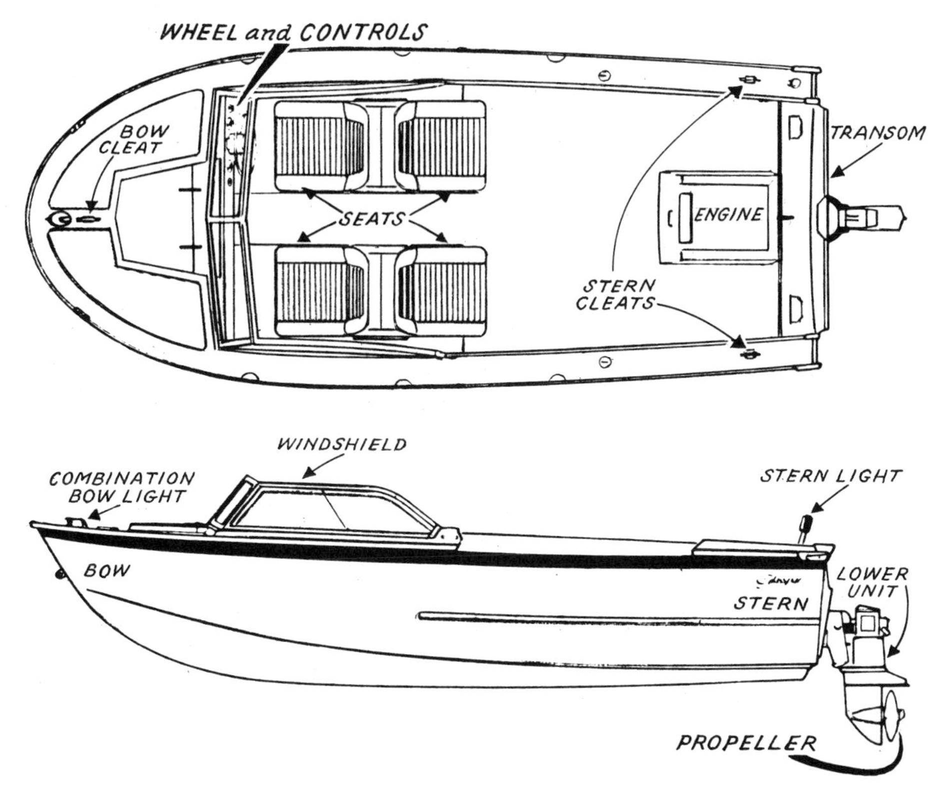

Fig. 163

safety equipment must be aboard, the rules of the road, safe boating habits, etc., all of which are necessary to safe boating.

Once aboard make the required daily boat and engine check, then start the engine according to instructions. When starting small motors with rope-pull starters, be sure you are sitting or kneel (Fig. 164). *Never* stand, as the initial thrust or pull might throw you off balance into the motor or over the side. Once the motor is running, check to be sure the immediate area is free of traffic; then cast off your lines. Push or let the wind move the boat clear of the dock and other craft. Be careful not to bump or scratch another boat. When clear, shift into forward and proceed slowly out to a practice area. Don't bother waiting for the engine to warm up. Modern power plants warm up best under a slight load. At the practice area, while still moving slowly, feel out the steering wheel or tiller by moving it a bit to the port then the starboard. Notice how the stern tends to swing out further than the bow (Fig. 143). This occurs because powerboats steer from the stern. In automobiles the opposite is true, because steering is done from the front. This characteristic of boats will be a factor when docking and moving in crowded waterways, so learn to compensate for it while practicing. Next slowly increase speed up to the recommended

Fig. 164

cruising range and continue to move the wheel or tiller occasionally a bit to port then starboard. As speeds increase the boat will respond to controls more quickly and heel (lean) more. This action is normal for all planing powerboats and within safe speeds will actually help the boat maneuver. At high speeds, however, it can be dangerous during tight turns or running in choppy seas. Spend a few minutes speeding up, checking headway (slowing down), running in a straight line, and making slight direction changes. If, while practicing, the boat tends to pull a bit to the port, don't become alarmed. This pull is only the effect of your right-hand propeller. Boats with left-hand propellers will pull to the starboard. You can, if you wish, overcome this pull by mounting the motor a bit off center of the transom. How much to move it is best determined by trial and error. Rarely, however, is the pull noticeable enough to warrant such action. In extreme cases of pull look for a warped or damaged hull.

The procedures for *Stopping* and *Quick Emergency Stops* with outboard and in-outboard engines are generally identical to those with inboard engines described on page 157.

Reversing. To move in reverse, come to a stop, check for traffic behind you, shift into reverse and throttle up to a slow safe speed (2 to 3 m.p.h.). Steer as if moving forward; just point the propeller in the direction you want to go. The only difference is that the propeller is rotating in reverse. If while under way the boat tends to steer a bit off course, don't become alarmed. It is only the effects of propeller rotation. To get back on course move the propeller thrust slightly in the opposite direction of the pull. How much to compensate will be a matter of trial and error. Smart skippers use propeller rotation to advantage by planning their reverse turns, where possible, to favor the pull.

The procedures for *Turns, Kick Turns, Docking,* and *Mooring* with out-

Fig. 165

board and in-outboard engines are generally identical to those with inboard engines described on pages 158-165.

Beaching. Outboard power boats, because the lower unit tilts up, can safely be beached (run up gently, bow first on a soft beach). This characteristic makes outboard craft ideal for island and out of the way exploring, picnicking, fishing, etc.

Landing on a Beach (Fig. 165):

1. Approach the beach slowly. Have a crewman at the bow to watch for rocks.
2. When the bow is ten or twelve feet off shore tilt up the engine's lower unit and let the boat's momentum drift you in.
3. When the bow comes to rest put ashore a bow line, or anchor.
4. Secure the bow line or set the anchor and bring any passengers ashore.

On strange shores be extra watchful for rocks and other hazards that could damage the hull.

Leaving a Beach (Fig. 166):

1. Position the stern so it is at a ninety degree angle with the shore line.

Fig. 166

2. Push the bow off the beach to the water's edge so the stern is afloat.
3. Have passengers go aboard and move to the stern.
4. Take in the bow or anchor line and go aboard over the bow. Give the boat a push outward as you go aboard.
5. Pole or row out to deep water, drop the lower unit and get under way.

In shallow or rocky water push the boat out until she is completely afloat before bringing passengers aboard. The passengers may have to go barefoot or be carried but it will save the hull from heavy scratches.

Beaching in Tidal Waters. On tidal waters check the tides before going afloat. A boat beached at low tide will float free on the rising tide and drift off unless anchored. Carry the anchor ashore, paying out line, and set it above the high water mark. This procedure will let you retrieve the boat from land at high tide.

If the tide is in when you beach your boat, it will be left high and dry on the ebb tide. To avoid having to wait for the next tide do the following: Set the anchor close to the shore line, put out lots of anchor line, and push the boat afloat. As the tide goes out so will the boat. Just make sure the anchor is well set.

When the tide is still coming pick a smooth clear stretch of beach you can carry or pull the boat across if the tide is out when you are leaving. When pulling be extra careful not to scratch up the hull. Many boatmen carry air rollers for such situations (See Chapter 14, "Trailers and Trailering").

Running Aground. Most outboard skippers have an affinity for exploring out of the way spots and strange waterways which increases the chance of running aground. Should this happen to you, and there is no major hull or propeller damage, proceed as follows in the order listed:

1. If the stern and propeller are still afloat move all the passengers aft to raise the bow then back off under power. When the stern is grounded or the lower unit tilted up don't attempt to power free.
2. Tilt up the lower unit and pole off or have some crewmen, wearing protective footwear and life jackets, go over the side and push the boat free.
3. On a rising tide wait for the tide to float you free.
4. Request assistance from other craft nearby. Preferably a larger more powerful boat if towing is anticipated. When stuck fast secure towline around boat to avoid ripping out cleats or transom (Fig. 167).

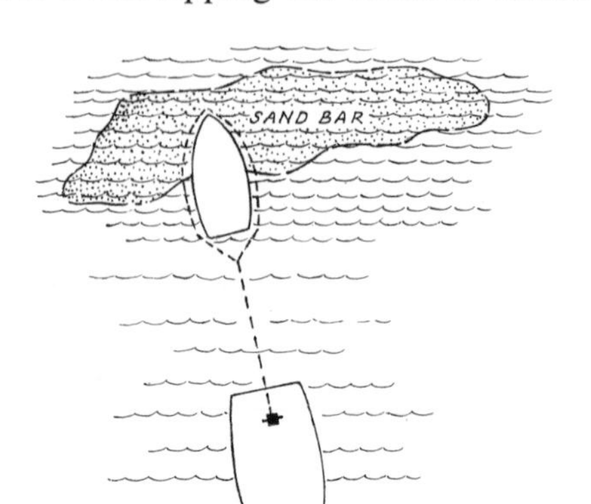

Fig. 167

Circle tow line around grounded craft's hull or sturdy super structure. This allows an even steady pressure and prevents cleat or transom damage. Rig tow boat the same way if not equipped with towing bitt or post.

10

Seamanship in Rough Weather

Seamanship ability covers many functions, one of the most important of which is boat handling during a storm. This does not mean you should purposely go afloat during a blow to master these techniques—just the opposite, use your weather eye to reach port safely before the storm hits. But if at some time this becomes impossible, a knowledge of rough weather seamanship can save your life. The first step in this direction is a thorough understanding of your boat and her ability. Do not expect miracles of a boat designed for small bodies of water when caught far offshore in a large lake or bay. And above all, do not make the same mistake, as so many other pleasure boatmen who learn only the basic requirements necessary to pilot their craft. Instead, become a part of your boat. Learn to make her jump at your commands. And, most important, be sure she is sound and well equipped before going afloat (see "Fitting Out and Storage," page 229). Learn these things which are an important part of your seamanship lore, and you automatically get a hullfull of luck in a storming sea.

HEAD UP

Running head up with the bow pointed directly into the waves or nearly so is the safest course to steer during a storm. Some spray and pounding of the bow against the sea can be expected, but this will have little or no effect on a well-designed boat. If the head-up course causes too much motion, run one or two points off the wind and the pounding and pitching will lessen. Take care though that the boat does not broach (swing broadside) to the waves causing her to swamp. Special care must be taken aboard light outboard powercraft, as these boats tend to be blown sideways into a broach more quickly than heavier inboard craft (Fig. 168).

When under power, throttle down the engine so as to just barely make headway. Excessive speed will cause the bow to plunge into oncoming waves in-

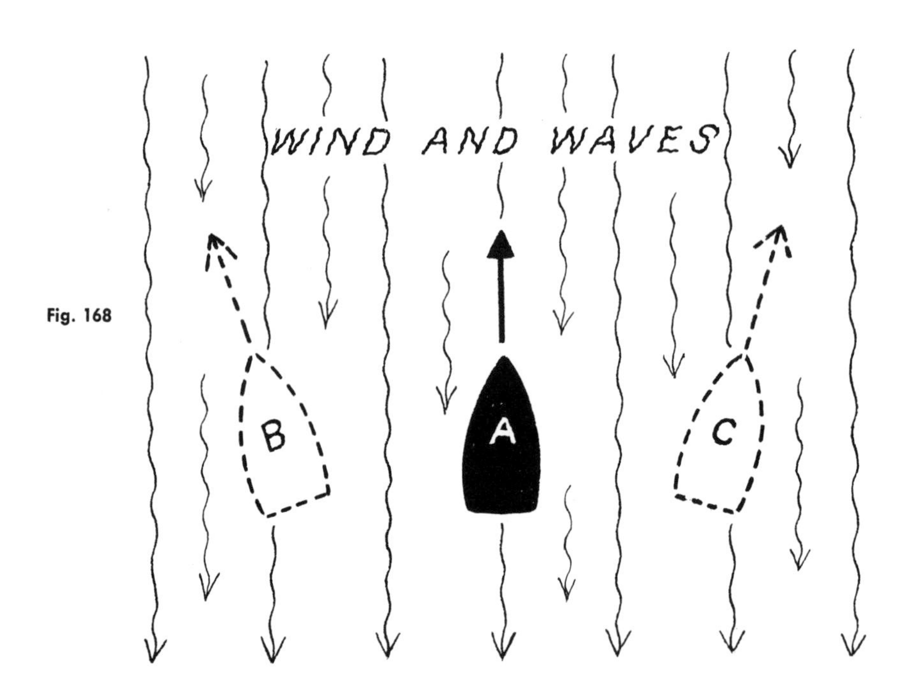

Fig. 168

stead of floating over them. Not enough speed to make headway will cause the boat to broach and possibly swamp. If the boat should start to broach, throttle up the engine until you just begin making headway into the waves. Stay on this course until the storm ends.

Rowboats and canoes use the same procedure as a powerboat except muscle power substitutes for engine power. Canoeists paddling alone will find it easier to keep the bow up if they paddle from the bow rather than amidships or the stern. In this position the bow is not effected by the wind, while the pointed stern acts as a wind rudder similar to a reefed sail on a sailboat.

When aboard a sailboat lower the jibsail and reef the mainsail. Sails are reefed by lowering them about one-third down the mast with roller reefing gear or by tying the lowered sail with the reefing points (lines) attached to the sail or other line aboard. Then sail close-hauled to the wind. If the wind increases in velocity, reef the sail lower. When reefing with reefing points or other line, lower the sail completely, make your reef, then rehoist the sail. If possible anchor while tying down the sail (Fig. 169).

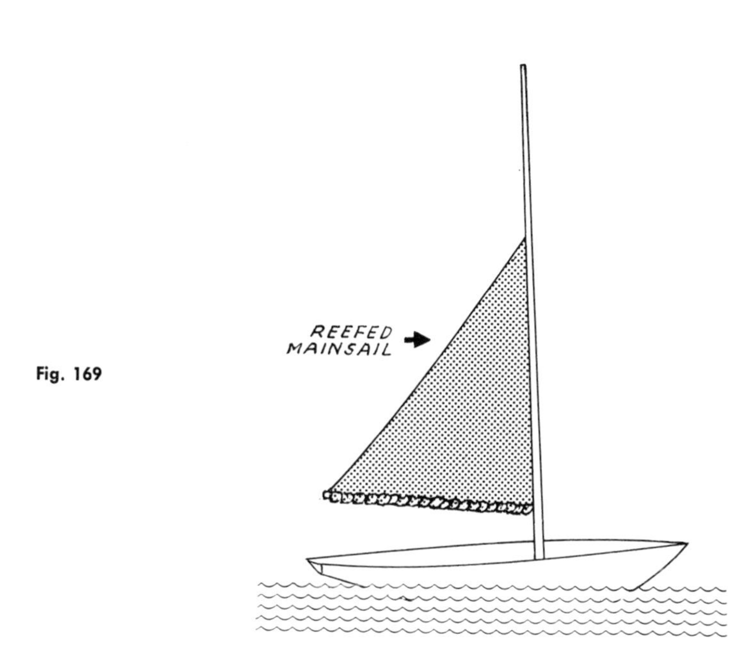

Fig. 169

ANCHORING

If the storm becomes so violent that you can not make headway and your anchor line is at least ten to twelve times the water's depth in length, point the bow directly into the wind and drop anchor. Be sure the end of the anchor line is securely tied to the bow bit or cleat and, if aboard a sailboat, all sails are lower and lashed down. Seat everyone aft on the floor to allow the bow to ride up and over the swells or waves. Once the storm hits, keep everybody calm and in his place until the blow subsides. Aboard powerboats it is a good practice to keep the engines idling in case the anchor starts to drag.

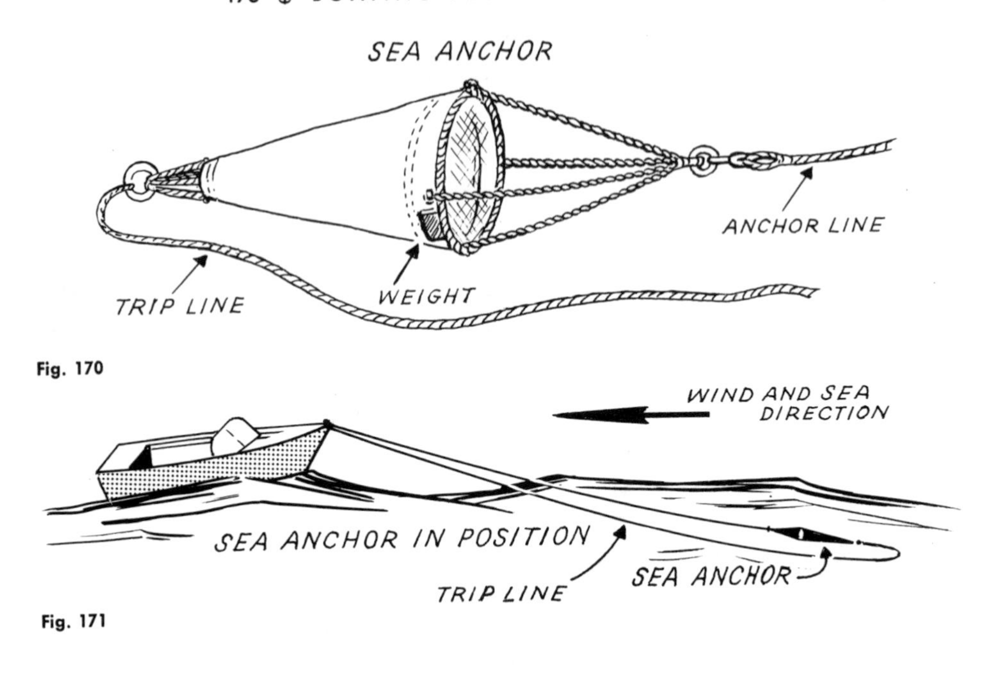

Fig. 170

Fig. 171

SEA ANCHOR

When headway is impossible and the water is too deep to drop anchor, put out a sea anchor.

A sea anchor is a cone-shaped canvas bag with a metal loop at the mouth and a trip ring at the cone end (Fig. 170).

To use the sea anchor, fasten the loose end of the line to the bow bit and throw the anchor overboard. The anchor works by the leeward drift of the boat. As the boat is pushed downwind, the sea anchor which floats only a few feet underwater causes a holding action against the bow so it will not swing broadside into a broach. After the storm is over, pull the trip line, spilling the water out of the bag, and haul it in (Fig. 171).

When no sea anchor is aboard use a pair of pants, sweater or anything that will cause a firm dragging action and hold the bow up. If the makeshift anchor does not cause enough drag, make another and put it out alongside the first. Do not pull the first anchor in to add dragging weight because the boat will swing broadside while you are adding more drag.

RUNNING BEFORE A FOLLOWING SEA

The ordinary swell encountered offshore rarely causes trouble while running before a following sea. Except for a slight fore-and-aft pitching motion, swells slide easily under the stern or can be ridden over in comparative comfort. During a storm this all changes. The once gentle swells turn into high cresting waves offshore or steep breaking waves in shallow water. In such a situation trying to keep the stern from being swamped, broached, or lifted out of the water takes the utmost in seamanship ability. Before the seas get too rough, canoes, rowboats, sailboats, and small outboards should come about and head up into the waves. Powerboats can, if handled by an expert, run before a following sea by slowing down and letting the seas pass under them or by riding on the upswell of a wave. Such maneuvering requires delicate throttle and rudder control. Too slow a speed will allow oncoming cresting waves to come in over the stern, causing a swamping or lifting action (Fig. 172). Too fast a speed will send the boat over a crest sliding down the other side, causing her to pitch pole end over end (Fig. 173). In an emergency a long heavy drag line is sometimes put out over the stern to check a boat's speed and keep her on the proper course. But special care must be taken when handling such a line to avoid its fouling the propeller. Because running is a constant touch-and-go proposition, sailing head up or anchoring is recommended as the best way to ride out a storm for all but expert skippers.

During a storm your boat will ship some water and catch a lot of spray. This is to be expected, so stay calm and bail out any water as it comes aboard. When passengers are aboard make sure they are all wearing life preservers. Seat them on the floor over the keel and hold a running conversation to keep them calm.

Fig. 172

Fig. 173

RUNNING IN THE TROUGH

During a storm no small craft should try to hold on a course that puts it abeam (broadsides) of the wind and waves, unless in dire emergency. Such a course is called "running in the trough" (valley between waves) and automatically puts a boat in a broached position. If such a course is ever necessary make it in a series of zigzags. First angle upwind into the sea, putting the wind broad on the bow. Run in this position for a few minutes, then angle

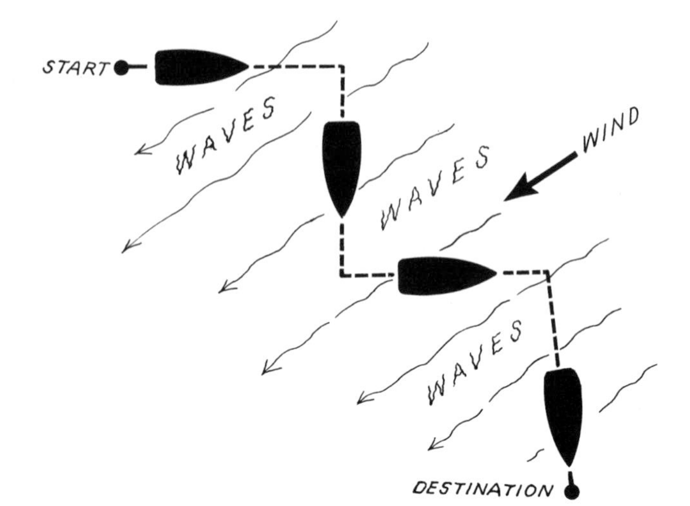

Fig. 174

downwind, putting the wind broad on the stern. Repeat these turns until you reach your destination. These zigzag turns will keep the boat out of the trough except when changing angles. Again I must caution that running in this position is highly dangerous and should be resorted to only in an emergency (Fig. 174).

RUNNING INLETS

Running the channels or passageways of breaking inlets demands the same abilities required to ride out a storm. As offshore swells pile up on the shallow water surrounding inlets, they often become steep breaking waves. Until you gain experience in boat handling it is best that you try to avoid such waters. New boatmen often make the mistake of assuming an inlet channel will be quiet all day just because it was calm when they went afloat in the morning. Sailboats, rowboats, and canoes, because of their lack of reserve power and maneuverability, should never attempt to run a breaking inlet. Powerboats of adequate size and design will find the following suggestions helpful when navigating these trouble spots.

Try to plan on entering the inlet channel during flood tide rather than ebb tide. On flood tide the waters move with the waves, whereas on ebb tide the waters are backing out against the waves, causing them to become steeper.

Stand off the channel inlet and watch the action of the waves. Usually they will come in groups of three or more, but at least three, with the last one the largest. After you have timed a series, wait until a big one has broken or spent its energy, then run in behind it. Or ride the upswell (backside) of the next lesser wave.

When running strange inlets have a local boatman take you through or wait

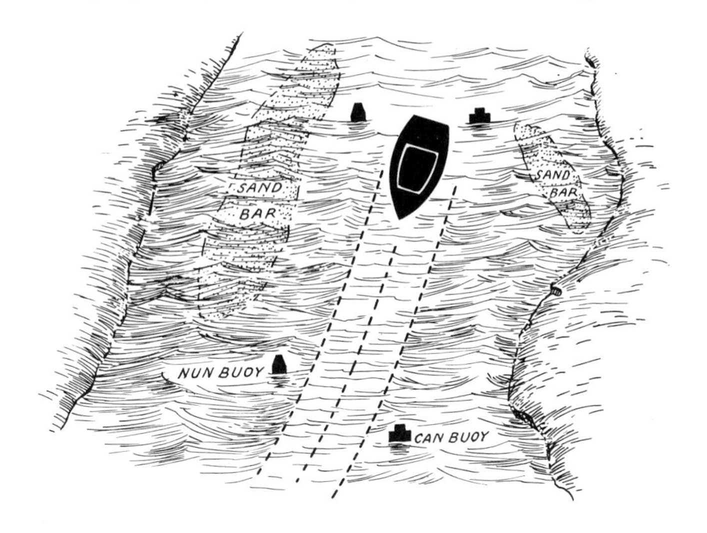

Fig. 175

offshore and watch how local boats navigate. If the channel entrance is unmarked, watch the wave action to determine where the channel or deepest waters are. Steep breaking waves will mark the shallow areas, while swells or smaller breaking waves mark deeper waters. So look for calmer water with less violent wave action to mark the best navigation waters (Fig. 175).

Even though the channel may be marked in an inlet, shifting sandbars often make the buoys inaccurate. Here again, having a local boatsman aboard or following local boats in are the safest practices.

One other important safety practice to observe during rough weather is: Secure and batten down all loose equipment. Once the storm breaks, you won't have time to worry about equipment rolling or banging around the boat.

CAPSIZING

Although I hope you will never be aboard a boat that capsizes, you should know how to handle this emergency. Boats capsize two ways, by either tipping over or being swamped by water coming in over the bow, stern, or sides. In tipping, take a deep breath and jump out, away from the boat, holding your arms over your head. This will usually put you clear of the overturned boat, or your arms will protect your head if the boat should come down on top of you. Should you be caught under an overturned boat or sail do not panic, just swim underwater a few yards until you are clear. This is one example of why all sailors should be good swimmers.

NOTE: Before jumping out, be positive the boat is tipping. If she should right herself after you abandon ship, she might drift downwind faster than you can swim, leaving you stranded. Here again experience in boat handling is the only teacher.

Fig. 176

Once you are clear, check the passengers and be sure they are all present and have their life jackets on. On overturned boats too large to roll upright, climb on or gather around and hold on to the hull. On smaller boats simply roll the boat over until she is right side up. She will roll easily, even with an outboard motor attached to the transom, so do not try to spin her. Once she is right side up, distribute the passengers evenly on both sides and have them hold on to the gunwales. Then have them slide aboard one at a time from opposite sides and sit on the floor over the keel. Anyone hurt or injured should be put aboard first. Check to be sure an injured person's life jacket will keep his head out of water in case he becomes unconscious. As soon as possible explain the method you plan to use in getting ashore. Under no circumstances should anyone leave the boat and attempt to swim ashore. This cannot be stressed too strongly. *Never leave the boat, regardless of how good a swimmer you are.*

If the boat is swamped but does not tip over, just hang on and sit on the floor over the keel line. A well-built boat full of water will support you and your passengers until help arrives, or you explain how to empty the water out. The only exception to this rule might be large inboard powerboats that occasionally sink because of their excessive engine weight. Should this happen and there is no "tender" (small boat) or inflatable life raft aboard, gather your passengers in a group and pair off the good swimmers with the injured or poor swimmers. Slowly start to swim toward shore, making sure everyone stays together. Usually you will be picked up within a short time. The main thing to remember is to stay together and don't panic. This procedure is only used if a boat has sunk. As long as the boat floats, stay with her. Search parties will spot a capsized craft much quicker than the heads of swimmers (Fig. 176).

11

Rescue and First Aid

Although boating holds an enviable safety record, accidents do happen and not, as we are prone to think, always to the other person or boat. Most of these mishaps are avoidable. Too often what starts out as a minor incident ends up as a disaster and tragedy—all because those aboard lacked the know-how to stabilize or correct the situation. This is why every boatman should learn and practice rescue procedures and first aid. Both these skills make you a better skipper and will, if the occasion arises, allow you the immeasurable satisfaction of saving a life.

The key to success in a rescue operation is the ability to act automatically, fast, and correctly. This is best done by having a plan of action with which to meet the more common emergencies, and practicing it until it becomes second nature to you and your crew. Following are the more common boating emergencies and the procedures used to overcome them.

MAN OVERBOARD

In all "man overboard" situations four things must be done automatically, fast, and correctly.

1. Alert the crew by yelling "Man overboard!" stating either the port or starboard side.

2. Swing the stern of the boat away from the person in the water so as to protect him from the propeller and rudder.

3. Throw him a lifesaving device, even if he is a strong swimmer. Normally a life ring is best because it can be thrown far and is easy to grab and hang on to. But when a ring is not handy, don't wait, throw a life jacket, buoyant seat cushion, or any other object that will keep a person afloat. Speed and accuracy are what count. Get the device out and as close to the person as possible without hitting him. Be sure it is not secured by a line that is fastened to the boat, otherwise if the person misses on his first grab the ring will be pulled out of reach as the boat moves on.

4. Keep the person in sight at all times. At night use the available lights on board to take and keep the fix.

Once these operations are done, quickly size up the situation and act according to existing conditions. If the water is calm, visibility good, and the person overboard a good swimmer wearing a life jacket, carry out a normal rescue operation. Circle, if need be, and approach from into the sea or downwind, whichever is the stronger. Slowly move up until the person is alongside, then pass or put a line around him and shut off the motor. Now, depending on the size boat and the condition of the person being rescued, lift him in over the side. On a small craft with a narrow beam take him in over the stern. Be careful to avoid the hot engine. When a fracture or severe injury is suspected, position the victim so he faces you, then lift him from under the armpits, straight up and over the side. Try not to bend his body as he comes in the boat.

If conditions are poor (choppy seas, frigid water, low visibility, etc.) or the person overboard is in poor physical shape, cannot swim, or is without a life jacket, common sense must dictate the rescue procedure. The main thing is to get him aboard as quickly as possible without injury or aggravating an existing injury. In rare emergencies you may even go over the side wearing a life jacket and tied to a lifeline to make the rescue.

Often when making rescue in heavy seas the biggest problem is keeping the person in view. One excellent way to assure this is by attaching a long mooring buoy wand with a high visibility pennant to a life ring (Fig. 177). Then, even when the person is out of sight, the pennant will still be visible. For nighttime sailing, a water light (light that goes on when in water) or a waterproof flashlight can supplement the pennant.

ASSISTING A DISABLED BOAT

Fortunately, most of the "rescues" made by pleasure boatmen consist of giving assistance in minor emergencies during fair weather on gentle seas. Standard procedure in such cases is to come alongside the disabled craft as if landing at a dock, put out a couple of fenders, and tie up. Once aid is given—usually some gasoline or a minor engine repair—cast off and move out as if leaving from dockside.

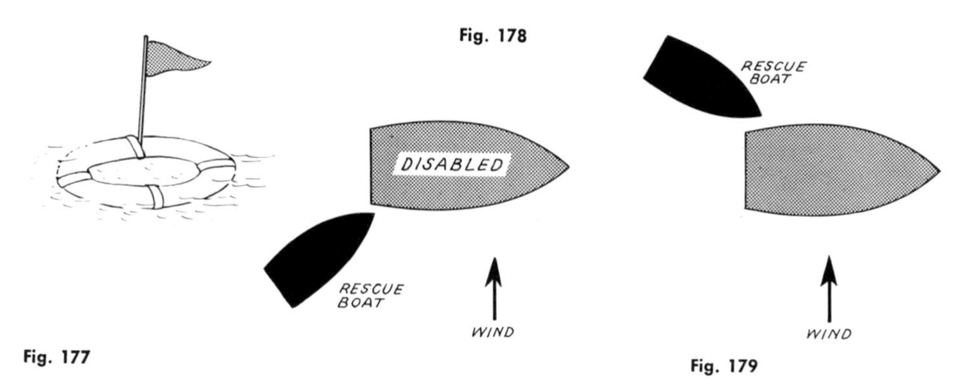

Fig. 177

Fig. 178

Fig. 179

If, however, the disabled craft is in serious trouble (fire, leaking, capsizing, etc.) or the sea is running, you must appraise the situation and act accordingly. Under no circumstances put your boat or crew in any serious danger. It will serve no purpose and could lead to your becoming disabled.

When the seas are swelling but not breaking, come alongside the disabled craft from her leeward side (downwind). The water will be calmer there, and unless the boat is much larger or has a higher freeboard than your craft, you will find it easier to transfer supplies or passengers. (This is the one time you might ignore your boat's passenger capacity rating and slightly overload. Be careful not to overload so much that you run the danger of capsizing or swamping. In cases where the disabled boat is larger or has a higher freeboard than your own, there is a constant danger that it will lift or heave up on a swell and come crashing down into the rescue craft. Avoid this by moving in from the weather side and angling your bow until it just lays off the disabled craft's stern (Fig. 178). Or, move in with your bow into the wind until your bow just lays off the disabled boat's stern (Fig. 179). In all of these positions a crewman will have to hold and fend off the disabled boat as it yaws and drifts. And under no circumstances should the rescue craft shut off its engine or tie up tight to a disabled boat in a running sea. Use a loose bow line if you wish, but be sure it can be quickly cast off.

FIRE

In a fire rescue there is always a danger that the rescue craft will also catch on fire, either by direct contact with the disabled boat, from an explosion, or by flaming gas or oil floating on the water. To safeguard against this always approach the boat on fire from upwind or upstream, whichever provides the stronger force. This direction prevents the disabled boat or any flaming water from drifting into your craft. And never attempt to board unless you are absolutely sure your craft is safe and your fire-fighting equipment is more than adequate for the job.

If the fire is out of control, stand off at a safe distance and throw or float one or more lifelines, attached to your craft, over to the passengers in the disabled boat. Have each one fasten a line around his chest and jump overboard. Once in the water pull them to the safety of your boat. Remember, as in any sea rescue, women and children first. When there is no flaming oil or gas on the water, make sure each one is wearing a life vest. But, if the water is aflame, have those who can swim remove their life jackets before jumping overboard, then swim underwater while being pulled toward your boat. Instruct non-swimmers, who will not know how to swim underwater, to take shallow breaths and splash the water away from their faces while being pulled to safety. This will keep the flames from their faces and prevent their lungs from getting scorched. Naturally, when the water around a disabled boat is on fire you will look for an open area or alley to pull the victims through.

All of the foregoing rescue procedures are predicated on gentle or non-breaking seas. Don't attempt any rescue that will take you alongside a disabled craft when the seas are violent with high breaking waves. Assistance under such conditions calls for expert boat handling and specially trained crews such as are found in the Coast Guard. Unfortunately, the average pleasure boatman just doesn't have either the equipment or the time to develop the skills needed for such rescues.

If, however, you still feel you must do something and you have your craft under control, use the lifeline method described in fire rescue. This assumes, of course, that the disabled craft is in serious danger of capsizing.

TOWING

Quite often a disabled boat cannot be repaired while afloat and must be towed to port. When both boats are about the same size and the seas are gentle, this is a relatively simple procedure. Come alongside the boat to be towed, and fasten a line (nylon preferably) on the stem eye or a bow cleat. Then coil out about four to six lengths of the line and fasten the other end to a bitt or cleat on your craft. Wherever possible secure the line on your craft as close to midship as possible (Fig. 180). Be sure the bitt or cleat is strong enough to hold. Tugboats are great exponents of this type of towing because it allows the pulling boat's stern to swing free while turning with a minimum of drag.

Once the line is fastened on both boats, start moving slowly ahead, paying out line as you go. When the line is all out, slowly increase engine r.p.m.'s until you reach a comfortable speed that is pulling easily without overtaxing the engine. Any sudden burst of speed at this point will put a shock strain on

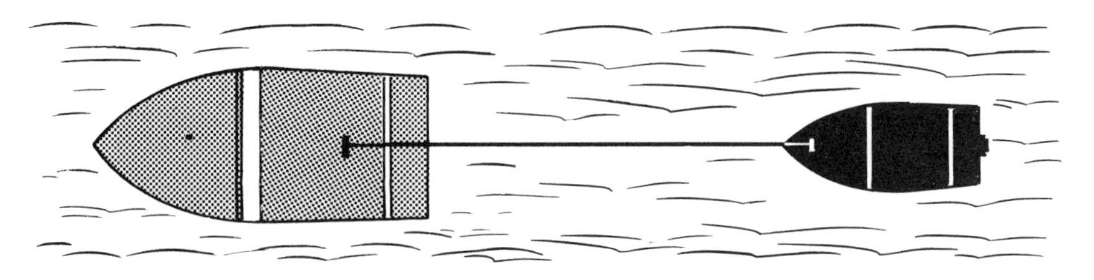

Fig. 180

the towline causing it to part or rip out a cleat or bitt. While pulling, always have someone at the towline in case it must be cast off or cut in a hurry.

In situations where the sea has a moderate swell it is a good idea to add another three or four boat lengths to the towline. And, as most moderate seas are uniform, adjust the position of both boats so they rise and fall together on swells. This prevents the disabled boat from dragging uphill while the towboat is moving downhill, or vice versa.

If, during the time you are towing, surface conditions should worsen, cast off the towline when you start to lose headway or the strain is too much for your boat. This again is another time when you must consider the safety of your own boat and crew. A smart skipper will cast off before the critical point, so he has time to pick up any passengers left on the disabled boat.

FIRST AID AFLOAT

Most boating accidents are run-of-the-mill cuts, scratches, bumps, and bruises that a dab of antiseptic and a little sympathy will cure. This is fortunate in that the nature of boating often takes you hours away from professional medical care. But it also gives you a greater responsibility toward your passengers and crew. This means you must, if the occasion arises, be prepared to handle any serious injury until a doctor takes over. The smartest way to do this is by taking a Red Cross first aid course designed specifically for boatmen. These courses have been developed by doctors and experienced boatmen to cover many areas not normally included in a regular first aid course.

Along with first aid training, which is paramount, you also need a good first aid book and first aid kit. The book should be in large easy-to-read print with a fast reference index so anyone can quickly find instructions for aid to an injury. The first aid kit, called a medicine chest aboard ship, should have standard basic items plus medications necessary to your locality. An example of the latter is a poison snakebite kit. In New England it would be useless, whereas in parts of the South where poisonous snakes are known to exist, it is standard equipment.

The supplies should be contained in a buoyant watertight metal or plastic box (if need be the box can be made buoyant by gluing or taping styrofoam strips to the sides), the kit should contain:
assorted Band-Aids,
two-, three-, and four-inch-square sterile gauze compresses,
individually packaged one-, two-, and three-inch-wide sealed rolled gauze bandages
one-half-inch and one-inch rolls of adhesive tape,
sterile absorbent cotton,
large triangular bandages,
tourniquet,
two mouth-to-mouth resuscitator tubes (one child and one adult),
sterile cotton-tipped applicators,
scissors with rounded ends,
tweezers, three-inch splinter forceps,
card of safety pins and needles (assorted sizes),
oral thermometer and case,
eye cup,
wire or thin-board splints,
tincture of Merthiolate,
salt tablets,
baking soda,
aromatic spirits of ammonia,
sterile mineral oil, tube of petroleum jelly,
insect repellent,
sunburn lotion,
calamine lotion,
seasick pills,
aspirin,
plus the items necessary to your locality.

The quantity of supplies is determined by the number of persons who will be aboard at any one time.

You may have noticed while reading the list of supplies that none require a doctor's prescription. The reason is self-explanatory. No matter how expert you become in first aid, the cardinal rule to remember is: you are only giving aid, not treatment. When a victim is hurt so badly that medical treatment is necessary, get him to a doctor as soon as possible. This in no way limits your usefulness; in fact, medical men all agree proper first aid is all-important. With this in mind, familiarize yourself with the following injuries that can happen afloat. When cruising away from home it is a good idea to find out the name, address, and phone number of two or more local doctors and a hospital. This information is available at all yacht clubs, boatyards, the Yellow Pages in a phone book, etc.

ARTIFICIAL RESPIRATION

The possibility of drowning is always present in aquatic sports. Therefore, anyone who uses the water as a playground should understand and be able to administer artificial respiration.

Cause: Drowning, choking, lightning, electric shock or any other incident that could cause victim to stop breathing.

Symptoms: Victim has stopped breathing and is unconscious.

First Aid: Start artificial respiration immediately, every second counts. The most efficient and practical method is the mouth-to-mouth resuscitation technique (blowing your breath into the victim's lungs). Anyone can use this method without help or equipment; even a child can save the life of an adult.

Fig. 181

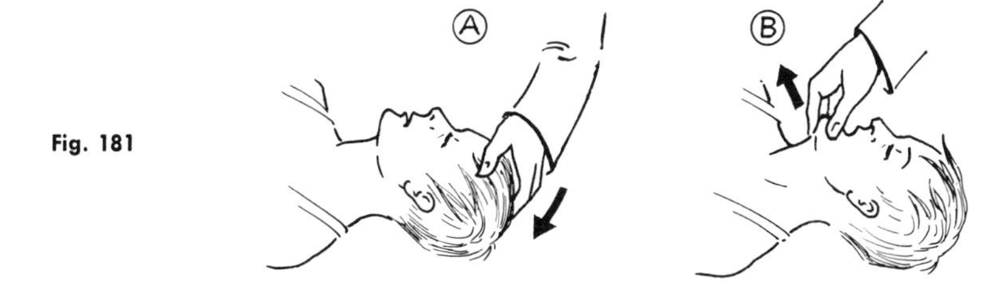

1. Tilt the victim's head back so the chin points upward (Fig. 181A).
2. Push or pull the jaw into a jutting-out position (Fig. 181B). This moves the base of the tongue away from the back of the throat, opening a clear air passage. If, during this step, any foreign matter (chewing gum, tobacco, partial plates, etc.) is visible in the victim's mouth, wipe it out quickly with your fingers or a cloth wrapped around your fingers.
3. Open your mouth wide, place it tightly over the victim's open mouth, pinch the victim's nostrils shut, and blow into the victim's mouth (Fig. 181C). In cases of external mouth injury it may be necessary to close the victim's

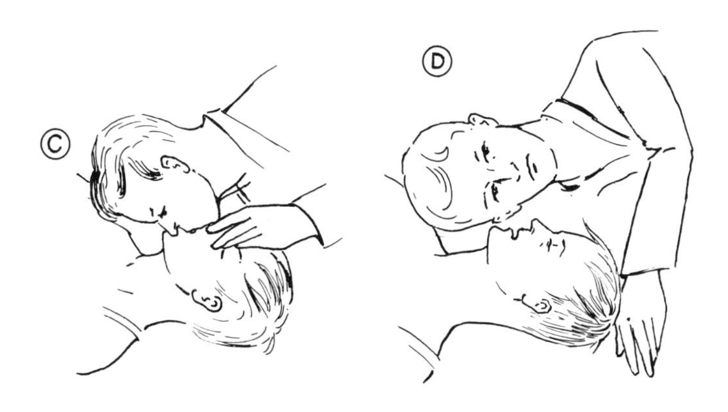

mouth and place your mouth over his nose. On small children put your mouth over both mouth and nose.

4. Remove your mouth and listen for the return outflow of air from victim's lungs (Fig. 181D). On adults repeat #3 and #4 at a rate of about twelve vigorous breaths per minute. On small children repeat at the rate of about twenty shallow breaths per minute.

If you do not get an air exchange (expansion of victim's chest and return outflow of air) after the first or second breath, recheck #1 and #2. If this doesn't start an air exchange, the chances are some foreign matter is lodged in the victim's throat. Turn him onto his side, give him several sharp blows between the shoulder blades, and again clean out his mouth. With small children, suspend them from their ankles or hold them head down over your knees and give several sharp *pats* between the shoulder blades.

Continue artificial respiration until the victim begins to breathe for himself or is pronounced dead by a physician. Although normal recovery is fairly rapid, it is not uncommon to work on a person for two or three hours. In fact, records show instances where a victim was revived after five hours. Frequently the patient stops breathing again after a temporary recovery. Therefore, he must be constantly watched, and should natural breathing stop, artificial respiration must be resumed. Once the victim is breathing normally treat him for shock.

To some people the idea of direct oral contact with an injured person is distasteful. To overcome this feeling, an inexpensive aid called a "resuscitation tube" has been developed (Fig. 182). One end is inserted over the victim's tongue while the other end projects and serves as a mouthpiece through which the rescuer can breath into the victim's mouth. These tubes come in adults' and children's sizes. Be sure to follow the instructions carefully or you could do more harm than good. In cases where a tube is not instantly available don't wait, begin direct mouth-to-mouth resuscitation. The few seconds

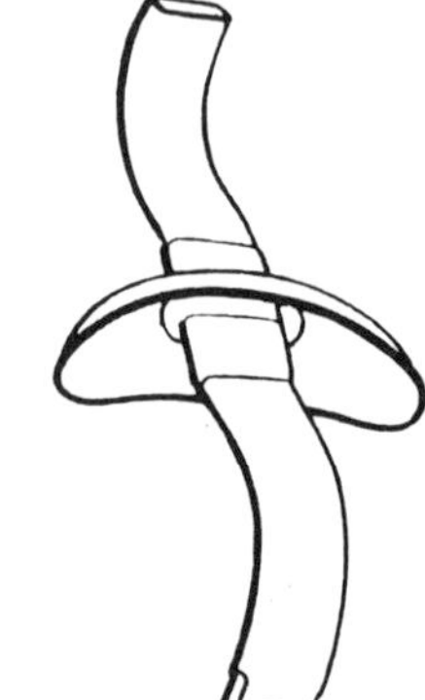

Fig. 182

you gain could save a life.

Boatmen who wish can learn two other methods of artificial respiration from their local Red Cross first aid instructor, the back-pressure arm-lift method and the Holger-Nielson method. Neither of these systems is as effective as mouth-to-mouth resuscitation but on rare occasions must suffice in cases of serious facial injury.

SHOCK

Every serious injury is accompanied by some degree of shock which, if not checked, can be fatal. So when a serious injury does occur, give shock first aid as soon as possible, even while giving artificial respiration or trying to stop bleeding, if possible. Do not wait for symptoms to appear.

Cause: A reaction from serious injuries, heart attacks, strokes, etc., which slows or stops the body's circulatory system.

Symptoms: Pale face, cold sweat, blue fingernails, shallow irregular breathing, rapid pulse, weakness, thirst, nausea, and vomiting. In severe cases, blood pressure will be extremely low.

First Aid: 1. Lay the patient flat with his head lower than his feet (except in head injuries, where the head should be elevated slightly).

2. Keep the patient warm. Cover him with blankets, coats, sweaters, etc., but do not overheat. The object is to prevent cooling by loss of body heat.

3. If the patient is conscious, not vomiting, and does not have an abdominal or head injury, give him a shock solution made from one or two salt tablets dissolved in one pint of water. Get him to drink all he can. When available, aromatic spirits of ammonia, a cup of strong tea, or coffee is also helpful as a stimulant. Under no circumstances give alcohol in any form.

SERIOUS BLEEDING

All serious bleeding must be stopped as quickly as possible if the victim is is to survive. When help is aboard and the victim has stopped breathing and is bleeding badly, have someone else work on the bleeding while you give artificial respiration, or vice versa. The seconds gained using this method will often save the victim's life.

Cause: Deep cuts, punctures, severed veins or arteries.

First Aid: 1. Remove any clothing from around the injured area so you can see the wound clearly.

2. Cover the wound with a sterile compress and, using your hand, apply a firm steady pressure directly over the injury until bleeding stops. Do not under any circumstances release the pressure to allow the blood to clean the wound. Loss of blood is more dangerous than the immediate risk of infection.

3. When bleeding has stopped, apply a pressure bandage just tight enough to prevent bleeding from starting again. Make the bandage from two or more sterile compresses, and hold it in place with bandage gauze. If the edges dig into the flesh, or the wound starts to swell, the bandage is binding and must be loosened. On the other hand, if blood starts oozing into the compress, the bandage is too loose. Tighten by wrapping with more bandage gauze. Once bleeding has stopped, treat for shock if it has not already been done. On arm or leg wounds where there is no sign of a fracture, elevate the limb so it is above the level of the body.

If for some reason sterile compresses are not handy, use any clean material, such as folded handkerchiefs, fresh towels, or strips from sheets. In fact, when necessary, use soiled materials or even your bare hand if nothing clean is available. Here again, stopping the flow of blood supersedes the immediate risk of infection.

Pressure Points

When bleeding still continues after a compress bandage and pressure are placed over a wound, press the heel of your hand or a finger at a point above the wound where a blood vessel passes across a bone. Such areas are called pressure points and will, when pressed on, stop the flow of blood in a way similar to that of clamping off rubber hose. Figure 183 shows where these

Fig. 183

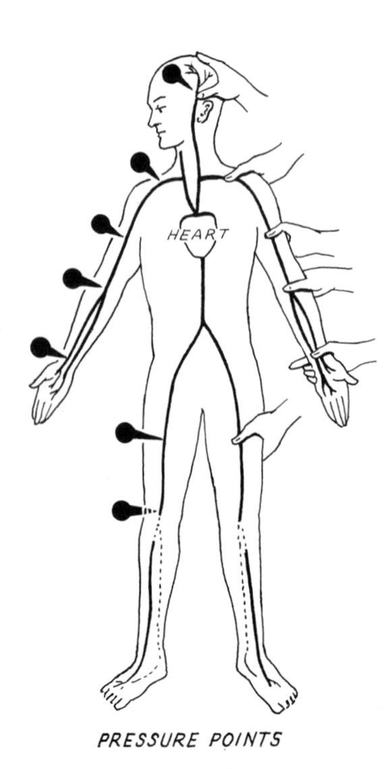

PRESSURE POINTS

points are on the human body. Be sure that a compress bandage won't stop the bleeding. Like tourniquets, pressure points can do more harm than good if not used properly.

Tourniquet

A tourniquet is a dangerous instrument in the hands of the untrained and should only be used where there is a partial or complete amputation of a body part. When used to stop the bleeding of any other type of wound, a tourniquet halts all the flow of blood below it and can, if left on too long, cause gangrene in the lower blood-starved tissues. Therefore, never use a tourniquet unless absolutely necessary. And when it is necessary, tie it as close above the wound as possible, making sure there is no broken skin above the tie. This saves the maximum amount of limb if amputation becomes necessary, by keeping the amount of tissue open to gangrene to a minimum.

Tie a tourniquet with any band of limp material one to two inches wide and long enough to go twice around the cut limb with ends left over for tying. Belts, scarfs, strips of sheets or clothing all make good bands when a regular tourniquet is not readily available. Do not use fish line, string, wire or any material that can cut into the flesh, except in dire emergency. Apply a tourniquet in the following manner:

1. Wrap the band loosely twice around the limb and tie with a half knot. Then place a small stick or dowel over the knot (Fig. 184A).
2. Tie another knot over the stick (Fig. 184B).
3. Twist the stick so that the band tightens down on the limb until the bleeding just stops (Fig. 184C). Do not tighten more than necessary; it serves no purpose and can bruise the tissues.
4. When bleeding has stopped, tie the free end of stick with another band (Fig. 184D).

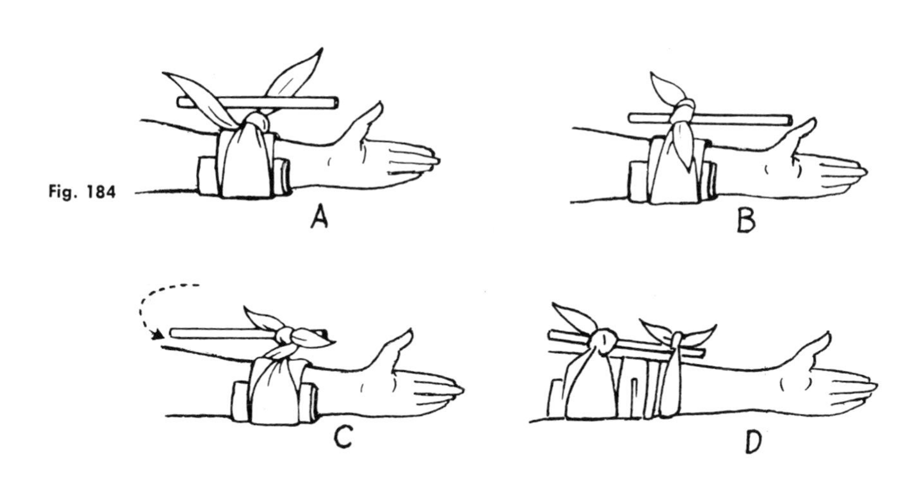

Fig. 184

Once the tourniquet is in place and bleeding has stopped, do not loosen it or a fatal blood loss may result.

If there is any chance you will be separated from the patient before a doctor arrives, mark the letters "TK" on his forehead and note the time you applied the tourniquet. Use iodine, Merthiolate, lipstick, etc., as a marking device.

INTERNAL BLEEDING

After any severe bump, blow, or crushing injury to the chest, abdomen, or torso, suspect internal bleeding, even though there may be no immediate outward sign of blood loss.

Symptoms: General Signs: restlessness, weakness, pallor, anxiety, constant thirst, and rapid weak pulse.

Significant Signs: Chest injury—coughing up red frothy blood. Stomach injury—vomiting blood shortly after an injury followed by material that looks like large dark coffee grounds a few hours later. Upper intestines—stools that contain black clumps (partially digested blood). Lower intestines—stools with bright red blood.

First Aid: When internal bleeding is suspected, keep the patient warm, quiet, and lying down. If he vomits or starts coughing, turn his head to the side so as to keep his breathing passages open. In lung injuries the patient may not be able to breath lying flat and will have to be propped up until he can breathe. Do not give liquids to internal bleeding patients.

MINOR CUTS, SCRATCHES AND ABRASIONS

Most boating injuries are the common everyday cuts, scratches, skinned knees or elbows. Wash the injured part well with clean water and soap. (Drinking water is safe). Rinse under tap or water poured from a pitcher. Coat with an antiseptic (Tincture of Merthiolate) and cover with gauze bandage or Band-Aid. In cases where the cut or scrape is from a rusty nail, or around an old dock, check with your doctor when you get home regarding a tetanus shot.

SPRAINS AND STRAINS

Sprains and strains are among the more common boating accidents for weekend sailors who try to cram a week's exercise into two days.

Cause: Tearing of ligaments that hold bones together at joints and pulled muscle tendons. It is often hard to distinguish between a sprain and a broken bone. When in doubt treat as a fracture.

Symptoms: Intense pain when injured part is moved, rapid swelling, tender to the touch, discoloration (black and blue) after several hours.

First Aid: 1. Relieve pain by resting injured joint.

2. Apply cold compresses for two or three hours after accident. Do not apply any heat for at least thirty-six hours or on doctor's orders. Cold tends to contract blood vessels minimizing swelling, whereas heat speeds up the flow of blood, encouraging swelling.

3. When ashore check with a doctor about having an X-ray taken for a bone break.

When an ankle is sprained and you must walk to get help, keep on your shoe or sneaker, loosen the laces, and wrap the bandage firmly but not so tight as to stop the circulation (Fig. 185).

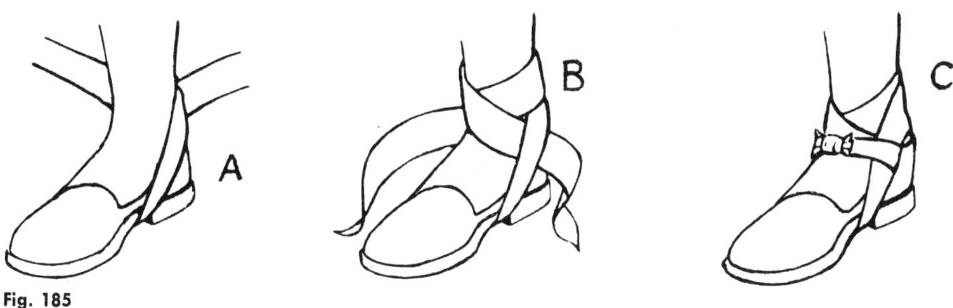

Fig. 185

A — Place middle of bandage below shoe in front of heel
B — Cross ends at back of heel and in front of above instep
C — Loop ends under rear of bandage; tie over instep

BROKEN BONES

Bone breaks fall into two categories, simple fractures, where the broken bone remains hidden under unbroken skin, and compound fractures, where the bone protrudes through the skin.

Cause: Falls, bumps, or blows

Symptoms: Simple fracture: 1. Suspect a simple fracture if the victim cannot move the injured part and is in intense pain when he does try to move it.

2. The injured part has an odd shape or looks deformed.

3. Swelling starts almost immediately and often there is no feeling below the fracture.

Compound fractures: The broken bone protrudes through the skin and usually there is serious bleeding.

First Aid for Both Simple and Compound Fractures: Do not move the patient except under extreme emergencies, such as to give artificial respiration, stop serious bleeding, or remove from danger. If none of these situations exists, the fracture in itself is not an emergency that calls for great speed in treatment. Just keep the patient warm and quiet until you get ashore and help arrives. Under no circumstances try to splint a fracture unless you have been trained in splint first aid, and never attempt to set a fracture.

SUNBURN

Sunburn is one of the few "accidents" skippers can prevent by using a little common sense. Do not allow any passenger or crewman to overexpose, and when they are "sunbathing," make sure they use a tanning lotion or cream.

Cause: Overexposure of bare skin to sun.

Symptoms: Mild sunburn will turn skin a pinkish hue and be sore to the touch.

Severe sunburn will turn skin a deep pink, be extremely painful to the touch, and blisters will form on burned area after a few hours.

First Aid: In mild sunburn cases, coat the burned area with a homemade burn remedy, such as wet baking soda paste, or one of the many commercial antipain burn ointments now on the market.

In severe sunburn cases, keep the patient quiet and have him rest. Spray the burned area with a commercial antipain burn medication that comes in a throwaway spray can. Do not rub a burn ointment on a severely burned area. Along with being painful, the rubbing will also break some blisters, increasing the chance of infection. Watch the patient for shock and, if his temperature goes over 102 degrees, call a doctor.

SUNSTROKE

Sunstroke, also called heatstroke, can be fatal if first aid measures are not started immediately. Like severe sunburn, which often accompanies sunstroke, prevention is a simple matter of wearing a hat and not overexposing your body while in the sun.

Cause: Overexposure of sun, especially on bare head.

Symptoms: 1. Rapid breathing, dizziness, mental confusion, weakness, panting, followed by unconsciousness.

2. Extremely high body temperature; 106 or 107 degrees is not uncommon.

3. Skin very hot to the touch and absolutely dry, no sweating anywhere.

First Aid: 1. Move victim out of the sun or erect a sunshade over him.

2. Cool him as rapidly as possible by drenching with cold water and applying cold cloths to his head (use ice when it is aboard). If there is a sheet on board, take off the victim's outer clothing and wrap him in the sheet. Keep the sheet cold and wet.

4. Rub his arms and legs, through the sheet, toward the heart.

5. Check body temperature every eight or ten minutes, preferably by thermometer, or by feeling his skin if a thermometer is not available.

Keep cloths, sheets, or clothes wet and cold until temperature drops to 101 or 102 degrees. If temperature rises again, repeat cooling procedure. Get victim to a doctor.

SEASICKNESS

Although seasickness is not a serious malady, it can ruin a trip afloat. This fact and the knowledge that anyone, including "old salts," can end up at the lee rail on a given day, make carrying a motion sickness remedy a must. Although these cures are not always 100 per cent effective, they do help in most cases. Bonine and Dramamine are two of the more popular commercial remedies. And when using them be sure to follow the directions. For a prescription type of remedy, see your doctor.

Cause: Rolling and pitching motion of the boat.

Symptoms: Pale face, dizziness, nausea, vomiting.

First Aid: 1. Keep patient out in fresh air and, when possible, in the shade.

2. Place him as close as possible amidship, over the keel. Here the rocking and rolling are at a minimum.

3. Try to get him to sip Coca Cola or strong tea. This will sometimes settle a stomach.

4. If the seasickness is only mild, try to keep the patient busy. This will sometimes take his mind off the motion of the boat and the queasiness of his stomach.

5. In severe cases, get the patient ashore as quickly as possible.

For some reason seasickness has become the butt of many jokes and has given some skippers the idea that a seasick passenger should be kidded out of his misery. Don't become one of those skippers; seasickness is very real to the ill person and should be treated as any other semiserious emergency.

FISHHOOKS IN THE FLESH

Chances are if a survey was made, it would show that fishhooks have caught more humans than fish. So boatmen who are also fishermen should know what to do when a hook gets caught in a part of the body.

First Aid: When the hook is imbedded in a critical area, such as the face, eye, or against a bone, do not attempt to remove it. Keep the patient from touching or picking at it and get him to a doctor as soon as possible.

When the hook is in a noncritical fleshy area, remove it as follows:

1. Push, *not pull,* on the shank end of the hook until the barbed end pushes

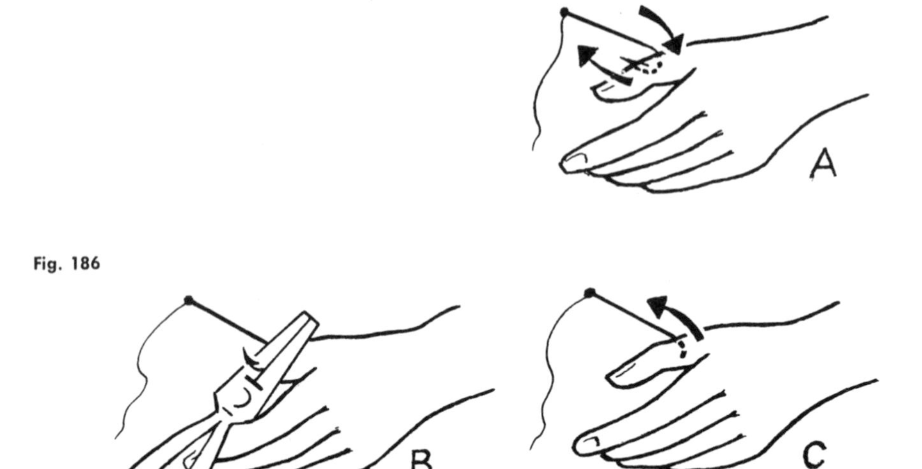

Fig. 186

through the skin (Fig. 186A).
2. Clip off the barb with a pair of cutting pliers (Fig. 186B).
3. Remove the shank by pulling back through the original entry (Fig. 186C).
4. After the hook has been removed, squeeze the wound for a minute or two to encourage bleeding (this washes the wound internally), then wash the wound with soap and water.

When ashore check with a doctor for a tetanus shot.

EYES

First aid for eye injuries must, because of the delicate nature of the eye, be limited to chemical burns which require immediate attention to prevent blindness and to simple eye cleaning (specks of dirt, eyelashes, cinders, etc.). All other injuries, such as foreign bodies imbedded in the eye, contusions of the eyeball, or eye wounds, need professional medical care as quickly as possible. Cover the eye with a sterile gauze compress to keep the patient from picking or feeling the injury, and get him to a doctor.

Chemical Eye Burns

Cause: Any acid or alkaline chemicals (powder or liquid) that get splashed or spilled into the eye(s).

Symptoms: Victim will be in extreme pain and will usually be holding hands over eyes stating, "I'm blind," or "My eyes! My eyes!"

First Aid: Once you know it is a chemical burn, immediately start flushing out the eye(s) with large amounts of cool water.

Don't waste time finding out whether the chemical is an acid or alkali. For the purpose of first aid it makes no difference. Keep flushing the eyes with water for at least ten minutes or until you are sure every trace of chemical is removed. One of the better flushing methods is: lay the patient on his back and pour water from a clean container into the corner of the eye (next to the nose) so that the water streams over the eyeball, under the eyelids, and down away from the other eye. This method gives massive, thorough, continuous irrigation and keeps the chemical from being washed into the other eye. Remember to keep flushing if you hope to prevent blindness. Your action in the first few seconds and minutes is more important than what the doctor will do later.

Eye Cleaning

Cause: Specks of dirt, eyelashes, cinders, etc., in the eye.

First Aid: When the specks of dirt or other foreign bodies lie loosely on the eyelid, remove them in one of the following ways:

1. Pull the upper eyelid out and down over the lower lid (Fig. 187A). This starts tears flowing and will usually wash out the particle.

2. Fill a medicine dropper or eye cup with warm water or a mild boric acid solution and "flood" the eye to wash out foreign matter (Fig. 187B).

3. If speck is visible, after pulling lower eyelid gently out for inspection, remove it with a moistened cotton applicator on the corner of a clean handkerchief (Fig. 187C).

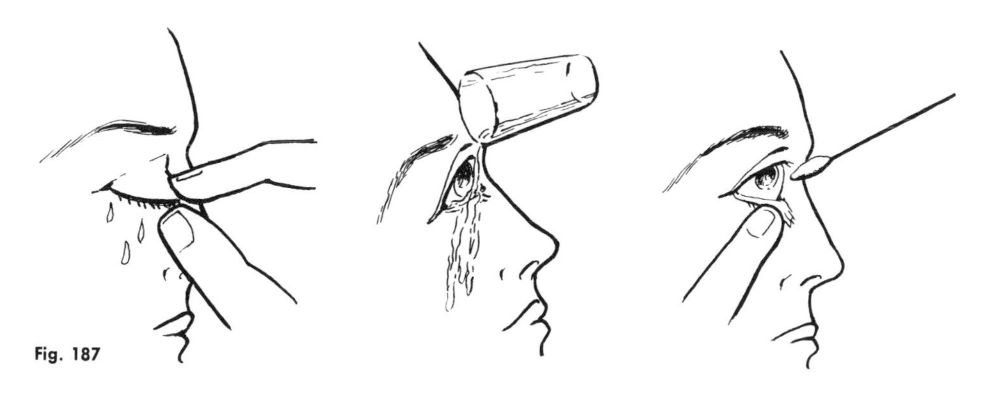

Fig. 187

Do not attempt to remove any particles that are imbedded in the eyeball or eyelids. In such cases cover the eye with a sterile gauze compress and get the patient to a doctor.

INSECT BITES

Boatmen in every part of the country must, to varying degrees, put up with biting or stinging insects. Smart skippers plan for this by carrying plenty of insect repellent and by screening all doors and windows on their boats. These preventive measures make boating much more enjoyable and keep the bites to a minimum.

First Aid: For insect bites that become itchy, apply some calamine lotion or rubbing alcohol to bitten area. This will usually stop the itching. Do not scratch the bite for fear of infection.

For stings, hold the stung part underwater for a few minutes, then cover it with a dressing of wet baking soda paste. This usually gives the best relief from the pain.

The stinger, when left in the skin, will look like a tiny dark speck in the center of the sting. Remove it by scraping outward with a clean fingernail or nail file. Do not pinch the stinger with a pair of tweezers, as this will only force into the skin any venom left in the stinger, causing more pain.

Watch a sting victim for shock. Although stings are not usually serious, some people are so sensitive to insect venom that they go into shock and must be treated by a doctor.

After studying how to care for some of the injuries with which boatmen are confronted, it is hoped you will agree on the importance of first aid training. The foregoing information is not intended to be a substitute for such training, but rather a reference guide for the more common boating injuries.

12

Anchoring, Mooring, Tying-Up

The right anchor, ample anchor line (called a rode), and the knowledge of how to use them correctly are the best and cheapest insurance you can buy to protect your boat. Along with being a parking brake during short stops to eat, fish, swim, etc., an anchor also serves as an emergency brake when your boat is left afloat unattended. And during storms or breakdowns, it can be the difference between safety or tragedy. Experienced skippers learn this early in their seamanship training and equip their craft with two or more anchors, a working anchor for short stops and a storm anchor for emergency use. Two anchors also give added protection in case one is lost through fouling or a broken rode. This seemingly overprotection is quickly justified when you consider that the price of both anchors and rodes rarely exceeds 1 per cent of a boat's cost. With this in mind, and the knowledge that anchors often protect lives as well as boats, choose your ground tackle (anchors and rodes) with care. Make sure the anchors match your boat as to type and size, will hold firmly in the bottom you anchor over, and the rodes are large and long enough to do their job properly.

TYPES OF ANCHORS

Anchors can be classified in three groups: the modern patent designs, the old traditional types, and mooring anchors. In general, small craft skippers prefer the modern patent designs because they are light in weight and fold

Fig. 188

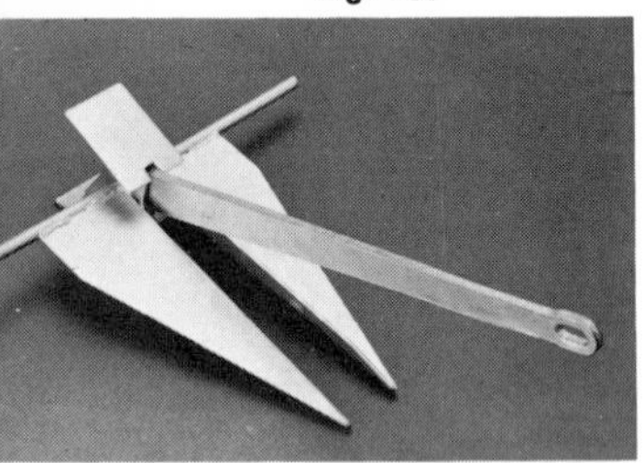

Danforth Standard

Danforth Hi-Tensil

Northill Utility

compactly. This makes for ease in handling, even by women or older children, and limits the area needed for storage. Storage space is usually a critical factor on small boats. The most popular patent types are the Danforths and Northill Utility (Fig. 188). Both designs have proven their worth under the worst conditions and on a variety of bottoms. Although they differ radically in design, each utilizes broad flukes that quickly dig in and set. This is especially helpful when dropping a hook in a crowded anchorage, fast current, or tide rip. The only faults to be found with either are: the Danforths occasionally get a stone or shell caught between their flukes and the shank, which prevents them from digging in at the proper angle; and the Northill Utility will sometimes foul a rode on an exposed fluke and pull out. None of these faults is major, and they should not deter you from selecting either anchor. It only proves that even the best ground tackle needs watching. Another patent type that has found wide acceptance in the British Isles but as yet not in this country is the C.Q.R. plow anchor (Fig. 189A). Although I have not personally used this "hook," comparison tests rate it favorably with the Danforths and Northill Utility. From the illustration its major fault would seem to be storage.

In the second group, the old traditional type anchors, only the yachtsman kedge or a modified version (Fig. 189B) can be considered a small craft anchor, even then only on the larger class boats. Its one claim to fame, because of its weight, is an uncanny ability to hold on ledge and rocky bottoms. Large cruising boats often carry a yachtsman just for this purpose. Otherwise its faults are many. It is heavier and larger than comparable modern patent types (the weight to holding ratio can run as high at 10 to 1), making it awkward to handle and bulky to store. And like all anchors that leave one fluke exposed, it will on occasion foul a rode on the exposed fluke (Fig. 190). So unless your boating area demands a yachtsman kedge, stick to the lighter compact modern patent types.

Another traditional anchor I feel needs mentioning, just so you will not be stuck with one by an overzealous salesman, is the stockless navy kedge (Fig. 189C). This backbreaker has an even higher weight to holding ratio than the yachtsman. At best it is a fair to middling mud anchor, but it does not compare with the modern patent types.

The last group, mooring anchors, consists of the mushroom designs (Fig. 189D) and large blocks of granite or metal. These are not anchors in the accepted sense because they are not carried aboard, but are left permanently or for the season buried in the bottom. Their primary purpose is to act as a mooring bit at a home anchorage where you can safely leave a boat unattended over long periods of time. The exception to the above statement is the accepted practice of using lightweight mushroom anchors (fifteen pounds or less) as "lunch hooks" aboard canoes and boats under sixteen feet, the object being to hold a small boat temporarily while you are still aboard. Under no circum-

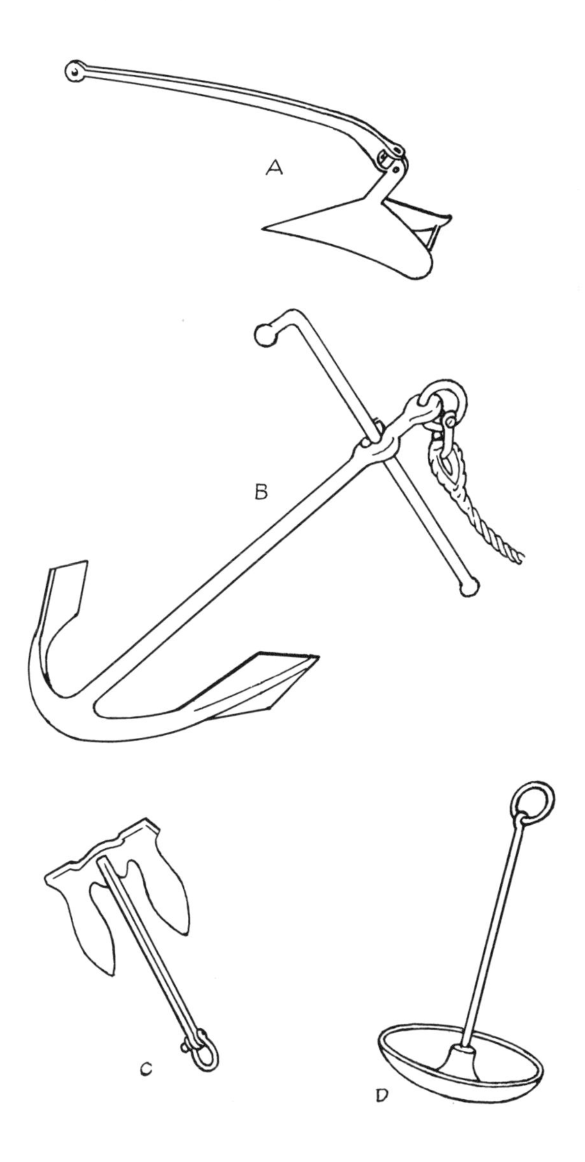

Fig. 189

Fig. 190

stances should a lightweight mushroom anchor ever be used to hold an unattended boat. Selection and setting of mooring anchors are fully covered under the heading "A Permanent Mooring," on page 218.

SELECTING AND MATCHING ANCHORS

When selecting your anchor(s) decide first on the type, then match it to your boat. If your boating will be limited to local waters, choose the anchor most popular in the area. This information is easily obtained by asking experienced boatmen or any reliable marine dealer. On the other hand, if you plan on trailering or cruising to distant waterways, information on anchors for those areas may not be available locally. In such cases, study the charts for those waters. They will show the general bottom make-up plus the ground conditions at different established anchorages. If there is some doubt as to where you will be boating, the following rule of thumb is a good guide when choosing anchors. The modern patent type designs are used successfully on all but rock or ledge bottoms. Here the heavier yachtsman kedge gets the nod. An excellent compromise on boats over twenty-five feet is to carry two patent types and a yachtsman. This equips you for any bottom and in an emergency the extra patent "hook" gives you added holding power. I have used this system for years, and through experience, one hurricane and numerous blows, have found it an excellent method. On boats twenty-six feet and under, two patent type anchors are normally adequate.

When matching anchors to your boat use the "recommended anchor size" tables put out by the anchor manufacturer as a guide. These tables, available at all marine dealers, give an idea of the length boat each size (weight) anchor will hold in fair to average ground on semiexposed waters. Unless stated otherwise, consider the test boats in all anchor tables as motorboats of average construction. When using these tables keep in mind that the type of boat and conditions are constant. A change could mean a larger size anchor. Using the table (Fig. 191), which has been compiled from tables of the anchors discussed in this chapter, you will see how this can happen. Let's assume you own a light sixteen-foot outboard runabout; the bottom conditions (exposed or protected waters, current, tides, etc.) are well protected with no currents or tides. Under such conditions you would simply look at the table and check the size anchors recommended for a sixteen-foot boat. In a Northill Utility the working anchor would be a 3R and the storm anchor (always a size larger) a 6R. In a Danforth standard the working anchor would be a 8-s and the storm a 13-s. Now let's assume, instead of owning a light runabout, your boat is a thirty-foot heavy-built inboard motorboat or a thirty-foot heavy-keeled, high-masted sailboat. In this case one of the conditions has changed, the boat is heavier than the table boat. So you would go to the next larger size anchors, a 6R and 20R in the Northill Utility and a 13-s and 22-s in the Danforth standard. The same would hold true if either or both of the other conditions (ground or surface) rated below the tables. On rare occasions when all three conditions are below standard, some skippers jump two sizes in their storm anchors. Probably the best rule to guide one is the fact that no boat has ever been lost because she carried too large a "hook." So when in doubt, play safe and go to the next larger size.

Fig. 191 **Suggested Anchor Sizes**

Boats Length in Feet		0–16	16–24	25–32	33–38	39–44	45–54	55–70
Danforth Hi-Tensil	working	—	5-H	12-H	12-H	20-H	35-H	60-H
	storm	—	12-H	20-H	20-H	35-H	60-H	90-H
Danforth Standard	working	4-S	8-S	13-S	22-S	40-S	65-S	85-S
	storm	8-S	13-S	22-S	40-S	65-S	85-S	130-S
Northill Utility	working	1-F	3-R	6-R	6-R	6-R	12-R	12-R
	storm	3-R	6-R	20-R	20-R	20-R	30-R	30-R
Yachtsman Kedge	working	20 lbs.	25 lbs.	35 lbs.	45 lbs.	65 lbs.	75 lbs.	—
	storm	25 lbs.	35 lbs.	45 lbs.	75 lbs.	100 lbs.	100 lbs.	—

NOTE: The above suggested anchor sizes are for fair holding ground. In areas with poor bottoms and or exposure to high winds the next larger size may be indicated. Check with local experienced boatmen.

ANCHOR RODES

Anchor rodes (a rode is the rope or chain for an anchor) are selected in much the same way as anchors. First, decide on the type (material), then match it in length and strength to your boat. On small boats where ground tackle is usually worked manually, nylon rope is the favorite rode material. Aboard large craft, equipped with chain lockers and anchor winches, BBB chain is usually

Fig. 192

the choice. And on crusty bottoms that could cut or fray a line, a short piece of BBB chain is often used between the rope and anchor (Fig. 192). Under no circumstances use manila rope for a rode. Although manila was once the mainstay of small craft tackle, it is now obsolete. Nylon in the same size is two and a half times as strong, has up to eight times the elasticity to absorb shocks, will outwear manila three or four to one, and sells in the same price range. A

Fig. 193

Size-Weight and Approximate Breaking Strength of Ropes and BBB Chain

Diameter in Inches	(1) Nylon Weight (lbs.) per 100 feet	(2) Pounds Breaking Strength	(1) Weight per 100′	Dacron (2) P.B.S.	Polyethylene (1) w/100	Polyethylene (2) P.B.S.	Manila (1) w/100	Manila (2) P.B.S.	BBB Chain (2) P.B.S.
1/4″	1.7	1,800	2.2	1,250	1.3	1200	1.9	650	2700
5/16″	2.6	2,800	3.4	1,850	1.9	1750	3.2	1150	3700
3/8″	3.8	4,000	4.5	2,600	3.0	2500	4.0	1550	4600
7/16″	5.4	5,500	6.1	3,500	4.0	3400	5.1	1900	6200
1/2″	7.1	7,100	7.6	4,500	5.0	4100	6.5	2900	8200
9/16″	8.3	8,300	9.8	5,600	6.0	4800	8.5	3800	10200
5/8″	10.5	10,500	12.4	7,100	8.1	5700	11.2	4800	12500
3/4″	15.0	14,200	19.3	9,800	11.5	7800	13.8	5900	17700
7/8″	20.5	19,000			16.2	11000	20.8	8400	24000
1″	27.0	24,600			19.6	13300	25.2	9900	31000

*w/100 = weight (lbs.) per 100 feet
P.B.S. = Pounds Breaking Strength

Fig. 194

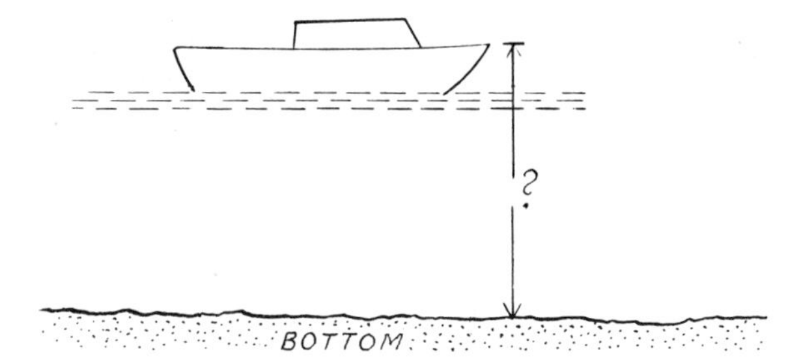

look at the table (Fig. 193) shows the weight per 100 feet and breaking strength of various sizes of nylon, BBB chain, and manila.

Although there are no hard and fast rules governing the length and strength necessary in a rode, the following have proven to be excellent guidelines. All rodes should be strong enough to lift the boat they will hold. The minimum length should equal ten times the distance from the bow chock to the bottom (Fig. 194). On tidal waters, figure this distance at high tide. The reason and purpose of this length formula, called the scope, are fully explained in "The Art of Anchoring" (page 206).

For boatmen who sail many waterways, the following table (Fig. 195) gives a suggested rode length and size for different-sized boats. When using this table, keep in mind that for an extra large or heavy boat, or poor surface con-

Fig. 195

Suggested Rode Size and Lengths

Over-all Boat Length	Anchor Used	Power Boats Nylon size/length		Power Boats Manila size/length		Sailing Boats Nylon size/length		Sailing Boats Manila size/length	
0′–12′	work	3/8	75′	3/8	75′	3/8	75′	3/8	75′
	storm	3/8	100′	3/8	100′	3/8	100′	3/8	100′
12′–20′	work	3/8	100′	1/2	100′	1/2	100′	9/16	100′
	storm	1/2	150′	3/8	150′	9/16	150′	5/8	150′
20′–25′	work	1/2	100′	1/2	100′	1/2	125′	5/8	125′
	storm	9/16	160′	5/8	160′	9/16	200′	3/4	200′
25′–30′	work	9/16	100′	5/8	100′	9/16	125′	3/4	125′
	storm	5/8	180′	3/4	180′	3/4	250′	3/4	250′
30′–40′	work	5/8	125′	3/4	125′	3/4	150′	1	150′
	storm	3/4	200′	1	200′	7/8	250′	1-1/8	250′
40′–50′	work	3/4	150′	1	150′	7/8	200′	1-1/4	200′
	storm	1	250′	1-1/8	250′	1-1/8	300′	1-1/2	300′
50′–65′	work	7/8	180′	1-1/4	180′	1	250′	1-3/8	200′
	storm	1-1/8	300′	1-1/2	300′	1-1/8	350′	1-5/8	300′

Fig. 196

ditions, the next size rode plus a 15 per cent increase in length is in order.

Another important point to remember is: keep your rode in one continuous piece. Two lines tied together lose 40 to 50 per cent of their strength at the knot. Splices only lose 10 to 15 per cent. So when securing a nylon rode to its anchor, the best method is to work an eye splice tightly around a thimble. Be sure it is tight; otherwise the nylon will stretch, enlarging the eye, and cause the thimble to fall out. Then use a galvanized shackle with a breaking strength greater than the rode to join the anchor and eye (Fig. 196). A good practice when attaching the shackle is to wire the pin locked as shown in Figure 196. Also use a little graphite grease on the threads to prevent rusting. BBB chain should always be attached to an anchor with a shackle. When a knot is used to secure the rode and anchor, an anchor bend or anchor bowline will do the best job (see Fig. 14 in Chapter 3).

THE ART OF ANCHORING

The use of ground tackle is a necessary part of every boatman's basic seamanship training. It does not matter whether you will use an anchor every day or just a few times a season. The peace of mind and self-satisfaction of knowing how will make your time afloat more enjoyable. And, when the time comes, as it always does, that you must ride out a blow or other emergency, the skills learned from a few hours' study and practice will become the means of saving your boat and passengers.

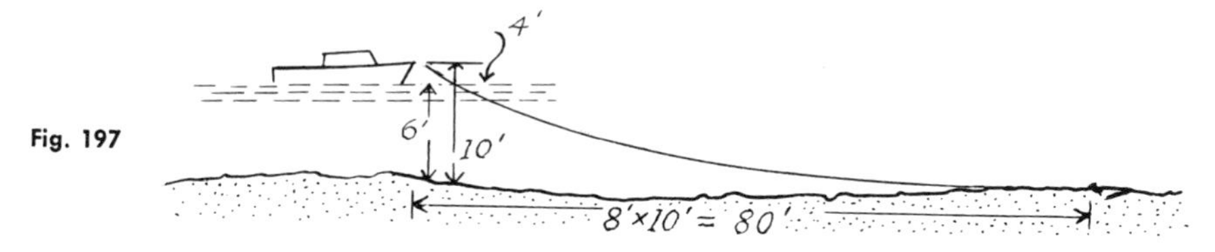

Fig. 197

Scope

Scope, the length of rode from the bow chock to anchor, is the key to using ground tackle. The amount of scope necessary in a given anchoring situation depends on the depth of the water, holding ground, and surface conditions. Under average conditions an anchor holds best with a scope of eight times the distance from the bow chock to the bottom. This means if you were anchored in six feet of water and the height from the surface to bow chock was four feet, your rode should be eight times ten feet, or eighty feet long (Fig. 197). On tidal waters remember to compute water depth for high tide. Otherwise a tide of five feet could, as in the previous example, cut your scope ratio almost in half. In all probability this would increase the angle of the rode to such a degree that the anchor would break out. The eight to one formula is based on the use of nylon or manila for a rode. When BBB chain is used the scope can usually be reduced to five or six to one safely.

Naturally all anchor situations are not made under average conditions. As skipper, you must decide whether a shorter or longer scope is necessary. Here again is where experience plus knowing your boat and equipment comes to the fore. No doubt there will be times (lunch, fishing, etc.) when you will drop anchor for short stops and remain aboard. During these breaks, if conditions are favorable, a scope of four to one may be more than adequate, thus saving you the job of handling unneeded rode. If before getting under way the anchor should break out and start dragging, the fact you are aboard and *awake* insures against any damage being done. Just pay out a bit more rode until the anchor resets. Note the word *awake* is underlined. Catnaps and siestas leave a boat unattended, which automatically puts it in an eight to one scope ratio.

At other times, during storms, expected blows, or poor conditions, a scope of ten to one or twelve to one may be in order. This added length serves two purposes: decreases the angle of the rode so the anchor can lie more parallel to the bottom, its best digging and setting position; and the added weight causes the catenary (sag) along the rode to become more pronounced (Fig. 198). This sag is the shock absorber between boat and anchor. Without it the

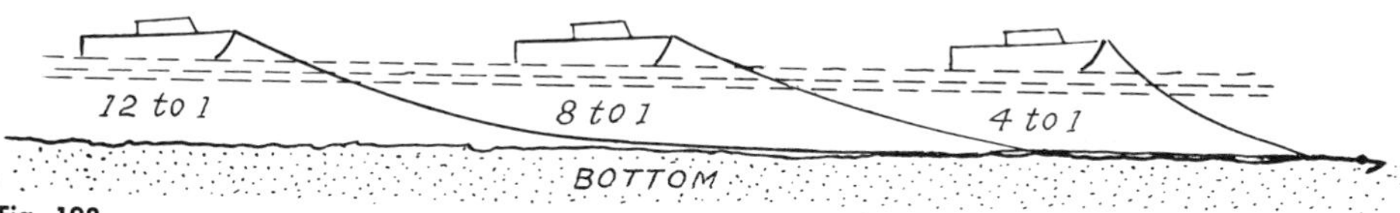

Fig. 198

Fig. 199

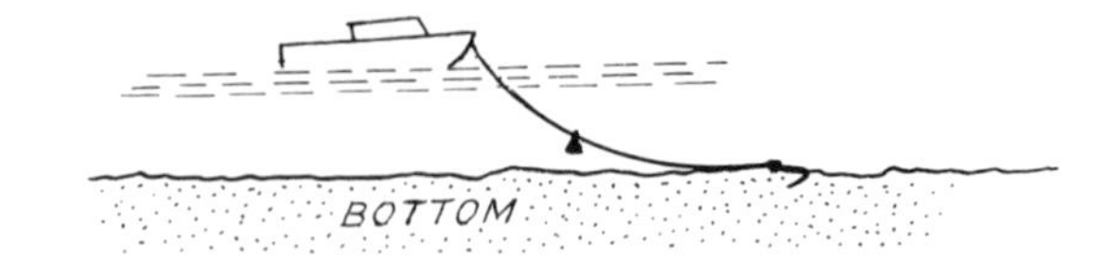

sudden strains from a boat pitching and bucking in choppy or rising seas would travel along a taut rode and quickly break out the anchor. Numerous ways are used to increase the catenary. The two most popular are a short heavy piece of BBB chain placed between the anchor and rode, as shown in Fig. 192, and a back-up anchor, called a kellet. The back-up anchor is a small weight with an attached ring or snap hook large enough to slide loosely on the rode. When added catenary is wanted the kellet is clipped to the rode and allowed to slide halfway down, controlled by a light line, as shown in (Fig. 199). Although both methods work well, I prefer the kellet because of the ease with which it can be handled and stored. On my own boat I carry a twenty-pound mushroom anchor for a kellet. The drawback to a BBB chain is in handling it. When it is permanently attached, the extra weight must be raised and lowered each time you anchor. This is a problem if women or children are the regular anchor crew. If it is not permanently attached, but used similar to a kellet, storage becomes a problem unless you have a chain locker. So unless a length of BBB chain is needed between the anchor and rode for sharp crusty bottoms that might cut or fray a line, I would recommend the use of a kellet.

To eliminate the guesswork when paying out a scope, mark your rode every fathom (six feet). Pieces of colored yarn or string worked into the line are ideal for nylon. Paint is the easiest and best for BBB chain.

Selecting Your Anchorage

Selecting an anchorage calls for careful and considerate planning. This applies to both established and emergency storm anchoring areas. Always keep in mind that a good choice insures a comfortable, safe layover. A poor location can ruin an otherwise enjoyable trip or endanger your boat. Before entering any strange anchorage area consult your charts. They show what shelter it provides, the depth of water at low tide, and bottom make-up. Try to find a spot where the water will be at least three feet deeper than your keel at dead low tide, be not more than twelve to fifteen feet deeper at high tide, and have a bottom of firm sand, clay, or a mixture of mud and clay. Avoid soft mud, soft sand, or rocky bottoms. The need for shelter will depend on the type of anchorage. During a blow, shelter from prevailing winds will protect you from the brunt of the storm. At other times, during hot, muggy weather or in an area infested with insects, a more open anchorage with a cool breeze

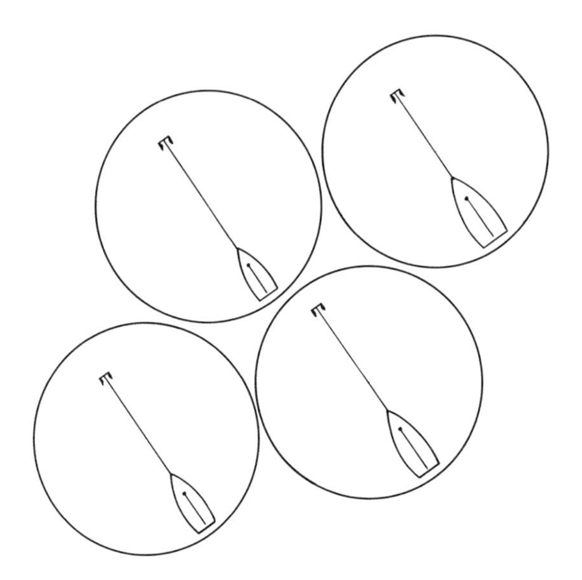

Fig. 200

will be desired. Be sure when on an open anchorage that the weather forecast is favorable and you have plenty of room to let out scope should the need arise.

At established anchorage areas use the following rules of courtesy and common sense to make your layover more enjoyable.

1. Always drop anchor in a spot that assures your boat a clear 360-degree circle at full scope (Fig. 200). This protects your boat should she or others swing around during a change in tide or wind. In crowded areas, which are becoming the rule rather than the exception, you may have to swing on a short scope to have a clear 360 degrees. Here is another good spot for your kellet.
2. When possible, anchor among boats of the same type and size as your own. Chances are they will all have about the same scope, and if the tide or wind should change, everybody will swing together. A mixture of "strangers" often means trouble. Deep-keeled boats swing fast in currents but slowly in winds; shoal draft (shallow) boats react in just the opposite manner.
3. Never anchor in or let your scope reach out into a channel. Not only does it cause a navigation hazard, but also it is against the law.
4. Keep your noise level at a minimum, especially at night when other boatmen may be sleeping.
5. If the area is supervised, call or write ahead asking for a mooring or berth. This saves time and confusion when you arrive.
6. At night keep a small light burning to show other boats moving through the anchorage where you are. When anchored outside an established anchorage area, you must show your thirty-two-point white light.

7. While moving through the anchorage keep your speed and wake down so as not to disturb others. Remember you are responsible for any damage done by your wake.

If a storm moves toward you faster than you can reach an established anchorage, the following rules will help see you safely through.

1. Try to find a nearby area with good protection from the prevailing winds. A land mass makes a good shelter if you remember to guard against shifting winds. Otherwise you may find yourself blown up on the beach.
2. When anchoring in a small cove or bay, try to put a sand beach, rather than docks or rocks, at your back. Then if the anchor should drag, the chance of saving your boat is much better.
3. Never race into a storm anchorage. Proceed with deliberate caution. Chances are, unless the area is an established anchorage or often-used waterway, your charts will not show recent obstructions that could stove in a hull.
4. Avoid the mouths of rivers or inlets whose current will run against the prevailing winds. Such conditions add to the height and turbulence of rising seas.
5. Aboard powercraft, unless you are very low on gasoline, always keep the engine idling in neutral during a blow. Then, if the anchor does not hold, you can immediately start up to avoid drifting or broaching.

Letting Go the Anchor

Once you decide on an anchorage, send a crewman forward to handle the ground tackle. Have him check to make sure the anchor and rode are securely fastened together and the "bitter end" (loose end) is secured to a sampson post,

Fig. 201

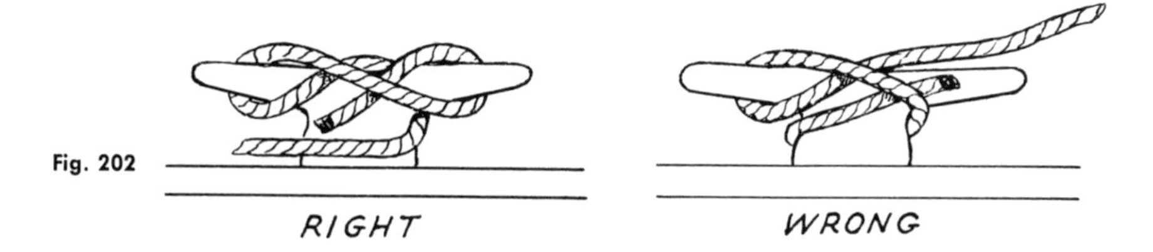

Fig. 202

bitt, or cleat. A tied-down "bitter end" will save your ground tackle and "face" if—and it often happens—the rode should slip or be pulled out of your hand. When alone check and prepare the ground tackle before entering the anchorage area. Do this by hanging the anchor off the bow or placing it next to you in the cockpit and run the rode through a closed bow chock back to the wheel or tiller. Then when you lower anchor you can still control the boat (Fig. 201).

When everything is ready, head up into the wind or current, whichever is the stronger, and start losing headway (slowing down). Powerboats should shift into neutral and keep the engine idling. When the boat comes to a dead stop, slowly start lowering the anchor until it touches bottom, crown first. Make sure the boat has stopped, otherwise you might run over the rode fouling it on a propeller or rudder. *Never throw or drop the anchor overboard.* It serves no useful purpose and may foul the rode on a fluke. As the anchor is being lowered, keep count of the fathom marks on the rode. This will tell you the depth of water and how much rode you need for an adequate scope. Once the anchor touches bottom, start paying out rode as the boat falls off in the wind or current. Be careful to see that the rode is free to run by keeping your feet and all equipment clear. When you have a scope of about four to one, put a strain on the rode, which in turn should start the anchor digging. It is a good idea to take a turn around a bitt or cleat when putting strain on the rode. Then if the anchor bites quickly or snags, the pressure will be on the bitt, not you.

Once you are sure the anchor is holding, pay out more rode until it reaches the scope you want. Then tie it down with a clove or cleat hitch (see Fig. 14 in Chapter 3). Occasionally on a poor bottom a four-to-one scope won't start an anchor biting. In such cases just pay out more line until it does start. With a little practice you will soon know when an anchor is biting or just skittering across the bottom.

Once the anchor has set, check the hitch to make sure that the strain is on the lower turns to prevent jamming (Fig. 202). If you should shorten the scope be sure to clear the bitt or cleat before bending a new hitch. This also insures against jamming, which is a nuisance when weighing anchor. Before going ashore or retiring, stand an anchor watch for twenty or thirty minutes. This lets you double check to be sure that the anchor is holding and gives you time to take an anchor fix.

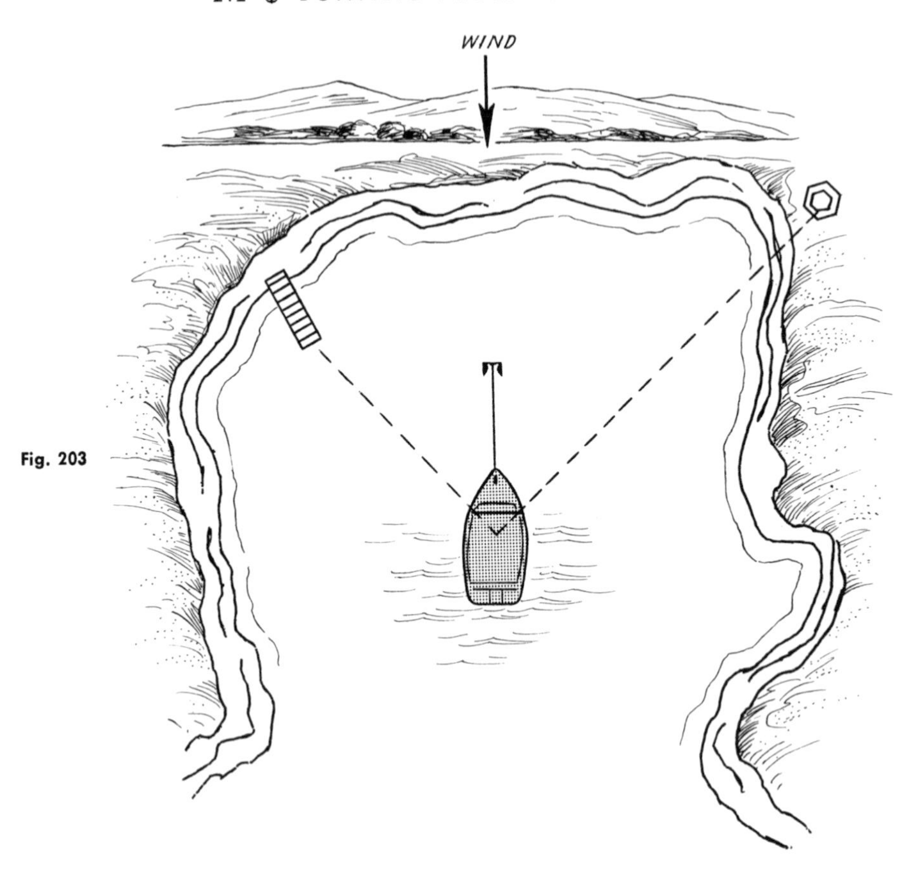

Fig. 203

Taking an Anchor Fix

The fact that your anchor is holding at 4:00 P.M. is no guarantee it will still be set at 7:00 P.M. Rising winds or a changing tide could break it out and start it dragging. Unless you have taken an anchor fix there is a good possibility you won't know you are moving until too late. The easiest way to take a fix is from two or more stationary objects, preferably on shore, two of whose bearings intersect at an angle as close to ninety degrees as possible. Using your compass or another stationary mark aboard, take a bearing on each object (Fig. 203). Then by taking occasional bearings later you will know at a glance by comparison if the boat has moved.

Weighing Anchor

When ready to weigh anchor and get under way, first, unfasten the rode from the bow cleat. Then start moving the boat slowly ahead, taking in the rode as you go. When directly over the anchor (the rode will be straight up and down) have a crewman give the rode a few sharp tugs. This will usually

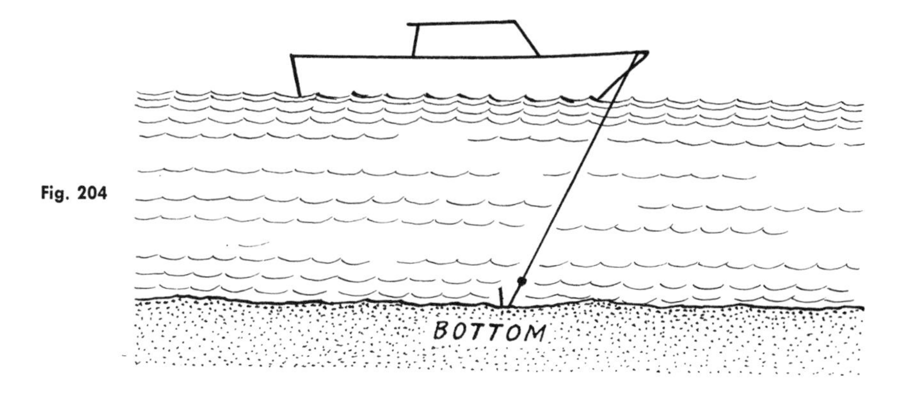

Fig. 204

break the anchor free. If not, snub the rode on a bow cleat and slowly run ahead past the "hook" so the angle of strain is pulling against the anchor's natural holding position (Fig. 204). Unless the anchor is fouled this will do the trick. Be careful the rode does not snag on the prop or rudder as it swings up under the hull.

Stop the boat as soon as the anchor is free, and start hauling it in. Before it breaks surface slosh it up and down a few times to wash off any mud or dirt picked up on the bottom. When clean, bring it aboard carefully so a fluke or the stock does not bang or scratch the hull. After all ground tackle is aboard, secure the anchor in its chocks (Fig. 205) and coil the rode in loose free loops. If the rode is left on deck it is a good idea to fasten it down with a lanyard (light line). This will prevent it from falling or being accidentally kicked over the side. Boats with chain lockers will, of course, store their rodes in the lockers. Be sure the lockers are well ventilated so the lines or chain will dry quickly; otherwise the dampness will soon cause a bilge odor and start dry rot in any exposed wood.

If on any occasion, you should use manila line for a rode or other purpose, never store it wet. As it is a vegetable fiber, it will soon rot. Always dry it thoroughly before storing.

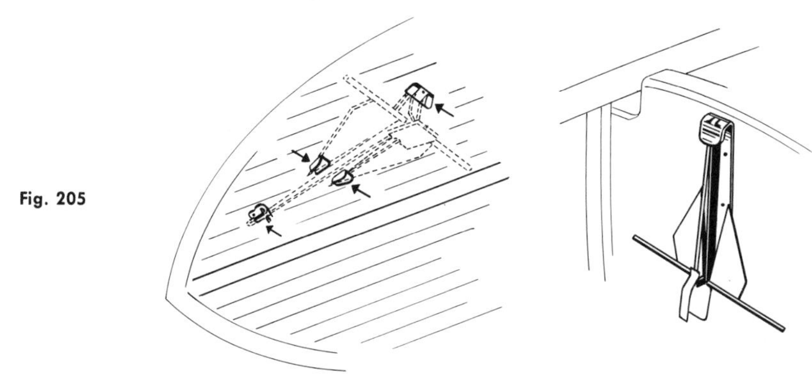

Fig. 205

Freeing a Fouled Anchor

A fouled anchor is one of the most exasperating problems in boating. Along with having to work "blind" (the anchor is usually out of sight below the surface), nine times out of ten you will be over a strange bottom. And if you are like most boatmen, fouling only occurs when you overstay a visit and must make home in a hurry.

Although there is no guaranteed way of freeing a fouled anchor, here are some methods that have worked in seemingly impossible cases. So when you find yourself with a stubborn "hook," try them in the order listed until you break out.

1. Pay out a scope of two or three to one and slowly circle the anchor, keeping a steady pressure on the rode (Fig. 206). The many angles of pull exert a worrying strain on the anchor and will, in all but the most stubborn cases, break it out.

Fig. 206

2. If a *good* swimmer is aboard and the water is not too deep or dirty, let him go over the side, tied to a lifeline, and free the anchor manually. Note: A *good* swimmer is one that has passed or is capable of passing a Senior Red Cross Swimming Course.
3. When a powerboat is nearby and will come to your assistance, try a trip line. Start by lengthening your scope to eight or ten to one. Then pass a heavy line or chain under the rode and fasten both ends to the stern of the other boat. On your signal have the assisting craft slowly run directly away from you, over and past the anchor. This pulls the trip line down the rode, under the head and shank of the anchor, to the crown (Fig. 207). By pull-

Fig. 207

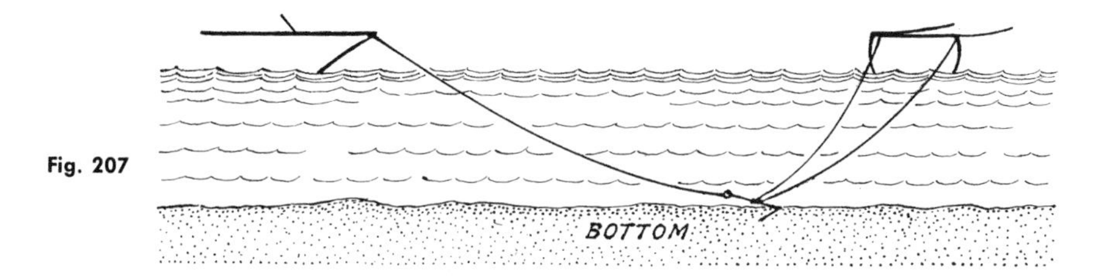

ing from the crown end, you reverse the anchor's normal setting position, which should break it out.

4. A last-ditch and somewhat dangerous method is heaving the anchor on a tight rode at low tide or in swells. As the tide rises or the boat is lifted on a swell, the tight rode will heave the anchor up and out. The danger in this method comes when the anchor remains immovable. Unless carefully watched, the rode can break or, even worse, rip out the bitt or cleat to which it is fastened, tearing out part of the deck.

If all these methods fail, you might just as well abandon the anchor by cutting off the rode as close as possible to the head. In areas where scuba diving is popular, it is a good idea to take a bearing before cutting the rode. Often a diver will salvage your anchor for much less than it would cost you to replace it.

Foul-Proof Anchors

Because fouling is a problem, some anchor manufacturers have developed foul-proof anchors. These special hooks incorporate a shear pin or other device that breaks when given a hard vertical pull. In theory the idea is very sound, but unfortunately experience has shown that they have a tendency to break when they are not supposed to. For this reason I do not recommend them if there is any chance they might be used in a blow.

Ground Tackle Maintenance

The care you give your ground tackle will be reflected in the length of service it returns to you. Like all boating equipment, anchors and rodes should be checked each time they are used and thoroughly inspected periodically. The usage check can be a simple look to be sure that the rode is not wearing or rusting, especially where it rubs against a chock, cleat, or hull, and that all moving parts of the anchor are in working order. The best way to prevent a rode (nylon) from wearing where it rubs is with chafing gear (Fig. 208). Chafing gear can be made from canvas strips or a rubber hose cut spirally. It is also available at most marine dealers.

When shackles are used, check the shackle pin and wire tie-down.

Periodic inspections should be made at least twice a year, in the spring be-

Fig. 208

fore putting your boat over the side and about midseason before the late August and September blows. Wash down the rodes thoroughly with fresh water. Clean all sand and grit from nylon or manila lines, and check for rust on chain. When washing nylon or manila use a low-pressure hose. High-pressure hoses tend to drive the sand and grit deeper into the fibres rather than wash them out. Twist open nylon or manila line and check for broken fibers. If 10 per cent are broken, the line is weakened by 10 per cent, 20 per cent by 20 per cent, etc. Spots where the line rubs or bends are usually the best areas to check for broken fibers.

On anchors inspect all moving parts and clean off any rust down to the bare metal with a wire brush or grit cloth. Then prime and paint the area with a marine grade rust-proof paint. Rust on a chain rode should be treated the same way unless the rust has eaten deeply into the links, then you must replace the rode or the sections that have rusted out.

Take apart all the shackles and make sure no rust has started on the threads. Use plenty of graphite grease when reassembling them. And do not forget to wire the pins locked (Fig. 196).

If you use nylon line in sizes three-eighths of an inch or less, store it out of the sunlight whenever possible. Strange as it seems, the sun's ultraviolet rays will attack and weaken nylon in these small diameters over a long period of time. In larger sizes (one-half inch and over) sunlight has little or no effect. These larger lines develop a white fuzz around their outside circumference which acts as a protection coat. So do not try to rub or wash it off.

Although manila rope is not recommended for rode, there may be occasions when you will use it for other purposes. Be sure to dry it thoroughly before storing, and keep an eye out for dark discoloration in the inner fibers. The latter is a sign of rot and means the line should be destroyed.

Special Anchoring Situations

Every so often you will find yourself in a situation that calls for a special anchoring technique. It may only be to increase your comfort by dropping a

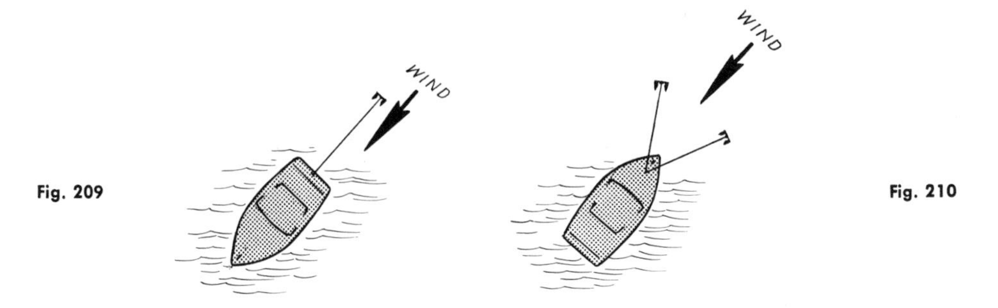

Fig. 209

Fig. 210

stern anchor to catch a breeze. Or it could be the need to bridle a high-bowed light boat with two anchors in a blow. Whatever the reason, knowing "how" in all situations insures your safety and makes you a better skipper. Following are the most common situations in which you may have use for special anchoring techniques:

1. On hot days when stopping for lunch aboard a cabin cruiser you may want to take full advantage of any prevailing breeze. Instead of tying down off the bow cleat, use the stern cleat. This will put the stern into the wind giving the after cockpit and cabins the full breeze (Fig. 209). If for any reason the boat must be left unattended, return it to the normal bow-up position.

2. Many modern designed planing hulls, especially outboards, have a bad habit of yawing and tacking (moving back and forth) at anchor. Their high freeboard and lack of draft at the bow make them fair game for shifting winds. This tendency not only makes the boat uncomfortable for those aboard but also will on occasion worry (shake) the anchor free. To stop the yawing, especially in a blow, it is sometimes necessary to put out two anchors off the bow at about a forty-five-degree angle (Fig. 210). Drop the first hook, set the scope, and make fast as in a single-anchor situation. Then slowly move ahead off to the side until the boat is abeam of the first anchor. Keep the rode snug but not tight as you maneuver. When abeam, lower the second anchor and settle back, paying out rode until both scopes are equal. If done properly your boat will now be held by two anchors in a bridle position and should not yaw or tack.

The two-anchor system is also used during especially hard blows to increase holding power. The important thing to remember in such situations is that two small anchors are not a substitute for one large anchor. Tests show a single large anchor will outhold two small anchors. So do not sacrifice your storm hook. If the occasion arises where you need extra holding power, use the working anchor to compliment your storm anchor.

3. At crowded anchorages boats are sometimes asked to lay anchors bow and stern. In such a situation put down the bow anchor first and pay out an

extra long scope. Then drop the stern anchor and move ahead, adjusting both the bow and stern scope as you go. When both are of equal length and holding, make fast the bow and stern. Although this method of anchoring is becoming more and more popular at crowded anchorages, I have never liked it. As long as the current or tide is the only factor to be considered, it works fine. But if a wind comes up abeam it raises havoc with unattended boats.

Windlasses

Up to this point it has been assumed all ground tackle on small craft is handled manually. This, of course, is not the case. Many boat owners take advantage of mechanical power, using a windlass to raise and lower their "hook." Until a few years ago only large boats (over thirty-two feet) had the space for these work savers. Today engineering advances have made them available in all shapes and sizes, and at prices that are practical for even a rowboat. The main advantage in having a "grinder" is the ease with which you can wind an anchor in or out. This becomes especially appreciated if you do any serious cruising where the anchor is used daily. The fact that a "grinder" gives you up to ten times greater pulling power than by hand is also useful when fouled or aground.

When selecting a windlass take advantage of the tables and charts put out by the manufacturers. They will tell the size drum and handle to use for the size and length of your rode. If chain is used be sure the wildcat on the windlass matches it.

When installing a "grinder" place it so any friction or chafing by the rode, as it goes over the side, is held to a minimum. Often a stemhead roller or other device to prevent chafing can be purchased as an accessory.

A PERMANENT MOORING

If you plan to leave your boat in the water all summer, the problem of where to park it arises. Should it berth at a dock or swing on a permanent mooring? At a commercial anchorage this question is usually answered by the owner, who will assign you a spot. On the other hand, if you plan to use public anchorage or your own private facilities, you must decide. A good guide, used by many commercial operators, is that all powercraft twenty feet and over plus deep-keeled "sailers" generally summer best on permanent mooring, while shoal draft boats under twenty feet usually make home at dockside. Both methods, when properly prepared, will hold a boat safely under all conditions.

When a permanent mooring is to be used, keep in mind that it will be left in the water all season and must be strong enough to hold your boat unattended over long periods of time, through storms, changing tides, and high winds. Or as any "old salt" will tell you, "strong enough to hold on days too wet to take

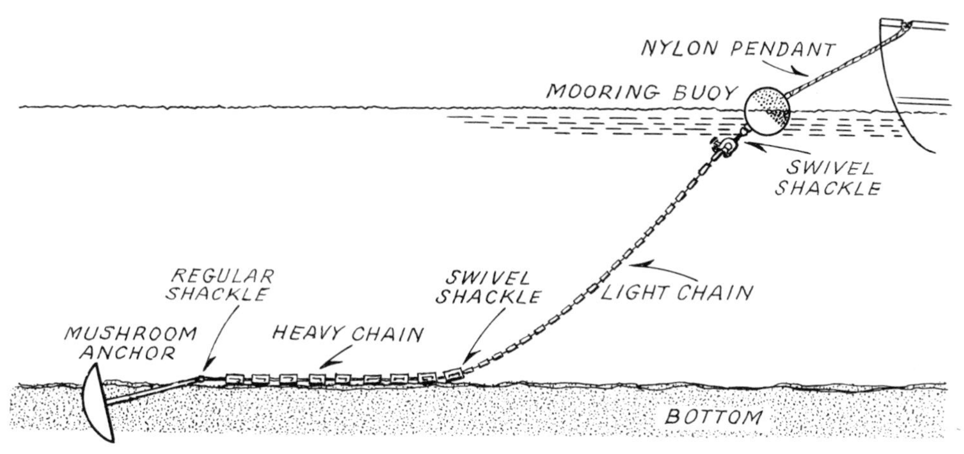

Fig. 211

her out." Figure 211 shows a diagrammed illustration of a well-designed permanent mooring.

The first consideration is to select an anchorage spot, taking into account the same requirements as those for a good layover or storm anchorage: ample water depth (at low tide), good bottom, shelter from prevailing winds, and plenty of room to swing. Try to fulfill as many of these conditions as possible and avoid the mouths of rivers or inlets that build up a heavy chop when a wind or tide bucks the current. Naturally finding a perfect mooring is almost impossible, but for the safety of your boat and your own peace of mind, do not settle for less than 75 per cent of the prerequisites, with ample water a must.

Once the site is chosen, mooring tackle should be selected. You will need a mooring anchor, two sizes of BBB chain for the rode, shackles, a mooring buoy, pennant (line) and, if your anchorage is overly exposed, a kellet.

The anchor can be a manufactured design, a heavy piece of granite, or scrap metal. As it will be handled only twice a season, the weight factor, so important aboard a boat, can be ignored. This makes possible the use of much heavier "hooks." Please note that cement has been omitted as a mooring material. Cast cement weights make poor mooring anchors because cement loses almost one-half of its normal weight when underwater and quickly breaks down in salt water. Scrap metal, although listed and used frequently, is not much better than cement. Only rarely is it shaped to set and hold properly. Granite, on the other hand, when large enough and cut with square corners, will compare favorably with most mooring anchors. Its one drawback is price. Unless you live along the coast of Maine, where a few dollars will buy a ton delivered, the cost is absurdly high.

This leaves the manufactured anchors, which are the easiest to obtain and in the long run give the best service. The mushroom type is the most popular of

Fig. 212

Suggested Mooring Anchor and Rode (Line) Sizes for Power and Sailing Craft

Over-all Length of Boat	Anchor Size (lbs.)	Nylon Rope Diameter	Manila Rope Diameter	*BBB Chain Diameter
0′–20′	200	3/4″	13/16″	3/8″
20′–25′	250	7/8″	1-1/8″	7/16″
25′–30′	250	1″	1-1/4″	1/2″
30′–35′	300	1-1/8″	1-5/16″	5/8″
35′–40′	300	1-1/4″	1-1/2″	3/4″
40′–50′	500	1-5/16″	1-5/8″	1″

*Denotes heavy ground chain. For vertical chain go one or two sizes smaller.

NOTE: The above figures are based on fair holding ground in a semi protected area. Under poor conditions go to the next larger size or check with local experienced boatmen.

the "store-bought hooks," with the stockless kedge (navy) used in some areas. A new fixed fluked design, manufactured by the Danforth Company, is gaining popularity in multianchor moorings. How it is used is explained under "Special Mooring Situations" in the next section.

Assuming that the mushroom anchor will be your choice, take the time while buying it to look at three or four different makes; then select the one with the greatest fluke area. Pound for pound it will hold the best. The tables in Figure 212 show the approximate size of anchor needed to hold different sizes and types of boats under average bottom and surface conditions. These same tables also show the size of chain and line to use for a rode and pennant. Keep in mind, poor conditions call for the next larger size anchor or rode.

After the "hook" is purchased, the next item is the rode. You will notice in Figure 211 that two different sizes of chain are used. The weight of a heavy chain gives better catenary (sag) during a blow, while the vertical chain is kept as light as possible, without sacrificing strength, to minimize the strain or pull on the mooring buoy.

The buoy, which acts as a marker and takes the weight of the rode off the bow, should be made from styrofoam or other good floating material. Avoid hollow cans or globes that could leak and sink if dented or punctured. The size buoy necessary depends on the weight of the vertical chain. When afloat it should be large and buoyant enough to show at least half its bulk with the rode attached and be visible at least one hundred yards on a clear day. Sometimes a small flag and reflective paint are used on a buoy to make sighting easier. Well-made buoys will also have metal rods or chain running through the center with an eye or ring at each end (Fig. 213). The rod and eyes allow the rode and pennant to be attached directly to the buoy. Buoys not using this type of construction depend on an eye bolt or eye screw to hold up the vertical rode. Often these will pull out, allowing the chain and pennant to sink to the bottom.

The last two items needed are a pennant, which is the line used to hold the boat, and three shackles, one regular and two swivels. The pennant can be either nylon or stainless steel, while the shackles should be galvanized or rust-proof metal that equals or betters the breaking strength of the vertical chain.

Fig. 213

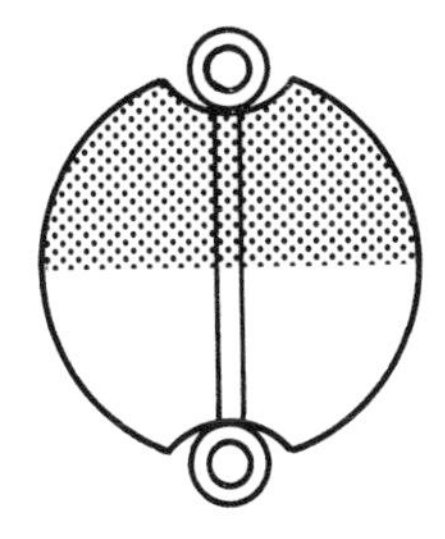

How the mooring is assembled and the length of chain and line needed are diagrammed in Figure 211. The heavy bottom chain should be at least three times the depth of the water. The vertical chain, one times the water's depth, and the pennant two and a half to three times the distance from the surface to the bow chock.

To assemble the mooring, attach the heavy bottom chain to the anchor and vertical chain. Use a regular shackle at the anchor end and a swivel shackle at the vertical chain end. Then secure the buoy to the loose end of the vertical chain with a swivel shackle or with a fastener supplied with the buoy. And, last, bend the pennant to the buoy. Splice an eye, if the pennant is nylon, or form the eye and clamp it with wire clamps if it is stainless steel. (When the buoy does not have a through bolt, be sure to attach the pennant to the top shackle on the vertical chain.) When the mooring is all assembled, tighten and wire down the shackle pins and coat each one with graphite grease. On overly exposed moorings, a kellet weighing 10 per cent of your anchor can be fastened to the shackle between the heavy and light chain.

When setting the mooring, have plenty of strong help along. Gently place the anchor aboard your boat and carry it out to the anchorage. Then, with assistance from your help, slowly lower it to the bottom, being careful not to scratch or mar the deck or hull. If help is not available and there is any question of your being able to handle the mooring alone, do not touch it. Hire a local work boat to do the job. The few dollars it will cost is excellent insurance against a hernia that could ruin a whole boating season.

Once the mooring is over the side, give it a day or two to dig and settle in.

It should then be ready to serve as your boat's parking bitt all season. If assembled correctly, the only maintenance should be the inspection and care of the nylon pennant or wire clamps on the stainless steel pennant.

SPECIAL MOORING SITUATIONS

As anchorage areas become more crowded each year, the problem of laying out sufficient scope has brought about the development of special mooring techniques. Of the many types used, the multiple-anchor arrangements seem to do the best job. They allow almost vertical anchoring without sacrificing scope, by bringing two or more rodes to a single buoy and pennant. Illustrations of several such moorings using lightweight Danforth fixed fluke anchors instead of mushrooms are shown in Figure 214.

The best is, naturally, the five-anchor system, which gives optimum security against winds from any direction. The three-anchor mooring, although not quite as efficient as the five-anchor, is the most popular and is the choice of most commercial marina operators. The two-anchor system is used only in

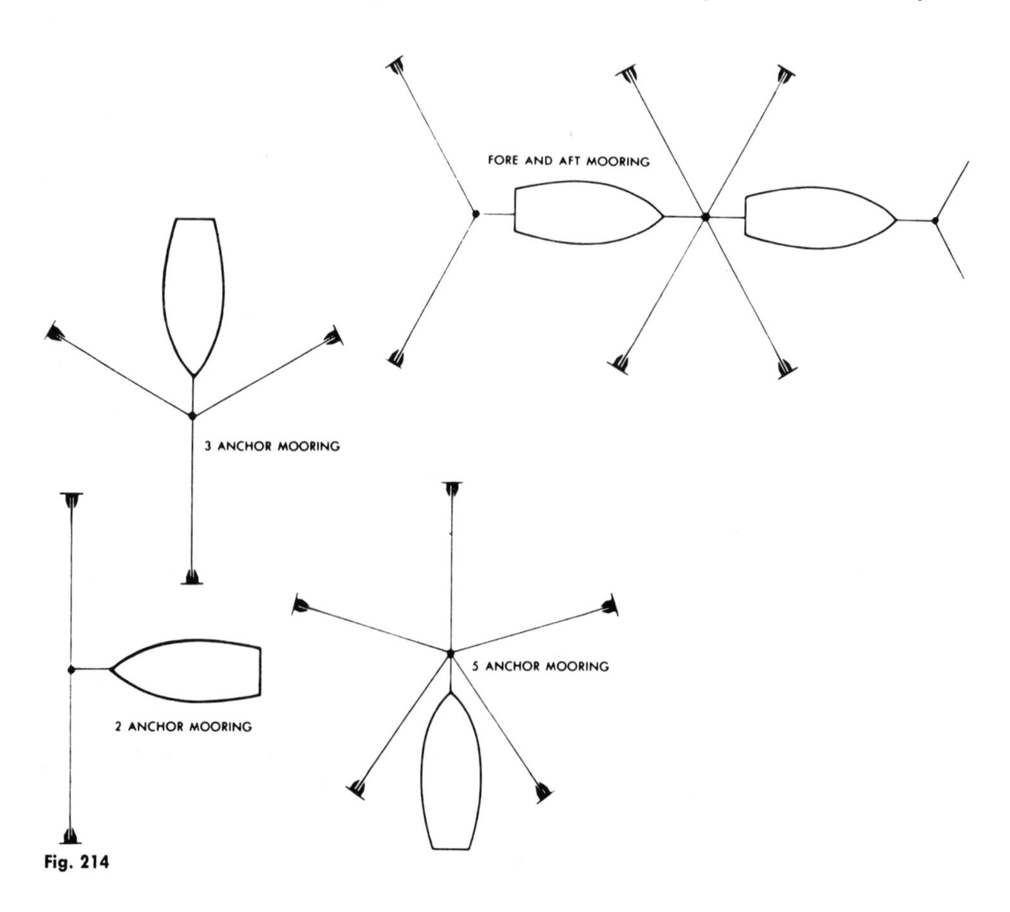

Fig. 214

special situations, such as tidal rivers or tidal anchorages that are well protected. Any strong wind blowing across this type of mooring would tend to worry the anchors. The last method, called fore-and-aft mooring, is just another way of holding bow and stern. Although this arrangement is popular in some areas, I feel that it has the same weaknesses inherent to bow and stern anchoring. An abeam wind raises havoc because the bow cannot swing up.

The selection of rode and anchor sizes for a multiple mooring is based on how many anchors will be working in any given wind direction. By studying Figure 214 you can see in a two- or three-anchor mooring that it is possible for only one anchor to be holding. Therefore, each anchor and rode should be treated as a single mooring. Look at the tables in Figure 29 and select the anchor you would normally use, then buy two or three instead. Purchase your rodes the same way. If you plan to use Danforth fixed fluke anchors or other makes, check the tables issued for those anchors.

In a five-anchor mooring, three anchors are always holding (a main and two helpers). Because of this extra help, anchors and rodes with only 70 per cent of a single mooring anchor's holding power can be used. (Seventy per cent holding power does not automatically mean that you can go to the next smaller size anchor or rode. Ask to see the holding power charts for the anchors and rodes you are buying and compute the 70 per cent from the chart.)

A trick used by many pros who use a five-anchor mooring on exposed waters is to sink a regular size hook in the direction of prevailing storm winds.

TYING-UP

Every boatman, regardless of the type of craft he owns, will use docking facilities at one time or another. Therefore, you must know how to tie up alongside a dock or in a slip. Fortunately, this part of seamanship training is simple to master. A few minutes study and one or two practice sessions will have you tying up like an old deckhand.

Mooring lines, also called docking lines, should be made of either nylon or manila rope, with nylon the first choice. Under no circumstances use discarded anchor line or other rope. No matter how strong it may look, the fact that it was thrown away can only lead to an embarrassing scrape or damage to your or someone else's boat.

Aboard small boats, sixteen feet or under, that tie up only occasionally, two mooring lines will usually be sufficient. If, on the other hand, the boat is tied up most of the time or is exposed to rough waters, four lines should be used. On larger craft a minimum of four lines is necessary. And where strong winds, waves, or currents are prevalent, six lines may be needed.

All mooring lines must be at least as long as the boat they are holding, and in tidal waters with a large tide range, they should be twice the length of the

Fig. 215

Suggested Docking Line Sizes

Overall Length of Boat	Nylon
0′–12′	3/8″
12′–20′	1/2″
20′–30′	5/8″
30′–40′	3/4″
40′–50′	1″
50′–60′	1-1/8″

NOTE: At docking areas that have strong surface conditions the next larger size line may be needed. Check with local experienced boatmen.

boat. This is especially important where docks or mooring facilities are stationary rather than floating and do not move up or down with the tide.

The size of lines to use depends on the size and type of your boat, plus surface conditions. Assuming that the boat is of average construction, the surface conditions are fair to good, and you will be using nylon line, the table in Figure 215 shows the size line needed for different length boats. Remember, as with an anchor rode, if the boat is extra heavy or conditions are poor, go to the next larger size line. This also applies when manila is used instead of nylon.

To insure the line's holding under adverse conditions, check your mooring hardware. Make sure all cleats and bitts are strong and large enough to do the job, that each one is through-bolted to a strong part of the hull, and that all have smooth, rounded edges. Aboard boats that use a dock as a permanent mooring, additional docking hardware is sometimes needed. There should be a cleat or mooring bitt forward near the bow plus cleats at the stern and amidships on both sides of the boat. To minimize line wandering and chafing, chocks should be installed with each cleat. Place the chocks so they are in line with the direction of pull. Whenever one cleat will have two lines running away from each other, two chocks should be installed. Chafing gear should also be used on permanent docking lines.

In addition to cleats and chocks, it is a good idea to install some fender hooks. These hooks hold the fenders which protect your boat from banging and scraping against the dock.

Lines to Use

Except for unusual or storm conditions, six lines are the most any small craft would ever use when tying up. In fact, four lines are usually more than adequate. The names of these lines are shown in Figure 216. After you learn

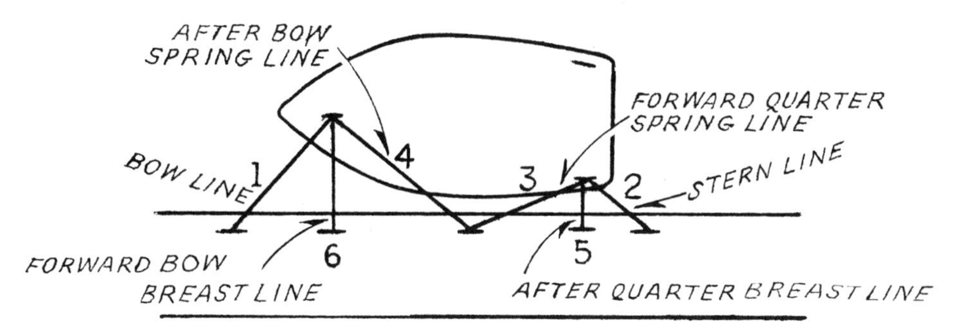

Fig. 216

them, study the different ways of tying up as shown in Figure 217.

Boat #1. The single line tie-up is used for short stops such as at a service dock. *Line A*. The bow line is used when the bow is heading into the wind or current or the boat is on the windward side of the dock. *Line B*. An amidship breast line (not shown in Figure 217) can be used if the boat is on the leeward side of the dock with the wind or current abeam. *Line C*. The stern line is used when the wind or current is coming in over the stern. When only one line is used, be sure someone is always aboard to handle any situation that might arise.

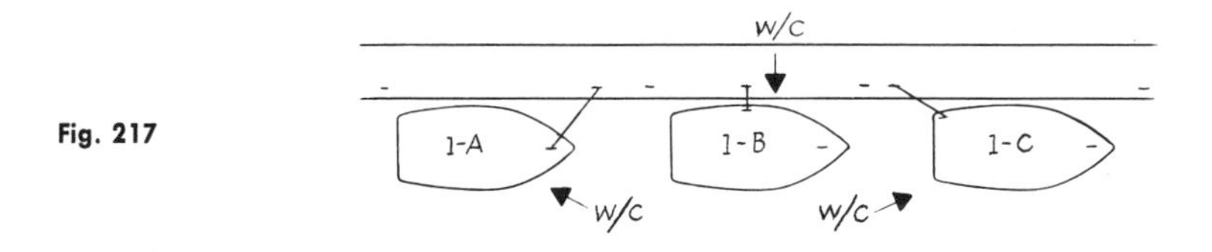

Fig. 217

Boat #2. The two-line tie-up, bow line and stern line, is the most commonly used when a boat is left unattended for a short period under favorable conditions. In a sheltered area this tie-up can be used as a permanent dockside mooring for very small boats (under fourteen feet).

Boat #3 shows a three-line tie-up, bow and stern lines with a forward quarter spring line. The spring line acts as a helper when a boat is moored in an exposed area. It prevents the bow and stern from swinging out or in with a forward and backward movement.

Boat #4. The four-line tie-up adds an after bow spring line. This is the tried and accepted method of dockside mooring for all but very large boats. The addition of the second spring line restricts any forward or backward swinging in high winds or fast currents. If you plan to moor at dockside and there are no unusual conditions, this is the method recommended for tying up.

Boat #4A shows another four-line tie-up, a bow and forward quarter spring line with two stern lines, one coming off each side of the boat. The purpose of

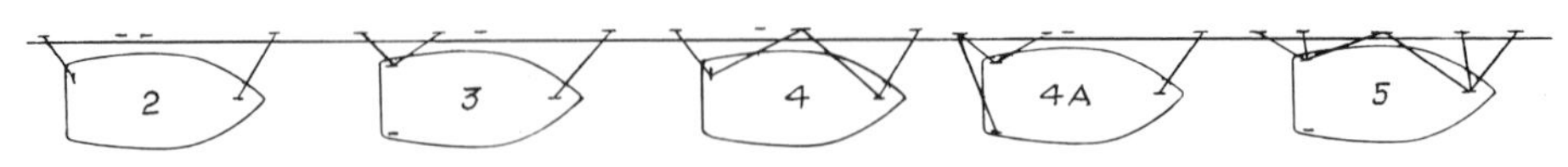

Fig. 217

the extra stern line is to help absorb the shocks and strains when a strong wind or current pushes the boat away from the dock. The trick in this tie-up is to make sure both stern lines are working together. If one is slack, it means the other is taking all the strain and will probably break.

Boat #5 shows the six-line method of tying up. In addition to the four regular lines, a forward breast line and after breast line are used. This method of tying up is generally used by larger boats (over fifty feet). The only time a boat smaller than this would need breast lines is during foul weather when strong winds and currents put her on the leeward side of the dock.

Boat #6 shows how lines must lengthen when a boat is moored in an area with a large tidal range. The extra length allows for the falling tide. If this is not done, the boat will be hung up high and dry or have all its cleats ripped out.

Fig. 217

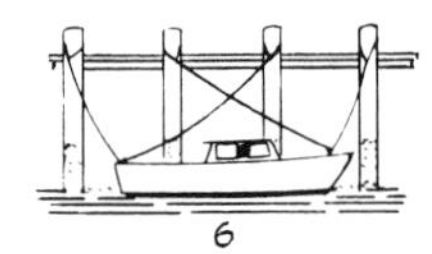

Mooring in a Slip

If you are fortunate enough to obtain a slip to moor in, the following methods of tying up, shown in Figure 217, have proved to be the most practical.

Boat #7. When the slip has a dock on two or three sides, use a normal tie-up on one side plus a bow and stern line on the other. This keeps the boat from banging against the dock. Boat #7 shows a four-line tie-up plus the bow and stern lines on the opposite side. A two-, three-, or six-line tie-up could also be used.

Fig. 217

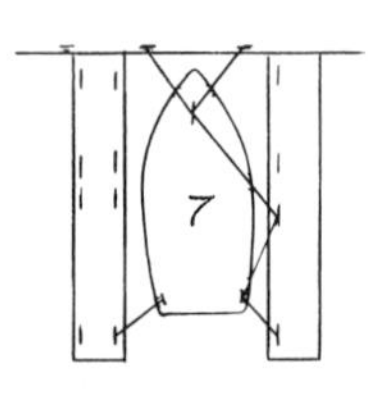

Boat #8 shows a simple twin bow and stern tie-up in a slip that uses pilings for securing. Bow and stern lines are put out off both sides to keep the boat from swinging into the dock. Be sure when using this type of slip that the pil-

Fig. 217

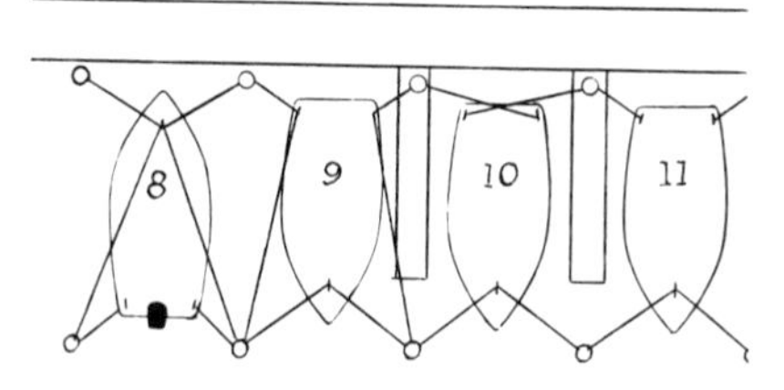

ings are far enough forward so that the bow lines have at least a thirty-degree angle. Otherwise, the bow lines will only act as breast lines.

Boat #9 is secured in the same way as Boat #8 except that the stern lines are crossed. This further restricts any sideways movement if there is a cross-current or wind. When using this method be careful to see that the boat does not surge forward because of the extra length of the stern lines. If it does, add two more stern lines as in Boat #8.

Boat #10 shows how to secure in a slip when the wind or current crowds the stern against the dock. Run two lines from the pilings to the stern cleats. This will prevent the boat from moving backward.

Boat #11. Outboard owners often like to put their bow rather than the stern to the dock. This makes going aboard easier without having to step over the motor. It also protects the motor against banging into the dock. The tie-up is the same as Boat #10 except that the spring lines run aft to the pilings from the bow cleat or bitt.

All docking lines, both dockside and slip mooring, should be doubled when a large storm or hurricane is forecast for your area. When using double lines be sure that each one is working. The least amount of slack in one line puts added strain on its partner.

Use of Fenders

Fenders are the bumpers for parked boats. Without them any boat that ties up alongside a dock or in a slip is asking for trouble. A badly scraped side is guaranteed, and, if the weather turns foul, serious damage could occur. For these reasons make sure that you carry at least two fenders aboard boats under eighteen feet and three or more on boats eighteen feet and over. Fortunately, with the creation of new materials, the cost of fenders has become a minor outlay in the necessary equipment category. When buying fenders, keep in mind that large-diameter fenders put the least amount of strain on the hull and long vertical fenders resist the tendency to ride up into the dock.

Boat #12 shows where to place the fenders when only two are used. Aboard small boats (under eighteen feet) this protection is usually adequate under fair to good conditions.

Boat #13 shows three fenders out and how four would be placed if the boat was large enough or during foul weather.

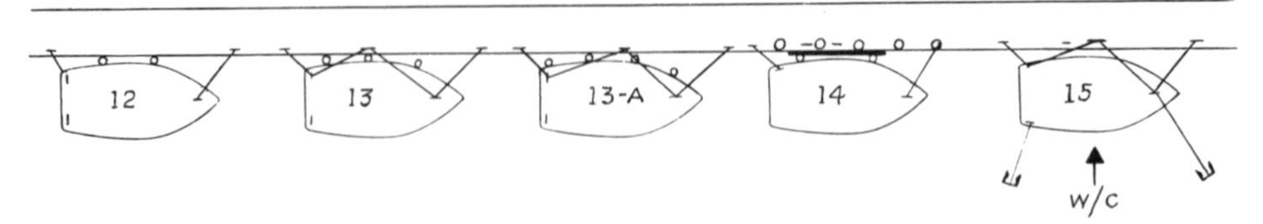

Fig. 217

Fender Boards

Boat #14 shows how a fender board complements fenders when a dock is sided with pilings. The fender board spans the pilings, allowing the fenders to do their job. Without the board, the fenders would slip in between the pilings and lose their effectiveness. To work properly, fender boards should be at least eight to ten feet long and four to ten inches wide. On boats with a storage problem, they can be cut in half and hinged to fold when not in use.

Boards shorter than eight feet or the practice of turning fenders horizontal at pilings is at best a poor substitute. Boards can be made from any wood that will stand up under wettings and rubbing. Close-grained hardwoods are usually preferred.

Docking on the Windward Side

Occasionally you may tie up on the windward side of a dock in an area of strong winds or currents. When there is plenty of room, you may find it feasible to drop an anchor or anchors off the windward side of your boat. This will keep her from crowding or jamming against the dock and overworking the fenders.

Boat #15 shows a windward anchor tie-up using two hooks. If one anchor is used, secure it amidship.

Set the anchors the same way you would normally anchor.

13

Fitting Out and Storage

At least once a year every boat should be thoroughly inspected and put in shipshape condition. In boating circles this is called "fitting-out time," and it usually takes place in late winter or early spring just before the start of a new boating season. The importance of doing this job well cannot be stressed too strongly, as it will, to a great degree, predict the kind of season you can expect. Sloppy, half-done work brings about a rash of breakdowns and maintenance headaches, whereas a thorough conscientious job will go a long way in assuring a safe, fun-filled season of boating. Experienced skippers realize this and plan their work schedule to allow plenty of time for necessary repairs before the season starts. This prevents having to rush through a job or "going over the side" (launching) late. Plan your schedule the same way, and use the following information to get afloat in jig time and "Bristol fashion."

Start fitting out by ventilating all areas that might collect pockets of inflammable fumes (gasoline, oil, etc.) during winter storage. This would include bilges, cabins, engine pits, storage lockers, etc. While ventilating, keep the smoking lamp out and shut off and remove any source of ignition from the immediate area.

When the ventilating is completed, wash or dust down your boat, depending upon her condition, in preparation for a survey inspection. If washing is necessary, use a good detergent or boat cleaner plus plenty of elbow grease; and don't overlook the hard-to-reach areas, since they tend to become mid-season trouble spots.

SURVEY INSPECTION

Whether your fitting out program involves a major overhaul or just a yearly face-lifting, a survey inspection which includes everything from stem to stern is necessary to insure a thorough job. The easiest and best way to make the survey is with a master checklist especially designed for your boat. It should cover all items that need inspection, grouping them under appropriate headings. For large boats or yard-stored craft, you can go a step further and organize the work for dry weather, wet weather, at home, and evenings. Then, regardless of the time or weather, you will not be held up. In Appendix C page 294 is a master checklist guide designed for all major types of boats made of wood, fiber glass, or aluminum. From it, you can develop a checklist for your craft, adding any special items not found on a stock production boat. Be sure to leave plenty of room for notes.

While making a survey, new skippers are often unaware of what to look for and how to inspect certain items. To help overcome this difficulty, I have listed some of the more common boating problems and how they are found.

HULL, DECK AND SUPERSTRUCTURE

When surveying hulls, decks, and superstructures, it is important that both inside and out are gone over with the proverbial fine-tooth comb.

On wooden boats look for fractures and dry rot in framing members, planking, and where cabins or other superstructures join the deck. Fractures are most easily found while washing or dusting, whereas dry rot is best located by tapping with the handle of an ice pick at all discolored varnish, dark water-stained wood, blistered paint, and spots where a shaft or fitting extrudes through the hull. A solid ring or thump signifies sound wood, while a soft dull thud usually means dry rot. Use the point of the ice pick to probe all suspected spots and to find the outer limits of the damage. Outline all affected areas with a crayon or marking pencil, and fill in all probe holes made in sound wood with a waterproof wood filler immediately. By waiting you may forget and leave the bare wood open to dry rot.

While looking for dry rot on plank-constructed boats, also inspect the caulking used in the hull and deck seams. If still pliable, it will compress back to its original shape when the planking swells in the water. If, however, the compound is hard or brittle, replace it, as it will only pinch out or cause uneven expansion when the planking swells. Bleeding at a seam is another indication that caulking in that area should be replaced. Run a marking pencil along all seams that need repacking.

On aluminum boats look for cracks along welded or riveted seams, the stem and transom. If the boat is painted, use a penknife to scrape away any paint around a suspected area. Look for corroding or pitting in the metal by running your hand over the entire hull. This could mean an electrolysis or chemical action is taking place and must be neutralized.

On fiber-glass boats examine for hairline cracks that extend past the top jell coat into the glass cloth and any high or low spots in the surface of the hull. Cracks are usually found around the keel, keelson, stem, and transom; wherever a fitting or shaft extrudes through the hull; and where the deck and hull are joined. High or low spots can best be found by sliding your open palm over the entire hull, inside and out. Examine any severe crazing in the jell coat, as it could mean the area is subjected to undue stress and needs to be strengthened. Outline all areas needing repairs with a marking pencil.

On all boats, regardless of construction, carefully examine through fittings, bolts, and screws for tightness. Any play should be inspected as to why it exists and what must be done to correct it. When a boat uses inboard power, check the stuffing box for leaks and the propeller for nicks and gouges, both of which could be signs the propeller shaft is warped. If there is any question in your mind, have it tested for alignment. Wherever leaks are found, be sure to trace them to their origin. Don't make the mistake of sealing a leak from below deck or inside a cabin. At best this will only be a temporary solution that will still allow the water to collect from the outside and find another outlet elsewhere.

DECK GEAR AND FITTINGS

Deck gear and fittings should be inspected next. Look for rust, pitting, and cracks in all metal parts, looseness in bitts, cleats, and stationary deck gear, and excessive play due to wear or strain in sheaves and winches. Be especially sure all winches work properly and lock if they are equipped with a locking device.

STEERING GEAR

Usually on small boats only normal maintenance of moving parts is required for mechanical steering devices. However, on types where wires or lines are led through a series of sheaves and wound on a drum, check for chafing, nipping, and broken fibers. Also check any pins that are used around a rudder or steering column to make sure they have not been sheared or bent. On large craft using linkage or hydraulic steering systems, inspect for broken links and gear teeth or excessive play, and leaks in the hydraulic system. Tag each item that must be repaired.

ENGINE AND ENGINE ACCESSORIES

Unless you are mechanically inclined and understand the workings of marine inboard and outboard engines, limit your inspection to looking for excessive rust around gaskets, cracks in metal parts, broken clamps and wires, split lines, broken brackets, and oil or gas leaks. Where a tune-up or overhaul survey is needed, have a qualified mechanic make the inspection unless you are capable of doing this work. Be sure to use the maintenance manual supplied with the engine as a guide. If you do not have a manual, send to the manufacturer for one.

SAILS AND RIGGING

Sailboat owners must also survey all sails, running rigging, and sailing hardware. The sails, in all probability, were inspected and dried before being stored for the winter. Even so, it is a good idea to reinspect all seams, bolts, ropes, reef lines, cringles, batten pockets, grommets, and track slides. Sailing hardware, which would include blocks, fairleads, goosenecks, winches, travelers, and other miscellaneous items, can be inspected at the same time you survey your deck gear and fittings. Mast and booms are best inspected before they are raised and stepped. Look for cracks, splits, dents, and warping, all of which are signs of structural weakness. Also examine the sail track for dents, bends, or looseness, which must be corrected to keep track slides from jamming. Next, inspect all stays, halyards, and sheets (lines) for fraying, rot, rust, and chafing. Mark or tag all items needing repair.

PAINTING AND VARNISH

Aside from appearance, a good paint job acts as a barrier seal against moisture, fungus, and marine life, which, given the opportunity, will attack most materials used in the construction of boats and boating equipment. Therefore, inspect all painted and varnished surfaces for peeling, blistering, scrapes, scratches, and discoloration, any of which must be removed and repainted.

GROUND TACKLE, SAFETY EQUIPMENT, AND OTHER EQUIPMENT

Inspect all ground tackle, safety devices, and other equipment to be sure they are in good condition and working order. A compass that is off or an empty fire extinguisher is as great a hazard as a life jacket that has lost its buoyancy or a weakened line. These items are good evening or rainy-day projects. Tag each piece of equipment, stating what, if any, work needs to be done on it.

DO-IT-YOURSELF OR PROFESSIONAL HELP

When your survey inspection is over, list all the repairs you plan to do yourself and those to be done by yard personnel or a mechanic. While making this list, don't overestimate your abilities or attempt jobs that will require special tools you do not own or cannot obtain. Both these mistakes are fairly common among new boatmen and are usually the reason for going over the side late. A good guide to follow is: don't attempt any work that involves major structural members, a large amount of siding, or a major overhaul, unless you are trained to do this work. Rarely is a handyman skilled enough to do a good safe job. Work the average boat owners can do includes cleaning, minor repairs to boat, engine, sails, and equipment, and painting. The trick is to keep abreast of minor items, and the major repairs will not materialize.

DOING THE WORK

As each boat has its own special needs, it is impossible here to prepare a specific worksheet for any one boat. However, the following list of accepted repair and maintenance procedures tells you how to correct the more common

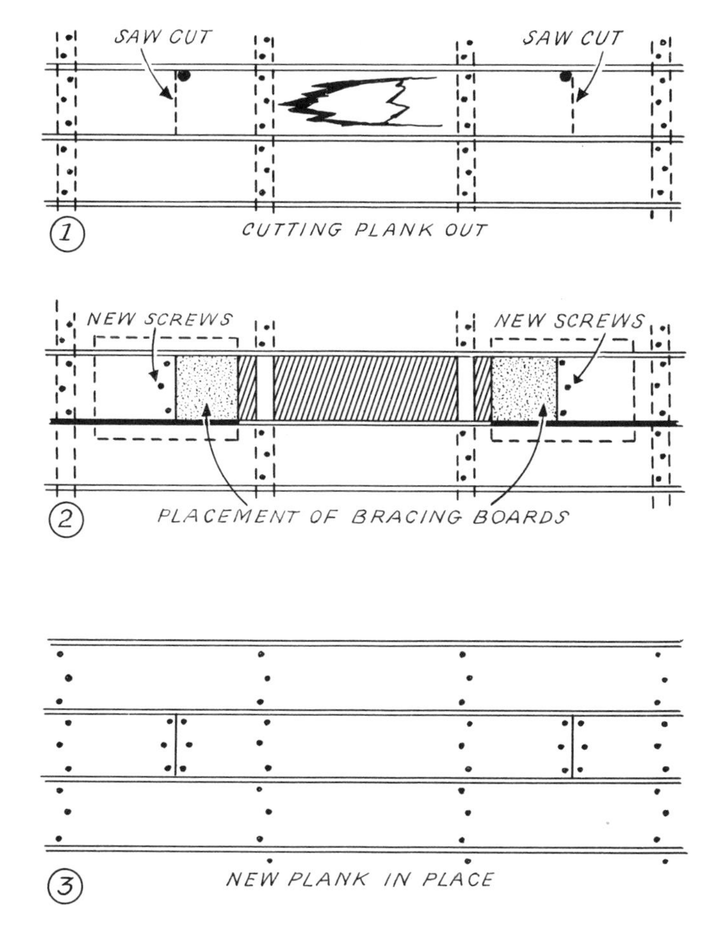

Fig. 218

boating ills. By using these as a guide, following the directions when using commercial preparations, and going to experts for specialized help, you will be able to put and keep your boat in shipshape condition.

Hull, Deck, Superstructure

⚓ Cut away all existing dry rot and replace with new wood or an accepted patching compound. If one of the new chemical compounds is used, follow the directions explicitly, as many of these "miracle" products have a very short "pot life" (harden very quickly) and must be mixed with care. Wherever structural members are involved, brace around the area to be repaired to prevent sagging or collapsing.

⚓ When new planking is being installed in a dry rot or fractured area, make sure it is held by a framing member or backed with a bracing board (Fig. 218).

⚓ Use white lead or a similar sealing compound generously wherever wood and wood, or wood and metal, are joined. Be especially generous where end of the grain is involved.

⚓ When using a fiber-glass compound to patch a large hole, back the hole with a semiflexible sheet of fiberboard or heavy cardboard. The purpose is to mold the patch along the same curve or bend as the siding surrounding the hole. Figure 219 shows how this is done.

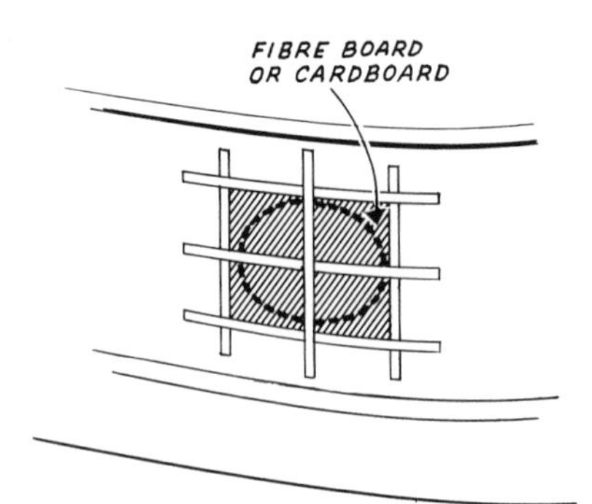

Fig. 219

⚓ When sealing a tear or hole in aluminum boats, hammer out the jagged metal until it is smooth and conforms to the curves or bends around it. Then glue with a special adhesive or rivet an aluminum patch, larger than the hole itself, over the hole. When using rivets be sure a sealing compound is used between the patch and hull. On large boats or large holes a patch on both sides of the hole is recommended for additional strength. Figure 220 shows a single and a sandwich patch.

⚓ When repairing aluminum or fiber-glass boats, use the patching kit recommended or supplied by the company that built the boat, and follow the

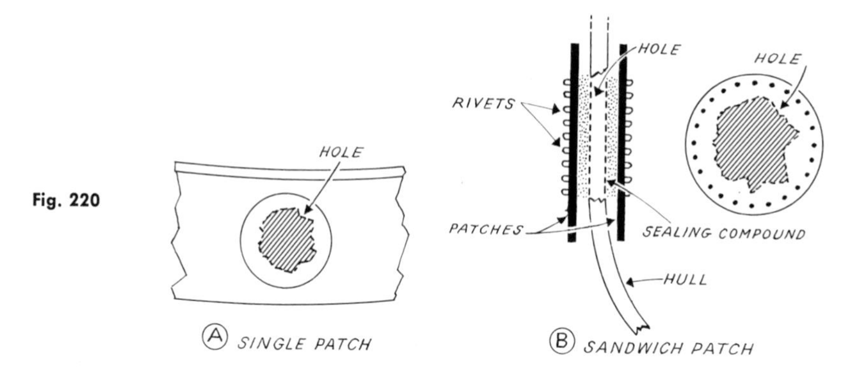

Fig. 220

directions to the letter. This is necessary, as many different alloys and plastic compounds used in the production of aluminum and fiber-glass boats are not always compatible.

⚓ Where necessary, reset or move screws that work loose in siding or decks. When resetting, plug the holding member with a dowel, and white lead the countersunk holes before replacing the screws. When set, the screws should be below the surface of what they are holding. This allows them to be covered with a plug or caulking compound (Fig. 221).

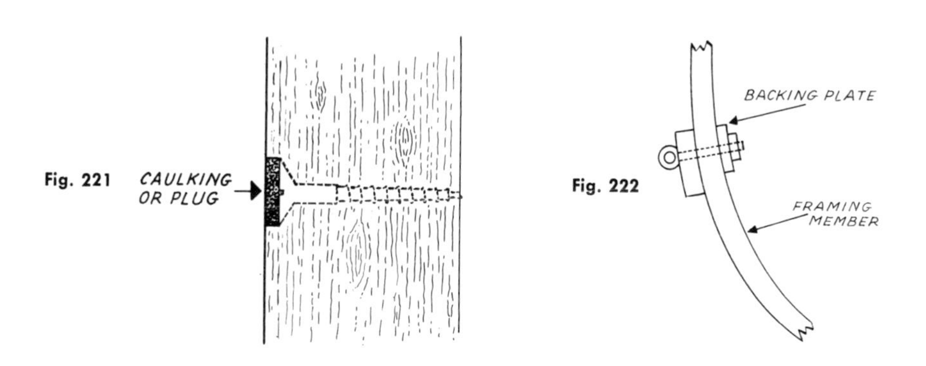

Fig. 221 **Fig. 222**

⚓ Wherever canvas or other deck or roof covering has rotted, blistered, or stained, remove the affected section and replace it with new material. Before replacing, check to be sure dry rot or other repairs are not needed in the wood underneath.

⚓ Hand rails and grab rails should always be through bolted; never screwed into wood, aluminum, or fiber glass.

⚓ When framing or structural members are drilled to receive a bolt, make sure the drilling will not appreciably weaken the member. Where this might happen, reinforce the member with a backing plate or a side stringer (Fig. 222).

⚓ Countersunk bolts will keep a watertight seal longer if soft cotton string soaked in white lead is wound around the shaft just under the head before tightening.

⚓ Clean out all drain vents in window and hatchway tracks to assure complete drainage when water collects in them.

⚓ Seal all small leaks around windows, hatchways, screw and nail holes, seams, and other areas that work (expand, contrast, or bend) with one of the new silicone or polysulfide type sealing compounds. These products stay pliable for years and will expand or contract to meet existing conditions.

Much of the trial and error that goes into stopping small leaks where superstructures join the deck can be avoided by resetting existing molding in a new bed of caulking compound.

Seam Caulking

⚓ When repacking a seam, use the same type(s) of caulking materials as were removed. Don't use oakum to replace cotton "rope," or vice versa, as each differs in swelling and absorption characteristics, just as the different types of chemical caulking sealers are often incompatible.

⚓ Use the right-size reefing and caulking iron when using oakum and cotton "rope." Otherwise, you could overspread the seams. Ask a yard owner or experienced boat repairman to look at the seams and recommend the size. Where a lot of seam work is involved, you would be better off having the work done by a professional.

⚓ When working caulking "rope," tap it gently, but firmly, so it fills the seam evenly. Any driving or heavy hammering will force it in so tight that the siding will be pushed away from framing members when the planking starts to swell.

⚓ When bleeding is found along seams, reef out all the water-stained "rope" plus two or three inches of sound "rope" on each side. Then repack with the same type of material(s) you removed.

When repacking a bleeding seam, check to be sure there isn't another reason for the leak. Often, small cracks just above or below the seam are the culprit. In such cases, don't use "rope" to fill the crack, as it will prevent the crack from swelling shut when wet. Instead, fill it with white lead or another pliable compound which can ooze out as the crack swells shut.

⚓ Where two or more planks abutting one another need caulking, finish each stage before going on to the next. In this way you will not drive the first seam so tight that it will close the seam above or below it.

⚓ Do not use wet or packed "rope" for caulking except in an emergency. Oakum and cotton work best dry, and if fluffed a bit just before using.

Fittings, Stationary Equipment, and Rigging

⚓ Wherever practical, all screw-fastened fixtures such as bitts, cleats, and stationary equipment should be refastened with through bolts for added holding strength.

⚓ Remove all rust and stains from metal parts. Many excellent cleaners are now on the market that will help make this job easier. Where rust or pitting is severe, replace the fitting.

Wherever cracks or metal strains are found, either replace the fixture or have it repaired. Signs of metal strains are paint crazing caused by bulging, warping, or twisting in the metal underneath, bumps or humps on metal plates, and bending or warping in metal bars, tubing, or horns.

⚓ Oil or grease—whichever is called for—all moving parts on equipment and fittings. Use only an approved water-resistant marine oil and grease.

⚓ Replace or have repaired any equipment that is not in top working condition.

⚓ Grease and wire lock all shackle pins. Replace the shackle if the pin is rusted.

⚓ Give all turnbuckle threads a coat of grease. Never use paint, as it makes turning next to impossible when making an adjustment.

⚓ Make sure all turnbuckles have a locking device to prevent accidental turning.

⚓ Replace all rope rigging lines that are frayed below the outer strands, have many broken fibers, or show signs of rot. Replace wire rigging lines that have broken or rusted-out strands.

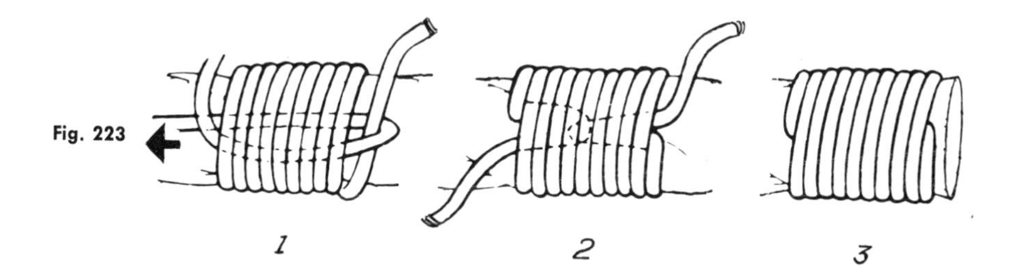

Fig. 223

⚓ Whip (wrap) the ends of all rigging lines to prevent unraveling. On rope lines uses a commercial whipping thread and wax (Fig. 223). On wire line use a good serving wire to whip ends and sections where chafing protection is needed. A trick used to whip the ends of various types of synthetic lines (nylon, Dacron, etc.) is heat sealing. Slowly rotate the end of the line over a low flame until it fuses together into a solid strand.

⚓ When replacing rigging always use new line that has a breaking strength equal to or better than the line being replaced.

Sails, Sailing Hardware, and Running Rigging

⚓ Patch all tears, rips, or holes in a sail by sewing or taping. The taping method is the easiest and, many experts feel, the best way to patch a sail. The tape has a special adhesive on one side and is pressed onto the sail with a hot iron. Chances are, the women sailors of the family will recognize these patches as similar to those they use to mend the children's pants and jackets.

⚓ If sails are mildewed or have acquired rust spots while in storage, wash them in warm water and a mild soap solution. If this does not clean them, ask the advice of a local dry cleaner. Under no circumstance use a strong bleach or detergent. In cases where rust spots have burned through the sail leaving pinholes, you might try patching if only a small area is affected. On large areas the only thing to do is replace the sail. Rust burn and mildew are caused by storing sails wet and dirty. So be sure your sails are both clean and dry before storing.

⚓ Repair or replace any grommets or sail track slides that are bent or missing. Bent grommets can be flattened by hammering them lightly with a ball-peen hammer on a wooden block, while bent sail track slides can sometimes be straightened with a pair of pliers.

⚓ Replace all halyards and sheets (lines) that are heavily frayed, have many broken strands, or show signs of rot.

⚓ Sailing hardware should be greased or oiled and repaired or replaced at the same time you work on deck gear and equipment. Be especially careful when examining blocks. Make sure the sheaves (wheels) turn freely and the pins are not worn or bent.

Steering Gear

Proper maintenance of steering gear is a prerequisite to safe boating.

⚓ Make sure all cables or lines are free from kinks, rust, broken strands, chafing, or rot. Repair or replace where needed.

⚓ Clean and inspect all blocks. Any sheaves (wheels) or pins that are worn or bent should be replaced; where called for, grease or oil, per instructions.

⚓ On linkage-type steering gear replace all broken or bent links and any gears that have broken teeth.

⚓ On hydraulic systems look for leaks at the pistons and along oil lines. Wherever piston leaks are found, tighten the packing nut at the piston head. If this doesn't stop the leak, replace the gasket. Where a line is leaking, tighten the flare fitting nut or, in cases where the line is split, replace that section of line. While checking for leaks look for rust, pitting, and scoring along piston shafts. If any of these symptoms is found, have a hydraulic mechanic check out the system.

Safety Equipment and Instruments

All safety equipment and instruments should be tested and put in first-class working condition before the start of a new season.

⚓ Lifesaving devices, such as life jackets, lifelines, flares, and fire extinguishers, must be replaced if there is any doubt as to their dependability.

⚓ All equipment and instruments should be oiled, greased, adjusted, or refilled according to manufacturer's directions. Wherever special adjustment or attention is needed, have a qualified person do the work. Don't try to fix highly technical instruments that must be in perfect working order to function correctly.

Ground Tackle (Anchors and Rodes)

⚓ Treat ground tackle the same as deck gear: remove all rust from metal parts, grease moving parts and replace the rodes (lines) if they show any sign of deterioration. (*See* ground tackle maintenance in "Anchoring, Mooring, and Tying Up," page 199.)

Engines

Assuming your engine was completely winterized before storing, and no major damage occurred during the lay up, putting it in shape for a new season is relatively simple. Most boatmen equipped with an average set of tools can do the job in a few hours. If, however, the engine was not winterized, has been damaged, or needs a complete tune-up, have a qualified mechanic inspect and repair it. How to do a general tune-up on inboards and outboards is explained in Chapter 9, "Powerboating," page 133. Do not run any engine after de-winterizing until it is in the water.

Inboards

⚓ Clean the engine with a good commercial engine-cleaning compound to remove the coating of preservative used when the boat was put in storage.

⚓ Clean off any rust spots and touch up with a metal paint primer. Look for cracks or leaks wherever there is rust.

⚓ Replace all water drain plugs and lines that were removed before storing, or drain off the antifreeze that was put in the cooling system for the winter lay-up.

⚓ Flush out the cooling system and fill with water.

⚓ Drain the engine preservative oil and replace with fresh oil of proper grade.

⚓ * Grease the propeller shaft and couplings, starter, and generator shafts, all control levers, springs, linkage, and rods, plus all grease fittings. Check the engine maintenance manual for the grade and type of grease to use.

⚓ * Clean out the carburetor bowl(s) and any other filters or screens.

⚓ * Check all lines for tightness and leaks.

⚓ * Check fuel tanks for "gum" deposits. These can be removed with a cleansing agent made especially for gas tanks. When checking the tank, make sure you use a sparkproof light and have removed all causes of explosion.

⚓ * Inspect all engine wiring and replace any where the insulation covering has become cracked, crazed, or oil rotted.

⚓ * Replace all spark plugs and be sure they are properly gapped (distance between the electrodes) for your model engine. The engine manual will give you this information. If you don't have a gap gauge, ask the seller if he will gap them.

Under no circumstances should marine spark plugs be cleaned via the sand-blasting method. If any lead deposits are present, they will be driven up into the plugs. Then, when the plugs are run again, the lead will melt from the heat and flow down onto the electrodes causing preignition. If you must clean the plugs, soak them for a few hours in carbon tetrachloride; then wipe each one dry and reset the gaps.

⚓ After your boat is outside or in the water, fill the fuel tank(s). Never fuel up while still under cover, as the chance of a fuel vapor explosion is ever present. In all probability, if your boat is at a yard, there will be numerous signs telling you this.

⚓ * Hammer or file down any small nicks and dents on the propeller. If the damage is severe, have a mechanic do the job using a pitch block to assure proper balance and alignment.

⚓ * Do not ground any electrical circuit on a metal fixture that does not pass directly into the water. Breaking this rule will set up an electrolytic action causing the metal to break down.

⚓ * Trace out all electrical wires. Replace any that show signs of cracking, crazing, or oil rot.

⚓ * Once the engine is running, check the exhaust system for leaks. This is important, as carbon monoxide exhaust fumes are highly poisonous.

⚓ * Replace and connect battery(s) in battery box. Batteries should be fully charged when brought on board. After the battery cables are secured, coat the battery terminals with grease to prevent them from becoming acid coated.

Outboards*

⚓ Drain the preservative oil from the lower gear case and replace it with the type and grade of grease recommended in the engine manual. When draining the lower unit, watch for metal chips or filings, which could mean the gears are wearing out or breaking up.

⚓ Lubricate all parts needing oil or grease as stated in the engine manual.

⚓ See that the shift lever operates properly. Hard or sluggish response usually indicates lack of a lubricant or bent linkage.

⚓ Remove the propeller to check the drive pin, and grease the drive shaft with a marine waterproof grease. If the drive pin is bent, kinked, or shows signs of wear, replace it.

* Many of the jobs necessary to fitting out inboard engines are also applicable to outboard engines. These are shown with an asterisk in the preceding section on inboards.

⚓ Don't start the motor out of water. Even a few moments of running dry can ruin the water pump impeller.

⚓ Squirt a few drops of light motor oil in each cylinder when the plugs are out. Then, hand crank the engine a few times to lubricate the cylinder walls.

Painting

Experience has shown that good paint, when properly applied, is the best protection a boat can have against the elements, dry rot, and rust. New boatmen often overlook this fact and paint only what will be seen, omitting the hard-to-reach or out-of-the-way spots. To avoid this mistake always obey the rule that paint is a protection agent first and a beautifier second.

To insure a good job, the surface to be painted must be clean and dry. Wherever old paint has peeled, blistered, crazed, or cracked, it must be completely removed down to the bare wood, metal, or plastic. This is best done by sanding or with a paint remover. Do not burn off the paint unless you have had a lot of experience with a blow torch. Charred wood doesn't take paint, and burned boats don't float. Where old paint is in fair to good condition, sand it down to a dull finish so the new paint will have a better gripping surface. Once the sanding or stripping is completed, wipe down the areas to be painted with a tac rag (rag moistened with thinner) to pick up any hidden dust particles. When this is done, the surface is ready for paint. Following are some painting tips that will help make the job easier:

⚓ Paint only over dry surfaces and during dry clear weather. Temperatures should be between fifty and eighty degrees for painting and sixty to eighty degrees for varnishing. Cold slows drying time, while extreme heat causes paint to blister or wrinkle. The relative humidity should be below 65 per cent. Never paint or varnish in damp or foggy weather.

⚓ Paint only over surfaces that are clean and free from sanding dust, oil, grease, wax, etc. Put off painting on windy days if your boat is outdoors.

⚓ As moisture usually accompanies evening time, it is a good idea to allow at least two hours drying time before sunset.

⚓ Use a primer coat when painting over new or clean wood and metal. (Read electrolytic action on metal boats on page 242 before putting a primer on metal hulls.)

⚓ Apply the prime coat (base coat) before puttying nail and screw holes or using white lead. This helps prevent the oil in the putty or white lead from being absorbed in the wood.

⚓ When using a primer paint be sure it is compatible with the finish coat. The surest way to do this is by using the primer recommended by the manufacturer of the finish paint.

⚓ Where possible remove all hardware in areas to be painted or varnished. If removing is impractical, cover each item with masking tape.

⚓ Stir the paint thoroughly from the bottom up. Then pour about one half into a clean can or pail. Stir again (both cans) until all pigment is dissolved, and then pour from one can into another several times.

⚓ Do not paint from the original can. Pour three or four inches of paint into a clean can, and use it as the paint "bucket." When finished, throw the paint in the "bucket" away. Don't pour it back into the original can.

⚓ Do not thin paint unless specifically stated to do so in accompanying directions. Only use thinners that are recommended by the manufacturer.

⚓ Always use an exterior marine finish on exposed surfaces.

⚓ Brush out each coat thoroughly. Avoid too heavy a coat or scrubbing with a dry brush.

⚓ Stop every few minutes and scan for holidays (misses) and runs (sags).

⚓ Always varnish masts and spars. Paint tends to hide any cracks or splits that develop during the season.

⚓ Always start painting from the top and work down. When working above a deck, use a drop cloth.

⚓ Allow ample time for drying between coats of paint.

⚓ Give your paint brushes and equipment a good cleaning when finished.

⚓ Don't leave paint- or thinner-soaked rags laying around. Put them in a covered metal fireproof can or destroy them.

ANTIFOULING PAINTS

All boats, regardless of construction material, that are used in salt or brackish waters, need an antifouling bottom paint to repel the many organisms that cling to the underside of a hull. This may come as a surprise to fiber-glass and metal boat owners who think their craft are impervious to fouling agents. The truth is that bottom foulers, except for shipworms (borers) which only attack wood, will cling to any surface at rest in quiet waters. Fouling does not occur in fast current or when a boat is moving.

So if your craft remains at dockside or on a mooring for lengthy periods, use a strong, soft leaching type of antifouling paint with a copper or mercury base. If, on the other hand, your craft is trailered to and from boating areas and is rarely motionless while afloat, use a hard racing-type antifouling paint, which stands up better under high speed and hard usage. When applying antifouling paint it is absolutely necessary to follow the directions on the can to the letter. Failure to do so can neutralize the antifouling properties or, in the case of metal boats, set up a severe electrolytic action.

Electrolytic Action on Metal Boats

When copper or other metal used in an antifouling paint comes in contact with the aluminum or steel on a metal boat, a chemical action caused by the salt water takes place, causing the aluminum or steel to pit and corrode. The action is similar to that in a dry cell battery, with the salt water acting as the sulfuric acid. To avoid this happening on your boat, paint the hull below the waterline with a coat of special barrier primer before applying the antifouling paint. This will prevent the electrolytic action by separating the metals. Most of the zinc chromate primers make excellent barrier paints. A check with your paint dealer will tell you which one is recommended by the manufacturer of the antifouling paint you plan to use. When a hard finish is called for, look into the new antifoulers that use a plastic rather than metal base. A barrier coat is not needed with many of these paints.

STORAGE AND WINTERIZING

As fall approaches, all boatsmen, except those in the deep South, must start planning on where, how, and when to store their boats for the winter. The where and how will depend a great deal on the boat's size. Small trailered craft can be stored in backyards or garages with the trailer acting as the holding crib. Large boats, however, because of size and weight, must be stored in boatyards or marinas and use custom-made holding cribs. This is also the case when large plank-constructed boats are stored "wet" (left in the water). Unless the owner can check his boat daily, wet storage should be done only in a supervised boatyard. This is especially imperative in the North, where ice can be a serious problem. When to store a boat will depend on the weather and the owner. Most skippers come ashore at the first sign of fall, while the remaining diehards are chipping ice from the tiller before calling it quits. Those in the latter group are usually in the best yard position (closest to the ways or slings) to go over the side come spring. This is the origin of the saying: "Last out, first in."

Choosing a Lay-Up Yard

Skippers who plan on storing their boats in a commercial yard should be certain it has a reputation for responsibility, capability, and sound management. These are usually indicated by proper fire protection, good maintenance of plant and equipment, an absence of congestion and refuse, sound yard rules for both yard personnel and boat owners, and yard owners who show a sincere interest in caring for your boat. Some of these requisites may sound a bit stiff until you realize that a boat out of water is subjected to many stresses and strains not normally encountered afloat, and can sustain severe damage if not stored properly. So avoid the "cut-rate yard" that professes to save you money on storage bills. Nine times out of ten any savings you make will be spent three times over trying to get your boat back into shape come fitting out time.

Fig. 224

Storage in the Open or in a Shed

Where to store your boat, out in the open or undercover in a shed, will depend to a great degree on its construction material. Planked boats that dry out when ashore are best left outside or in an unheated shed. This minimizes seam drying and makes caulking easier the following spring. Molded wooden hulls and boats with a lot of bright work (varnish), on the other hand, store best undercover where the elements can not attack the finish or start dry rot. Boats constructed of plastic or aluminum can be stored either inside or outside, preferably inside when winter work is contemplated. Regardless of where your boat is stored, be sure to cover it with tarpaulin to act as a dust cover inside and a weather cover outside. When used outside, build a framed ridge pole to hold the tarpaulin; this allows rain and snow to run off onto the ground and assures adequate hull and cabin ventilation. Figure 224 shows how a framed ridge pole is placed on a boat. When placing the tarpaulin, be careful not to leave any rain pockets (sags), and check to be sure ample air can get up under the sides or through any vents.

Cribbing

When a boat is stored ashore it is essential that the hull be adequately supported in a holding crib. The object of this is to duplicate as closely as possible the position in which the boat would lie when afloat. With small trailered boats, the trailer bed can act as the crib. Just block up the springs and wheels so they will not have to carry the load all winter. A couple of cement blocks under the axle and a sawhorse under the tongue do an excellent job of blocking. On large craft, cribbing must be custom-made to meet each boat's specifications. Unless you have had previous experiences in this type of work, it is best to let yard employees construct it. Figure 225 shows how a crib is constructed and where the blocking and shoring should be placed. Things to look for when checking a crib are:

⚓ Average-size boats should have at least three keel blocks, one in the area of greatest weight, one near the fore foot, and one in the stern area. Larger craft may need more than three keel blocks. Here is where choosing a reputable yard pays off.

⚓ Boats with long overhangs should have special shoring for these areas to prevent sagging.

⚓ Keel blocks and shoring timbers must be set against framing members or other strong points along the hull. Breaking this rule can lead to hull breaks or warping.

⚓ After the cribbing is checked out and the boat is sitting evenly, tie the cribbing together with one-by-three-inch and two-by-four-inch boards.

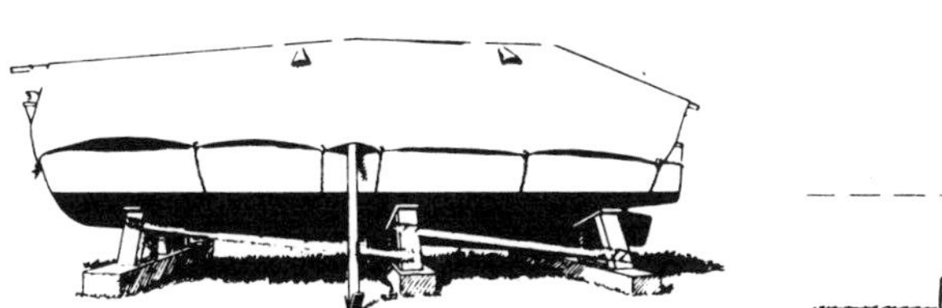

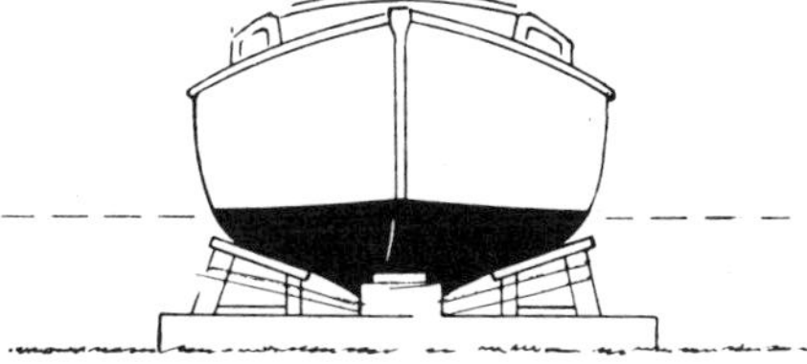

Fig. 225

⚓ Make sure all sea cocks (drain holes) in the hull are left open. This will prevent flooding if rain or snow should fall into the boat.

Winterizing Your Boat

Every boat should be winterized as part of its lay-up program, in order to protect it from the elements and the ravages of enforced idleness. How well this job is done will be a determining factor on the amount of work necessary come fitting out time in the spring. A sloppy, half-done job will mean extra hours of labor and probably major repairs; whereas a conscientious winterizing job makes fitting out a pleasure and will have you over the side in jig time. The best and easiest way to winterize is by following a program similar to fitting out. In fact, except for some procedures which are reversed, winterizing is done the same way. The main thing to watch for is a tendency to take short cuts or put off necessary jobs. This often happens if the weather takes a turn for the worse. When possible pick bright sunny days to winterize, even if it means having to give up a few days afloat.

As winterizing is so like fitting out, I am not going into a detailed explanation of each procedure. Instead, there appears in Appendix D, page 301, a comprehensive lay-up checklist that covers all types of boats. From it you can develop a checklist suitable for your craft. Once this is done, you will have a guide and reminder to help make winterizing easier and complete.

14

Trailers and Trailering

The days when only large cruising craft could sail to distant waterways are gone forever. Today, with a modern boat trailer, any body of water that can be reached by automobile is sailed by "go-by-tow" skippers. In fact trailering has become so popular that most new boat buyers automatically include a "tow rig" as part of their equipment. Along with "highway cruising," well-engineered trailers also act as backyard mooring cradles and winter storage platforms. Both these features should be considered when debating the necessity or cost of a trailer. Usually the money saved in mooring and storage charges will, over a few years, more than pay for the complete outfit. This fact is especially important if you plan any intensive traveling. Do not sacrifice practicality for economy.

SELECTING A TRAILER

When selecting a trailer keep in mind it must safely support your boat and track (follow) smoothly behind an automobile. Unless it performs both these functions well, it is not properly matched to your boat. The first consideration should be adequate support. Make certain of this support by selecting a trailer as long or longer than the boat it will carry. (Length is measured from the bow stop to the rear chocks or rollers [Fig. 226]). This insures ample support for the transom, and outboard engine when carried on the transom. Transoms that hang over the end of a trailer unsupported are prone to warp or spring. Either of these faults can amount to an expensive repair bill. With length,

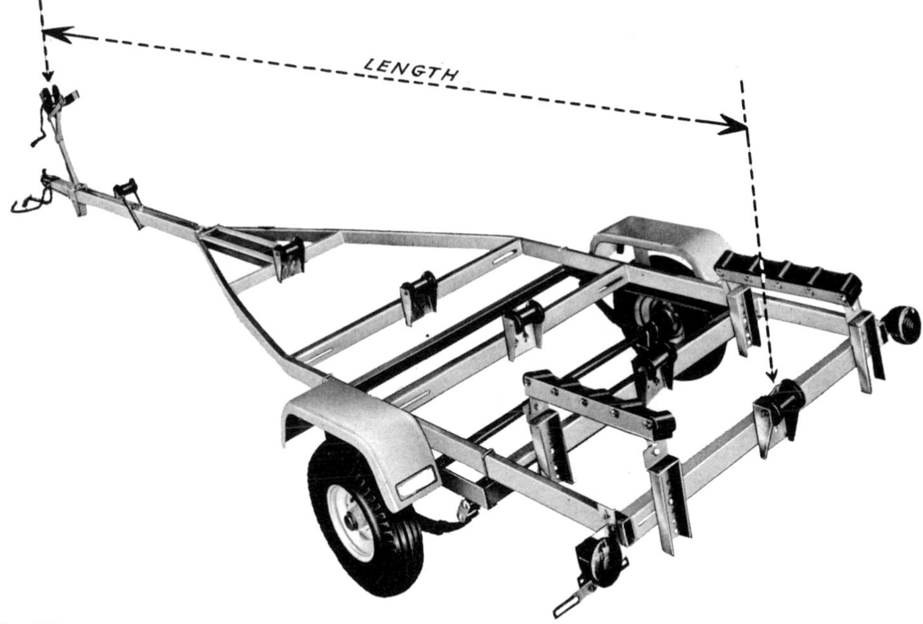

Fig. 226

check the gross load capacity (the maximum weight a trailer can carry at rest or in motion). To be safe it should be 10 to 15 per cent greater than the combined weight of your boat, motor, and all equipment normally left aboard. This extra safety factor allows for traveling over rough roads and the extra gear that somehow always finds its way on board. The load capacity of all trailers built by reliable manufacturers will be plainly marked on the frame. Stay clear of any trailer minus this information. When figuring load capacity don't confuse net weight (weight of trailer alone) and gross weight (maximum weight of trailer, boat, motor, and gear), which is often marked on the trailer with the load capacity.

Once you have made certain the length and load capacity are correct, check the rollers and chocks which hold and support the boat. The rollers should spin easily and have anticorrosive metal or nylon bearings and bushings. The chocks should be well padded to avoid scratching the hull. Both should be adjustable to insure adequate support at key spots on the hull. If up to this point everything checks out, have the dealer place your boat on the trailer. This is necessary even if it means taking the trailer some distance to your boat. While putting the boat on the trailer, adjust the rollers and chocks so they give firm support at the keel, the transom, and at the turn and bottom of the bilge. Figure 227 shows the strategic areas to cradle a hull. Wherever necessary, replace existing rollers or chocks with larger ones, or add more if additional support is needed.

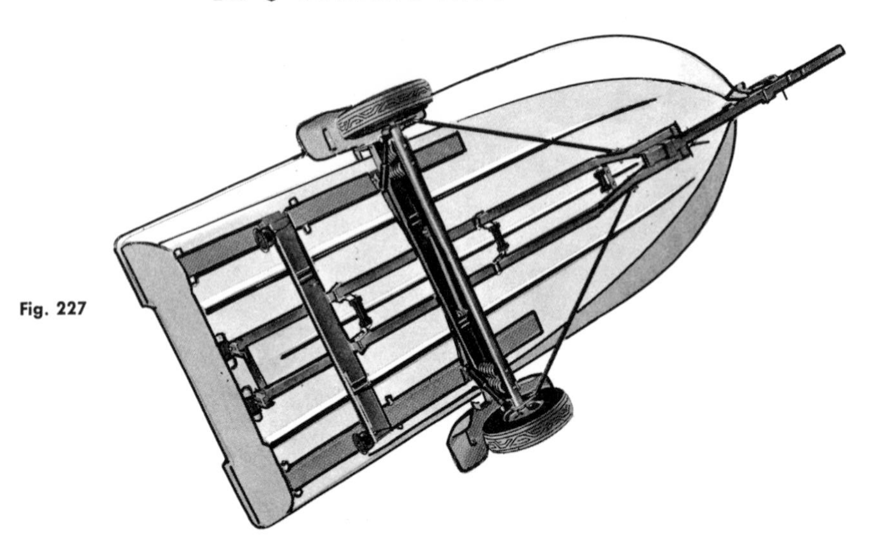

Fig. 227

Once the boat is properly supported and secured to the trailer, take it for a road test and, if possible, a launching test. Use your own automobile for the road test. If it lacks a hitch, have one installed before shopping for a trailer. (See "Hitches" under "Necessary Accessories.") The road test should be made in two stages, with you observing from a second car and with you driving the tow car. When observing, follow the tow car at a safe distance (a minimum of ten car lengths) and watch for the following:

Walking (moving sideways) on straightaways, curves, or turns. Probable Cause: an unbalanced load or one weak spring. Remedy: balance and center boat on trailer. If boat is already balanced and centered, chances are one spring is weak and should be replaced with a new spring of the *same make* and *model.*

Excessive leaning or swaying on curves or turns. Probable Cause: boat too heavy for trailer or weak springs. Remedy: Try next larger size trailer. If you own the trailer, install a set of helper springs or road levelers. Unless the boat is far too heavy, this will usually cure the trouble.

Excessive bouncing (boat only) on rough roads. Probable Cause and Remedy: same as excessive leaning.

Excessive bouncing, both boat and trailer, on rough roads. Probable Cause: boat too light for trailer. Remedy: try a trailer with a smaller load capacity. Be sure it is not shorter. Or, if the dealer is willing, install a set of lighter springs.

Jerking while stopping or slowing down. Probable Cause: loose hitch, boat not tightly secured to trailer, or brakes grabbing. Remedy: tighten hitch, refasten boat, or adjust brakes.

Rear of tow car sagging. Probable Cause: too much weight over front of trailer or weak auto springs. Remedy: shift equipment amidship or to stern, or in the case of weak car springs install helper springs or road levelers.

While making the above tests, check out any accessory that would be used on the move, such as lights, directional signals, and brakes.

When driving the tow car, listen and feel for any of the following causes of troubles:

Squealing trailer tires on turns and curves. Probable Cause: excessive speed, low tire inflation, brakes partially on or grabbing. Remedy: slow down, check air pressure of tires, check brakes.

Tow car rocking or swaying. Probable Cause: trailer load too far forward, weak car springs, car too small. Remedy: shift trailer load to amidship or stern; install helper springs or road levelers. In rare cases a large boat and trailer will be too big and heavy for a small or lightly powered auto to pull.

Automobile sluggish (especially climbing hills). Probable Cause: boat and trailer too big and heavy for tow car (assuming engine and transmission are functioning properly), clutch slipping. Remedy: have clutch checked; try larger auto (more horsepower).

Trailer pushes when tow car slows down. Probable Cause: trailer brakes not working properly. Remedy: have brakes adjusted, or in the case of brakeless trailers, the boat could be too heavy for car or the trailer should have brakes installed.

After driving several miles (some over bumpy roads) stop and look things over. Feel the wheel bearing cups. They should be comfortable to the hand. If one or both are overly warm or hot, it means the wheel bearing needs grease, the bearing is bad, or the wheel nut is too tight and must be loosened a half turn or so. Check all fastenings and tie downs. Any excessive looseness shows the boat is working on the trailer. Look for this especially at the bow tie-down.

If there is an outboard engine on the transom, check to see if it is still fastened securely. This also applies to any equipment secured aboard. Nothing will damage a hull quicker than a sharp or heavy piece of gear rolling around the bilge.

Next, check the trailer hitch. If it needs more than a single tightening turn, it is working loose and should be repaired or replaced.

And, last, check the tires. If they look low or feel soft, it could mean a slow leak, assuming, of course, they were properly inflated when you started. (See "Wheels and Tires" under "Necessary Accessories.")

Except for a launching test, which is covered under "Launching and Retrieving," you should now be able to decide on whether or not to buy the trailer. If it has passed all the foregoing checks and tests, feel confident that the rig is well matched. In cases of minor adjustments or repairs, the trailer could still be a good buy once they are fixed. But, if a major replacement is needed or poor performance was noted, do not buy. Shop for another trailer.

NECESSARY ACCESSORIES

Trailers, like boats and automobiles, can be bought as stripped-down models void of accessories, up through deluxe rigs with everything but the kitchen sink. This gives a boatman the opportunity to buy a production model ready to roll or to build a custom rig suited to his individual needs. With this in mind, the following parts and accessories are usually, but not always, included as part of a trailer package. They also include the accessories that are compulsory equipment in many states. Before buying a trailer, check the laws of your state to see what equipment is needed.

Wheels and Tires

When there is a choice of wheels and tires, always choose the larger size. They outwear smaller tires and give a smoother ride on rough roads. The table in Figure 228 shows the recommended load capacity for different-size trailer tires at various inflations. Adherence to this table will give longer tire life and better trailer performance.

Fig. 228

Tire Size	Recommended Load Capacity	Air Pressure
480 x 400/8—4 ply	up to 1,000 lbs.	65 lbs.
570 x 500/8—4 ply	1000 lbs. to 1300 lbs.	50 lbs.
530 x 450/12—4 ply	1000 lbs. to 1400 lbs.	55 lbs.
690 x 600/12—4 ply	1000 lbs. to 1700 lbs.	40 lbs.
690 x 600/12—6 ply	1200 lbs. to 2000 lbs.	60 lbs.

Spare Tire

Boatmen who plan extensive traveling or trips to rural areas should always carry a spare wheel and tire for emergency use. Do not make the mistake of depending on a tire repair kit. In cases of cuts or blowouts they are useless.

Trailer Jack

One of the most overlooked pieces of trailer equipment is a jack. Most boatmen assume their auto bumper jack will also serve a trailer. Then, when a flat or other emergency occurs, they find much to their despair that bumper jacks do not always fit under the trailer's axle. So check to see if your auto jack will fit under and raise the trailer when fully loaded. If it does not, purchase a hydraulic or scissors-type jack strong enough to lift the gross load and low enough to fit under the trailer's axle when a tire is flat.

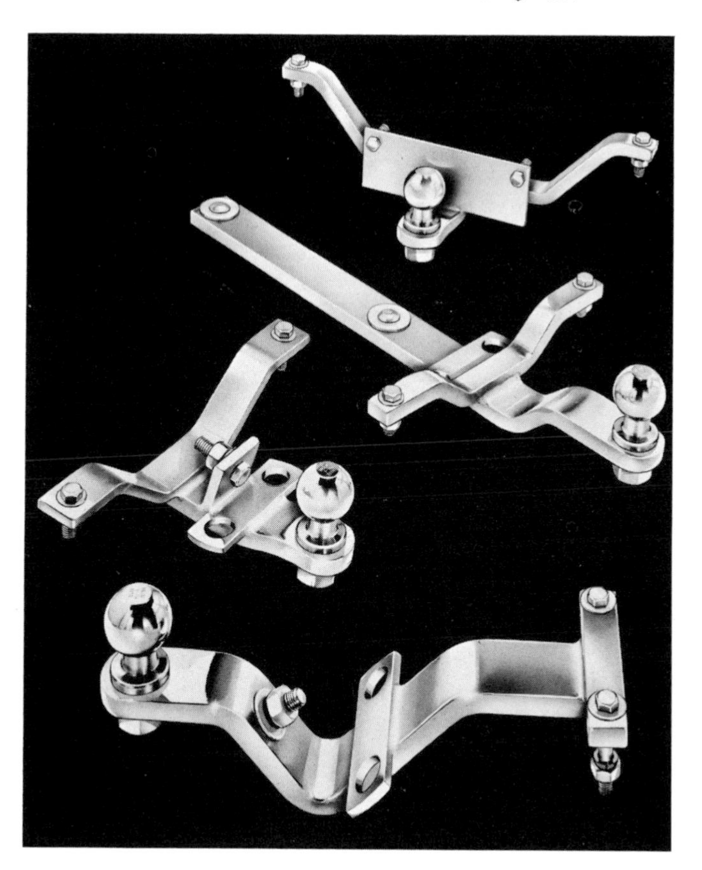

Fig. 229

Hitches

When selecting the hitch that will fasten your car and trailer together, choose a model that bolts directly to the auto's frame (Fig. 229). These hitches, called frame hitches, are the strongest and have proven to be the safest way to pull a trailer. The size needed can be determined from the gross weight to be pulled. Class A hitches for Class A trailers include all nonpassenger utility rigs with a gross weight not exceeding 2,000 pounds. When a ball-type hitch is used, the minimum diameter of the ball should be one and seven-eighths inches. Class B hitches for Class B trailers include both passenger and nonpassenger rigs having a gross weight of 2,000 pounds but not over 5,000 pounds. The minimum diameter of the ball should be two inches. And Class C hitches, rarely used by boatmen, are for Class C rigs, which include all trailers having a gross weight of 5,000 pounds but not over 10,000 pounds.

The minimum diameter of the ball should be two and five-sixteenths inches. Size or towing capacity will be marked on the hitch or the carton it comes in.

Another type of hitch, often used as an auxiliary, is the bumper hitch which attaches directly to the bumper of an automobile. When clamped on a front bumper these hitches allow much greater visibility and maneuverability while launching and retrieving (see "Launching and Retrieving," page 263). Under no circumstances should a bumper hitch be used for over-the-road towing. The danger of breaking free is much greater than with a frame hitch. For this reason, many states have forbidden their use on public roads.

Safety Chain

A safety device that must be used on all trailers is a safety chain. When attached to the trailer and automobile as shown in Figure 230, the safety chain prevents the trailer from running amok or ramming the tow car should it break free. When selecting a chain, get one with a breaking strength at least 10 per cent greater than the gross weight of the loaded trailer. It should also be galvanized against corrosion. Owners of fancy rigs can purchase rubber- or plastic-coated chains which protect the hull, trailer, and car from scratches. These chains are available at all marine and trailer dealers.

Another use for the safety chain is to lock your trailer to a post, tree, or car while afloat. All that is needed is a padlock.

Fig. 230

Lights

Most states require a trailer to show the same lights and signals as those found at the rear of an automobile. The purpose is to reproduce the view an overtaking motorist is accustomed to seeing. The lights required are dual tail lights, stop lights, directional blinkers, and a number-plate light. All of these

Fig. 231

can be bought individually or as a package kit at most marine and trailer dealers. A word of caution: unless you are familiar with automobile wiring and electricity, have the dealer or other competent person install the lighting system. The hookup involves tying into your automobile's electrical system, and unless it is done properly, it will foul up the auto's lighting. When buying lights and signals, make sure they meet the following specifications:

1. All lights and lamps must be as bright as those on your automobile.
2. Lights and signals must be waterproof, and all parts corrosion-resistant.
3. All wiring must be insulated with crack and craze proof covering such as neoprene or its equivalent.
4. Sockets for car connecters must be of the locking type. This insures against their coming disconnected while traveling.
5. Voltage system must be the same as your automobile, usually twelve volts but occasionally six volts on foreign cars.

In addition to required lighting, red reflectors and reflective tape make excellent border markers to show overtaking motorists the outside edges of the boat and trail. Figure 231 shows how reflectors can be used with a tie-down bar to mark the outer edges of a trailer boat. These reflective markers also act as emergency outlines in case of power failure. On my own rig, I go a step further and carry amber reflectors that point forward. This lets oncoming motorists see that I am pulling a trailer with a load wider than my car.

Tie-Downs

The lines, straps, or bars used to secure a boat to her trailer should be selected with the same care given mooring and anchor lines. First consideration should be the bow tie-down. Trailers equipped with a winch can use the winch line as the bow fastener.Trailers without a winch can use either Dacron line, light chain, or elasticized snubber cord. Of the three, snubber cord has proven the best because it holds tight without putting undue strain on the stem eye.

Moving aft there should be one or two tie-downs, depending on the size of the boat. For small boats, a strap with a clamp buckle that can be pulled tight makes a satisfactory tie-down. Its only drawback is that it will pinch and mar the gunwales if too tight. My own preference is a tie-down bar, made from a piece of one-and-a-half-by-three-inch hardwood cut six to eight inches wider than the boat's beam where it rests over the trailer's axle. The bar is placed across the gunwales and held down on each side by snubber cords, chain, or Dacron line. These lines are held by eye bolts placed at each end of the tie bar and by three-quarter eye bolts on each side of the trailer frame. When chain is the holding line, wing nuts are used for tightening. To prevent scratching or marring the gunwales, pad each end of the tie bar with a piece of carpet. Figure 232 shows how to construct a tie-down bar.

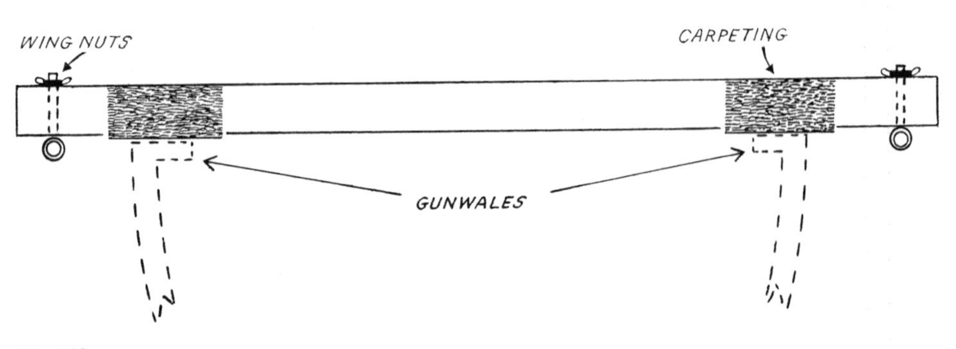

Fig. 232

On boats eighteen feet and over, transom clamps can be used with a tie-down bar. These extra tie-downs are attached to the rear of the trailer and the top edge of the transom with snubber cord or chain.

Brakes

The need for trailer brakes is governed by the weight of the rig being pulled, size of tow car, and local state laws. Generally it is smart to have brakes on any trailer with a loaded gross weight of over 2,000 pounds. Most states with compulsory brake laws use this figure.) Brakes should also be used if a light car (compact or foreign) is the pulling vehicle and if long over-the-road trips are the rule rather than the exception.

The two types of brakes most commonly used are electric and hydraulic. Both are good when well made, just as both can be a constant headache if poorly constructed. When selecting brakes look for the following:

1. Waterproof components at the wheels and power connector. Brakes that are not waterproof quickly short out or corrode.
2. Trailer brakes should be coordinated with the tow car's brakes system so that both work in unison. Trailer brakes that are independent of the tow car brakes tend to grab and release too soon or too late.
3. Make sure the brakes release when backing up. This was a major fault on many older types of trailer brakes.

Trailer brakes, like automobile brakes, are a precision accessory that need fine adjusting. So have a competent mechanic do the insulation and adjusting.

Winch

Every skipper who owns a boat weighing over three hundred pounds and must depend on women or children for crew should consider a trailer winch as necessary equipment. To appreciate why, try wrestling a boat onto a winch-less trailer. Even with adequate help and under ideal conditions it is cumbersome. On the other hand, with a winch that matches the boat, anyone, with a minimum of help, can reel in a boat quickly and easily.

The type and size of winch needed will depend on the weight of the boat. The pulling weight to winding ratio should be high enough to assure easy cranking, and the winch must have a clutch or ratched brake to stop the boat from slipping backward. In such cases the crank spins out of control and could break an arm or jaw. Owners and skippers of large craft, who must often retrieve their boat alone, should look into an electric power winch. These labor savers can be operated at the power head or by remote control (Fig. 233) and only draw a minimum of power from the car battery. The remote control feature is especially handy when retrieving alone in a current or wind.

Fig. 233

As all winches occasionally get wet, they should be rust-resistant or well painted and the gears kept well greased.

Dacron line or stainless steel wire make the best winch lines. Do not use nylon, as its stretching qualities make a poor bow tie-down, or manila, because it wears or rots out quickly. The line should be twice the length of the boat and strong enough to lift it. The hook attached to the end of the line should be a self-locking type and have a breaking strength equal to the line's.

Side-View Mirror

Most trailered boats partially block the view from a car's rear-view mirror. To compensate for this loss of view have a side mirror installed on the driver's side. When particularly wide boats (over seven feet) are being towed, a second side mirror placed on the passenger's side is a great help in heavy traffic or city driving.

Repair Kit

To make emergency repairs, you should carry a few tools and spare parts not usually included in the boat's toolbox. They are a wrench with jaws large enough to handle the largest nut or bolt on the trailer, a wheel bearing kit, a small can of bearing grease, and a tube repair kit. Carry these items aboard in the boat's toolbox to insure not leaving them at home when using someone else's car.

Line

At least a hundred feet of extra line strong enough to lift the boat should be part of every trailer's equipment. This can be the spare line normally carried on board. The times and places this line will be used are too numerous to mention. But it is safe to say it will be used more than any other piece of equipment.

DESIRABLE ITEMS

Following are a few items that, while not essential, are desirable equipment and will make hauling, launching, and retrieving much easier. Some you can build yourself; the others can be purchased from marine or trailer dealers.

Tilt Bed

Trailers built so the cradling section of the frame tilts up to aid in sliding the boat on or off are available from some manufacturers (Fig. 234). They are used mostly in areas where the water does not fall off fast enough to keep the car on dry land while launching or retrieving.

Fig. 234

Catwalk

A board five or six inches wide placed parallel to the trailer's keel supports makes a wonderful catwalk for guiding a boat on or off the trailer without getting wet. When placing the board, be sure it is securely fastened and does not interfere with any rollers, chocks, or the hull when the boat is cradled.

Dolly Jack

If your loaded trailer is hard to move manually, an investment in a dolly jack may be worthwhile. The dolly jack, a jack with a wheel (Fig. 235), lets you raise or lower the bow to push or pull the trailer into coupling position. This eliminates the need for lifting the trailer tongue manually, saving a lot of effort and strain. The dolly jack can also be used to support the trailer tongue during short storage periods. When choosing a dolly jack, keep in mind that the larger the wheel, the easier it will be to roll the trailer.

Fig. 235

Sand Boards

A set of sand boards used in sand or mud for traction under the rear wheels of the tow car or to prevent trailer wheels from sinking are invaluable aids to the skipper who launches and retrieves in out-of-the-way areas. The boards, which can be made from any type of construction lumber, should be eight to ten inches wide, three-fourths to one and a half inches thick and six to ten feet long. While en route they can be stored in the boat. How sand boards are used is explained in "Special Launching and Retrieving Techniques," page 265.

Motor Tilt Bar

When trailering an outboard motorboat, the engine should be tilted up, with the head leaning in away from the transom (Fig. 236). This position allows the engine to ride securely with a minimum of weight over the transom. To insure against the engine flipping upright while under way, a tilt bar, also shown in Figure 236, is often used as an auxiliary to the engine's tilt-up mechanism.

Fig. 236

Wheel Chocks

A couple of four-by-four-inch blocks of wood cut on a bevel make excellent wheel chocks for parking on steep inclines (Fig. 237). Placed under the front or rear car wheels they act as safety wedges and supplement the brakes.

Burlap Bags

A half-dozen burlap bags placed under a car's rear wheels give wonderful traction when stuck in soft sand or mud. Store them in your auto's trunk all year around as they can also be used on snow or ice.

Fig. 237

Outboard Engine Cover

If by chance you tow an outboard motorboat that does not have a boat cover, make sure you cover the engine. Otherwise road dust will raise havoc with the carburetor.

Rubber Transom Pad

A rubber transom pad placed between the transom and engine mount (Fig. 238) helps cushion road shocks and prevent much wear and tear on your engine. Many "trailer sailors" feel this is a necessary piece of equipment.

Transom pads are normally used on small motors. Plates are used on larger motors that are through bolted to transom.

Fig. 238

Air Rollers

Boatmen who must launch or retrieve across rocky beaches, mud flats, or steep banks will find a set of three air rollers indispensable. The rollers, which are elongated air-filled bags, let you roll your boat across or down these areas with a minimum of effort. Although the rollers come two to a set, I have found a third is necessary to handle any boat over twelve feet.

HANDLING A TRAILER

Anyone who drives in a safe, intelligent manner can quickly master the art of handling a trailer. All that is needed is a little common sense combined with a few key rules and maneuvers. Once these are understood, a few practice sessions, the first with an experienced "trailer sailor," will give you ample know-how and confidence to "go by tow" anywhere.

Safe Driving Rules

1. When starting, accelerate slowly.
2. Shift through all gears to avoid excessive clutch wear.
3. Once under way hold a steady rate of speed, from one-fourth to one-third under the posted speed limit.
4. Use your rear-view mirrors frequently. They show you how the trailer is tracking and let you watch for other drivers who start tailgating.
5. To avoid rear-end collisions keep a minimum of ten car lengths between your car and those ahead of you. Let tailgaters pass.
6. When going down steep or long hills, shift into a lower gear. *Never* coast down hills in neutral.
7. Try to plan ahead when you want to stop. This rule is especially important when a trailer is not equipped with brakes.
8. Plan a check stop every couple of hours. Inspect the hitch and safety chain, tie-downs, lights, signals, outboard motor, boat cover, tires, wheels, and wheel bearings. How to make this inspection is explained in "Trailer Maintenance," page 267. A check stop also, makes a wonderful stretch and wake-up period. Just be sure to pull safely off the road. Rest areas and eating spots are good stopping places because they afford ample parking well away from road traffic.

DRIVING MANEUVERS

When moving over the road, always remember that a trailer adds sixteen or more feet to a car's length, which means many of the ordinary driving maneuvers must be exaggerated or changed.

Stopping

When towing a trailer not equipped with its own brakes, you must be particularly careful when coming to a stop. The thousand or so pounds rolling behind you greatly increase the distance usually needed to stop. Pump the brakes when stopping and allow plenty of room. Never jam on the brakes or try to pull up short. This is an invitation for the trailer tongue or boat to break free and move up into your lap.

Trailers equipped with brakes make stopping much easier. When the trailer and car brakes are coordinated, apply the car brakes as you normally do and allow for a bit more stopping room. When the trailer brakes are independent, work them in conjunction with the auto's and allow for extra stopping room. Never use the trailer brakes alone; this puts too much strain on the hitch and brake mechanism.

Curves

When approaching a curve, your trailer will make a shorter arc than the car. Therefore, you must swing wider than usual, allowing the trailer extra roadway to prevent it from running up a shoulder or crossing over into the opposite lane. This means that where a curve is to the right, you keep the car as far to the left as safely possible (Fig. 239). And where a curve is to the left, you keep the car as far to the right as safely possible (Fig. 240).

Turns

Turns should be treated as sharp curves. Do this by exaggerating the swing into an extra wide arc (Fig. 241). At intersections, allow for the extra length by giving yourself more time against oncoming traffic. And be especially watchful for pedestrians and cars moving into the intersection. You must assume they do not realize that the trailer will swing short.

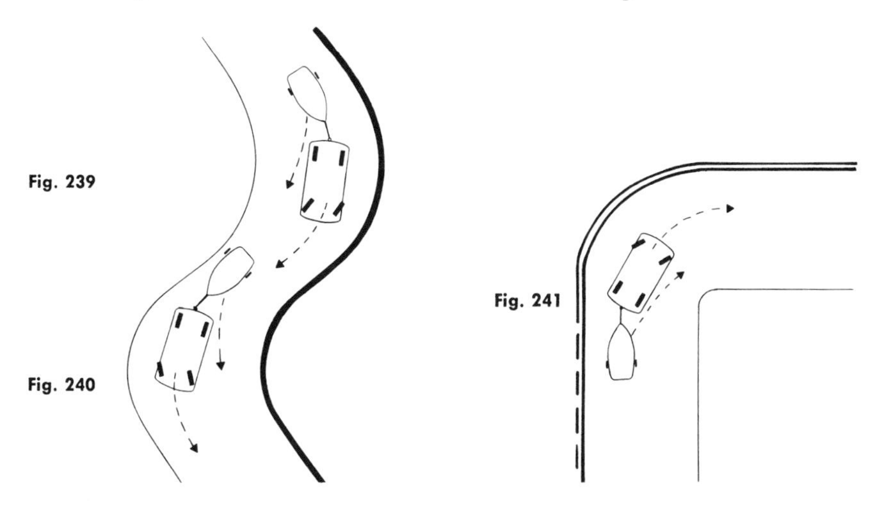

Fig. 239

Fig. 240

Fig. 241

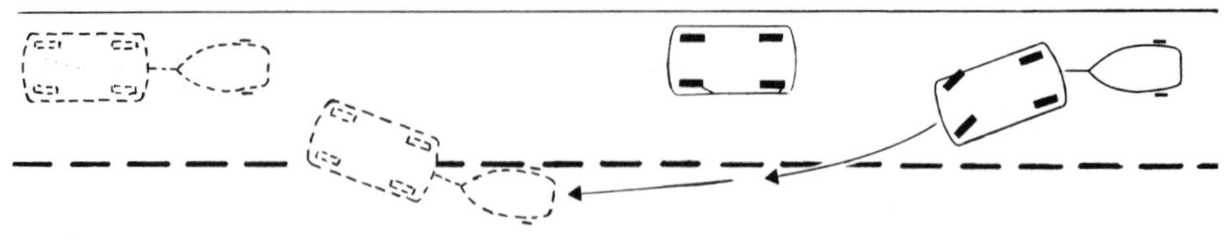

Fig. 242

Passing

Try to avoid passing other vehicles unless absolutely necessary. When you must pass, allow plenty of time and room. Move slowly to the left into the passing lane. When in the passing lane increase your speed and pass. Once you have passed, wait until you are far enough ahead to return safely to the driving lane (Fig. 242). Never cut in sharply on the passed vehicle; remember, you are driving two vehicles, not one.

Backing Up

Backing up is the hardest maneuver to master while learning to handle a trailer. The main things to remember are: when moving straight back, the car and trailer must be directly in line with each other (Fig. 243). Any wandering from this line will cause the trailer to start jackknifing.

When making a turn, the trailer will swing in the opposite direction from that of the auto's wheels. So when backing the trailer to the left, you turn the automobile's wheels to the right (Fig. 244). If you want to back the trailer to the right, turn the wheels of the auto to the left (Fig. 245). Try when possible to make wide turns. Sharp turns are harder to straighten out and quickly send

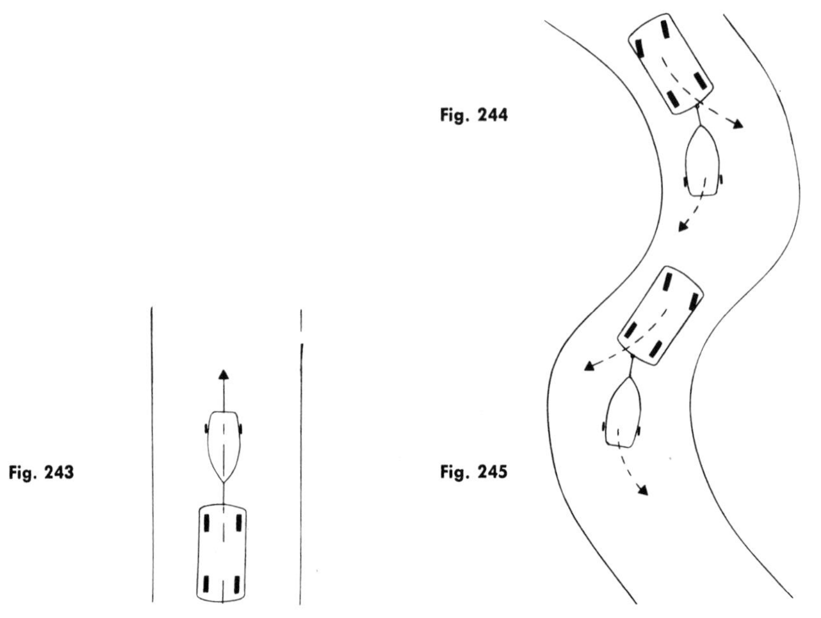

Fig. 244

Fig. 243

Fig. 245

Fig. 246

the trailer into a jackknife. While learning, you may on occasion find yourself in an impossible position. In such circumstances, unhitch the trailer and turn it manually. Even the best go-by-tow sailors occasionally must get out and push. Here is where a dolly jack is invaluable.

LAUNCHING AND RETRIEVING

Once you feel secure towing over the road, head for the nearest launching ramp. If it is heavily used, check first to find when the traffic is lightest. This would be the best time to go over the side, transom first.

To Launch

1. Back the trailer to within a few feet of the water's edge, pull the emergency brake, and put the car in a forward gear. On steep ramps, use wheel chocks.
2. Unplug the lights at coupling to prevent a short, remove the boat cover, tilt outboard engine up and lock, unfasten all tie-downs except the winch line.
3. Re-enter the car and back the trailer into water until the stern of the boat starts to float (Fig. 246). Reset emergency brake and chocks; put the car in forward gear. During this operation keep a constant check on water depth. Try not to let the trailer's hub caps get wet, and *never* let the water reach the auto's tail pipe. If it looks as though this will happen, tie a loose line to the car's bumper and the trailer's tongue, unhitch the trailer, and continue to back it manually. Or raise the front end of the trailer, which will automatically lower the rear end, and allow the boat to slide off slowly into the water. Before the front end is raised, the winch should be unlocked (as explained in 4, below).
4. When the stern is afloat, unlock the winch and slowly push the boat off the trailer (Fig. 247). Once afloat, secure the boat to shore with bow line and detach winch line.

Fig. 247

5. Reel in the winch line. Drive the trailer off the ramp to the parking area.

To Retrieve

Retrieving and loading a boat are the reverse of launching, with a few innovations.

1. After the trailer and car are on the ramp, secure the winch line to the boat's stem eye and position the boat so that it lines up directly behind the trailer (Fig. 248).

Fig. 248

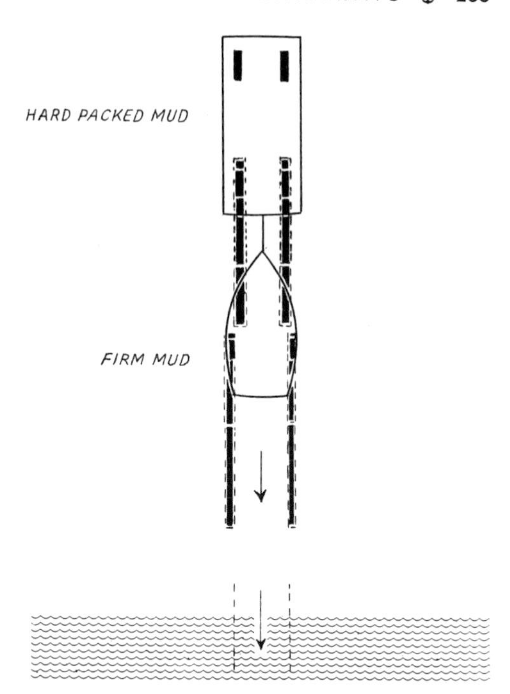

Fig. 249

2. Wind in the boat, making sure the bow rides in over the guide rollers.
3. When the boat is properly cradled, lock the winch, and drive up the ramp until the trailer is land-bound.
4. Then fasten the tie-downs, secure the motor, check the hitch, lights, signals, and brakes.

Special Launching and Retrieving Techniques

In your travels to distant waterways, there will be many times when sand beaches, mud flats, or even worse will be your launching and retrieving ramp. At first, some of these spots will seem impossible, but after a while you will learn that trailer sailors are rarely, if ever, left high and dry on the beach. Following are some of the special techniques they use to get over the side.

On soft sand or firm mud, sand boards make going in or coming out a lot easier. Place the sand boards under the car so that the rear wheels can move slowly over and along the boards. As the rear wheels pass over one set of boards, pick them up and place them to the rear of the second set so that they touch and are in line (Fig. 249). Continue this procedure until the boat is in launching position. Use the same procedure, only in reverse, for retrieving.

Once in a while the problem of retrieving across a mud flat that it is impossible for the tow car to enter must be solved. The best and easiest way is to unhitch the trailer and sand board it manually across the flat to the boat. Load the boat. Take off the winch and attach it to the car's bumper. Then with the spare line, winch the boat and trailer across the flat, again using the sand boards to prevent the trailer wheels from sinking.

Another method used on sand is to remove about 40 per cent of the air from the auto's and the trailer's tires. This gives the tires a wider traction surface. The major problem with this method, and the reason I rarely use it, is that too often you are miles away from a gas station. By the time you refill the tires, they can be cut up inside from going over bumps.

In extreme problems of rocky beaches, soft mud flats, or steep banks, where neither a car nor a trailer can navigate, air rollers are often used. Unload the boat onto the rollers as if you were setting her afloat and roll her sand board fashion into the water; retrieve her in just the opposite way.

Where a steep bank is the problem, use the trailer winch and spare line in conjunction with the air rollers.

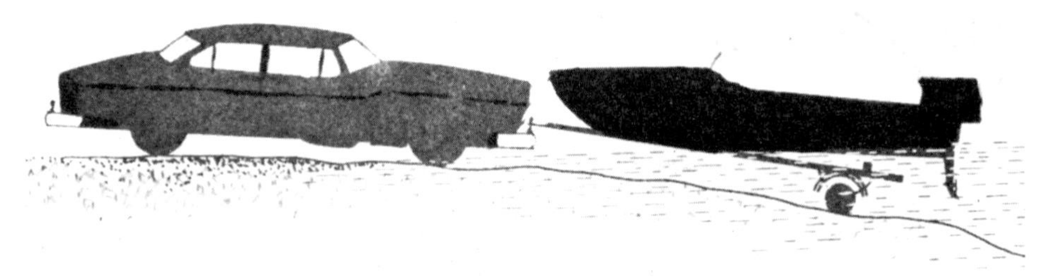

Fig. 250

At confined or crowded ramp area, a trick used by many trailer sailors is front-end maneuvering, using a bumper hitch (Fig. 250). With this set-up, you attach the hitch to the front bumper and maneuver the trailer from the front end of the car. This method is much easier than backing and will keep the car's rear wheels high and dry if traction is a problem. Front-end launching also makes an ideal nighttime rig, as the car's headlights act as launching lights.

Fig. 251

The most common retrieving problem is crosswinds or currents that push the boat's stern downwind while trying to line it up for loading. To overcome this leeward drift, fasten a line to a stern cleat and have a crewman stand on-shore holding the line so it keeps the stern in position (Fig. 251). When loading alone, this same method can be used if your rig has an electric power winch with remote control. Just take the remote control line and move to where the crewman would stand. Without remote control, look for a spot to tie or stake down the line.

TRAILER MAINTENANCE

Today's modern boat trailers need little care or upkeep when a regular system of preventive maintenance is maintained. This is best done through a usage check, periodic lubrications, and a yearly overhaul. The usage check is carried out each time the trailer is used and rarely takes more than ten minutes. Things to check are:

Hitch and Chain

A quick look and shake of the hitch and ball coupler are all that are needed to know if it is snug and tight. Any movement shows a bolt is loose and needs tightening. Make this check before each trip. At the same time check the safety chain for rust and wear.

Tires

Before each trip, check tires for proper inflation and cuts or bruises. On long trips make a habit of checking inflation during gasoline stops. After a long haul on a hot day, however, do not bleed air if the pressure gauge reads a slight overinflation. This is perfectly normal and is caused by the heat. See Figure 3 for recommended trailer tire pressures.

Lights and Signals

Check the lights and directional signals before each trip and after every retrieving. Even though these parts are waterproof, they do on occasion leak, which can cause a short circuit. Also check the plug and connections, clean off any dirt or sand, and make sure they are dry.

Rollers and Chocks

After each launching, take a minute while the trailer is empty and inspect the rollers and chocks. Spin the rollers and pivot any movable chocks. The rollers should turn freely and the chocks more easily. If they do not, a few drops of oil or grease on the bearings or shaft will usually free them. Look for nicks and gouges on the rollers and worn or torn padding on the chocks. Replace or repair as soon as possible.

Winch Line

The winch line should be inspected each time it is used. Look for kinks, knots, broken strands, frayed sections, and rot (if it is manila). Replace when necessary.

Tie-Downs

Inspect the tie-downs each time you load the trailer. Any undue wear, rot, or broken fibers means a replacement is needed. Do not take the chance of having your boat jump off the trailer because a tie-down gave way.

Hose Down

After each salt water use, give the trailer a thorough hosing down with clean fresh water. This protects the paint and unpainted surfaces from salt corrosion. Be especially thorough with wheels and other parts that come in direct contact with the water. A periodic hose-down is also advisable when the trailer is exposed to sea air or polluted fresh water.

Paint Touch-Up

After each hose-down, inspect the trailer for rust, chipped paint, and scratches. Any that are found should be sanded with a medium-grade grit cloth, then touched up with a good paint primer. I use a zinc chromate primer in a throwaway spray can. The zinc chromate is an excellent primer and the spray can eliminates the muss and fuss of a paint brush and clean-up. Boatmen who want to spend a few extra minutes matching the trailer's color can spray on a finish coat once the primer is dry. Matching color paints are available for most makes of trailers.

PERIODIC LUBRICATIONS

Grease and oil are your most important preventive maintenance tools. Without them, a trailer's moving parts would soon rust or wear out. Therefore, it is necessary to give periodic lubrications to help insure trouble-free operation. Generally, on trailers owned by weekend sailors, three or four lubrications per season will do the job. Naturally this figure would increase if the trailer is used around salt water, makes long over-the-road trips, or is subjected to rough use at undeveloped launching areas. In such cases the usage check and common sense will dictate when oil or grease is needed.

When doing a "lube" job, consult the instruction book that comes with the trailer. It will have a section on lubrication, showing all the points and parts that need oil or grease. If you buy a secondhand trailer, have the dealer get you a book or show you how to do a lube job. Usually it is done in two stages, first the oiling, then the greasing. Starting at the front and working aft is also helpful, as it lets you keep track of the fittings more easily. The major parts that use oil are hitch components, winch bearings, winch lock cam, roller bearings (when not self-lubricating), all swiveling parts and levers. Use only S.A.E. #30 motor oil or a high-grade machine oil. Other oils are too light or heavy and will break down or get gummy. Parts needing grease are winch gears, roller shafts, shock pins, wheel bearings, and all grease fittings around the springs or axle. Use only a water-resistant bearing grease such as Lubriplate 70 on these parts.

While oiling, check each fastening with a screwdriver or wrench. Every nut and bolt should be tight yet removable. Any that are frozen must be freed or replaced. A drop or two of oil on each fastening will usually prevent rust freezing.

REPACKING WHEEL BEARINGS

Wheel bearings are in a sense the heart of a trailer and should be repacked at every lubrication, more often if the wheel hubs constantly get wet while launching or retrieving. This also applies to the so-called waterproof bearings that boast a watertight seal. Even they leak occasionally when dunked in cold water immediately after a trip over a hot road. Figure 252 shows the parts of a wheel bearing in the order they fit into the wheel. When disassembling, remember the first part to come off is the last part to go on.

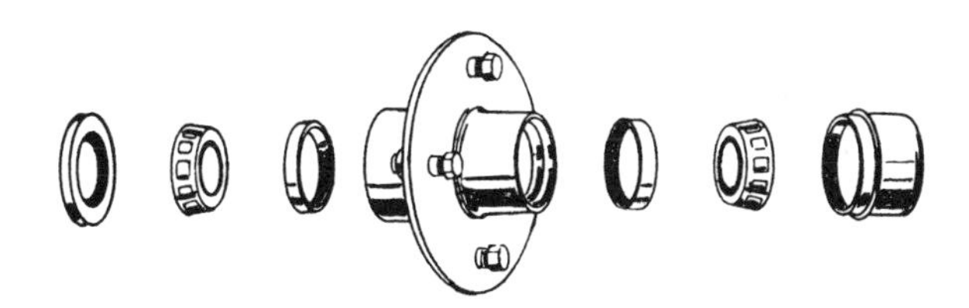

Fig. 252

Trailer wheel parts. From left to right: grease seal; inner wheel bearing; inner wheel bearing cup; hub; outer bearing cup; outer wheel bearing and hub-cap.

Pack wheel bearings as follows: 1. Jack up axle until wheel is off the ground. Then remove the wheel cup, the cotter pin holding the retainer nut, and the retainer nut. Tools needed are a screwdriver, pliers, and wrench. 2. Loosen wheel by pulling toward you and remove outer wheel bearing and outer bearing cup. Next slip off the wheel and remove inner bearing cup, inner wheel bearing, and grease seal. If the wheel pulls off as you loosen it, just reach into the hub and remove the above-mentioned parts. 3. Wash each piece thoroughly, including the axle and inside of the hub, with gasoline. Be sure the room is especially well ventilated while using the gasoline. If it cannot be, wash the parts outside. While washing check for wear and hardened grease particles that sometimes stick to the inside of the hub. Wipe dry and place parts on clean cardboard in the same order in which they were disassembled (Fig. 252). 4. Assemble bearing, packing each part with a water-resistant bearing grease. Be especially sure bearing races are well greased. 5. When bearing is assembled and the wheel is on, tighten retainer nut until snug; then back off one quarter turn to cotter pin hole and replace cotter pin. The wheel should now turn freely without any side play.

OVERHAUL

At the end of each season, give your trailer a complete overhaul. This puts it in shipshape condition for the long winter storage and, come spring, it will be all set to take off after a quick inspection. Start the overhaul with a usage check, giving extra emphasis to the hose-down and painting. Instead of the usual hosing, wash the entire trailer with a good car-wash detergent. After it dries, inspect the frame, axle, and springs for cracks, breaks, or warping. These are usually found at welds or bends and should be repaired by an experienced auto body mechanic. Next, sand, clean, and prime all rust spots and loose paint. After the primer dries, depending on the number of touch-up areas, you can paint either the whole trailer or just the primed spots.

Finally, give a complete lubrication and block up the wheels so the tires are off the ground while in storage. This is best done by placing concrete blocks under the axle at each spring. If the storage area is outside or damp, it is a good idea to spray a light film of oil or silicone all over the trailer to guard against rust.

SPECIAL TRAILERS

Until recently, sailboat and inboard owners had to be content with one body of water because there were no trailers beds suited to their types of boats. Now, however, many manufacturers are building special trailer beds designed to fit various-shaped hulls. With this in mind, sail or inboard enthusiasts should find out if the boat they are buying can be matched to a trailer. If not, they might want to look at some models that can be towed.

15

Cruising America's Waterways

A map of North America quickly shows why cruising is so popular among American boatmen. Point a boat in any direction and there will be a waterway to travel and explore. It does not matter whether the boat is a luxurious yacht or a simple outboard utility, complete with trailer and camping gear, there are enough water and fun for everyone. Family groups are especially partial to cruising. The adults find the low-pressure atmosphere both relaxing and stimulating, while the children rate it tops in fun and adventure. Cruising is also an excellent way for the serious boatman to improve his seamanship and boat-handling skills, since different waterways present different problems.

CAPTAIN'S WAR COUNCIL

Planning a cruise is almost as much fun as making the trip, and it is a wonderful way to help pass the time while awaiting spring. Usually the first attempts will find charts and road maps spread all over the living room floor with each crew member plotting a different trip. At this point a smart skipper will take command and call a "captain's war council" to set up certain ground rules and answer some basic questions.

Size and Type of Boat

From the start, the crew must realize the limitations of their craft. Small runabouts cannot be used to cross large bodies of water or roam miles offshore,

Fig. 253

just as large inboard cruisers make poor lake-hopping boats that must depend on trailer portages between waterways.

Cruise Objective

To insure that everybody on board has a good time, the trip's purpose and objectives should be agreed on well in advance. The quickest way to start a mutiny is by spending a day fishing when half the crew want to go exploring or sightseeing. Knowing what you are going to do and where also gives the "supply officer" a chance to bring aboard any extra special equipment.

Supplies en Route

When plotting a long-distance cruise, be sure there are adequate marinas or stores in the right location to replenish gas, food, and other supplies.

Accommodations en Route

A lengthy cruise also calls for layover accommodations. So, be sure the course has adequate anchorages and marinas for sleeping aboard or campsites, motels, and cottages if you plan to sleep ashore. If the trip is made during the height of the insect season, try to pick anchorages and campsites that have a prevailing breeze. This information is usually available from other boatmen who cruise the area.

What Time of Year to Go

For short, one-day or weekend cruises, departure dates will depend on time available and local weather conditions. On longer cruises, lasting a week or more, it is a good idea to check prevailing weather conditions along the route. Picking your way through a New England fog is no way to see one of the prettiest coastlines in the world. Nor does sweating out a storm during the hurricane season do justice to the famous waterways of the South. A check with local U. S. weather stations will supply you with seasonal forecasts for any part of the North American continent.

Entertainment

To have a good time is the primary objective of everybody on a cruise. This could mean visiting lively marinas, exploring out-of-the-way beaches and coves, touring historical areas, sightseeing at quaint seaside fishing villages, camping at national parks, or just plain relaxing to get away from it all. Fortunately, it is not difficult to plot a cruise that will include any one or several of these forms of entertainment, so try if possible, to let everyone do the things they like best. When time does not allow this, put the omitted entertainment on the top of the list for the next cruise.

Timetable

Many things go into making a cruise a memorable experience, but none is more important than using the time available to the best advantage. Experience has shown that the skipper who sets a leisurely course has the happiest ship. A race to see how many miles or activities can be crammed into a weekend only leaves everyone tired and, in most cases, disappointed. Frequent stops each day to swim, beachcomb, explore, do a little sightseeing, or for just plain leg-stretching seem to be the key to success.

Arriving back in port on time is another necessary ingredient to successful cruising. The surest way to accomplish this is by alloting 40 per cent of the time available to the outgoing leg and 60 per cent for the return run. This allows ample time for minor delays and a chance for a bonus activity near home port if no delays occur. Naturally the above percentages would change if a prevailing condition, such as a current or winds, remained constant.

Supplies and Equipment Checklist

Every cruising skipper should have a carefully itemized checklist of all the supplies and equipment needed on board to insure a safe, carefree trip. Nothing spoils a trip more quickly than to leave an important piece of equipment or some supplies onshore. Before shoving off, have one of the crew go down the list, item by item, checking off each article on board. Don't mark off items still on the dock or in the car. The list in Appendix E, page 307, is intended as a guide. From it you can develop a checklist suited to your own needs. The first category, general equipment, is divided into two parts: essential equipment, most of which is required by law, and desirable equipment, which will make your trip safer and more comfortable. The next two categories, clothing and food, can be amended to suit the needs and taste of your crew.

SHAKEDOWN CRUISE

Once your crew understands how to plot a cruise let them work up a few shakedown trips to nearby areas. Restrict the first couple to all-day affairs; then graduate into overnight and weekend trips. This is the best and quickest way to develop a seasoned boat and crew. During these training trips concentrate mainly on the following: proper boat trim with a cruise load, fuel consumption at various cruising speeds (r.p.m.'s), stowage of equipment and supplies for trim and ease of accessibility, food consumption per day, and equipment that should be added or deleted. These trips are also an excellent time to experiment and see how menus, sleeping accommodations, duties, and watches are working out. When possible, make the shakedown trips in the company of experienced cruising boats or to areas frequented by cruising craft. This puts help within hailing distance if an emergency should arise and lets you observe how the "pros" make it look easy.

GROUP CRUISING

For boating families who enjoy sharing experiences with others, group cruising offers many attractions not normally found while traveling alone. High on the list are planned social affairs, a wider age range of companions for the children, plus safety in numbers should assistance be needed. Generally speaking, group cruising falls into two categories: the informal trip made up of a few close friends who usually belong to the same yacht club and enjoy doing things together; and club cruises, which are highly organized affairs with upward of a hundred or more boats participating. These cruises range from one-day affairs on up to vacation trips lasting two or more weeks. New boatmen are especially attracted to club cruising because it is a wonderful way to get acquainted with other boatmen, and the variety of activities are almost endless. Some of the more popular are beach parties, swimming, moonlight sails, handicap boat races, sightseeing tours, fishing contests, barbecues, and the ever popular "boathopping" and smorgasbord dinners in which many boats contribute one dish each toward a multicourse meal. Information on how and where to join a cruising club can be obtained at most yacht clubs or marine dealers.

KEEPING A LOG

On board all naval and commercial vessels an official record, called a log, must be kept of every voyage. The purpose of this record is to make it possible to reconstruct the trip, in whole or part, at any time in the future should the need arise. Many pleasure boatmen also keep a log, even though it is not compulsory. They find it the simplest way to keep track of fuel consumption, engine hours, and other items pertaining to the operation and safety of a boat. Cruising skippers usually go a bit further and include a list of passengers, crew, various courses, and a daily journal of happenings and events. This gives them a detailed account of every cruise and makes enjoyable reading during the off-season when thoughts occasionally roam the blue water. For skippers who would enjoy developing their own personal log, the sample log form in Figure 254 can be used as a guide. When only a basic log is needed, use section A. If a more detailed record is desired, use sections A and B. Ready-made books, styled after commercial logs, can be purchased at most marine dealers. If you plan to keep a detailed log, don't attempt to fill in the journal section hour by hour. Such a practice tends to become a chore and will cause you to lose interest quickly. Instead, fill in the necessary items when called for and save the journal section until you have a few moments to reflect and think about the day's events. I have found just before turning in, when the crew is all below, my best time to log.

Another point worth mentioning is the effect photography can have on keeping a log. In recent years taking movies and snapshots has become standard procedure aboard pleasure craft. Unfortunately this has caused many boatmen to drop the journal section of their log. Don't you make this mistake. Your log can record all the events the camera missed and, like a good book, will become a treasured possession.

DEVELOPING A CRUISE LIBRARY

Too often boatmen, when back from a cruise, are disappointed to learn that they missed some important sights or could have returned home by another route. The reason usually is that they knew little or nothing of the cruise area.

Fig. 254

SAMPLE CRUISE LOG

A. Name of Boat ________________________ Date __________
Registry No. ________________ Type Boat ______________
Length ____________________ Color ________________
Other Distinguishing Features ____________________________
Departure From ______________________ Time __________
Destination ______________________________________
Anticipated Stops __________________________________
Route or Cruise Plan ________________________________
Estimated Date and Time of Return ______________________
If radio is aboard:
Transmitting Frequency ______________________________
Receiving Frequency ________________________________
Time when monitoring ______________________________
Names of People aboard ______________________________
____
____
If overdue, contact ________________________________

B. Weather ____
Fuel (gallons) ______________
Fresh water (gallons) __________
High water (time) ______________Low water (time) __________
Days run __________________miles ______________
Journal: ____
____
____

NOTE: Make a habit of leaving a copy of section A with a responsible person or harbor-master. Then if trouble develops while afloat the Coast Guard or rescue parties will know where to look for you.

To be sure this does not happen to you, start now to develop a cruise library. Collect all available charts, pilots, and road maps of the various waterways and areas you would like to travel. Next gather information on anchorages, campsites, recreation facilities, and other points of interest along the proposed cruise routes. The charts and maps will show you how to go, while the other information will help you to decide where to go, what facilities are available, and the things you can do and see. Fortunately building such a library is not the job it seems at first glance. Most of the needed information can be obtained from federal or state agencies, with the rest available from private and commercial sources.

Following is a breakdown of available materials and their sources. To simplify matters each major source (federal, state, private) is listed separately. Most items will have a small charge to cover printing costs and handling. Wherever a free catalogue is available, a cost breakdown will be included. When a catalogue is not available, cost can be obtained by writing to the source.

United States Government

Coastal Charts. United States Coast and Geodetic Survey, Washington 25, D. C. These charts cover the Atlantic, Pacific, and Gulf coasts plus the Intracoastal Waterways, the Hudson River north to Troy, Alaska, the Hawaiian Islands, and other U. S. possessions. On the East Coast the 1,200 series charts are the most commonly used. Each one shows an area of about 30 miles running north to south. On the West Coast, which includes the Columbia River and Lake Mead, the 5,000 series small-scale large-area charts are the most frequently used. The U.S.C. & G.S. charts are considered the most accurate and finest in the world. A free catalogue, available from the above address, lists all of these charts, the areas they cover, and cost per chart or set of charts.

Lake and Canal Charts. U. S. Lake Survey, 630 Federal Building, Detroit 26, Michigan. These charts include the Great Lakes and connecting waterways, St. Lawrence Seaway, New York State canals, Lake Champlain, Lake of the Woods, Fox River, Lake Winnebago, and Rainy Lake. A free catalogue listing these charts and the areas they cover is available from the above address.

Illinois Waterway. Corps of Engineers, U. S. Army, 475 Merchandise Mart, Chicago 54, Illinois. A book of charts showing navigable waters from Lake Michigan to the Mississippi River. A free index map is available from the above source.

Mississippi River. Corps of Engineers, U. S. Army, 475 Merchandise Mart, Chicago 54, Illinois. Charts from Minneapolis, Minnesota, to Cairo, Illinois, from Cairo, Illinois, to Grafton and from Cairo, Illinois, to the Gulf of Mexico. Individual sets of charts are available for each of the above sections.

Ohio River. U. S. Army, Engineer Division Ohio River, Corps of Engineers, U. S. Army, P. O. Box 1159, Cincinnati 1, Ohio. Charts from Pittsburgh, Pennsylvania, to the Mississippi River. Available in three sets.

Mississippi River Tributaries (including the following rivers). Mississippi River Commission, Corps of Engineers, U. S. Army, P. O. Box 80, Vicksburg, Mississippi, Arkansas-Atchafalaya, Big Sunflower, Ouachita, Red, St. Francis, White, Yazoo.

Missouri River. Corps of Engineers, U. S. Army 1709 Jackson St., Omaha 2, Nebraska.

Tennessee and Cumberland Rivers and Kentucky Lake. U. S. Army Engineer District, Nashville Corps of Engineers, P. O. Box 1070, Nashville, Tennessee.

Lake Texoma on the Texas and Oklahoma Border. U. S. Army Engineers Office, Corps of Engineers, Denison, Texas.

New Small Craft Charts. United States Coast and Geodetic Survey, Washington 25, D. C., or any U.S.C. & G.S. sales outlet. These new charts have been designed especially for the small craft skipper. All information is related to small craft use. A request to the above address will bring you a list of the waterways which these maps now cover and the areas presently being mapped.

Coast Pilots. United States Coast and Geodetic Survey, Washington 25, D. C., or any of their sales outlets. These are government publications intended to give further aid to boatmen by supplementing the information given on charts. New boatmen will find them invaluable as they contain a wealth of information on courses, routes commonly followed, distances between points, piloting information, weather, local harbors, repair facilities, etc. A request to the above address will get you a list of available Coast Pilots.

Great Lakes Pilot. U. S. Lake Survey, Corps of Engineers, 630 Federal Building, Detroit 26, Michigan. This is an annual publication kept up to date with seven supplements per year. Similar in content to the U. S. Coast Pilots, it covers all areas under the jurisdiction of the U. S. Lakes Survey, Corps of Engineers, U. S. Army.

National Parks, Campsites, Historic Sights, and Recreation Areas. Superintendent of Documents, Government Printing Office, Washington, 25, D. C. In addition to charts, pilots, and maps your cruise library should have information on any national parks, campsites, historical areas, etc., that you might visit. Following is a list of publications giving such information.

The National Park Story in Pictures.
Areas Administered by The National Park Service.
The National Park System, Eastern United States.
The National Park System, Western United States.
National Parks, Historic Sites, National Monuments, a price list of many publications entitled "PL-35".
Camping Facilities in the National Park System.

National Forest Areas. Forest Service, U. S. Department of Agriculture, Washington 25, D. C. There are nearly 200 million acres of national forest, many with excellent recreational waterways. The booklet *National Forest Vacations* lists these forests by states and tells of their facilities and attractions.

Canadian Government

Charts. Canadian Hydrographic Service, Department of Mines and Technical Surveys, 249 Queen Street, Ottawa, Canada. A complete catalogue of all Canadian charts covering the Atlantic, Pacific, and Arctic coasts, the Great Lakes and St. Lawrence Waterway, plus all inland charted navigable lakes and rivers is available from the above source. Also available are booklets on the canals of Canada and the rules and regulations for the canals.

Canadian Pilots and Sailing Directions. Canadian Hydrographic Service, Department of Mines and Technical Surveys, 249 Queen Street, Ottawa, Canada. These pilots are published as a supplement to Canadian charts. They are available in the following sets: *Great Lakes Pilot*, Vol. 1, covering Lakes Ontario, Erie and St. Clair; *Great Lakes Pilot*, Vol. 2, covering Lake Huron, Georgian Bay and the Canadian shore of Lake Superior; *St. Lawrence Pilot*, covering the coast of Quebec and the Atlantic Provinces; and the *St. Lawrence Pilot* from Quebec to Kingston Harbor, plus the Richelieu and Ottawa rivers.

Worldwide

Charts. U. S. Hydrographic Office, Washington 25, D. C. These charts are intended for the deep-water sailor. They cover offshore waters, foreign waters, oceans of the world plus Great Circle sailing charts for long-distance cruising. A general catalogue, listing these charts, is available from the above address.

States and Canadian Provinces

All fifty of the United States and all of the Canadian provinces have commissions or departments whose primary purpose is to attract vacationers and tourists. Toward this end they have developed and published reams of information on the various attractions of their states or provinces. Boatmen especially will find a wealth of information, since all these sources realize boating has become a major recreation sport. To obtain general or special information on any waterway in a given state or province write to the following addresses:

Alabama: Division of State Parks, Dept. of Conservation, State Administration Bldg., Montgomery 4, Alabama

Alaska: Division of Tourism and Economic Development, Room 310, Alaska Office Bldg., Juneau, Alaska

Arizona: Development Board, 1521 W. Jefferson St., Phoenix, Arizona

Arkansas: Publicity and Parks Commission, State Capitol, Little Rock, Arkansas

California: Division of Beaches & Parks, Dept. of Natural Resources, P. O. Box 2390, Sacramento 14, California

Colorado: Colorado State Game and Fish Dept., 1530 Sherman, Denver 1, Colorado

Connecticut: Connecticut Development Commission, Hartford 15, Conn.; and Park & Forest Commission, Hartford 15, Conn.

Delaware: State Development Dept., 45 The Green, Dover, Delaware

Florida: The Florida Development Commission, Carlton Building, Tallahassee, Florida; and Florida Park Service, P. O. Drawer 1487, Tallahassee, Florida

Georgia: Dept. of State Parks, 418 State Capitol, Atlanta 3, Georgia; and Game and Fish Commission, 401 State Capitol, Atlanta 3, Georgia

Hawaii: Hawaii Visitor's Bureau, 2051 Kalakaua Ave., Honolulu 15, Hawaii (cable address "VISBU")

Idaho: State Parks and Recreational Areas, Dept. of Public Lands, Boise, Idaho

Illinois: Division of Parks & Memorials, Dept. of Conservation, Springfield, Illinois

Indiana: Department of Conservation, 311 West Washington Street, Indianapolis 9, Indiana

Iowa: Public Relations Section, State Conservation Commission, E. 7th St. & Court Ave., Des Moines 8, Iowa

Kansas: Kansas Forestry, Fish & Game Commission, Box 581, Pratt, Kansas

Kentucky: Kentucky Tourist & Travel Commission, Frankfort, Kentucky

Louisiana: State Parks & Recreation Commission, P. O. Box 2541, Baton Rouge, Louisiana

Maine: The State of Maine Publicity Bureau, Gateway Circle, Portland 4, Me.; and State Park Commission, Augusta, Me.

Maryland: Division of Tourist Development and Publicity, Department of Economic Development, State Office Building, Annapolis, Maryland

Massachusetts: Dept. of Natural Resources, Division of Forests & Parks, 15 Ashburton Place, Boston 8, Mass.

Michigan: Michigan State Waterways Commission, 1004 Cadillac Square Bldg., Detroit 26, Mich., and Michigan Dept. of Conservation, Office of Information & Education, Mason Bldg., Lansing 26, Mich.

Minnesota: Division of State Parks, Dept. of Conservation, State Office Bldg., St. Paul 1, Minn.

Mississippi: Mississippi Park Commission, 1104 Woolfolk State Office Bldg., Jackson, Miss.

Missouri: Missouri Division of Resources and Development, Jefferson Bldg., Jefferson City, Mo.; and Missouri State Park Board, Box 176, Jefferson City, Mo.

Montana: Fish and Game Dept., Helena, Mont.; and State Parks Director, Helena, Mont.

Nebraska: Nebraskaland, State Capitol, Lincoln 9, Nebraska

Nevada: Nevada State Park Commission, Carson City; and State Fish & Game Commission, 51 Grove St., Box 678, Reno, Nev.

New Hampshire: New Hampshire State Planning & Development Commission, Concord, N. H.; State Parks and Historic Sites and New Hampshire Recreation Division, State House Annex, Concord, N. H.

New Jersey: Division of Planning & Development, Dept. of Conservation and Economic Development, 520 E. State St., Trenton 25, N. J.; and Division of Fish & Game, 230 W. State St., Trenton 25, N. J.

New Mexico: State of New Mexico, Dept. of Game & Fish, Capitol Bldg., Santa Fe, N. M.; and State Parks Commission, P. O. Box 958, Santa Fe, N. M.

New York: Division of Parks, Conservation Dept., State Campus Site, Albany 1, N. Y.; Division of Lands and Forests, Conservation Dept., State Campus Site, Albany 1, N. Y.; and Dept. of Conservation Div. of Motor Boats, State Campus Site, Albany 1, N. Y.

North Carolina: State Advertising Division, Dept. of Conservation & Development, Raleigh, N. C.

North Dakota: Public Relations Director, North Dakota Game & Fish Dept., Bismarck, N. D.

Ohio: Chief, Div. of Parks, Ohio Dept. of Natural Resources, 1500 Dublin Rd., Columbus 12, Ohio

Oklahoma: Tourist Division, Oklahoma Planning and Resources Board, 533 Capitol, Oklahoma City 5, Okla.

Oregon: Oregon State Highway Dept., Travel Information Division, Salem, Ore.

Pennsylvania: Travel Development Bureau, Pennsylvania Dept. of Commerce, Harrisburg, Pa.; and Director of Public Information, Dept. of Forest and Waters, Harrisburg, Pa.

Rhode Island: Publicity and Recreation Div., Rhode Island Development Council, Roger Williams Bldg., Hayes St., Providence 8, R. I.; and Division of Parks & Recreation, Dept. of Public Works, Providence, R. I.

South Carolina: South Carolina State Development Board, P. O. Box 927, Columbia, South Carolina

South Dakota: Division of Forestry & Parks, Dept. of Game, Fish & Parks, Pierre, S. D.

Tennessee: Division of State Parks, Dept. of Conservation, 203 Cordell Hull Bldg., Nashville 3, Tenn.; and Tennessee Game and Fish Commission, Cordell Hull Bldg., Nashville, Tenn.

Texas: Texas State Parks Board, Drawer "E," Capitol Station, Austin, Texas; and Texas Game and Fish Commission, Walton State Bldg., Austin, Texas

Utah: Utah Tourist and Publicity Council, State Capitol, Salt Lake City, Utah

Vermont: Dept. of Forests & Parks, Montpelier, Vt.; and Dept. of Public Safety, Montpelier, Vt.

Virginia: Dept. of Conservation and Economic Development, 823 State Office Bldg., Richmond 19, Va.

Washington: Department of Conservation, General Administration Bldg., Olympia, Wash.; and Washington State Parks and Recreation Commission, 522 So. Franklin, Olympia, Wash.

West Virginia: Industrial & Publicity Commission, State Capitol, Charleston 5, W. Va.; and Division of State Parks, Conservation Commission, State Office Bldg., Charleston 5, W. Va.

Wisconsin: Wisconsin Conservation Dept., Madison 1, Wisc.; and Recreational Publicity Section, Wisc. Conservation Dept., P. O. Box 450, Madison 1. Wisc.

Wyoming: Wyoming Travel Commission, 213 Capitol Building, Cheyenne, Wyo.; Superintendent, Grand Teton National Park, Moose, Wyo.; and Superintendent, Yellowstone National Park, Yellowstone Park, Wyo.

Canadian Provinces
Alberta: Travel Bureau, Legislative Building, Edmonton, Alberta
British Columbia: Government Travel Bureau, Dept. of Recreation and Conservation, Victoria, B. C.
Manitoba: Travel and Publicity Branch, 254 Legislative Bldg., Winnipeg 1, Manitoba
New Brunswick: Travel Bureau, P. O. Box 1030, Fredericton, N. B.
Newfoundland: Newfoundland Tourist Development Office, Confederation Building, St. John's, Newfoundland
Northwest Territories: Northwest Territories Tourist Office, 150 Kent St., Ottawa
Nova Scotia: Nova Scotia Travel Bureau, Provincial Bldg., Halifax, N. S.
Ontario: Dept. of Travel and Publicity, 67 College Street, Toronto, Ontario
Prince Edward Island Travel Bureau: P. O. Box 1087, Great George St., Charlottetown, P.E.I.
Quebec: Provincial Publicity Bureau, 106 Grand-Allee, Quebec
Saskatchewan: Travel Bureau, Dept. of Industry & Information, Legislative Annex, Regina, Saskatchewan
Yukon Territory: Yukon Travel Bureau, Box 419, Whitehorse, Y. T.

Commercial and Private

In their advertising programs many businesses and promotional groups publish informational literature aimed at boatmen and others who might use their product or visit their area. An excellent example of this is the road maps and cruising guides offered free by all major oil companies and distributed through their local gas stations. Following are some of the major sources for this type of information. When writing for material be specific about what you want in the way of information. This will save you and the sender time and unwanted material.

Oil companies
Insurance companies
Chambers of commerce
Yacht clubs
Tourist associations
Hotels
Motels
Outboard Boating Club of America,
307 N. Michigan Avenue
Chicago 1, Illinois

Related Publications

As a supplement to the normal information gathered for a cruise library, the following publications are available and should be included when they apply to your cruising plans.

Notice to Mariners. United States Hydrographic Office, Washington 25, D. C. This pamphlet is published weekly by the U. S. Coast Guard and the U. S. Hydrographic Office. Its purpose is to keep boatmen up to date on any chart or pilot changes. To receive a free weekly copy write to above address.

Local Notices. Commanders of Local Coast Guard Districts. This information on chart changes, new hazards, etc., is limited to an area within a respective Coast Guard District.

Tide Tables, Current Tables, Current Charts. United States Coast and Geodetic Survey, Washington 25, D. C. These publications are especially valuable while coastal cruising, for they give the times of high and low tide, directions of currents, etc.

Light Lists. Superintendent of Documents, Washington 25, D. C. These lists describe the lighted aids, unlighted buoys, day markers, fog signals, and radio beacons found on various sections of the U. S. Coast, the Great Lakes, and Mississippi River System.

Inland Waterway Guides. Inland Water Guide, Inc., 101 North Andrews Avenue, Fort Lauderdale, Florida. Three books: The *Northern* volume covers the areas from Boothbay, Maine, to Norfolk, Virginia, the *Southern* covers the area from Sandy Hook to New Orleans; the *Great Lakes* covers Lake Erie, Lake Ontario, the St. Lawrence River, and the New York Canal System. These books give brief but excellent descriptions of the waterways, harbors, and anchorages, where supplies and equipment are available, plus a host of other helpful information.

Yachtsman's Guide and Nautical Calendar. Motor Boating Magazine, 572 Madison Avenue, New York 22, New York. This has been a reference guide for cruising boatmen for over eighty years. It includes coast pilots, tide tables, yacht club directories, cruising tips, plus a lot of down-to-earth information on cruising and cruising equipment.

Great Lakes Waterway Guide. Great Lakes Publishing Company, 843 Delray, Grand Rapids, Michigan. An excellent book listing the waterways, harbors, available supplies and equipment outlets, etc., of the Great Lakes, St. Lawrence River, Richelieu River, Lake Champlain, and New York Barge Canal.

Pleasure Boat Cruises. New York Times, 229 West 43rd Street, New York 36, New York. A booklet of 26 selected cruises with a wealth of cruising information and tips.

Yachtsman's Guide to the Bahamas. Nassau Development Board, 608 First National Bank Building, Miami 32, Florida. A must for the skipper who hopes to put the Bahamas on his cruise list.

Recreation on the T.V.A. Lakes. Tennessee Valley Authority, Knoxville, Tennessee. A free guide to the boating and recreation attractions found on the T.V.A. lakes.

Rangely Lake System. Rangely Lakes Publicity Association, Rangely, Maine. Charts and information on camps, recreation areas, etc.

Moosehead Lake. Sadlers Store, Greenville Village, Maine. A chart of Moosehead Lake, published by the Kennebec Water Power Company.

Shasta Lake. Shasta, Cascade Wonderland Association, Redding, California. Maps and information on the various attractions of California's largest inland waterway.

Lake of the Ozarks. Lake of the Ozarks Association, Box M-1, Lake Ozark, Missouri. Its length of 129 miles, with over 1,300 miles of shoreline, makes the Lake of the Ozarks one of America's major inland boating centers.

Appendices

APPENDIX A

Sea Talk

A GLOSSARY OF NAUTICAL TERMS

Along with learning boathandling and seamanship, new sailors who want to become proficient seamen must also learn a new language—Sea Jargon.

Floors will become "decks," toilets "heads," stairs "ladders," right "starboard," left "port," etc., etc. Fortunately, like most aspects of boating, sea jargon is colorful and fun to learn. Just a few minutes of study, and the everyday words used in the operation of ships and for signaling will be part of your vocabulary. The remaining words and terms can be studied at your leisure or picked up in conversation and by listening to other sailors.

To get you aboard and under way in jig time, an asterisk (*) precedes the more commonly used words. Learn these now to handle your boat safely, then learn the others at your leisure:

Abaft—toward the stern

*__Abeam__—at right angles to the keel

*__Abreast__—side by side

*__Aboard__—on board, within a boat

*__Adrift__—drifting without power, broken from a mooring or anchor

*__Afloat__—on the water, waterborne

Alongside—by the side of (ex., alongside a dock)

*__Amidships__—the middle of a boat, halfway between the bow and stern

*__Anchor__—an implement used to hold a boat while afloat in a desired spot

Anchorage—an area reserved for anchoring boats

*__Astern__—behind a boat or in a backward direction (when a boat moves backward, it is going astern)

Bail—remove water from inside a boat with a bucket or bailer

Bailer—a container or device used to remove water from a boat

*__Bar (sand, mud)__—a bank or shoal of sand or mud formed by currents or wave action. When a bar is just below the surface, it becomes a navigational hazard. Bars are usually found at the mouths of rivers and inlets

*__Beacon__—a signal or marker used as an aid to navigation

*__Beam__—widest part of boat

Bearing—the direction of an object from a boat

Bear-off—to stay clear of, steer away from, to avoid a collision

*__Below__—below deck or in a cabin

Berth—space allotted a boat when at anchor, moored or docked. Also, any bed aboard a boat

*__Bilge__—lowest part of a hull's interior. Usually below the floorboards on small craft

Binnacle—a protective housing for a compass

*__Bitt__—A strong perpendicular timber going through the deck, to which lines may be secured

Bitter end—the inboard end of any line

Block—a pulley

*__Blow__—a strong wind or storm

*__Bow__—the forward part of a hull

Bring about—to reverse the direction of a boat

*__Broach to__—when a boat is broadside to the wind or waves and is in danger of being rolled over

Bunk (berth)—a bed on board a boat

*__Buoy__—a floating navigation aid anchored in place to mark channels, obstructions, and special areas

*__Burdened vessel__—the boat which must give way to another when they meet (see Rules of the road)

Capsize—to upset or overturn

*__Cast-off__—cast loose from a dock or mooring in preparation to get under way

Chart—a marine map showing water depths, channels, buoys, obstructions, land areas, etc.

Chock—a metal or wooden fitting with short horns curved inward which acts as a guide for anchor, docking, and other lines

*__Cleat__—a metal deck fitting used to secure lines while afloat

Coaming—a raised plank rail designed to keep water out of a sailboat's cockpit

Cockpit—open section of a boat lower than the deck which contains seats, steering controls, and compass

*__Current__—a horizontal flow of water, usually caused by gravity such as a river current. Other types are tidal currents caused by incoming and outgoing tides, and wind currents caused from a steady wind

*__Dead ahead__—directly ahead, in line with the boat's keel

*__Dead astern__—directly behind, in line with the boat's keel

Dead reckoning—the determination of a boat's position based on its run since the last-known position, figured from her corrected course and distance logged

Draft—the depth of a boat from the waterline to the lowest point of the keel. Depth of water needed to float a boat

Dry rot—wood decay caused by dampness and lack of ventilation

*__Fathom__—six feet, used in measuring water's depth

Fender—Semisoft cylinders, made from various materials, hung over a boat's side to protect her from chafing when tied up at a dock

Fitting-out—preparing a boat for use after a lay-up; usually done in the spring after winter storage

*__Fore and aft__—stem to stern, anything lying parallel to the keel

*__Forward__—in or toward the front of the boat

*__Freeboard__—the vertical distance from the waterline to the gunwale

*__Gale__—a storm with winds from 32 to 63 miles per hour

__Galley__—boat's kitchen

__Gear__—a generic term for the equipment used in boating

*__Ground tackle__—generic term for anchors, rodes, and other anchoring equipment

__Gunwale__—the top edge of a hull. Often used to strengthen hull and as a railing

__Hatch__—an opening in a deck or cabin top giving access to the interior

__Hatch cover__—door or covering over hatch

__Head__—boat's toilet

*__Heading__—direction a boat's bow is pointed. Used mostly in reference to a compass course

__Headway__—forward motion of a boat through the water

*__Heave to__—to bring a boat up into the wind with little or no headway; a boat is usually "hove to" when riding out a blow

*__Hull__—the main body of a boat; cabins, deckhouses, etc., are superstructures

__Keel__—the main structural member of a boat's hull running from stern to stern along the centerline at the lowest point of the hull

*__Knot__—point where two lines or two parts of the same line are tied together. Also, a nautical unit of speed equal to one nautical mile (6,080 feet per hour)

__Latitude__—distance on the earth's surface northward or southward from the equator

*__Leeward__—the direction away from the wind

*__Life preserver__—a lifesaving device designed to support the weight of a person in the water. Life preservers are compulsory equipment and must be carried aboard all boats, one per person. Jackets, vests, cushions, and rings are the most commonly used

*__Line__—nautical term for rope made of vegetable fibers, synthetic fiber, or metal

__Lubber line__—a mark or line on a compass bowl to indicate the fore and aft centerline of a boat. When installed properly, the lubber line will be parallel to the boat's centerline, fore and aft, and will show the boat's heading by compass

*__Navigable waters__—water that is deep and wide enough to sail safely

__Navigation__—the art of directing a boat and fixing her position by using landmarks or navigational aids (buoys, charts, compass, etc.)

__Painter__—a line at the bow of small boats used for tying up or towing

__Piloting__—the art of guiding the movement of a boat from one point to another

__Plot__—to lay out a course or position on a chart

*__Port__—left side of boat when facing forward

*__Privileged boat__—the boat which has the right-of-way when it meets another (see Rules of the road)

*__Rudder__—a flat plate attached vertically to the stern used to steer a boat

*__Rules of the Road__—a set of rules and regulations designed to regulate the flow of traffic afloat

__Sea anchor__—a device used to hold a boat head up into the wind during a storm (see Chapter X, Seamanship in Rough Weather)

Sounding—the depth of water at a given spot or as marked on charts

***Starboard**—the right side of a boat facing forward

Stem—the main framing member at the bow to which the sides of the boat are fastened

***Stern**—the rear part of a boat

Superstructure—any part of a boat built above deck except for masts, booms, and rigging

Swamped—when a boat becomes filled with water from seas coming in over the sides or by leaking

***Transom**—the rear end of a boat. On an outboard motorboat the engine is hung on the transom

***Trim**—the attitude with which a boat sits in the water when the carrying weight is correctly positioned

***Under way**—a boat moving through the water in any direction.

Wake—trail of disturbed water left astern by a boat under way

***Waterway**—any area of water suitable for navigation. Most commonly refers to navigable channels

Weigh anchor—hoist the anchor in preparation to get under way

***Windward**—the direction from which the wind blows

APPENDIX

B

Publications

The following publications are available from: The Superintendent of Documents, United States Government Printing Office, Washington, D. C. 20402. A small fee is usually charged to offset the cost of printing and mailing.

WEATHER PUBLICATIONS

1. The Aneroid Barometer—Cat. #C 30.2: B 26/2
2. Hurricane Warnings—a brief description of hurricanes, warnings and safety precautions. Cat. #30.2: H 94/3/962.
3. Storms Warnings, Coastal warning facilities charts: Each, 12x19 inches.
   Canadian Border to Eureka, Calif. and Alaska. Cat #C 30.22/3: C 16.
   Cape Hatteras, N.C. to Brunswick, Ga. Cat. #C 30.22/3: C 17h.
   Eastern Florida. Cat. #C 30.22/3: F 66.
   Eastport, Maine to Montauk Point, N.Y. Cat. #C 30.22/3: Ea 7
   Eureka to Point Conception, Calif. Cat. #C 30.22/3: Eu 7
   Hawaiian Islands. Cat. #C 30.22/3: H 31
   Manasquan, N.J. to Cape Hatteras, N.C. and Chesapeake Bay. Cat. #C 30.22/3: M 31
   Montauk Point, N.Y. to Manasquan, N.J. Cat. #C 30.22/3: M 76
   Morgan City, La. to Apalachicola, Fla. Cat. #C 30.22/3: M 82
   Point Conception, Calif. to Mexican Border Cat. #C 30.22/3: P 75c
   Puerto Rico and Virgin Islands Cat. #C 30.22/3: P 96
   Small craft, gale and whole gale warning facilities charts, Great Lakes: each 12x19 inches.

Huron, Erie, and Ontario. Cat. #C 30.22/3 G 79
Superior and Michigan Cat. #C 30.22/3: G 79/2

4. Weather Forecasting—Verification of the Weather Bureau's 30-day outlooks. 1961. 58 p. il. Cat. #C 30.28: 39.
5. Weather Forecasting—An excellent booklet for the layman who has an interest in forecasting the weather and how it is done. 39 p. il. Cat. #30.2 F 76/3.
6. Weather Maps, Daily weather map (including Sundays and holidays) Cat. #C 30.12.
7. Cloud Code Chart, Prepared with view of aiding in interpretation of cloud reports in international figure code. Cat. #C 30.22: C 62/2/958.
8. Forrester, Frank H. *1001 Questions Answered About the Weather.* New York: Dodd, Mead & Company, Inc., 1957.

NAVIGATIONAL AIDS, PUBLICATIONS

1. Aids to Marine Navigation of the United States—An excellent booklet describing the various types of U. S. Marine Navigation Aids, their history, purpose and uses. :CG-93.
2. List of Lights and Other Marine Aids
   List of Lights and Other Marine Aids commonly called light lists, describing the aids to marine navigation maintained by or under the authority of the United States Government, are published by the Coast Guard. Revised editions appear each year. The following volumes are issued:

Atlantic Coast

Volume I. First Coast Guard District, from St. Croix River, Maine, to Watch Hill, Rhode Island.

Volume II. Third Coast Guard District, from Watch Hill, Rhode Island, to Fenwick Island, Delaware.

Volume III. Fifth Coast Guard District, from Fenwick Island, Delaware, to Little River Inlet, South Carolina.

Volume IV. Seventh Coast Guard District, from Little River Inlet, South Carolina, to Apalachicola River, Florida and the United States, West Indies.

Volume V. Eighth Coast Guard District, from Apalachicola River, Florida, to Rio Grande.

Volume I-V (Combined). Complete List of Lights and Other Marine Aids, Atlantic Coast. This volume is a composite list of Volumes I to V, inclusive, with suitable cross-references to facilitate its use by navigators operating in more than one Coast Guard District.

Pacific Coast

Volume I. Eleventh Coast Guard District, from Mexican border, to Point Arguello, California.

Volume II. Twelfth Coast Guard District, from Point Arguello, California, to St. George Reef, California.

Volume III. Thirteenth Coast Guard District, from St. George Reef, California to Alaska.

Volume IV. Seventeenth Coast Guard District, Alaska.

Volume V. Fourteenth Coast Guard District, Hawaiian and Pacific Islands.

Volume I-V (Combined). Complete List of Lights and Other Marine Aids, covering the Pacific Coast and Islands. This volume is a composite list of Volumes I to V, inclusive, with suitable cross-references to facilitate its use by navigators operating in more than one Coast Guard District.

Great Lakes

List of Lights and Other Marine Aids, Great Lakes, United States and Canada.

Mississippi River System

List of Lights and Other Marine Aids, Mississippi River System.

3. Radio Beacons and Lorans
   A. Charts of radiobeacon system, Atlantic and Gulf coasts, Pacific Coast and Great Lakes.
   B. Radio Navigational Aids (H. O. Pub. No. 205):
   C. Loran charts and tables.
4. Additional Publications are listed in Chapter 15, Cruising America's Waterways, under section: Developing a Cruise Library.

APPENDIX

C

Fitting-Out Checklist

Boat's name________________________Reg. no.__________

Type____________________Length____________________

Engine make________________Type__________H.P.____

Builder________________________Year__________

Owner's name________________________________

Address________________________________

City____________________Zone______State__________

Home phone______________Business phone______________

Initial and date each item that is inspected and found okay, or when the work needed is completed.

OKAY	ITEM	TO BE DONE BY OWNER	TO BE DONE BY YARD	WORK DESCRIPTION	WORK COMPLETED
	Hull, Deck, Superstructure				
	Ventilate all closed areas				
	Wash or dust inside and out from stem to stern				

Okay	Item	To Be Done By Owner	Yard	Work Description	Work Completed
	Dry rot				
	Fractures, Cracks, Crazing				
	Caulking				
	Canvas				
	Through fittings: screws				
	bolts				
	nails				
	Through hull openings				
	Hull and deck hardware				
	Deck gear				
	Cabin(s) sides, top				
	Stern bearing				
	Shaft(s)				
	Stuffing box(es)				
	Propeller(s)				
	Rudder(s)				
	Ground plate				
	Transducer				
	Prepare for paint				
	Paint prime coat				
	finish coat				
	antifouling coat				
	Check and close: hull drains				
	seacocks				
	water closet				
	fresh water system				

Okay	Item	To Be Done By		Work Description	Work Completed
		Owner	Yard		
	Other: 1.				
	2.				
	3.				
	Ground Tackle, Safety Gear, Equipment Anchors				
	Anchor line				
	Dock lines				
	Extra lines				
	Splices and whippings				
	Chain				
	Shackles				
	Winches				
	Fenders				
	Boat hook				
	Life preservers				
	Ring buoys				
	Emergency life rafts				
	Approved fire extinguishers				
	Horn, bell, whistle				
	Lights				
	Flashlight				
	Searchlight				
	Portable battery				
	First aid kit				
	Tools				
	Spare parts				
	Bilge pump				

Okay	Item	To Be Done By Owner	Yard	Work Description	Work Completed
	Bile blower				
	Vents				
	Compass				
	Charts, piloting tools				
	Binoculars				
	Distress signals				
	Radio				
	Direction finder				
	Depth sounder				
	Radar				
	Other electronic equipment: 1.				
	2.				
	3.				
	Convertible top				
	Tarpaulin cover				
	Mattresses, seat cushions, bedding				
	Cooking utensils				
	Steering Apparatus Wheel, bracket, and shaft				
	Gear box, or cable, drum lube				
	Cable				
	Cable guides				
	Cable clamps				
	Blocks, sheaves, and straps				
	Forward linkage				
	Stern linkage				

Okay	Item	To Be Done By Owner	Yard	Work Description	Work Completed
	Other: 1.				
	2.				
	3.				
	Engine Clean outside				
	Clean and check all rust spots				
	Paint touch-up				
	Replace drains and other plugs or drain off anti-freeze				
	Flush cooling system				
	Replace engine oil				
	Grease and oil all parts per engine manual				
	Check lines for leaks, cracks, and tightness				
	Clean filters and carburetor bowl(s)				
	Check fuel tanks, clean if necessary				
	Inspect all wiring				
	Replace and gap spark plugs				
	Charge and replace battery				
	Tune up engine				
	Other: 1.				
	2.				
	3.				
	Rigging, Sails, Sailing Hardware Step mast(s), attach boom(s)				

Okay	Item	To Be Done By Owner	Yard	Work Description	Work Completed
	Check, replace, or repair all: rigging lines				
	sheets				
	halyards				
	stays				
	fairleads and jam cleats				
	gooseneck				
	turnbuckles				
	straps				
	chainplates				
	winches				
	tiller				
	rudder, rudder fittings				
	centerboard				
	roller reefing				
	battens				
	grommets				
	sail track				
	slides				
	stops				
	Grease and wire all shackles (replace if pin is rusted)				
	Grease turnbuckle threads				
	Grease or oil where needed, all hardware				
	Wash, if needed, and repair all sails and sailbags				
	Other: 1.				
	2.				
	3.				

Okay	Item	To Be Done By		Work Description	Work Completed
		Owner	Yard		
	Additional Items 1.				
	2.				
	3.				
	4.				
	5.				
	Last-Minute Double Check Before launching, be sure all hull drains and seacocks are closed				
	Before running engine, be sure that cooling system blocks are removed, all hose clamps tight, and intake and outlet valves open				

APPENDIX

D

Winter Lay-Up Checklist

Boat's name____________________Reg. no.__________

Type____________________Length____________________

Engine make________________Type__________H.P._____

Builder__________________________Year____________

Owner's name____

Address____

City______________________Zone_____State__________

Home phone_______________Business phone____________

Okay	Item	To Be Done By Owner	Yard	Work Description	Work Completed
	Portable Equipment Remove for off-the-boat storage all:				
	charts and navigation equipment				
	compass				
	binoculars				

Okay	Item	To Be Done By Owner	Yard	Work Description	Work Completed
	radio				
	radar				
	depth finders				
	other electronic equipment: 1.				
	2.				
	3.				
	tool kit and spare parts				
	flashlights				
	life jackets and cushions				
	anchors				
	lines				
	boat hook and ladder				
	convertible top				
	hobby or sports equipment				
	bedding				
	clothing				
	oily rags or other fire hazards				
	cooking and eating utensils				
	food				
	portable gas cylinders				
	portable gas stoves				
	battery(s)				
	other: 1.				
	2.				
	3.				

Okay	Item	To Be Done By Owner	To Be Done By Yard	Work Description	Work Completed
	Note: Wash, clean, grease, or oil, as called for, the above equipment before storing. Keep batteries charged over the winter.				
	Storage Area and Cribbing *Clean storage area of all refuse and highly inflammable materials				
	*Check to be sure there is adequate space surrounding your boat to allow for maneuvering in case of an emergency (fire, flooding, etc.)				
	Check cribbing timbers for length and strength. Short or weak timbers will cause sagging or warping				
	*Make sure the ground under the crib is firm. Soft or swampy land will cause the crib to tilt which puts dangerous strains on the hull				
	*Be sure all blocking and shoring or trailer pads and rollers are placed at framing members or other strong points along the hull				
	Check to be sure the crib is securely braced against sway and thrust 1″ x 3″ x 2″ x 4″ boards are commonly used for bracing. Boats stored on trailers should be tied down snugly, but not so tight that a strain will be put on the hull				
	Other: 1.				
	2.				
	3.				
*Also applies to trailer-stored boats					

Okay	Item	To Be Done By		Work Description	Work Completed
		Owner	Yard		
	Hull, Deck, Superstructure Open all hull drain seacocks and clean off any strainers. Run water through to be sure drains are working. This check is necessary to prevent a freeze-up in cold weather				
	Drain water tanks and water system. Pour a pint of liquid aqua cleaner into the tank a few hours before draining, to prevent internal corrosion and the possibility of sour drinking water next season				
	Drain toilets. Use a sponge where necessary to remove water from traps				
	If the unit lacks a drain plug, fill the bowl with antifreeze				
	Drain bilge pumps and hoses				
	Wash hull inside and outside. Be especially thorough below the waterline and in the bilge. Pour a can of bilge cleaner in the bilge a few days before washing				
	Repair or mark for future repair, all dry rot, cracks, crazing, loose fittings or fasteners				
	Prepare interior for winter cover. Partially open all doors, hatches, and drawers to insure adequate ventilation. Turn bunk boards on their side, exposing compartments below. Hang a few bags of moisture absorbing slica gel in normally damp areas				

Okay	Item	To Be Done By Owner	Yard	Work Description	Work Completed
	Inspect winter cover for rot, tears, broken grommets, etc. Repair or replace where necessary				
	Install winter cover and lace it securely with sound line or snubbers that won't part in a blow. While placing the cover, be extra sure you are leaving adequate ventilation areas				
	Other: 1.				
	2.				
	3.				
	Engine and Accessories If engine is an outboard, remove it from the boat and run it for 10 minutes in a flushing tank or flush water through the cooling system with a hose. Then, drain the lower units and relubricate with lower unit gear lube. Remove the propeller, grease the propeller shaft, and replace the propeller. Next, perform the jobs below that bear an asterisk (*). When all jobs are completed, cover motor and gas tank and store in a dry place				
	*Close fuel valve and let engine run until it stops				
	*Clean engine exterior with a commercial, non-flammable engine cleaner				
	*Remove any rust and prime with a touch-up paint				
	Drain cooling system, then refill with anti-freeze				

Okay	Item	To Be Done By Owner	Yard	Work Description	Work Completed
	Drain the crankcase and refill with new oil				
	*Remove the spark plugs and pour an ounce of top cylinder oil in each cylinder. Replace spark plugs and turn engine over a few times to coat the cylinder walls and pistons				
	*Grease: (Check the engine manual for recommended type and grade grease) starter shaft, generator shaft, propeller shaft, and couplings, all control levers, rods and springs				
	Spray entire engine with a preservative oil. (Throw-away spray cans can be purchased at most yards or boat stores)				
	Additional Lubrication Grease the following items with a light density grease such as Lubriplate 105: seacocks				
	tank filler caps				
	pumps				
	winches				
	steering system: wheel, drum, shaft, pulleys, gears, wire lines, leads, shackles, etc., throttle and shift controls				
	Wipe a thin protective coat on: all metal deck hardware such as cleats, chocks, lights, etc. Plus, window and door tracks, hinges, door knobs, locks				

Okay	Item	To Be Done By Owner	Yard	Work Description	Work Completed
	Other: 1.				
	2.				
	3.				
	Sailing Equipment Unstep mast and boom. Inspect for damage				
	Store mast and spars flat, off the ground to prevent warping				
	Wipe a thin coat of grease on all metal hardware. Do this while coating regular hardware				
	Inspect and wash rudder and tiller assembly. Do this while washing the hull				
	Inspect, wash, and repair, if necessary, all sails before storing in a dry place. If major repairs are needed, take the sails to a sailmaker				
	Other: 1.				
	2.				
	3.				
	4.				
	5.				

APPENDIX E

Cruising Checklist

Essential Equipment

___ Life jackets for all hands
___ At least one U.S. Coast Guard approved fire extinguisher (full and in working order)
___ Horn or whistle
___ Lights, red and green running lights and a white stern light
___ Two anchors, one working and one storm, with appropriate length lines
___ Wrist watch
___ First aid kit and manual
___ Spare coil of 100 feet of line
___ Paddle or oars
___ Bilge pump or bailer
___ Compass, charts, navigation tools, and pilot instructions
___ Water Jugs (full)
___ Flashlights
___ Seaman knives
___ Matches
___ Water purification tablets
___ Flares in a watertight container, or a flare pistol and cartridges
___ Emergency hull repair kit
___ Fenders
___ Insect repellents
___ Inflatable life raft for offshore cruisers
___ Sun glasses
___ Sunburn lotion
___ ________________________________
___ ________________________________
___ ________________________________

Desirable Equipment

___ Portable radio
___ Binoculars
___ Bucket and line
___ Emergency food rations
___ Hatchet
___ Sponges and swab
___ Skillets, nesting pots, and pans and coffeepot
___ Folding boxes
___ Bottle and can opener
___ Toilet kits
___ Dish and bath towels

___ Bar soap and detergents
___ Ice coolers
___ Toilet paper
___ Gasoline lantern for use ashore
___ Canvas boat-top and side curtains
___ Tent(s)
___ Bedding
___ Air mattresses
___ Portable gasoline stove and folding stand for use ashore
___ Camera and film
___ Fishing equipment
___ Toys, games, beach toys
___ Waterproof box that will float, for currency and identification cards
___ Reading material
___ ______________________
___ ______________________
___ ______________________
___ ______________________

*CLOTHING

(*on distant cruises be prepared for all weather conditions*)

ITEM	DAD	MOTHER	BROTHER	SISTER	OTHERS
Underwear	___	___	___	___	___
Shirts	___	___	___	___	___
Pants	___	___	___	___	___
Dresses	___	___	___	___	___
Sweaters	___	___	___	___	___
Jackets	___	___	___	___	___
Shorts	___	___	___	___	___
Sneakers	___	___	___	___	___
Shoes	___	___	___	___	___
Boots	___	___	___	___	___
Socks	___	___	___	___	___
Stockings	___	___	___	___	___
Foul weather gear	___	___	___	___	___
Bathing suits	___	___	___	___	___
Handkerchiefs	___	___	___	___	___
Hats	___	___	___	___	___
Nightwear	___	___	___	___	___
Sunday go-to-meeting clothes	___	___	___	___	___
______________	___	___	___	___	___
______________	___	___	___	___	___
______________	___	___	___	___	___

*FOOD

Nonperishables (*When space permits, keep the galley well-stocked*)

___ Coffee
___ Tea
___ Sugar
___ Salt
___ Pepper
___ Dried fruits
___ Canned meats
___ Canned sea food
___ Soups
___ Potatoes

*Clothing and food can be checked off at home and placed in portable supply lockers; then, only the lockers have to be checked on board.

- ___ Instant Milk
- ___ Instant Cream
- ___ Cereals
- ___ Pancake mix
- ___ Biscuit mix
- ___ Canned fruits
- ___ Onions
- ___ Crackers
- ___ Cookies
- ___ Cooking oil
- ___ ______________________
- ___ ______________________

Perishables (*On boats lacking refrigeration, a picnic-type ice cooler will keep most perishable foods up to 48 hours*)

- ___ Milk
- ___ Butter
- ___ Eggs
- ___ Bacon
- ___ Meats
- ___ Frozen juices
- ___ Vegetables
- ___ Bread
- ___ ______________________
- ___ ______________________

NOTE: Some cooks bring aboard food in labeled menu boxes, each box holding all the ingredients for a certain meal or snack. If you prefer this plan, make your checklist by menu instead of items.

Index

Index

(Italicized page numbers refer to illustrations)